Trans**Pacific**

Collected Poems of

Ernest **G. Moll**

Edited by Alan L. Contreras

Preface by Patrick Buckridge, Griffith University

Hope Arnold, Editorial Assistant

This collection has been published with the gracious encouragement and permission of Ernest G. Moll's granddaughters Judy and Nancy.

Poems by Ernest G. Moll (1900-1997) are © Judy Moll and Nancy Moll, except for poems from *Blue Interval*, which are © Alan L. Contreras by gift from the late Carolyn Moll.

Preface © Patrick Buckridge
Introduction © Alan L. Contreras
Front cover photo © John Simpkins, used with permission
Back cover photo of E.G. Moll courtesy University of Oregon

ISBN 979-8-218-39289-5

Oregon Review Books
Eugene, Oregon

Corrected December, 2024
Title Index added December, 2024

TransPacific

Collected Poems of

Ernest G. Moll

Books by Alan L. Contreras

Nonfiction

Afield: Forty Years of Birding the American West
A History of Oregon Ornithology (editor with V. Thompson and N. Clements)
Birds of Oregon: a General Reference (editor with D. B. Marshall and M. G. Hunter)
Collected Poems of Ada Hastings Hedges (editor with Ulrich Hardt)
Edge of Awe: Experiences of the Malheur-Steens Country (editor)
Far Afield
The Gay Imagination
The Mind on Edge: An Introduction to John Jay Chapman's Philosophy of Higher Education
Northwest Birds in Winter
Pursuit of Happiness: An Introduction to the Libertarian Ethos of C.E.S. Wood

Poetry

In the Time of the Queen
Firewand
Night Crossing

To the memory of Colin Brumby,
Australian composer of universal music

Contents

Native Moments and other poems (1931)

Campus Sonnets (1934)

Blue Interval: Poems of Crater Lake (1935)

Additional Poems from Crater Lake

Cut from Mulga (1940)

Brief Waters (1945)

Beware the Cuckoo and Other Poems (1947)

The Waterhole (1948)

The Lifted Spear (1953)

The Rainbow Serpent and Other Poems (1962)

Briseis (1965)

The Road to Cactus-land (1971)

The Well and the Star (1983)

The View from a Ninetieth Birthday (1992)

Recognitions at Ninety-three (1993)

The Children of Somalia 1992-1994 and Other Poems (1994)

Introductory Material

1

PREFACE

I first encountered the name 'Ernest G. Moll' about twenty years ago as the author of a book called simply *The Appreciation of Poetry*, published in New York in 1933. I was at the time investigating the idea of 'appreciation' – now regarded with some suspicion in the academy for being ostensibly un-political. Moll's book was (and is) a delightful read, certainly one of the most engaging of several similar books published in the interwar period. Informed by a strong and coherent post-Romantic philosophical aesthetic, it is nonetheless enriched by its wide array of fresh and appropriate poetic examples, by the sensitive and writerly commentary on them, and by a deep interest in the traditional forms and techniques of English poetry.

At the time I had no idea that the author of this unusually helpful and illuminating book was either a poet (though I could have suspected that) or an Australian. In due course I discovered that he was not only a compatriot but also a friend of several older Australian poets and scholars, including one, Cecil Hadgraft, just a couple of years younger than himself, who was a valued mentor to me as an undergraduate in Brisbane in the 1960s.

My discovery that he was a poet in his own right came even later, no doubt partly because, as Alan Contreras explains in his Introduction to this edition, his poetic output, though large, spans Australia and the United States in both subject matter and place of publication and reception, with the unfortunate result that his profile is lower than it ought to be on both sides of the Pacific. Furthermore, the traditional formalism of all his poetry would always have restricted his appeal for an Australian postwar poetry establishment in which – with a few honourable exceptions – 'rules' and canons were there to be cavalierly broken or ignored.

When I finally became aware, just a few years ago, of the sheer quantity of Moll's published *oeuvre* and – even more recently – of the undeniable excellence of so much of it, I felt – to quote one of his favourite poets – 'like some watcher of the skies /When a new planet swims into his ken'. Gerry Moll's poetry is not quite Chapman's Homer (and I am not John Keats), but perhaps the analogy can stand. Homer was certainly one of Moll's major poetic touchstones, and his brilliant and moving sonnet sequence *Briseis* (1965) develops with great psychological acuity and empathy one of the most fascinating and under-developed characters in the *Iliad*.

Moll has Briseis, the young woman over whom Achilles and Agamemnon quarrel, tell her own story in fifty-five Petrarchan sonnets. I mention that particular verse form because Moll was strangely addicted to it in the earlier part of his career, perhaps relishing the challenge its restrictive rhyme scheme poses for poets writing in English. In his early thirties he published *Campus Sonnets*, comprising 45 of them, nearly all crafted with a seemingly effortless facility, almost as natural, flexible and versatile as the blank verse pentameter to Shakespeare. Throughout his career he reverts to the sonnet, while at the same time relaxing into couplets, alternately rhyming quatrains, sestains and other forms – even, on rare occasions (as in the strange Biblical narrative 'Jonah at Nineveh') – into blank verse.

But he is much more than a gifted technician. The 'campus sonnets' themselves, written in his early years at the University of Oregon, are a remarkable record of the inner life of a passionately invested English lecturer. The occasionally anthologized sonnet 'On Reading a War Poet with a Class' even hints at the 'appreciative' direction the discussion must have taken:

You like this quiet poem that he madeIn gratitude because a
swallow brought Down the curved lanes of death a sudden
thoughtOf autumn sunshine in an English glade?

Reading his modest and sensitive reflections on the challenges and rewards of 'old-fashioned' university English teaching reminds us how seldom this rich vein of human experience has been mined for poetry.

Moll was a scholarly poet in the best sense: not bookish or stuffy, but heavily influenced by his life as a teaching academic. His writing nearly always feels fresh and original; but it is also deeply informed – one might almost say suffused, even saturated – by an awareness of the whole preceding tradition of canonical English (including American and Australian) poetry to which he devoted his academic life. Time and time again, in reading through his extensive oeuvre, one registers – as an added pleasure – a line that evokes Blake, Shelley or Keats, Dickinson, Frost, Hardy, Arnold or Yeats, even Shakespeare, Donne, or Marvell. The Australian poets Christopher Brennan, Mary Gilmore and William Baylebridge also make their presence felt; and then there are the explicit and extended explorations of Homer, the Old Testament, Wordsworth, Coleridge, Shelley, Browning, Arnold, Hopkins and Francis Thompson.

Still, Moll is not a 'bookish' poet – or only occasionally. The bulk of his poetry, drawn from every phase of his long career, has to do with the natural world, which he loved and revered in its very different Australian and Oregonian manifestations. Many of the poems of his middle period – *Cut from Mulga* (1940), *Brief Waters* (1945) and *Beware the Cuckoo* (1947) – dramatize, in sometimes shocking ways, the morally indifferent cruelty inherent to the natural world – 'Bottle Swallows'(CfM) and 'The Butcher-Bird' (BW) are both unforgettable in this regard! – but also, and even more disturbingly, the brutalising, morally numbing effect that dealings with the natural world, especially the drought-stricken rural districts in which he spent much of his boyhood, can have upon human moral sensibilities. That he traces this process, often enough, in his own consciousness makes for an even more chilling effect: see, for example, 'Parrot-Shooting' (BW) and 'Instructions to a Boy on Digging Rabbits' (BW).

Moll's mid-career preoccupation with the effects of growing up, and later living and working, in the Australian bush perhaps reflects the old colonial fear of moral degeneration in a harsh and unforgiving environment, though there is no reason to doubt that it also reflects his own lived experiences (recollected in the tranquillity of an American college campus).

But this is also part of a much broader pattern of interest and apparent anxiety, evident throughout Moll's nearly seventy years of writing, namely the unity and integrity of the self. From 1971, when he published the uneven but powerful 1400-line semi-autobiographical poem *The Road to Cactus Land,* that theme becomes ever more insistent, as does the urge to integrate the self across the decades from childhood to maturity, and to resist the fragmenting forces of dislocation, grief, and senescence. In a note to the poem 'In Praise of Mirages,' from *The View from a Ninetieth Birthday* (1992), he describes a moment in which he experienced that almost mystical sense of a self triumphantly unified against the entropic effects of age. Characteristically, that moment is immediately associated with the power of English literature:

> When, long retired and old, I was thinking about my early boyhood and the excitement and pleasure I had felt at mirages, suddenly, as though by the magic of Prospero, my youth and age were one in a being whole and indivisible, a being [in] which "The child is father of the man" and not something of assembled parts. The pleasure in that recognition is great indeed, especially when it occurs when the opposite one, that of disintegration is constantly forced on one by advanced aging. (p. 363)

Thanks to this comprehensive edition of Gerry Moll's collected poems, American and Australian readers alike can now trace the evolution of a varied, distinctive and altogether rewarding body of work, and above all *appreciate* its qualities, as if for the first time. It 'belongs' to both of us.

Patrick Buckridge
Griffith University, Queensland

INTRODUCTION

Ernest George "Gerry" Moll (1900-1997) was born in rural Victoria, Australia. He attended Concordia College (a boys' school at the time) in Adelaide, South Australia, then moved to the United States and graduated from Lawrence College in Wisconsin in 1922. He obtained a Master of Arts at Harvard University in 1923. Moll taught at Colorado College in the late 1920s, after which he was appointed Assistant Professor of English at the University of Oregon in 1928, where he taught until retirement in 1966. He died in Oroville, California in 1997 after living for a time in Brookings, Oregon, where he raised Australian plants.

Moll's Legacy as a Poet

Moll's poetry is little remarked in the U.S. today and is perhaps not as fully appreciated as it might be in Australia. There are several reasons for this unfortunate situation. His literary legacy was, and still is, split between Australia, where he was born, and the U.S., where he was a professor, mostly at Oregon. Three of his first four books were published by the small publisher Metropolitan Press in Portland, Oregon, which had mostly disappeared as a publisher not long after Moll retired (it no longer exists) and was hardly visible in Australia.

Most of his "middle" work was published in Australia and was apparently not very visible in the U.S. His most prestigious award, the Australian Book of the Year award, came fairly early in his career, for his collection *Cut From Mulga* (1940), which appeared during WWII from Melbourne University Press. His work appeared in collections of best Australian verse in 1950, 1956, 1968 and in the *New Oxford Book of Australian Verse* in 1986 and 1996.

Moll's last few collections, best described as chapbooks and somewhat quirky in content, were privately published through a print shop in Oroville, California, long after his academic career, and were effectively invisible except to a few friends.

His poetic reputation may have suffered from being divided in this way, rather than having a typical increase in visibility over time, as it does not bulk as large as it should in any one time or place. This divided legacy extends to his papers, some of which are at the University of Oregon and the bulk, some sixteen boxes, at the National Library of Australia in Canberra.

His poetic output, though substantial and usually excellent, was exceptionally varied and unique in tone and subject, though he tended to use rhyme and traditional forms, particularly sonnets. In short, he followed his own light and did not fall into a clear 'school' or category of poets, though in Australia he is considered something of a regionalist or poet of nature. Reviewer Thomas Gardiner, writing in the Australian literary magazine *Southerly*, disputes any such limits to the consideration of Moll's achievement, noting that:

To be sure, there are vivid poems on kookaburras, gums, and lambing paddocks, as well as a sonnet sequence (*The Waterhole*) that is practically a spiritual history of the Australian continent. There is a rustic simplicity, humour, and fidelity to colloquial speech rhythms in many of these pieces that Robert Frost might easily have produced in an Australian setting.

But there is something more: scattered throughout the collection are a number of lyrics and lyrical-descriptive poems that explore and express human emotions, social and philosophical problems in a profoundly effective way, ordering imagery, rhythm, syntax and thematic statement into beautifully balanced units that have the unmistakable character of first-rate poetry.[1]

Moll retained the capacity to write remarkable poetry until the end of his life. At ninety-three he had developed some difficulty in writing, noting that "even words I thought I knew well are beginning to act like strangers."[2] That said, he kept writing wonderful poems and at the extraordinary age of *ninety-seven* he wrote out "The Life Force" in sketchy longhand a few hours before he died; his daughter Carolyn typed it for him while noting that "I'm sure he would have reworked parts of the poem could he have stayed. Time ran out. He couldn't help me as I tried to read the script for typing."[3]

The Substance of Moll's Poetic Work

I have enjoyed Moll's poetry for many years and recently re-read his entire poetic output, including several unpublished pieces, as part of this effort to bring his work back into print. The sheer variety of his poetry cannot be overstated. *Blue Interval* (Metropolitan Press, Portland, Oregon, 1935) consists entirely of rhymed quatrains related to the history and physical aspects of Crater Lake, the national park in southern Oregon where he worked two summers as a ranger-guide. An example from this work follows.

Night on the Lake

Man is too frail to speak the power of this
Mysterious night or plunge with thought the gloom
Where Cloudcap hangs above the vast abyss
Tremendous in his probes of doom.

Nancy Moll, a retired professor of geology, wrote that E. G. Moll's son Richard, her father, also "worked at Crater Lake for a number of years on fire lookouts etc. and most of his ashes were scattered at various spots in the Park." She noted that "my

---

1   Gardiner, Thomas J. 1965. The Poetry of E.G. Moll, in *Southerly* (Sydney) vol. 25 no. 3, p. 173-181, at 173.

2   Letter from Moll to Thelma Greenfield, October 13, 1993, provided to the editor by Greenfield for this book.

3   Letter from Carolyn Moll to Thelma Greenfield, May 23, 1997, provided to the editor by Greenfield for this book.

Dad's tales of Crater Lake, which he would often tell me when I was scared of thunderstorms ... are one of the reasons that I went into geology."[4]

The poems in *Blue Interval* display a clear, direct diction characterized in most cases by a reference to either specific parts of the landscape of Crater Lake National Park or the plants and wildlife found there. Unlike some poets who write about the natural world, there is always much more to Moll's work than layered descriptions of what he sees. An appreciation for the joys and limits of human existence can often be found on or not far below the surface of his work. Nancy noted in a message to me that she "would certainly like to see it preserved and published."[5]

Contrast the direct observational lens of *Blue Interval* with the extraordinary sequence of fifty-five sonnets that constitute *Briseis* (1965), Moll's retelling of the core emotional events of the siege of Troy from the point of view of the woman who was traded back and forth like a sack of wheat during the heart of the battle. Here's an example of just how much action and emotional content Moll packs into a single one of these sonnets. This one is set just after the death of Patroklos (Moll's chosen spelling), with Agamemnon speaking first in quotes.

44

His joy was like a dog just off the thong
That ran before him, tripping up his voice:
"Achilles has forgiven me—rejoice!
Speed to him with my gifts! Hurry along
The women and Briseis and the strong
Fleet-footed horses, and tell them that I swear
In all these days and nights I touched no hair
Of her who brought upon us all this wrong!"

I heard him and felt nothing. "Brought upon?"
Let Helen's be such honor, and let the lie
Smile on its god-like father. Meanwhile I
Go to my lover who would cast me on
The camp's dunghill if by so doing he could
Unfreeze the current of Patroklos' blood.

This is Briseis the bold, a woman who has to manage her captivity and her relationships under extremely difficult conditions. The poet's clear and often colorful language embodies his heroine's thoughts and efforts and gives the familiar literary incidents of the siege of Troy an entirely fresh and entertaining flavor while remaining true to the events of Homer's original.[6]

---

4   E-mail from Nancy Moll to the editor.

5   E-mail from Nancy Moll to the editor, April 29, 2020.

6   There is some modern argument about who Homer was and what he did or did not write. That is a subject that we need not discuss here.

Then we turn to *The Rainbow Serpent*, a remarkably varied collection published in Sydney in 1962. The lead poem recounts a story connected to Australian aboriginal lore of the Alcheringa, the primordial Dreaming, in which the figure of the serpent in the shape of a rainbow takes on religious and cultural significance. In this eight-page poem the serpent, effectively in drag, meets some women after one of them, in a moment of ill-considered anger, calls for the snake to come. In a fine example of being careful what you ask for, he does, and their eventual meeting is foreshadowed, indeed, foreboded, by this beginning.

The Rainbow Serpent
  Summer Noon

  The Rainbow Serpent slid between
  The hills that lay with open thighs,
  (For so he saw them curving through
  The lens of lust behind his eyes).

  The sun he had not seen nor felt
  Through aeons of black loneliness
  Pressed on his moving back like hands
  In the twin rhythm of a caress

  But could not make him pause where he,
  Pulsating light in many a hue,
  Slid on between the straining hills
  To a more urgent rendezvous.

Feel the magnetic tension of the word "straining" in the last quatrain of this introductory section. Straining—away from the unexpected danger /horror/power of the Serpent. Straining—to accept the surprising joy of the profoundly male god-snake's imperial penetration of the earthly thigh-hills. Straining—to allow the Serpent passage in a filtered form upon which humans can gaze without fear or, indeed, that allows humans to see it at all. All three of these, at a minimum, are borne out in the eventualities of the poem. It is hard to imagine a more perfect, natural and multifunctional word choice.

His award-winning iconic work, *Cut From Mulga* (Melbourne University Press, 1940), is to some extent a poetic precursor to his autobiographical family recollection, *Below These Hills* (1957). The bulk of what it contains has to do with rural life in the transitional Australia of the early 20th Century. The general setting is much like the dusty, water-starved, varied outback and Riverina scene-setting in Arthur Upfield's mystery novels set in Australia at roughly the same time. Some of the specific events set forth in poems in *Cut From Mulga* can be found in a more linear narrative in *Below These Hills*, but some are universals of rural life in Australia:

The Bush Speaks

I will be your lover
If you keep my ways.
All delights I'll give you:
Gum-tree scented days,
Skies where kestrels hover,
Nights with stars ablaze.

But if you diminish
Care and think me won,
Other gifts I'll give you
Edged with thorn and sun,
And the crows will finish
What I have begun.

In addition, this collection includes a poem that connects all of Moll's geographic forays in one rolling poetico-ornithological tour:

Kookaburras

I've heard the skylark Shelley heard,
The ruffled thrush that Hardy knew,
The English nightingale that stirred
The dying heart of Keats when dew
Silvered the moonlit lawns where he
Had left so little time to be.

I've heard the wren in rocky glades
Darting his silver lance of sound,
And high among the white Cascades
The purple finch pour, round on round,
Fire-music that should swirl and swing
And loose the torrents of the Spring.

And all of these with joy or pain
Were lyrical, as though they wrought
In sunshine or in slanting rain
To free some urgent hidden thought
Whose brightness man at last should see
On the dark brows of Tragedy.

But Kookaburras when the west
Burns red behind the ring-barked trees,
And the dark earth sinks down to rest
And every flower has lost its bees

Shake the still dusk with sudden mirth
Flung recklessly across the earth.

In gusts of sound their laughter breaks
Against the steepening walls of night
And listening then my spirit takes
Backward through time the wings of flight
And hears among the ghosts at play
The lusty laugh of Rabelais.

I have personally heard purple finches singing in the Oregon Cascades and kookaburras cackling in riparian Queensland, as well as the wren and a number of ruffled or at least reasonably vigorous thrushes, some of which were in England, so I can certify the zoological accuracy of Moll's poetic vision.

Moll's other principal published works include *The Appreciation of Poetry* (1933, F. S. Crofts), *Poetry: the Problem of Appreciation* (1934, University of Oregon) *Collected Poems: 1940-55* (1957, Angus & Robertson) and *Below These Hills: the story of a Riverina farm* (1957, Melbourne University Press), written in collaboration with his brother Otto.

The poems are presented here in the same chronological order as the books, with the Lawrence poems preceding those collected in books, and a few previously unpublished poems appearing at the end. Editing has been minimal, which means that Australian words such as "warrigal" appear without notes (some appear in the Glossary), spellings of words such as "colour" are sometimes that of British English and sometimes in American, as Moll originally wrote them, and some unique Moll-isms in terms of spellings, contractions, and rare usages such as "wried" are left as-is. Obvious typos (very few) have been corrected, and in a few cases the existence of alternate versions is noted in a footnote.

Moll himself occasionally offers explanatory notes with poems. This is sometimes interesting, sometimes unnecessary (e.g. telling the reader who Shakespeare was) and, particularly in the later privately published work, distracting simply because of sheer length. That said, there are interesting nuggets in many of these asides and in some cases the poet's explanation of why he did some particular thing adds to our awareness of how he thought and wrote. In some cases these notes are retained and included with the segment for the volume in which they appeared.

Moll occasionally wrote about other writers. He was particularly fond of the work of Robinson Jeffers, taught his work, and sent Jeffers two poems, to which Jeffers responded in May, 1929:

I come to you as a penitent. My wife usually is good enough to look at and answer if necessary letters that come for me—because I never can get it done. When yours came several months ago she said "they are very good poems," and I said "Then let me answer the letter." But I did not read at that time; the letter was laid aside for me and I never found it again until to-night. I am very sorry.

They are, as she said, very good poems. So good that I was able to quite forget myself in reading, and not even wish that they had a better subject [*they were about Jeffers-ed.*]. Thank you sincerely and, and let me congratulate you on the power and music of the lines. ... if you are south sometime, I hope you will come see me and my stones.[7]

Attempting to revive the work of a dead poet is a chancy business. This is particularly true when the poet has been little studied and is even more true when the poet's general approach to the art considers beauty a perfectly legitimate goal and formal structures a normal and positive way to achieve that goal. Nonetheless, such efforts are made from time to time. This reissue of the work of Ernest G. "Gerry" Moll is in that category.[8] I feel justified in this attention because I agree with Thompson, who concluded his review in *Southerly* by saying that

> in terms of the number of first-rate poems in his main collection, Moll might rank near poets like Theodore Roethke and John Crowe Ransom, if his work were better known than it is at present. For a lyric poet, in any case, a handful of gems is enough to deck a crown.[9]

There may be poems of Moll that do not appear here simply because they were not included in his books or discovered by the editor, whose access to Australian sources was quite limited. A truly authoritative, definitive collection could be done, but only at considerable expense of time and money, given the need to work in both the U.S. and Australia. I hope that this substantial collection will serve to keep his work alive and generate increased appreciation for a poet whose work remains as vivid and sharply-cut as when he wrote it.

Acknowledgments

I mentioned the kindness of professor Thelma Greenfield who, in her mid-nineties, agreed to let me borrow her private correspondence from Moll. She died in July, 2023 at 100. Her children Sayre and Tamma, long-time friends of mine, have supported this reissuance project. The Lawrence poems were provided through the diligence, alacrity and kindness of Lawrence University archivist Lina Rosenberg Foley, to whom I was referred by my friend and Lawrence student Kai Frueh. Original material from *Southerly* was provided (with astonishing and greatly-appreciated speed) by Angela Rockel, an aptly named literary angel. My special thanks to Nathan Williams and Hope Arnold, who retyped most of the poems in this

---

7   *Selected letters of Robinson Jeffers*, Ann N. Ridgeway, ed., Johns Hopkins U. Press (1968), p. 159

8   Moll's middle name was George, not Gerald or Gerard. I don't know how he became known as Jerry or Gerry. He may have used both spellings of the nickname, mostly with a G.

9   Gardiner, Thomas J. 1965. The Poetry of E.G. Moll, in *Southerly* (Sydney) vol. 25 no. 3, p. 173-181, at 181.

volume. This collection was proofed against the original books by Hope Arnold and the editor, a task both gigantic and revelatory that took the entire summer of 2022.

Professor Patrick Buckridge of Griffith University, Queensland, was kind enough not only to contribute a preface for this collection but to assist with a number of questions I had about Australian terminology and material hard to get from Oregon. In a couple of cases in which modern usage may differ from the colloquialisms that Moll used in the early 20th Century, I have included both in the Glossary at the end of the book. Thanks to my Western Oregon Editors colleague, garden writer and editor Mary-Kate Mackey, for botanical expertise.

Although E. G. Moll's son Richard died before this project started, I had the privilege of corresponding with Moll's daughter Carolyn before her death in 2019. She was enthusiastic about her father's work, which she rightly considered to be of high quality and worth bringing back to the attention of the public. However, she was very reluctant to endorse a collection that in her view might not meet proper standards for publication. Although she never formally supported this collection, she did gift me with the copyright for *Blue Interval,* the most purely "Oregon" book that Moll did, as it is set entirely at Crater Lake. I reissued that book as a standalone publication that she liked. I hope that the present publication would also meet with her approval.

Ernest G. Moll's granddaughters Judy and Nancy, Richard Moll's children, graciously approved this rebirth of their grandfather's work. I hope they are pleased with the result.

Income from sales of this book will go to the Ernest G. Moll Faculty Research Award program at the University of Oregon in Eugene, Oregon. I appreciate the assistance of Jena Turner from the Oregon Humanities Center for background on the Moll award.

The first printing included errors that are corrected here through a gracious and careful review by Chris Tiffin (University of Queensland) with assistance from Patrick Buckridge (Griffith University). Chris Tiffin also prepared a title index that appears at the end.

Alan L. Contreras
December, 2024

Work Included in This Collection

This collection reprints seventeen previously published books by Ernest G. Moll, in chronological order. They were published in the U.S. and Australia, as noted below.

It also includes a number of poems that did not appear in these major collections. These include eight poems published in 1921 and 1922 in *The Lawrentian*, campus newspaper of Lawrence University, where Moll completed his undergraduate degree. These were not included in any later collections. They are not properly considered juvenilia because they deal for the most part with young adult themes of love, faith, dedication and family, but they vary more than his later work. A couple of them display the deep rolling cadences of outdoor diction so visible in the mature work; a couple of them are the moon-laden love poems of a college student. On the whole, they represent an interesting view of a young poet's development.

Also included are a few poems from *Crater Lake Nature Notes*, in-house newsletter of Crater Lake National Park in Oregon, USA, inserted here with the previously published text of *Blue Interval* for reasons of theme and chronology, one poem that appeared in *The Bulletin* (Sydney) and two previously unpublished poems from late in Moll's life provided by the late Thelma Greenfield.

It is inevitable that some of Moll's published poems that did not appear in his books are not collected here. Several incomplete and unpublished poems, stories and other material are held in the Ernest G. Moll papers at the National Library of Australia in Canberra. Additional material is held by the University of Oregon archives. A useful list of Moll's work has been compiled by Dirk Spenneman of Charles Sturt University.[10]

What Americans are now in the habit of calling the "n-word" appears in one poem, placed for poetic purposes in the sour mouth of a crusty old man with little good to say. I have retained it. In a few places aboriginals, sometimes called blacks, appear in a negative context, but this is far from universal and I saw no reason to tinker with any poem for this reason.

A few minor errors have been corrected when the mistake is clear. In rare instances, for example Moll's unusual use of the word breach instead of breech for the part of a firearm, the more standard word has been inserted when the meaning of the use is clear. Moll had an exceptionally broad vocabulary and thus his diction was so rich that in our editing processes, Hope Arnold and I had to look up a number of words that we thought were mistakes. We were usually wrong.

Owing to the great breadth of subject matter in Moll's poems, a discerning reader may encounter images that cause discomfort regarding human sexuality, relationships, war and other less beautiful aspects of life. This is also true in a set of poems related to personal life in a boys' school, set forth here in rather more intimate,

---

10   Spennemann, Dirk H.R. (2000). Ernest George Moll (1900-1997): a biographical sketch. URL: https://marshall.csu.edu.au/Marshalls/html/Literature/Moll.html.

not to say crusty, detail than usual. There are also some descriptions of station life and relations of humans with animals that may strike a modern audience, one hundred years later, as harsh and crude. Yet even today we need to remember that food does not come from stores, nor does clothing grow on its own. Large segments of the work are about topics as varied as aboriginal lore, a retelling of the biblical Jonah story, sheep ranching and gambling on horses.

I trust that readers will find the bulk of Moll's work to be worth the read.

1   US   Sedge Fire (1927, Harold Vinal)
2   US   Native Moments and other poems (1931, Metropolitan Press, Portland, Oregon)
3   US   Campus Sonnets (1934, Metropolitan Press, Portland, Oregon)
4   US   Blue Interval, (1935, Metropolitan Press, Portland, Oregon, reissued by Oregon Review Books, 2017)
5   AU   Cut from Mulga (1940, Melbourne University Press)
6   AU   Brief Waters (1945, Australasian Publishing Company)
7   AU   Beware the Cuckoo and other poems (1947, Australasian Publishing Company)
8   AU   The Waterhole (1948, Angus & Robertson)
9   AU   The Lifted Spear (1953, Angus & Robertson)
10   AU   The Rainbow Serpent and other poems (1962, Angus & Robertson)
11   US   Briseis (1965, Pageant Press)
12   AU   The Road to Cactus-land (1971, Edwards & Shaw)
13   US   The Well and the Star (1983, privately printed)
14   US   The View from a Ninetieth Birthday (1992, La Jolla Poets Press)
15   US   Recognitions at Ninety-three (1993, privately printed)
16   US   The Children of Somalia 1992-1994 and Other Poems (1994, privately printed)
17   US   A Gleaner's Sheaf of Poems (1995, privately printed).

Poems published in *The Lawrentian* (1921-22)

Ambition (November 3, 1921)

Give me not breathless, mountain-mirroring bays
Where languid folly toys a listless oar.
Give me not shallow, sedge-choked waterways
That slumber in the shadow of the shore.
Give me not that which costs no pain to win,
And, being won, lies passive in the hand;
Not the weak spark that smoulders into sin,
When purple shadows veil a palmy land.
But give me the wide sea, the hissing foam,
The flying spray that clings about the lips.
Give me a ship stout-braced to call my home,
And a brave heart when slow the cable slips.
Give me the ship, the compass and the wave,
To strive and live or find a worthy grave.

Perseverance (November 17, 1921)

Ah well! The mast hangs shattered by the board;
The tangled cordage heaps the slippery deck
Across our bows the black, salt seas are poured
As rudderless we float, a helpless wreck.
Before, a wall of lightning-riven black,
And boiling leagues of ocean stretched behind.
And in the gloom I hear the timbers crack,
And the loud shriek of sea-birds on the wind.
Yet, trusty comrade, hold the lantern high,
And give that axe into my willing hand;
We still shall live to see a calmer sky,
And tread the pathways of our native land.
While blow on blow we clear the wreck away,
See, yonder breaks the first faint light of day!

The House of Peace (December 1, 2021)

What shall it be, the red-veined marble hewn,
From all the ages or the blood-soaked sand
That glitters black beneath a pallid moon,
A bloody stain upon a bloodless land?
What shall it be wherewith we raise these halls!
The square-cut blocks of Truth that scorn the jeers
Or the soft lie that poison-reeking falls

Upon the anguish of a mother's fears?
Ah! give us Truth, the sum of Nature's law
And Love, the mystic, heaven-directing power,
And Hope to write in gold above each door;
So let us raise them battlement and tower,
The Halls where red-eyed Murder never trod,
Whose turrets tremble to the bells of God!

Song (January 26, 1922)

In noontide,
Or moontide,
By silent streams that flow,
The light shall rise,
Of paradise,
In lovelit eyes that glow;
And hushed shall be your troubled sighs,
In breathings soft and low.
I wandered to the sloping lawn,
The moon was in the sky;
And on the breezes clear was borne,
That haunty melody.
I turned my fevered brow to God
Beneath his lustrous stars,
And soothed was every burning pang,
As low that voice enraptured sang,
The simple artless bars:
In noontide,
Or moontide,
By silent streams that flow,
The light shall rise,
Of paradise,
In lovelit eyes that glow;
And hushed shall be your troubled sighs,
In breathings soft and low.

A Sonnet (February 9, 1922)

We are like children gathering broken shells
Upon the margin of a slumbrous sea.
Sometimes we hear the boom of distant bells
Or the low call of cattle on the lea.
Slowly the tall black ships move down the bay,
And we behold them like forgotten dreams
Come back to bless us from the Far Away,
Where children live and all is as it seems,

And all day long we gather useless things,
And hoard them gently with a miser's care;
Sharp bits of glass, and insect's gauzy wings,
A tangled braid of Autumn's crimson hair.
Then, when our mother calls us from the hill,
We leave them all and run to do her will.[11]

Song (February 23, 1922)

The birds are in the tree, love
The bees are on the wing
They sing for you and me, love
Through dreamy days of spring,
The flowers on the glade, love
The squirrels in the air
Are gifts of Peace, by heaven sent
To make us happier.

II.

The song the robins sing, love
The notes the wild bees make;[12]
What are the thoughts they bring, love
Beside the limpid lake?
I see it on your cheek, love
I read it in your eyes;
They sing a haunting sweet refrain
A song of Paradise.

Farewell (April 13, 1922)

Slowly the waves
Of the ocean are rising and falling;
Faintly from yonder mountain side
A voice is calling;
And from the valley chimes the vesper bell,
Love, farewell—farewell—

The Hour of Prayer (May 11, 1922)

It is the hour of prayer!
At yonder stream a thirsty herd is drinking,
From purple hills the evening shades are sinking,

---

11   "Distant bells" in line 3 appears as "listant" in the original, an apparent typo.
12   This appears as "wake" in the original, which is plausible, or perhaps a typo for "make,"
     which the editor has used here.

And one lone bird wings through the dusk his flight—
Goodnight! Goodnight!
The wide-eyed stars are beaming,
The weary world is dreaming,
And silence broods upon the sleeping air
It is the hour of prayer!

Poems from *Sedge Fire* (1927)

To a Friend

Your feet make quiet through my storm of days
A pathway for your radiant loveliness,
And though, close in, black-fronted angers press,
With you I walk down warm, dream-silent ways.

Thistle Stalks

I love the grim white thistle stalks
Upon the hills where Autumn walks
A yellow hag with breast all bare
And grasses sticking in her hair.

I love their twisted forms, the sneer
That marks them of a high career,
That reached at love and gathered dross
And rose in scorn above its loss.

I love the bleak old skeletons
That stare defiance at the suns,
For they were green, their leaf is dry,
And they can laugh as the hag goes by.

A Mother

You were stained with the dust of the road
When first I saw you;
You were strapped with a weary load,
Little son, when I bore you.

For your father's feet were light
On the highway ever;
He left one winter's night
And comes back never.

Your father's eyes were deep
With gypsy passion;
To lie, and kiss, and sleep,
Was not his fashion.

Your father's eyes were wild
With storm clouds drumming—

You are your father's child
And summer's coming.

Pause

The gray dawn hangs above the mountain top
As though afraid to touch her feet to earth;
Somewhere a wind, sensing that she is near,
Rises expectantly upon one elbow
And lifts a drowsy head above the ferns—
Then drops to sleep again. Birds, dew-awakened,
Ruffle damp wings and twitter dreamily
Like spirits lazing by a sea of sleep.

This is the pause;—the flowing is not yet;
But the ebb gathers from the waiting land
Its lingering waves. The dim-revealing stars
Are hushed away, and silent earth forms raise
Dark, shaggy heads to watch the imperious night
Slant her black wings above the crested sun.

The Gleaner

I am a gleaner where my dreams have run
With swift and shining sickles on before,
And silent are the lands beneath the sun
Where they will reap no more;

Yet all my days I gather broken grain
Content with little when each day is done,
For on the low horizon of the plain
Bright sickles flash the sun.

Arcturus
For A. H. D.

Arcturus comes when spring
Has half forgot her lovers,
When birds are on the wing
And the sick heart recovers,
But loves not anything.

Arcturus comes when leaves
Are beautiful in dying,
When all the summer thieves
In darkened hives are lying,

And frost is on the sheaves.

Arcturus' heart is deep
With pity for the lover,
And so he climbs the steep
When spring and love are over
And puts the world to sleep.

Crossing a Brook at Night

Alone, I had flung carelessly across
From brink to brink and never once looked down
To see if there were stars in the black water,
Or racing bits of foam. So had I often
Crossed that brook at night:—a short, quick step,
A leap, a rush of wind, a downward surging,
Hard earth again!—and so up over the ridge
And down the other side to the dark town.

But you were with me, gathered in my arms,
Your head against my shoulder, my cheek on yours,
Your shadowy hair like music on my eyes.
And I stood still and pressed you closer yet,
And poised, and leaped, and looked as we sped over,
And all the brook was filled with ghosts of stars!

Brown Eyes

Brown eyes that know the world but in a dream,
A haze of flowers
Sweet with new-fallen showers,
And all things lovely as in sleep they seem,
I ask for you
One only gift of what kind gods there be:
That, waking you may find amid the blue
Of opening vistas by a morning sea,
Truth but the gradual flower of your dream,
And all things lovely as in sleep they seem.

Brinsley Town

On Sabbath morn in Brinsley Town
The people wear their Sunday shoes
And creak to church and kneel them down
With foreheads pressed against the pews.

The drowsy elders kneel before—
For prayers are long in Brinsley Town,
While from the cherry at the door
God's laughter shakes the blossoms down.

Testament

Hide me not in the earth away,
Far from the flowers and the light of day;
Lay me not where the white roots creep
Pale from their bloodless winter sleep,
With a wall of earth about my head,
Dark with the secrets of the dead;
For I might hear the heavy beat
When the sexton walks across my feet,
And I might feel the fresh sweet air
When one lies down beside me there.

But on some quiet starry night
Shroudless let me sink from sight
Down to the valleys of the sea
Open-eyed to eternity.
Love of heaven nor fear of hell
Walled my soul from the ocean swell;
God I saw in the bird that clung
To the maple bough which the south wind swung;
And God, I know, in some deep sea place
Will wipe the darkness from my face,
And show me on some quiet day
The fish among the kelp at play.

Rondeau

Time, beware you touch her not in going;
Breathe no sorrow on her dusky hair,
Shade your sun and curb your storm-wind's blowing—
Time, beware.

Yours the rock that crumbles in thin air,
Yours the mountain where the clouds are snowing,
Yours the star that flames its last despair:

She has found a strength beyond your knowing,
Greater than your strength, for she is fair;
Come not you where beauty's pride is glowing—
Time, beware.

Drifting

To drift along forever with no aim
Save still to drift—no compass and no guide
To shock me with a purpose sanctified;
No hope, no fear, no triumph, and no shame—
To be but the cool shadow of a name
Elusive, that no house-wife pity chide
My gypsy waywardness, nor hate deride
My passing with the story whence I came—

Thus ever to be, and when the flood-tide fills
The sedgy creeks that whisper of the sea,
Hoist the swift sail, and ghost-like, stealthily
Drop from the last black pier of human ills—
Then should I grow sea-weary, let me be
A drifting shade among the moonlit hills.

Out of the Wind

There is no passion in your kiss tonight,
But the calm sweetness of a summer day
That holds the world in a deep hush of light
And pillows dreams among the new-mown hay.

Lost once in beauty's infinite desire
We rushed from crest to crest across the deep,
But we have learned the comfort of a fire
On the low shore, and the warm peace of sleep.

Dejection

The years lurch by like camels in a line,
Shuffling along an endless waste of sand;
And here and there an Arab waves a hand,
Or bright with death I see a dagger shine.
Above wide jaws round blood-shot eyes seek mine,
Piercing my heart like spears of Samarcand,
For they are cursèd eyes that know a land
Where flows the poison honey mixed with wine.

And must I join this herd that slouches by,
Going, it knows not whither, caring less,
Till all be blent in one vast nothingness
In its last gloomy caravanserai?
No, leave me here where quiet still may bless
The heart that longs for nothing but to die.

Timocles
(From Anatole France's "Thais.")

Here I sit with folded hands
Heeding neither cold nor heat,
Wintry blast nor burning sands
Blistering my naked feet.

Let who will be at their task,
Till their fields and sow their grain;
Though earth yield them what they ask
All their toil shall be in vain.

Let the thinker think his thought
Wandering far through starry space,
When his fleetest dream is caught
Dust will blow upon his face

Let the ants of commerce crawl
Round their sticky honey-bin,
Grasp and tug and clash and brawl—
Death will take their harvest in.

I will heed nor peace nor strife,
Nothing do, nor think, nor say,
So the fool who gave me life
Shall have nought to take away.

Warning to Love

Shadow hands of wind, my love,
Are on the wheat today,
Silent, stealthy fingers
Turning all to gray,
Robber hands of wind, my love,
That steal the bloom away.

Look not from your window, love,
On the wheat today!

A Spider

This gray monstrosity that crawls
From clod to clod a summer's day
Is like a thing that Time forgot

To crush and hide away.

And I would hate it if I could
And kill with eager speed;
But there's a spider in my heart
That will not bear the deed.

The lifted hand falls impotent,
The fires of anger die,
While we face lonely into life,
This monstrous thing and I.

Summer-Thought

Could I but lie in some sea-cavern deep
Where sheds the sun an emerald-filtered light,
Dim as the sickle-moon's when in the night
Gray phantom clouds turn over in their sleep;
And could I sink my elbows in the steep
Of some soft sand-bar gleaming coolly white
And flecked with sea-shells amber-clear and bright,
And gay with gaudy crabs that slowly creep
From under streaming weeds—could I thus be
Left with my dreams upon an ocean-bed,
With pale green waters kissing hands and head
And whispering of wide vales of mystery,
The world's faint echo trembling down to me,
I'd smile to hear men mutter: "He is dead."

Two Ghosts

They go pacing up and down
Through the shadow-haunted street,
Two pale ghosts in a dead town
That will never hear their feet.

By the well-remembered place,
Where love came and found them sleeping,
Slowly the wan lovers pace
Side by side, and both are weeping.

For the flesh of love is dead,
And the flame has soothed its gashes,
But desire holds his head
Sitting lonely in the ashes.

Searching through a maze of pain
For the kiss they dared not take,
Bound forever in the chain
Of the law they dared not break,
    Up and down, up and down,
      Two pale ghosts in a dead town.

If You Should Say

If you should say you love me not at all
In some still hour
That drowses like a flower
Heavy with slumber when the crickets call;
If you should say
Your kisses were untimely petals spread
By little winds of passion at their play
That tossed them up and left them lying dead—
If you should say, when dew is at the fall,
Some summer night, you love me not at all,
Though still the hour,
I shall not smell the flower,
Nor feel the dew, nor hear the crickets call.

Earth-Lover

I love the adventurous thought that brings
A sense of vast mysterious things,
Laws driving onward under chance
And meanings hid in circumstance.

I love the warmth of days that flood
With dreamy languorousness the blood
Till sleep has sealed with impotence
The last protest of waking sense.

I love dark eyes that hold the fire
Of deep, untamable desire,
And the wild beat of hearts that move
To the sweet earthiness of love.

I love all things that creep and run,
And wind, and rain, and the warm sun;
I love bright flowers and summer bees—
And death, a closer life with these.

Futility

They walk the jagged ridges of the night
In perilous abandon to the stars—
Dim, human forms against the uncertain light
That rises from below the world. Bright spars
Of false, alluring gold are at their feet,
And thin, sharp-fingered winds are in their hair;
But, all insensible, they keep their beat
Like ghosts intent on shadows of despair.

But morning gathers slowly like the drift
Of foam across a headland newly won
By the young tide; and soon, with stifled breath,
The phantom seekers turn them east and lift
Proud, pitiful faces, white against the sun,
That soon will flood their hollow eyes with death.

In September

I who but taste the sunlight
Shall drink it by and by,
For the first red leaves are falling,
And with them I shall lie
On a wide cool bed of earth
Beneath an open sky.

And I shall feel the winds blow
The flowers that are me—
The little winds that flutter
At dawning from the sea;
And I shall wait the coming
Of the first boisterous bee.

And I shall feel the stirring
Of his pollen-cumbered feet,
That bring the dust of other flowers
To make my seed complete;
And I shall yield him honey,
And he will find it sweet.

And I shall feel the rain fall
On the dead leaves overhead,
And feel its earthy sweetness
Around me in my bed;
And I shall send new flowers up
And never know I'm dead.

On an Amoeba

I who am strong to hold the world enchained
In vast proud thought—tomorrow I may be
Washed by slow rain down arteries of earth
That grope through darkness blindly to the sea.

And this slight thing that reason never touched
With searching fire, that is not bound nor free,
Moves down the ages indestructible
In Protozoan immortality.

Song

My love's eyes were filled with laughter
Beautiful and fleet
As the sun that follows after
Shadows on the wheat.

But her lips were sly-alluring
And I broke their pride—
Like a night-affrighted poppy
Her bright laughter died.

On a Mountain Top

A void is all about me and a calm
Of nothingness; the very air hangs dead
Cloud-like athwart the sun; the rocks are red
With shrivelled moss, and on the twisted arm
Of a sere pine, flung out in white alarm,
A sleepy lizard lifts a slow, flat head,
Dull as a figure cut in senseless lead
By barbarous hand to work a cursèd charm.

How easy now to step across the edge
And be forever nothing, with the stones!
Under the cliffs the sun will wrap my bones
In warm, white sleeping, and the withered sedge
Will lift the wind in low and languorous tones
To the brown hawk that drowses on his ledge.

Coquette

When you smiled I smiled again,
When you frowned I smiled the sweeter,
Till the game was on, and then
You pursued, but I was fleeter.

Where the roses made a blind,
Like an eager flame you sought me,
But you fell so far behind
That I faltered—and you caught me.

In the sunken field of clover
What should lovers say or do?
But the pity was, young lover,
'Twas the game I loved, not you.

Cosmos

Let me be glad in little things
Nor search afar to find
The law that shapes the beetle's wings
And the eternal mind.
A patch of thistles at the door
With summer bees at play
Can teach me all the mystic lore
Of things that leap and things that bore,
Of hearts that love forevermore,
And swift red hands that slay.

The Immortal Part

My love came down from the hills
In the time of anemone skies
With a splash of rain on her cheek
And the soul of the wind in her eyes.

She gave me her hand to hold,
Her hair to loosen and twine,
She gave me her lips to kiss—
And the joy of the wind was mine.

What now though the hills grow cold
When the sun is gone from the sky?
The joy of the wind is mine
And hers, and it cannot die.

For beyond the day and the night
The wings of the wind beat wide,
And she will ride on the wings of the wind,
And I shall go at her side.

To _____

(With the painting by Waterhouse of "Hylas and the Nymphs.")

The Nymphs that wooed young Hylas to the deep
While Hercules, deserted, vainly grieved,
I thought their wiles had long been sealed in sleep
By gloomy death, but I have been deceived.

For in your eyes, dark, haunting as the night,
They live again, seductive, phantom-dim;—
I know why Hylas left his world of light,
And though he died, I do not weep for him.

Flowers Blackened by the Frost

Why have these petals not fallen decently?
Their fragrance spent on the warm summer winds,
And all their eager lovers, dusky bees
And shadow-quiet moths grown satiate
With too much nectar, immortality
Safe treasured in the dark of hidden seeds,
Hope rounded, beauty gone, it had been well
To drop away from life and leave no scar.

But as proud drinkers when the feast is high,
Whose homing hour is long since overpast,
Still linger for the last sweet cup, so they,
Drunk with their beauty, pressed the edge of time
For one last hour of sun, and flung their all
In haughty payment down the black maw of death.

To a Girl in the Mountains

What has your spirit in common with these hills
That you should yield your fragile loveliness
To the hard rock? What subtle longing fills
Your eyes with shadows soft as a caress?
Is it that you have pierced this vast recess
Of senseless stone with the warm life that thrills
Through depths of primal being till rocks confess
A sympathy with human joys and ills?

But who shall tell love's ways or understand
The need that plucks from others' wound the dart,
Pressing it selfward till the red drops start
Only to lose themselves in the dull sand—
The need that bids you crush with fearless hand
This spiny brood of pain against your heart!

Miser Mother and Child

"What did the stranger give you
Who stopped you on the street?
Was it a bright new penny, child,
Or something nice to eat?"

"It was no bright new penny, mother,
Nor a sweet-cake to share,
But a wild hedge-rose he plucked close by
To twine in my black hair."

"A flower to wreathe in your long hair
And make you proud and vain!
The devil takes all those, my child,
Who seek for aught but gain!"

"I do not fear the devil, mother,
Who makes the wee black sheep,
For with the fragrance of my flower
I'll send him fast asleep."

Two by the River

Two by the river, and one looked up
To the heights where the winds beat free
And down over a world of sun-wide plains
To the edge of the quiet sea.

And the other gazed at the muddy swirl
Where the eddies made a ring
Round a fleck of foam that tossed and spun
Like a mad and frightened thing.

Two by the river, and one was filled
With the pain of a wild surmise,
While the other sat with placid hands
And a great calm in his eyes.

An Old Man Watering Cabbages

In the green quiet of his garden plot
This is his summer-morning happiness:
To drive the windy spray against broad leaves
And watch them quicken to the cool caress.

Cheeks sunk, head bent, an old and withered man;
Yet though his eyes are slow and dulled with pain
He feels the sweet conspiracy of life
And walks companion with the sun and rain.

Flooding warm peace about his quiet heart
The memories of his youth rise up once more
Like soft recurring melodies that break
Bright waves of gladness on a waiting shore.

And he is in the wide green fields again,
Hoe in his hand, with comrades young and gay,
Laughing amid the frolic of rain
In a far country and a buried day.

The Riders

My soul and I were once good friends together
Keeping sedately side by side, attuned
Each to the slightest song the other crooned
In long bright rides on purple slopes of heather,
Lulled by the rhythmic creak of saddle-leather,
And swing of easy pace. The long days swooned
In sunshine, and the night, with languor mooned,
Made lazy comfort of all times and weather.

Love brought a strangeness like a flight of birds
Sweeping far out from some sleep-heavy shore
That leave the silence deeper that before;
We clutched each other but found not any words.
Oh passionately now my soul and I
Ride side by side in silence steadfastly!

In Winter

Ever the loud wind urges,
And dead leaves winter-strown
In fretful gusty surges

Down empty ways are blown.

Ever strong passion urges
Across an ice-locked fen
In dark and dismal surges
The withered hearts of men.

Psyche's Task

Psyche with her slim white hands
Sorting from the slave-girl's heaping
Poppy seeds, and rye, and wheat;
Psyche with the bleeding feet
Sorrow-bruised in weary lands
Since she looked on Cupid sleeping.

Psyche long has passed away,
But whom Cupid's conquest numbers
Have her dreary task to do:
Thoughts to sift and deeds to rue—
This is the price that lovers pay
Would they see the god who slumbers.

Haven and Love

Not in a cold clear Thought
An Arctic circle of light,
Not where a pale Idea
Rustles her frigid gown,
Not in the radiance caught
From a luminous star at night
When the dawn is pulsing near
And the heavens are broadening down.

How should our lips confess
There, what our hearts reveal?
How should we fling our Truth
Sheer in the face of Law?
For a thousand angers press
With a sullen glint of steel
Where Mind lays bare a tooth
And Life unsheaths a claw.

We from the bitter light
Hide our love like a treasure;
Hands palm-up to Law—

Nothing for him is there.
Safe in our valley of night
Where Passion knows no measure—
There we can tell it o'er
In the dark of our mingled hair.

Love is a ship afloat
On wide flood tides of dream
With white Sense-sails high set
For every Mood to take;
The languor of your throat
In moonlight's fitful gleam,
Your eyes how dewy wet
When morning bids us wake.

And does the West wind blow?
We shall not lie unheeding;
Or North, or East, or South,
We quiver to the leap:
Your bosom soft as snow
And tender to my pleading,
The slow curve of your mouth
Where kisses break from sleep.

Is the red lightning swift
To lash his plunging thunder,
And wheel the storm clouds out
Beneath the rim of sea?
Like some pale flower adrift
On wide blue waves of wonder
Unmindful of the rout
You come in peace to me.

Is the warm earth aswoon
With hush of flowers awaking?
And do the wild birds tell
What mystery folds the land?
I know the meaning soon
On your sweet lips for taking,
All earth, and heaven, and hell
In the pressure of your hand.
. . . .
Not in a cold clear Thought,
A still sharp circle of light;
Not where a pale Idea
Rustles her frigid gown;

Not where the battle is fought
Between dark Error and Right
For Truth that is mostly Fear
And Law that is but a frown.

Let Mind lay bare a tooth
And Life unsheath a claw,
Let their conflict shake the deep
While Law stands sternly by;
We hold in our hands the Truth
They rend each other for,
Close in our valley of sleep
Belovèd, you and I.

Blindman's Buff

I did not seek to join the game, but hands
I could not see put darkness on my eyes,
And feet I could not follow led me on.
A whisper—a soft bosom—fragrant lips—
Love! but she slipped away. Knife on a stone—
Hate! but my lunge was futile. Laughter next
Tapped lightly on my shoulder, but when I turned
The sound of fleeing foot-falls died away.

So the game sped: blind gropings, sudden touch
Of warm elusive fingers, ecstasies
That came tip-toe, and paused, and leapt away;
Till, wild with terror of the false pursuit,
I plucked the bandage from my eyes, and there,
Hideously still, was one lone player—Death.

Night-Lily

Only for night-eyes your color,
Too bold for the light;
Only for luminous moth-eyes,
Vague in the night.

Red like the redness of blood,
Yellow as silk,
Black like a raven's feather
And white with the whiteness of milk.

Fever of marshy places,
Yellow and red;

Passion of days long vanished
And loves long dead.

One Who Scorned Love

Love will not find her here
In the deep halls of death
Where royal figures move
Yet breathe no breath

Where spirits ache for sound
And none is heard,
And lips are wild with speech
Yet say no word.

Where hearts are sick for rest
Yet may not sleep,
And eyes are filled with tears
Yet do not weep.

Where thin white fingers move
Through the still air
To soothe a loved one's brow
Who is not there.

Where Passion like a king
In some mute-play
Frames an eternal word
He may not say.
Where Death walks mockingly
In Life's fair guise
Love will not wipe the dark
Pain from her eyes.

The Senses

Handmaids of Thought are we that build her fires
And fashion subtle perfumes for her hair
That men shall gaze and claim her very fair
The while their hearts grow bold with high desires;
And when of their warm flattery she tires
And grows earth-weary in her queenly chair
Of our white backs we build a royal stair
To lead her feet up dream-enchanted spires.

And when at last her dreams prove vain, her trust
In the proud spirit of man lies trampled low,
Her sweetest fruits an idle heap of dust
And all her conquests for the winds to blow,
When she is deep in anger at all life
We know her need and stoop beneath her knife.

Flower and Fruit

I wore you like a flower
A summer's day,
But in a quiet hour
You dropped away.

And like the flower whose flame is
Put out by summer's breath,
You left a fruit whose name is
Death.

Dying Pauper to Attendant

This body, sir, this weary body though soon
It must be helpless in the void of death,
Has felt the wind, the rain, and the warm sun,
Ridged green sea-water with strong thrusting arms,
Pushed with exulting breast against the flow
Of inland rivers, scaled lofty peaks and stood,
In conscious power of the deep life-urge fulfilled,
Balanced to sense the circling speed of earth.

And will you lock this body in the dark
Deep from the winds that ran their ecstasy
Of motion through its veins, far from the sun
That gave it warmth, and sleep, and quiet dreams,
Cold in the earth that once it trod upon?
Deep, far, and cold, no wind, no sun, no rain?

Think No More of Love

Think no more of love when I am dead
Lest death should mock you with the loss you bear;
And should you die, I'll not remember hair,
Or lips, or breast, or dear love-pillowed head
In hush of kisses. Of us be it said:
" 'Tis but a day, and she seems not to care";
Or, "see how light his feet are on the stair
As if she still were listening for his tread."

For love like ours needs no eternity
Beyond its leap of vision; no pitiful
Sad lingering downward to insensate gloom;
Brief, proud in beauty, held, yet ever free,
The flush on the white breast of a wild gull
That goes with life, too lovely for the tomb!

A Face

I wonder what old passions made that face,
Sculpturing flesh in ages far remote
Till beauty found him, but too frail to bear
Desire with icy fingers at his throat.

An Old Woman

Age has subdued the spirit in her eyes
And shut her heart to beauty and to pain
That she might lay her self-hood in the dust
And quietly go back to earth again.

The Dreamer

In dreams he spent the languor of bright days,
Chiding the hours with passion-gloomy eyes,
His every impulse headed by constraint
And every purpose shattered by surmise.

The Invalid

You did not love me when my feet were set
In eager strength to hold you stride for stride;
Now that I am a thing I would forget,
Keep your pity, for I need my pride.

The Rebel

Hard by the ashes of his fathers' fires
He leans against a broken altar-stone
Triumphant, proud, yet one whose heart has learned
How terrible it is to dwell with Truth, alone.

The Impotent

I saw her spirit wounding her frail flesh
With passions from the dark of ages got,
And I who had the power could make no move
To set her free, because she loved me not.

A Silence Between Lovers

I must not speak tonight, for I should say
Things you would strive in vain to understand;
Dark bits of night left floating in the day,
Pain too elusive for your honest hand.

Winter

Earth, like a woman, has fallen to her knees
And covered up her eyes with sombre hair
Lest curious love should find old memories
Caught in a frozen stare.

The Venture

I thought to make her angry; with a word
Bitter as death to sting her sleep apart
That passion might lay hands upon her heart—
She only smiled as though she had not heard.

The Indifferent

"'Tis cold, you say? I do not feel the blast.
Venus is low tonight, and very clear?
I see no star. The night is deepening fast,
Come in, you say? No, I am happy here.

The Undertaker Speaks

"We turn their lips a little upward—so—
A sainted smile;—the happy soul let free
Forgot to shut the door. The soon-to-die
Take comfort, and the parson takes his fee."

A Puritan

Her spirit raised proud angry pinnacles
Pain-buttressed, far above life's sensuous deep;

Yet on the sheerest crag of that stern soul
Moonlight breathes softly and winds lie down to sleep.

Lifting Boards

We lifted boards; the grass beneath was white,
Thin yellowing stalks that held no hope of flower;
"I knew two women"—"O let be," I said;
He smiled: " 'Twill all be finished in an hour."

The Poet

Slowly he shapes the granite of a thought
To forms of life with passionate lips and hair,
Till on a day he finds that he has caught
Himself in immortal gesture of despair.

Poems from
Native Moments and other poems (1931)

Song of Myself

I have fashioned with gladness and pain
A thought in the dark of my brain,
A sword that will bite and prevail
And I swing it and cry it for sale.

Come and buy, come and buy! What's to pay?
Just a sword to meet my sword in play,
Striking blade along blade till the eye
Glow bright as the sparks where they fly.

I have made me a body beside
With muscles that ripple and slide
And laughter is shoes to my feet—
Now I cry it for sale in the street.

Come and buy, come and buy! What's to pay?
Just a hand to meet my hand in play
Till we sink on the grass breast to breast
And a kiss shuts the world up in rest.

Will none hear? Come and buy, come and buy,
While you've something to spend, ere you die!
For I go like the wind or the rain
And the street will be silent again.

Pierrot to a Timid Lady

Lie not still when Pierrot sings
At your window soft moon-things,

Songs that have the moonbeam in them,
For by moonlight he did spin them,

Spinning swift as spin he could
Sitting in the enchanted wood

Where the shy moon-elves had led him;
Spinning swiftly while they fed him

Fruit of many a magic tree
Ripe and dripping where the bee

Tasted first.His ditty done,
Swift he rose and swift did run,

Leaving far the wood behind him,
Running lest the gods should find him,

Thief who shook their sacred tree
And sucked nectar merrily.

And the ditty that he made
Sitting in the hoar-oak's shade,

(For the moon was bright as day),
In his heart he tucked away.

There too soon it warmed and grew
Sweeter far, and sadder too

Than a Pierrot's song should be
Writ beneath the enchanted tree.

Then, Pierrette, when Pierrot sings
At your window soft moon-things,

Lie not still lest you should wrong
Pierrot's heart in Pierrot's song.

Happiness

You're cold without there in the wintry weather,
And I'm all warm within;
With quiet hand I shake the logs together
And watch the fire-sprites spin.

I'm but a guest, and they who asked me hither,
Bade me to come alone;
You're cold without there in the gusty blither
Beyond that wall of stone.

To Earth

I strive with hot endeavor
To bend her to my will—

She gives me thorns for roses,
And laughs, and mocks me still.

I burn with ancient anger,
And turn, and walk apart;—
She sends, in half-derision,
A flower to break my heart.

So we shall strive together
While life and strength remain,
Each looking to the season
When we'll be friends again.

To N——.

For a Narcissus grown in winter

This perfect thing she gave my eyes
Before the coming of the Spring,
Or April clouds in April skies—
This perfect thing.

Earth felt her warm hands' lingering
And woke to life with sweet surprise
Half waiting for the larks to sing.

But she had used love's witcheries,
Conspiring with the sun to bring
One bloom from where lost summer lies—
This perfect thing.

Invitation

In his circle each shall go
Moving toward the solemn end,
This my friend and that my foe
And this other more than friend.

While we lay dispersed in Fate
Ere our lips had learned to move,
Hate had sown the seeds of hate
Love had sown the seeds of love.

He that finds me in his star
Let him speak and use no guile;
So shall two who come from far
Mingle and be one a while.

Mingle and be richer so,
Thought to thought like bells that chime
From the valleys far below
Where we slept so long a time.

But who finds no line of me
Graven in the secret book
Let him never wantonly
Shake my silence with a look.

In my circle let me go
Keep you yours until the end;
You my friend, and you my foe,
You that know me more than friend.

On the Beach—A Fancy

If a rock should plunge from the steep
Where we lie, you and I, half asleep,
Should plunge, and fall near us—not harm—
Would the sudden bright wave of alarm
Sweep us out of ourselves, drive us clear
From the slime of our Harbor of Fear,
To the wind and the blue and the sea
Where your hands would reach only for me,
Sweep us out to the sea and the blue
Where my hands would reach only for you?

Or we turn on the beach where we lie
And drowsily gaze at the sky:
"There's a palace with towers" you say,
"To the East there a little—all day
There are laughter and song in its halls
And at night a soft whispering falls.
And at night"—but a cloud, so you say,
Like a gate shuts the palace away.
If a wind should blow open that gate—
'Tis my word now—O love, would we wait?

A Hymn to Indifference

When from the dreams of men Olympus rose
A beacon for their upward bending prayer,
One goddess found that Crest a place of foes
And still lives nameless and forsaken there.

She is no partner of the hopes of men,
No mystic beckoner from imagined stars;
Fallen, she does not bid them rise again;
Or risen, smiles no approval of their scars.

No hand has traced her features on a shield
To charm the danger from some throbbing heart;
No eye has found within her name revealed
The prophet secret at the core of Art.

Outcast of men for that she will not lend
Her breast to the dark pressure of their woe,
For that she will not hate them nor befriend,
Nor lift them, nor in anger lay them low.

Yet in the quiet ways of life my eyes
Have learned to seek her form for she is fair;
No pain she shows nor any glad surprise,
Nor reads my brow to find what's written there.

Nothing she gives to me and nothing takes—
No shrewd exchange of notions made or bought;
Her eyes are cold and grey as winter lakes,
Her brow has never weakened into thought.

But still she sits, and I can lay me down
In my poor tatters of mortality
And seek her eyes and never fear a frown
And never fear that she will pity me.

And I can find her without gift or prayer
On the far mountain pinnacles of stone,
By winter aspens bleak in the bleak air,
Or in a bird's nest when the brood has flown.

In the Study

So she sits and talks of love
In my study here at night,
Gives the rug a thoughtful shove
With her foot, or smiling bright,
Bites the finger of her glove.

Lays her questions neatly out
Like so many snares to take

Captive all the brood of doubt;
Hears my answers; half awake,
Yawns and moves about.

Takes a book at last and goes;
Smiles her "Thank-you" from the door;
Trips away on flippant toes.
Good! but why upon the floor
Must she drop that crumpled rose!

Spring Song of the Unquiet Heart

The best flower's the bold flower
That lifts its head in Spring
Before the winds have sheathed their swords,
Before the robins sing.

When sunset in the gusty days
Burns red above blue hills
A little run of laughter shakes
The trumpet daffodils.

For they have heard a prophecy
And deep amid the earth
Have gathered bravely the first warmth
To bring a flower to birth.

The rose still is waiting
For the summer sun to shake her
And the jonquils and daffodils
Laugh softly lest they wake her.

She shall have summer
And the bright sun all day
But when she blooms the daffodils
Will wither back to clay.

She shall have summer
And the bees to make her proud;
But the daffodil's the light that falls
Between a cloud and a cloud.

She shall have summer
And a long while to die;
But the daffodil's laughter
Is as brief as a sigh.

For she's a queen, queenly,
Bent on a queenly part,
But the daffodil's an urchin
With a dream at his heart.

The best flower's the bold flower
That lifts its head in Spring
Before the winds have sheathed their swords,
Before the robins sing.

Pain-Song

Wind all night and fitful gusts of rain
Dark, all dark, and darkness in the brain
Darkness creased with livid streaks of pain.

All night long the droning of the sea
Deathless that, and moaning wearily,
Deathless that but there's an end to me.

Spring-Beckoning

Gather you daffodils, violets and aenemones,
And the shy fawn-lilies that grow among the hills;
Summer days are coming, loud with drowsy bumble bees
Soon along the brooks will blow the wild blue squills.

Gather the gay crocuses, and the gleaming buttercup
Shining where the tangled grass of other summers lies;
Hunt to find them eagerly, take their fragile beauty up,
They will give their gladness for the gladness in your eyes.

Take you what you will of Spring, running yon and hither,
All the flowers will yield them, feeling no annoy,
For they know you tender, know that when they wither
You will feel their beauty as now you feel their joy.

Content

I could go down tonight
Where no grass is, nor any breath of flowers,
Nor tree, nor bird, nor sudden beat of showers,
Nor wind, nor joy of light.

I could go unafraid,
Knowing myself not worth the trouble of fear;
Audacious, empty, smiling with wan cheer
Upon the wan ghost laid.

A Bow to Folly

Then look on Folly while her lips are red
And warm her breast to be desired;

Take her white hand while it is soft and still
Has something of the wanton's power to thrill;

Make her your mistress while she still may bear
Sons with the wind of laughter in their hair.

For by and by she'll creep into your bed
When she's grown old and strangely withered

And make you father on the day you die
To one you'll have no breath left to deny;

And when Death weaves a crown with quiet hand
To give you honor in the silent land,

On high the pale preposterous Clown will sit
Upon your brow and thumb his nose at it.

Native Moments

I
Beneath the lifted light of consciousness
Moths stirred the dark in wantonness of flight;
Their shadows crossed like fear upon my eyes
Till passion set her candle in the night.

II
The Potter's hand may shape, but ours on his
Moulds subtly to the pattern of our need:
A girl was born amid the falling years
Because I saw two linnets on a reed.

III
From one "good-bye" a wonder moved across
My soul like music heard at night afar,
Wakened a dream from toneless vasts of sleep
And startled the deep silence with a star.

IV
In gradual discernment on my eyes,
That had not seen for holding you too fast,
Planet by planet, warm and silently,
The heavens of your beauty break at last.

V
You are the memory of a thousand suns
That rose from misted seas before our birth
And looked on other lovers wistfully,
Seeing their paths of darkness back to earth.

VI
Your eyes are midnight; something I have dreamed
Dawns in their depths and lightens out to me;
Beneath the calm clear beauty a woman wakes,
And in the woman "La Belle Dame Sans Merci."

VII
One night I saw you leaning o'er a cliff
Of mad gray laughter, breast and shoulders bare,
Wild songs and wine upon your mouth, a rose
Caught in the streaming darkness of your hair.

VIII
I would not trust a singing bird to you
To love and care for; there would come a day
His pulsing throat would lure you to his cage—
And who should bid you keep your hands away?

IX
Never will men call you innocent,
For that you bear, in hands vague as a spell,
A blossom grown in dust of worlds; I bring
A flower you'll know, sprung from a cleft in hell.

X
Form weds with vision in the dreaming brain
And turns to substance all the mysteries:
A Grendel on the marshes of the North
A Venus in the foam of Southern seas.

XI
Into the spacious valleys of the soul
Blow wisps of fog that veil the far, sublime,

Cold pinnacles of thought, and drop a hush,
A twilight shadow in the stream of time.

XII
My lips have made a poppy on your breast.
See the warm petals, subtle-edged as rain,
Ache to the sudden rush of stormy weather—
The might of love and wizardry of pain.

XIII
I hold you in the hollow of my hand;
Exulting, I remember a far hour
When, mad with beauty and the wine of June,
I crushed the petals of a white moon-flower.

XIV
April makes riot in me where you curl
With slow soft motion, till a bud of fire
Opens wide petals round us and we lie
Cupped in the deep red lily of desire.

XV
You shall know all the pain that men have brought
To women in all ages; madly I press
Anguish upon your lips;—oh, wonder-eyed
You turn to meet that cruel tenderness!

XVI
Fluttering breath and broken falling hands!
Leave me not yet; my eyes are strange with pain;
Angers lie thick about us; go not yet—
We must not part till the stars come again.

XVII
Perhaps we came too near the Primal Fire,
Startling the old Earth-Giant seated there;
Almost he had forgot the shape of man—
(Let go your fingers from his tangled hair).

XVIII
What hand reached out to touch you from the dark?
You slipped from my embraces silently
A wan smile on your lips, and in your eyes
A heron dreaming by a moonless sea.

XIX

And in my heart, while you slept, having sinned,
Came one and danced me to a crazy tune;
And while he spun me round I heard the wind
Twist icicles of laughter from the moon.

XX

Why do you smile so strangely, drawing down
My face to where your breasts in languor part?
I have plucked orchids in warm Southern lands,
But always with a Fear about my heart.

XXI

Do you not feel them stirring in the dark?
Hot, twisting things that writhe about our knees,
Dragons of eld resurgent in the embrace
That sweeps us back to primal ecstasies.

XXII

All that I know of midnight and the moon,
The curve of waters, the wind's unreticence,
The pulse that beats within the pulse of noon,
I crush to you in one deep throb of Sense.

XXIII

Palely calm, from slopes of being afar,
You gaze at me; the close long pressure's over;
Somewhere are lands brooding in the wide sun,
And drowsy bees, and lush wet banks of clover.

XXIV

Weary from passion you droop within my arms;
How fair your brow, how sweet your plundered lips!
And in your eyes the gray still light of one
Who has looked often at departing ships.

XXV

Now, Passion silenced like an ancient rout,
In you is stillness and a path of stars;
I, from the mind's dark turrets gazing out,
Feel desolately human with my scars.

XXVI

The road was long—take not your hand away—
That led us to this moment from the wrong
Of many deaths and sad dark years of sleep—
'Tis but a moment, and the road was long.

XXVII
Tell me the things you came so far to say
That I might learn again with sweet surprise
What moor-birds knew beside the sedgy streams
When Omar was a boy with wistful eyes.

XXVIII
Were there temples in Old Egypt then?
What gods were richer for your baffling smile!
And did you worship Love? And was he man
Or strange half-brute beside the slumbery Nile?

XXIX
Or has your spirit caught a memory
Of April rains that called the grass to birth
Ere your soft throat was fashioned of desire,
Ere your white hands were flowers upon the earth?

XXX
The sunrise calls you from your dreams, I know,
With deeds unborn that cry upon repose;
Yet look behind; the stature of a soul
Is measured by the shadow that it throws.

XXXI
Proud is that stature when you and I make one
Of our two strengths to plunge the caves of time
And find along the rock roots of the world
The life germ moving darkly in the slime.

XXXII
Sure in that far beginning, the past is ours,
And all our days and nights too short to reap
In body's warmth its richness, till we fall
Upon the second and the darker sleep.

XXXIII
I wake. You lie beside me languorously,
Pale but half mocking in your tumbled place;
And from the valley of lost springs there sweeps
Something warm like joy across my face.

XXXIV
Your hand upon the pillow at my cheek:
Frail, wan bird, what yearning bade you start
In high bold flight across the years, what need
Dropped you at last in the warm nest of my heart!

XXXV
Thought drifts away to silence and desire
Seeks his cool bed of ashes. Hark awhile!
Outside I hear the clatter of passing feet
Bound churchward—how I love you for that smile!

XXXVI
From timeless space the dismal prophets peer
Like dry malicious mockers of our birth.
Fear them not, love—they will not see our fire
Lost in the wide and windy plains of earth.

XXXVII
Let no one tread where we have set our hands
To lift the earth in flowers; silence deep
Shall lie upon that bold sweet tenderness,
Lovely as Life, and terrible as sleep.

XXXVIII
Through Autumn to the month of brittle stars,
Our eyes upon each other, lost to men,
Wandering in some rich harmony we moved
Till the first snow—we saw the world again.

XXXIX
Midwinter, yet a potted tulip thrusts
Its bloom-stalk from the warm, conspiring earth;
Each day you tend it, and each day your soul
Leans shyly to the mystery of that birth.

XL
From you shall spring a strong and terrible man
Who will drink up our lives like water spilled
And turn his fingers to our throats that Earth
May love him well for her dark dream fulfilled.

XLI
We are too pale for heroes, too o'ercast
With hopes of harvests we shall never reap;
Yet through us Life will stretch a backward hand
To rouse a Viking from the dust of sleep.

XLII
Some lost old ancestor who wanly keeps
His dark unquiet where grass roots blindly thrust

Will feel that birth amid his forceless days
And chuckle, though his mouth be stopped with dust.

XLIII

It were not good the lusts of earth should die
Prisoned in the cold chambers of the brain;
Loose her wild soul in the sinews of a man,
Our son, though he must drink our lives like rain!

XLIV

Yet we would have him tender fitfully,
Abashed when girls' eyes seek him with their wooing,
Broken before a flower his heel has crushed,
Startled to wonder by his own hand's doing.

XLV

Not like ourselves, but like that part of us
That died beneath the daggers of our fear
When caution froze the laughter in our veins
And wisdom whispered darkly at our ear.

XLVI

He will take up the pageant where we fall,
Flaunt the gay colors that we feared to wear,
Shout the mad songs we choked on, stir our dust,
And, laughing, bind its fragrance in his hair.

XLVII

And so to Life one fearless, give him o'er;
We'll watch him move across the darkening land,
And when he waves from the last hill of all
We'll guess for whom the flower that's in his hand.

XLVIII

Earth shall not forget us yet awhile
For we have lived her longing joyously;
On a blue hill of summer we caught her smile,
Dared her dream, and set her spirit free.

XLIX

Alone, thought could not help, and body's strength,
Alone, was vain; but fashioned in one whole
By love the two grew beautiful at length
And worthy Nature's dearest dream—a soul.

L
That soul is ours, to live while Earth shall keep
One impulse of the life-urge up to light;
Long though our eyes be covered up with sleep,
Lovers will find us hid in their delight.

Snares for Beauty

I
Men set their snares for Beauty variously:
Some on clear summits of the tranquil mind
Spread nets of thought to hold her feet confined
As she slips softly sunward to the sea;
And some lay bare their bosoms anxiously,
Hoping the bird will drop there, passion-blind.
But all the same's the luck the hunters find—
Shadows and shadows where no bodies be.
       I am too young for wisdom and too old
       To think that kisses bring the treasure in;
       There's little hope in even the finest sin
       And none at all in thought whose lips are cold.
       One way: let passion burn the whole fabric thin,
       Then sift the ashes for the possible gold.

Still I can feel the tingling of your hair
Against my face upon the lonely beach
Where wondrously you slid within my reach
And taught my lips a strange forbidden prayer.
Still I can see your shoulder glinting bare
When I had learned what only you could teach
Among the dunes, with kisses all our speech—
So still it was we dared not whisper there.
       Behind the sand dunes on a summer night
       With far away the breathing of the sea
       Among the torn fantastic roots of earth,
       The long embrace, the bitter-brief delight,
       The beauty that we looked on fearfully,
       Born of our souls yet dragging shards of birth.

Lovely earth made you, lovely and too frail
To yoke with use in shaping of a deed
Or nourish in your blood a single seed
To plant against the reaping or the hail.
Too weak to win, and all too sweet to fail,

I see you press your lips until they bleed
Against the cold stone image of your need—
And yet not even that imprint shall prevail.
> Lovely earth made you, frail, and bitter so:
> Had there been dross there were no need of tears,
> Some baser stuff to make your gold complete.
> Had there been dross;—yet only this I know—
> I whisper it to you back across the years—
> Your bitter soul but made your kisses sweet!

Then sift the ashes, for the wind is right
That blows across the clear cold peaks of thought:
Where glints the gold so perilously caught
In the drab sieve of bitter gray delight?
Where gleams the treasure that we dreamed so bright
The little precious something that we sought?
Only your face in shadow-waverings wrought,
Your ghost-lips pressed against my soul tonight!
> And oh, the body is a quiet place
> When love is gone, and quieter than all
> For the last whisper of your blood in mine.
> What comfort that I keep your pale sad face,
> What comfort that I hear your soft foot-fall
> When never again for me you'll pour the wine!

Then sift the ashes, all has not been said—
A memory were a memory and no more—
But from the dunes along that windy shore
The past lifts up a dismal prophet head:
"Young man that took your love so quick to bed,
There is a dream no wise man would explore,
There is a need with sorrow at its core—
Remember me when all your hope is dead."
> And I remember: side by side we stood
> And dragged the veil of darkness from the Thing
> That some call Life, some God, and others Fate;
> Now like a mallard o'er the willow wood
> That sees the barrel's glint and bends his wing
> I hover, charmed, where the crouched hunters
> > wait.

II
Down Market Street on a dull day of rain
I wandered slow as tramps or sick men do;
The wet came seeping through a broken shoe,
And heavy were my eyes and hot with pain.

Then suddenly I saw you—hair like grain
That the last sun of Autumn glimmers through,
And on your wrist there perched a cockatoo;—
I paused and went, and turning paused again.
> Then came your smile—you saw me looking in,
> A beggar at the gates of Paradise,
> So woebegone I scarce can picture now;
> There was a sprite of laughter in your chin,
> Gloomed over by the pity in your eyes
> And something strangely gentle in your brow.

The rain has fallen since in Market Street
And you are gone from there and I am here;
And someone for the crested bird paid dear
And glows to hear his rattling tongue repeat
The words you taught him, simple words and sweet
Out of a heart so pure I shrink with fear
Remembering the pain that pressed you near
The time you asked me in to dry my feet.
> Today a brown hawk-wing above the hill
> Struck the birds silent; but he passed, and more
> Than ever before I heard their singing grow:
> The shadow of my soul that made you chill;
> I wonder is your laughter brighter for
> That shadow past—but I shall never know.

Then sift—but here's no ashes, only charred
Fragments the fire scarce touched; yet what the text,
And what the comment? Only a mind perplexed
With fear lest some slight beauty should be marred
Becoming greater, some perfection scarred
Being made human; only a thief that vexed
The fruited bough, left plucking to the next,
And sneaked away, leaving the gate unbarred.
> Unbarred! and with the morning comes the beast
> All lust and trampling, even such a one
> As he you danced with evenings now and then.
> Alone, he never had entered to the feast,
> Yet I'm not guilty of what I have not done—
> There's the world's comfort; shall I take it then?

III

Quiet as the green valley in which we live
Came love a little while to you and me;
There was no cloud of ambiguity,
But simply did you come and simply give
Gifts that a queen might offer, a king receive.
We leaped no chasms of passion recklessly,
Nor beat the gates of heaven for the key,
Nor tried to carry water in a sieve.
  And it is good sometimes to lay aside
  Hot, nervous graspings for the mystery
  That only maddened prophet-lips reveal;
  Good to sit down, and, knowing the world is wide,
  Like gentle pilgrims by a roadside tree,
  Break bread together and share the noonday meal.

Adventurers in love? It may be so—
But what land's better to adventure in?
Where's nobler treasure for the hand to win
Or clearer flame to set the heart aglow?
The highway's plain, and smooth and straight, I know,
But oh, the valleys where the streams begin!
Your lips, my lips; your heart, my heart. A sin?
Then draw the curtain on the sorry show!
  Tonight I found you standing by your gate;
  We talked awhile together and turned us home,
  You to your waiting loved ones, I to mine:
  Now, musing with my feet upon the grate,
  I feel that somehow, when the hour be come,
  The bitter drink will smack a little of wine.

IV

There comes a time—and then the man is blest—
When to one hand he yields his life's control
Knowing that thought and passion in her soul
Mingle like light and darkness in the West;
That, even with fingers on his eyelids pressed,
She still will lash with scorn to make him whole
And send him flashing onward to his goal,
Or draw him gently downward to his rest.
  Knowing, as I know, that your hand is bold
  To grasp at life and never fear the tooth,
  To dip in darkened places with deep thirst,
  Ready to take the ashes with the gold;
  Enough the cynic to be true to truth,
  Enough the lover to put beauty first.

DARTS

Arrow
I love the way an arrow does its job:
Not like a bullet in one thud of breath,
But slowly, with a half voluptuous throb
Till the wrenched lips smile outward into death.

Dregs
The last few oozy drops within the cup
Men sip at vaguely; but the other day
I saw one tip the beaker sharply up
And take one gulp—a bullet was his way.

Pause
I did not know how proudly a man could die
Until I watched him shut his eyes; the day
Hung like a frightened gull in the wide sky
For all her power of flight he took away.

Lost Creek, Oregon
Here, if love come, let him come with soul that remembers
Gray ghost-valleys loud with the sound of waters:
Tiger coals when the wind blew over the embers;
Swift man-lust for the breasts of the warm Earth-daughters.

Picture Gorge, Oregon
My Lady Earth is here a prostitute
With cruel lips and warm alluring breath:
Pay as you come—her fee is but your soul—
Her gift the passionate luxury of death.

A Dahlia
What brindled horns of madness in haughty pose
For what gay toreador of vanished days!
Earth remembers her old lusts and throws,
Strangely transformed, their shadows on our gaze.

Cavalier
Yours is a rose-rich mockery of love,
A bright audacity to flank desire,
With laughter subtle as a scented glove
And a blade that shakes blue fire.

Ameera
(*Without Benefit of Clergy*)

Let us walk quietly beneath the stars
Trusting our joy no further than a smile:
'Tis always better that the gods should think
Us not much worth their while.

Poems from Campus Sonnets (1934)

To An Entering College Freshman

And you have walked with streams for company
In quiet valleys; deep in sheltering woods
Have found the shy fawn-lily and the hoods
Of purple orchids caverned secretly.
And you have heard the dusky bumble-bee
Drone a gold drowsy track through solitudes
So deep not even the boldest thought intrudes
His wistful shadow on that infinity.

    I, too, have walked green meadows, and I know
    What loveliness they send about the heart
    Drawn from sweet wells where thought is laid asleep.
    Child, you are wise already, and being so,
    Why reach for knowledge that can but tear apart
    Your blessedness, nor tell you why you weep!

Pronouns and Spring

Spring on the Campus: azaleas bloomed again
And rhododendrons and the white May flower;
But in the class I spoke with learned power
Of pronouns till Spring died in every brain.
Then suddenly against the window pane
Two robins fluttered in a passion-shower,
And all along the ledges of the tower
I heard the ivy shaken as with rain.

    Sadly I mused, "desolating is man's law,
    That chills the native impulse at its spring,
    Till freedom's only in a robin's wing."
    And then along the second row I saw
    A girl's eyes seek a boy's; they met, and I
    Reached for my bag of pronouns hurriedly.

Examination in Romantic Poets

She knew the names of all of Byron's guesses
And had the dates on Wordsworth and Annette;
Talked Fanny Brawne until her eyes were wet
And her voice shook with phantoms of caresses.
She fixed poor S. T. C. his proper jesses,

How he and Sarah never could forget
Till all his days were dark and his feet set
In bogs and vast Satanic wildernesses.

> Then looked at me with clear and steady eyes
> Void of all evil; and I never knew
> Till then what life and thirst of life could do.
> I grabbed my hat and muttered on the rise:
> "You're fair and twenty and you may recover—
> Go, shut your book and get yourself a lover!"

Dragon-Killer
(Alumnus, Five Years After Commencement)

So, solemnly he gave into his hands
The Sword of Knowledge, blessed it, saying then:
"Go forth, my knight, into the world of men;
This sword beside you, seek through distant lands,
By pleasant valleys, wastes of burning sands,
Mountain and plain and bleak malarial fen
Till you have run the Dragon to his den—
Then, Truth and Beauty, strike him where he stands!"

> And that's five years ago. Today I found him
> At ease in his own inn—the very first
> Along the highway—quenching of his thirst
> And smiling proudly on the group around him
> Who gazed in awe no poet's tongue could utter
> To see him use his sword at bread and butter.

Faculty Clown

He's like a dog with a mad nose, forever
Baying the tree where 'possum never sat;
His mind's an endless jumble of this and that
Like the locked past of some ungracious liver.
Learned he seems, but his conclusions never
Fall in their proper places neat and pat
But sit his reasons like a crazy hat—
He sees the joke and makes the thing look clever.

> Come, laugh your fill; and since he's seated high,
> Increase yourselves thus much by laughing at him;
> What does it matter that a fool begat him
> Somewhere between his supper and a sigh?
> You've paid your fee, come, set your wits to school
> And grow in wisdom by laughing at a fool.

Intellectual Ferret, Muzzled

Life was unkind to grant you such a scent
For Truth and then provide your nose a muzzle;
Against the quarry's side you may but nuzzle
As helpless as a hungry man in Lent.
Your masters say the muzzle is well meant
That keeps you keen while others feed and guzzle;
You serve them better so—but still I puzzle
Is milk, alas, your only nourishment?

    Proud hunter, ranging through the Sacred Wood,
    You'll drive out Truth from many a secret hill
    And then stand by while others make the kill
    And grant you not one single drop of blood.
    And worse to come, your masters will, no doubt,
    Take off the muzzle when your teeth are out!

Professional Scholar

His mind's a sort of flypaper, a thing
Spread with bright honey for the legs of flies;
And joy it is to see them try to rise,
Lean madly upward from the feet that cling.
He loves them in his way—Ah see that sting!
And see that fellow with the goggle-eyes!
And then he counts, with something like surprise,
And gloats them over gently wing by wing.

    Why weep for gnats and flies? Well, here's the reason:
    Some quiet day, where he has set his snare
    A lovely thing will flutter unaware
    And find too late the honey is but treason;
    And he'll come lugging, proud and merrily,
    The crumpled thing—I know it—straight to me.

The Idealist

He liked her for the freshness of her skin,
The quiet laughter of her eyes, the bright
Quick movement of her hands that set aright
The curl that strayed too dangerously near sin.
He liked her for the spirit dark within
That called to his—he heard it—for the light;
The mind that looked in longing to his might,

The blade that only needed rubbing thin.

> So, just to give her manners and a soul
> He talked with her, went walking now and then,
> Taught her what words to say and how and when
> Laughter or tears the meeting should control.
> The lesson learned, she loved him starry-eyed,
> And he went back to Plato satisfied.

Linesman in Poetry Class

So there, a modern Caliban, you sit,
Vast, ominous, and grave as Ignorance;
A mighty thing left incomplete by chance
That gave the muscle but forgot the wit.
Now mine's the job on that bull-neck to fit
A mind—God bless us! Something to enhance
The carcass crude as Island Necromance
Had Caliban some morning mastered it.

> In the roped square where spit and blood and sweat
> Flow freely I would yell for you—but here?
> You've solved it, though: already droops one ear
> And only half an eye is open yet.
> Then sleep; I'll read; you'll like it better so:
>   --"Brought death into the world and all our woe."

For a Campus Poetess

Since Virgin visions grow a little tawdry,
Fair lady, pray the gods to make you foul;
Let the larks be, and listen to the owl—
Come, sit you down beside my gentle Audrey.
Throw phantoms over and take the truth aboard ye:
She's felt the sting of rain when the winds howl,
And she has sat with laughter cheek by jowl,
And known when earth puts fingers out toward ye.

> Fair lady, to the poet words are things
> With bodies swift and bright—so Shakespeare knew them;
> Let not your hand stick pins of Virtue through them,
> But let them drowse your breast with fluttering wings
> And teach you sweetest flowers grow deep and shady
> And the best honey's from not too fine a lady.

Faculty at the Game

Beer and philosophy no longer wake
The student pulse to rapture. There they go,
Shouting their war-song with young lips aglow,
Glad in the glamour of the noise they make.
"On to the fight there, pound them till they break!
March on! March on! hit hard and lay them low!
There's glory, glory waits on every blow—
O, give them hell for Alma Mater's sake!"

    John Keats—the shorter poems—yesterday
    I read them to my class: all silent there
    While minds rose up to beauty like a prayer,
    And eyes were drooped, and heads were turned away;
    Just one, mouth open, slumbered unafraid—
    That forty-two there—see the hole he made!

Success-Boy

The world was made to suit your talents, lad:
Shrewdness enough to know the right, not choose it:
Eyes that see virtue clear enough to use it
In gaining ends that virtue never had;
Hands deft to winnow out the good from bad
And push the bad aside, but not to lose it;
Tongue graced with truth sufficient to abuse it;
Heart that may feel, but never leave you sad.

    Go to your kingdom, for it waits your coming;
    The gods nod blessing, what is more to do?
    Gather the harvest that was sown for you!
    And if you hear some dismal prophet drumming,
    Smile—I'll smile with you—for we know right well
    You'll seek your plums, and find them, even in hell.

Professorial Hen-Coop

One learns to hate the dull domestic things
That come to perch where nightingales should be:
The tame ideas one fattens endlessly
Until they grow too heavy for their wings;
And then to mark their legs with little rings
White, red, and blue, and dated accurately
For classroom market—tender, don't you see,
Fit, (were there any), for the board of kings.

But yesterday from over the hill's crest
A hawk swooped—I but saw his shadow pass.
My fattest hen lay bleeding in the grass;
I took her up and laid her with the rest.
Warranted tender, but you'll never know
What shadow-thing it was that made her so!

Heroic Dullard

I had a kitten, just an alley cat,
That kept my childhood cheerful with a game
We played together, till years and wisdom came
And taught her that a cork was not a rat.
I'd swing the bauble high, and with a "pat"
She'd leap and miss and slink away in shame;
And then I'd tease, or if the sport grew tame,
Rid myself of her with a sudden "scat".

    Ah, but you're game, you with the slow dull eye,
    To go a-plodding after nimble things
    That will not fall but to an eagle's wings;
    To leap and leap, and miss at every try!
    I had a kitten—but I'm tired, I say;
    Lord, how I wish you'd quit and go away!

Falstaff in Class

Go easy, Jack; this isn't the Boar's Head,
And here's no Doll or friendly-bosomed Quickly.
Remember, we have grown a trifle sickly
Since you and Hal drank wisdom to his bed;
Remember, we are Custom-Honor fed,
And find your Shrewsbury talk a somewhat prickly;
So gloze a bit, and though it go down thickly,
Swallow less sack and eat more wholesome bread.

    Yet welcome! Here are gathered three or four
    Who'll meet your laughter and see the brain behind it;
    Who'll search your heart for youth eternal and find it,
    And love you well for that; and what is more,
    Who'll understand, when your proud spirit yields,
    'Tis right your lips should babble o' green fields.

Examination for a Teacher
(Before giving him a Class)

These men seek Love: and have you held her, say,
Close as desire in the secret night?
These men seek Truth: and have you seen the light
Burn full into intolerable day?
These men seek Beauty: have you seen the play
Of wind in grasses, curve of birds in flight?
These men ask Courage: have you, then, sat tight
When death clanked by nor turned your eyes away?

    Last—(please discuss), —these men have come to find
    At your hands Self-hood: can you give it them?
    Self-mastered, have you raised your hand to stem
    The mad mob hurry of the mad mob kind?
    Stood, have you, in their arrow-flight of jeers
    Like Christ or Satan, and like them full of tears?

An Instructor

In youth he dreamed that in the tempest-tossed
Deep seas of passion beauty might be found
So eyes were clear enough and courage sound
To strip against the south-wind and the frost,
Counting no danger, scorning every cost;
To dive till hands should touch the cold sea-ground;
And to that venture all his powers he bound,
Staked his whole soul on one proud plunge, and lost.

    Now in the classroom with the young around him
    From the dark past he digs the bones of youth
    And shows them where the worm has set his tooth,
    "So gay this corpse before the darkness found him."—
    Poor death-filled Hamlet with his Yorick skull,
    Youth gulps a yawn to show he's merely dull.

Question

How shall one plant in this too-healthy frame
The seed of beauty that will thrive alone
Where subtle fevers waste the flesh and bone
And stab the heart with arrow-heads of flame?
Little cares beauty whence her substance came
So it be pure, the glory that is blown
Sunward in flowers, the sweet that shall atone

For the pale roots that feed at wells of shame.

    Soul-health is soul-content, the clear sun
    Nourishing grain in days of laughing weather;
    But beauty's sprung where pride and shame together
    Make hot-beds of the soul, and one by one,
    Out of the mold where all fat things have died
    Rise blossoms that are neither shame nor pride.

Mind-Limits

Were there but rooms enough for you to explore
With this the light I place within your hand
You might go on and never understand
That past one point for you there's nothing more.
You might perhaps not ever reach the door
That will not open to your need's demand,
Nor stumble where the floor is shifting sand
With only utter darkness on before.

    Were there but rooms enough!—but presently
    Back to the first you will have made the round
    To gray rock walls, all that your search has found,
    With narrow windows where my eyes shall see
    Your soul, a conscious prisoner, through his bars
    Watching tight-lipped the dawn-retreat of stars.

On Reading a War Poet with a Class

You like this quiet poem that he made,
Bending the gracious outlines of his thought
To pastoral themes: a shy wood-maiden taught
To play on pipes deep in a forest glade
And, the tune learned, lifting all unafraid
Lips for the kiss her lover long has sought—
You like the quiet poem that he wrought
Softly amid Death's shrieking masquerade?

    Remember, too, he fell on that same day,
    Eyes wild with fear, a bullet in his breast;
    And his last sunset, yellow in the West,
    Saw, as the wild gun-fury died away,
    Only a corpse with blood upon its mouth
    And a few swallows, high and heading South.

On Asking a Class to Read Jeffers

There'll be no quiz: Who looks upon the seed
Of his own soul in the primeval slime
Sees that which locks his lips for after-time
With silence deeper than a miser's greed.
There'll be no quiz: I give you to the need
Your souls must feel to know the way they climb
Up the earth darkness, stern and white with rime,
Fierce eyed, proud mouthed, with hands that grasp and bleed.

    But having read, come back again to me
    That we might sit a little while together
    Quietly dreaming in the quiet weather
    After the storm that struck us from the sea;
    Quietly dreaming to the drone of bees
    And drift of voices speaking words like these:

Robinson Jeffers I: Poet in Stone

I watch you write stone poems, build stone towers,
Gathering that mind into one point of light
That lay dispersed for aeons in the night
Before earth knew the gentleness of flowers.
Out of the rock a hawk. In him a soul
Too clean for passion. Out of the hawk a man
Whom thought defiles with vision and a plan
Futile in all save its own stern control.

The cold thin agony of stone bites deep
In flesh of those that feel it. The proud dream
Of stone stabs bitter music through the mind.
For you I fear not—even in that wild leap
Of seeing that lays bare the eagle's scream
And shows the gray stone anguish that's behind.

Robinson Jeffers II: Builder of Tor House

I think I'd know the marks upon your hands
That have grown firm with the cool touch of stone
And the slow surge of strength along the bone
What time you built a tower in empty lands.
I think I'd know the light in your still eyes
That, when the work was done and quiet came
About you, and the wonder of a name,
Looked from that height with something of surprise.

I knew you in the granite long ago
On hills you'll never see; but you were proud
Beyond my strength—a spirit darkly met
In the faint glimmerings far beneath the snow.
And you'll go back, but round you like a cloud
Will be the memory of the tower you set.

To the Faculty
(On Behalf of a Brilliant Student)

My brothers, put no darkness on his sight
Nor tie a heavy stone about his feet;
Eagle-eyed he is and as the wind fleet
And knows the fiery taste of god-delight.
He will out-see, out-run us, flashing bright
Far down the road where wearily we beat
The steady deadly rhythm of defeat,
Tired and sick, and longing for the night.

The night will come, and sitting round our fire
We'll watch the glooming ridges far away
Toward which we urged our faltering steps all day—
The hills of Truth and noble Heart's-Desire.
'Twill be some comfort when we see the spark
Flung from his camp toward us in the dark.

Task-Master

To climb the ropes of darkness to a star
Upward and upward till beyond the rim
Of the dark earth new constellations swim;
Upward and upward dizzy bar by bar
Till in your brain the racing currents jar,
You think of the couched ox and envy him;
Upward with bleeding hands because the dim
Earth-plodders need the light that gleams afar.

This is your task; and set your hearts no trust
Of peace in failure; there will be no peace
Till earth grows cold and the last mortals cease
To hope, and cover up their eyes with dust.
Should you ask pity, being of woman born,
To the gods' dream I'll lash you back with scorn.

On the Way to Class
(Magnolia in May)

Lord, should I tell them that I saw a tree
Laugh!—in the classroom, they that wait me there—
How they would greet me with incredulous stare!
Yet, that's the very thing that I did see:
A great magnolia chuckling merrily
At crabbed winter with his dismal hair
And hunched receding shoulders gleaming bare—
Magnolia blossoms laughing silverly.

>That night it frosted; from behind the hill
>Winter reached back a sly malicious paw;
>My gay magnolia's lips were bruised and raw
>And all her silver laughter frozen still.
>Devil that took my beauty in her sleep!—
>Lord, should I tell them I heard a tree weep!

Half-Feeders

This is my torment, that you will not feed
Nor turn away, accept nor yet deny,
But sip and taste and lay the morsel by,
And pick the whole world over creed by creed.
Is there no passion in you, no soul-greed
For something dearly held though but a lie?
For spirit winds that care not whither they fly
So they but split the heavens with their speed?

>Sick half-believers, Truth is neither there
>Nor here, nor anywhere but in a thought
>Clutched till it bruise the hands that hold it caught;
>In hate that takes the victim by the hair;
>In love that burns the soul to bitter drouth,
>Or blow that breaks the fist against the mouth.

Students and Teacher

Not men and women, but patterns subtly wrought
On the mind-fabric far beneath the plane
Of conscious knowing, patterns in the brain
That the soul gropes for, blindly, passion-fraught;
Till on a day the elusive Vision's caught,
The lines come clear, and fade, and glow again,
Then steady into gladness, into pain

That brings you Self made conscious in a thought.

> I who must guide that marvelous alchemy
> Face what is unrevealed, lonely, afraid
> To bring to birth the patterns which, once made,
> Never erased, and never changed may be;
> Numb, while you wait the seed I must bequeath,
> Flowers and grain—and some is dragon's teeth!

On Paying Tribute to Pain

Since pain is still the mightiest of earth's lords,
With castles by each pass, that men must wend
Beneath his banners to their journey's end
And under the red lightning of his swords;
And since, his strength being great, it naught affords
To frown against him boldly or to bend
The bow and aim the dart that can but lend
Brief glory ere you join his slaughtered hordes;

> Reach for your tribute as you near the rise
> Where waits the robber with his cut-throat band,
> And drop your cold coin coldly in the hand
> That else will snatch your heart to be its prize;
> Even should he see, he will not understand
> The imp of scorn that lurks behind your eyes.

On Pain and Joy

I tell you men have drunk of tragedy
And the sick-sweet and subtle poison, pain,
Till they are beasts, not men. Their jangled brain
Sucks in the loathsome devil's-brew let free
Through church and state, spiced with the mockery
Of wars and laws and whores; again, again
Up with the glass, till, where all joy lies slain
Death sits with the barmaid, virtue, on his knee.

> O, trust them not lest you should sink within
> The shifting quagmires of their obscene woe;
> But leap to meet the morning winds and throw
> Your breasts against that splendor clear and thin,
> Caring not much that from the bogs below
> There rise against your joy the cry of "sin!"

On Virtue

She is "procuress to the lords of hell"
This same mild virtue whom you praise so much;
The rape of joy is in her every touch,
And in the arms of her Duessa spell
Courage and strength, whom fear could never quell,
Loose from the hilts the earnest fingers' clutch,
Coward-confessed, and yield them up as such,
Torn banners and a broken citadel.

> There is a being wherever runs the sea
> Flashing in sunlight when the great winds move,
> That mouths no rape of beauty, joy, and love,
> Nor lisps of virtue's amorous mockery,
> But shouts in thunder to the black rocks above,
> "Man knows not hell then only when he is free!"

On Man

A rat who in his freedom felt the glare
Of hungry eyes in ambush, mused one day,
"Life would be sweet were there a safer way
To win my food"; and as in answer to prayer,
A cage with cheese and safety!—You who care
May find him sitting, gaunt and somewhat gray,
Watching grim phantom cats that crouch and sway,
The bit of cheese untouched beside him there.

> Even so, man: lord of the newer age
> With earth's rich treasures heaped about his knee,
> Colors and forms, and all sense-witchery,
> Love, and proud thought, and learning's mellow page,
> God even of god—so only he be free—
> Caught by the Jester with cheese inside a cage!

On Woman

It is enough that round your being cling
Fragrance of dreams, my dreams; that softly where
Night fills with darkness your down-fallen hair
My nightingales of passion come to sing.
It is enough, when storms are on the wing,
That I should know your breast lies open there,
A harbor for the galleons rich and fair
My thoughts lead home from lonely wayfaring.

You are no greater than my thought of you
(O trust me, then, to lift that vision high!)
And, though I tread the pathways of the sky
And talk with gods amid the secret blue,
I am no more than what your love finds true,
And what of me you take not soon must die.

Love

The light that beats from under the blue rim
Of western hills the clouds break wondrously
Into swift colors till the burning sea
Is hushed in darkness and the cold stars swim.
And when man lifts, although his eyes be dim,
Their light on woman, round her form will be
The color of his being, even while she
Sees her own light made visible in him.

   For that one moment all the daylight hours
   Gathered their forces in the sloping west;
   For that one moment on his loved one's breast
   Man gathers all the fulness of his powers,
   To see, dim mirrored in her shadowy smile,
   Two far eternities made one awhile.

Love and Convention

Love will give all or nothing, and take all
Or spurn the pittance offered in its place.
Her gracious law is absolute as grace
And, scorned, her going as the day's foot-fall.
Kings she has laughed at who would make her thrall
And breathed clear heaven on the beggar's face.
Slipped through the bars to captives where they pace
And mocked the free lust-vulture's throaty call.

   Bargain you would? Then drive it, but beware
   Lest she should join you in your little jest
   And grant you even what your lips request;
   Then, rising gently, go and leave you there
   At breakfast with a mummy or a whore
   In the heaped silence of a closed door.

Beauty

I.

The Conditions of Beauty

The undiscovered past that in us lies
Yearns far beneath the conscious levels where
Our daily commerce is: a prisoner there
It beats against its dungeon-bars and cries
For Love to break the darkness on our eyes
And feed us wine of courage till we dare
Let free our buried Selves, and touch the hair
And meet the lips of all the things that rise.

> Who dares do that knows Beauty; only he
> Who by the love of Woman or of Earth,
> Or Thought, or Vision, pushes back his birth
> Beyond his day's beginning fearlessly,
> And looses through his heart in one full tide
> All that his fathers lived, and dreamed, and died.

II.

Illustration

A tree made me eternal yesterday
And thereby clothed herself with loveliness,
A cedar rising nobly from the press
Of crooked oaks; she set my blood asway
With sweet Earth-music, thought-effacing, gay
As country violins; from a recess
Within me a spirit, freed from its distress,
In wistful pleading whispered "let me stay!"

> That me which the soul-darkness held in shame
> Till the glad cedar swept that shame aside
> Shall live forever, wan and wistful-eyed,
> A part of the Life-urge from which I came,
> A part of all things dead in earth laid by
> And of all things unborn and yet to die.

III.

Conclusion

And therefore is she lovely marvelously
My dark-browed cedar, that her hands have made
At my soul-casement, a laughing serenade
That called one out from darkness to be free.
And therefore on my altar shall she be
A goddess crowned, that, smiling unafraid,
One finger on my lips for silence laid,
She sang the song that gave my soul to me.

    And grief will do what she with smiles, and pain
    And terrible things with faces bruised and torn,
    For man has devils waiting to be born
    That will not rest imprisoned in the brain
    But yearn for birth that man might know and see them—
    And Beauty's on whatever hand shall free them.

Immortality

I.

I watched a clever sculptor moulding clay
To forms of life: a frog beneath his hand
Stood with his swollen sides on marshy land,
Eyes bulged, mouth waiting open for his prey.
But the sly artist crushed him as in play
And wooed from his dull lump a girl to stand
Smiling in triumph with gesture subtly planned
To scorn the thing her birth had pushed away.

    Thus all forms change forever. The stuffs remain
    And that which shapes them, be it Death or Life,
    Or chemistry of cells with peace at strife
    Building through chaos to the conscious brain;
    And man shall feel that change for all his lore:
    Life, death, the worm that brings him life once more.

II.

There is a dance in which all things that live
Move to a cosmic music endlessly,
One speaks: "O, Soul, this measure must not be
Our last together, parted but to grieve;

Quick, hide with me before the Master give
The awful signal!" But two cold eyes see,
And with a shrug at man's impertinency
Death goes to find the amorous fugitive.

> Step, girl! 'Tis not forever, but 'tis sweet.
> Your laughing mouth, your shadow-pooled eyes!
> Dance! let the sunlight-flashing patterns rise
> Up through your kisses from your twinkling feet!
> The end! My other partner's at my shoulder?
> A hag?—My dance will be so much the colder!

III.

Thus for the dance and dancers. Here and there
Comes one, a being, who by strength of will
Or inner beauty lifts him to the hill
Where the gods sit; they watch with quiet stare
While he, transformed in that diviner air,
Writes in new measures with immortal skill.
Death ponders the deep magic of his quill
And marks the change in program with due care.

> Such is immortal, though like all his brothers
> He too must change with every tune that changes;
> For when his body through the darkness ranges
> With a dull partner, a vast world of others,
> While he is crawling to some sluggish beat
> Will dance his measure with triumphant feet.

Double Portrait

Truth lives in pictures: and the world will paint
Of you its dull unconscious caricature
With all the virtues that but made you poor
Set in a calm that was but uncomplaint.
Yet somewhere there, satirical and faint,
In eye or lip the world has called demure,
Like Mona Lisa's mockingly secure,
Will be the smile that made you not a saint.

> Truth lives in pictures: could I catch you fair
> 'Twould be a proud and rocky sea-ward place
> With glittering spray upon your brow and face
> And wet sea-wind like darkness in your hair;
> And in your eyes two wild and deathless things
> Watching afar the lift of sea-gull's wings.

By the Fire-Side

I have raised Helen even as Faustus did,
And Alexander with his paramour;
Roused Heloisa just when she was sure
Love could not find her past the coffin's lid.
I've called John Keats in pity when he chid
The laughing Fanny that her soul was poor.
And Burns has come slow-smiling to my lure,
A glass of beer and no one to forbid.

    Before the cock has crowed the break of day
    I've had them by my hearth, the gentle and fair,
    Nor wondered at the brightness in their hair
    From the Time-frost they walked through on their way;
    And they have made high converse with me there
    Watching the last red embers turn to gray.

One Reason

When in the balance of the mind I throw
Against the eternal cold my little spark,
My glint of light against the eternal dark,
Against the silence the one word I know:
And when I heap my dreams in trust that so
My balance may hold level to the mark,
My last, best dream just fallen there, then hark
The thin satiric Laughter clear and low!

    Then, then, O love, hold wide your arms to take
    One touched with scorn who yet would reach your side
    To spend the warmth he owns before he dies:
    And love him not for any other sake
    Than that he dared what coward never tried
    And comes to you with terror in his eyes.

Inscription for a Modern University

Man dreamed a dream beyond the Impossible
And shaped me then out of his noblest need
To mate with Truth and nourish the dark seed
Of Beauty to make lovelier the Will.
But Power and Use grew dearer to him still,
And the old toothless, withered lecher, Greed;
He sold me to them that I too might breed,
Shut out forever from the Sacred Hill.

Lovers who come with frankincense and myrrh,
Gifts for the child that shall be born of me,
Back to your deserts! do not wait to see,
For he will be but as his fathers were.
Back to your deserts where the far light hovers,
Lovers of Beauty, lovers of Truth, oh lovers!

Poems from *Blue Interval* (1935)

To the Memory of William Gladstone Steele

And to those men and women, still living, whose best thought
and effort are dedicated to making the National Parks
sanctuaries for meditation on Nature, and Science, and Beauty.

Editor's Note: Moll worked as a ranger at Crater Lake National Park in Oregon in the summers of 1934 and 1935. These poems originated from that experience. The original edition of *Blue Interval* included line art accompanying many of the poems. That art was included in the 2017 reprint of *Blue* Interval issued by Oregon Review Books.

Crater Lake
(From the Rim)

Time shuts the old earth giants all away
In cool far dungeons where his years lie deep
But rarely does he grant, as here, to play
Smiles that light with loveliness their sleep.

Night on the Lake

Man is too frail to speak the power of this
Mysterious night or plunge with thought the gloom
Where Cloudcap hangs above the vast abyss
Tremendous in his shadow-robes of doom.

Moonrise

So silverly above this quiet lake
The moon comes up, she scarcely seems the same
White queen that saw this crested mountain break
And paled before the terror of his flame.

Wizard Island

Where the great shadows waver, grim and gaunt,
Its roots are locked, but gently to the skies
It holds a sunlight-brimming cup, the haunt
Of humming-birds and lacy butterflies.

Wizard Island
(At Night)

Who watches there when moon-up time is near
Shall see a phantom moving swift and white,
And who with bent head listens there shall hear
The ghost of Llao wailing in the night.

Applegate's Paintbrush
(In the Crater on Wizard Island)

Where flame once wrought its awful symphonies
Whose theme was death, with darkness woven through,
They lift in summer silence to the bees
A fairer beauty than the fire-gods knew.

Under Cloudcap

Beneath these cliffs where the blue waters sleep
When the last fires of evening flash and die
It were not hard to slip into the deep
Lured by the singing of some Lorelei.

Dutton Cliff at Sunset

Lost in his grim austerity all day
Dutton awakes beneath the sunset glow
To gentler meanings, and in rose and gray
Blooms with a beauty only strength can know.

Tragedy

The world's great meanings rise from pain, as now
On this torn thing, consumed by its own flame,
There smiles a beauty such as Lear's brow
Knew when, in death, he breathed Cordelia's name.

Sublimity

To know this grandeur is to know how weak
How brief man's dreams and all his longings are;
Yet in that thought, with no surprise, I seek
And with my mortal fingers touch a star.

Color

Untouched by thought, I give myself to these
Rich intervals of blue, and rose, and gray,
Free as a white-winged ship that sails the seas
Knowing no port nor any homing-day.

Hemlocks
(In the Crater Wall)

Serene, where death once pitched his camp, they lift
Green spires against blue water far below
And the scarred slopes where their slow shadows drift
Drink the cool peace that only trees bestow.

A grove of hemlocks sloping to the west
like a full tide in calm majestic flow
With sunlight burning gold along each crest
And dark still pools of shadow flung below.[13]

Wind-Blown Pine

On this torn ridge he rooted, proud and free
Battling the wild earth-forces for control;
Life granted not his dream of beauty, so he,
Majestically dying, reached his goal.

Reflections
(Watchman and Hillman)

Their war of winds and mountain-strife laid by,
They seek in the blue wave a fairer goal
As man may find within a loved one's eye
Tranquil and clear, the image of his soul.

Llao
(From the Lake Below Cloudcap)

Great bird of fire, cold now, and grey, and lone,
Ten thousand years have seen you never wake,

---

13   Note: the second quatrain, which appeared with an illustration, was not included in *Blue Interval.* It appeared following the first quatrain in *Nature Notes From Crater Lake* Volume 7, No. 3, September 1934.

Ten thousand more shall know your breast of stone
Brooding far up above the silent lake.

Rock Patterns
(The Grottos)

Out of the ancient rage of fire and frost
And prisoned forces struggling to be free
Came beauty such as poets, vision-lost,
Dreamed long ago in dales of Arcady.

Tree Patterns on Erosion Slopes
(The West Crater Wall)

Down the long perilous slopes their lines extend
Flanked by the scars of thrusting water-spears,
Steadfast and close as friend might stand by friend
In some grim place upon a day of fears.

Erosion Pinnacles
(Slopes below Watchman and Hillman)

Weakness that yields to force, and strength that breaks
Up from the waves of conflict to the sun,
Yet beauty's touch is on them both and makes
Weakness and strength, death, life, forever one.

Man and Beauty

Where the torn rock like some spent giant clings
Before the last and fatal shaft is hurled
I muse how from this fearful conflict springs
The vast unconscious beauty of the world.

Rock Lichens

So life is born even from that which dies;
And, be this love or stern inhuman strife,
From this embrace in after-days will rise
Moss, fern and tree—the cool green brood of life.

Time

1. The Past

By the great lords of earth I count the years,
Each shut forever now from pain and bliss:
Long before Shakespeare knew the salt of tears
Before Christ walked the earth, you lay like this.

2. The Future

Man will do mercies more than gods might try,
Work horrors that might hell itself appall,
A thousand generations laugh and die—
And you will smile unheedful of it all.

3. The Present

Then hold me for a moment, awful thing
Impersonal, against your cold clean breast,
That I may free me of the mortal sting
And feel at last the nobleness of rest.

Farewell

Having been more than man, I turn again
To lift my burden of mortality,
Afraid no more of hope, nor joy, nor pain,
For what I have seen is greater than all three.

Additional poems from Crater Lake

Editor's Note: The following untitled poem did not appear in *Blue Interval* but was included in *Nature Notes From Crater Lake,* the park's internal publication, Volume 8, No.1, July 1935. Included with it was a description by Moll: "… a new scar in the out-jutting lava bore witness that a large mass of rock had split off and fallen away to the lake. Huge freshly-broken fragments, mixed with splintery remnants of tree trunks, lie scattered along the shore-line." I have assigned it the title "Broken Stone" for purposes of indexing and the needs of future readers.

The two poems following "Broken Stone" did not appear in the original edition of *Blue Interval* but were included in *Nature Notes From Crater Lake.*

[Broken Stone] (NN Vol. 8, No. 1, July 1935)

That which seemed strong as Time lies broken here,
A fearful discord of tempestuous stone;
And o'er that field still linger, sharp and clear,
The echoes of the wild earth-bugle blown.

Western Windflowers: Anemones (NN Vol. 8, No. 1, July 1935)

Before the hills are confident with flowers,
Columbine, paint-brush, phlox—the bee's delight—
Come these as silent as the silent hours,
Bridesmaids of Spring that fill her path with light.

Llao's Hallway (NN Vol. 8, No. 2, August 1935)

Sometimes earth-laughter rings like silver bells
Where brooks run crisping over glinting stone;
But here the earth, remembering ancient hells,
Grins at the joke she shares with death alone.

Poems from *Cut from Mulga* (1940)

For Critics

Don't, as you will as like as not
Tell me my mind's an ugly blot,
And all my thoughts a mangy lot.

That I'm half sick, half angry at
Desires that jump from this to that
Like fleas from a lean dog to a fat.

That there's no way on the round earth
To prove myself a little worth
What someone paid for me at birth.

No way? But there a starling unwound
A silver shaving of bright sound
And let it slip and slide to the ground.

And there a dandelion broke
The silence of its bud, and spoke,
And three square yards of earth awoke.

And somewhere in old ages fled
A poet heard these things, and said
A word, and lifted up his head.

So long ago—so far a land—
But you, by God, shall understand
That I, I have him by the hand!

Eagles over the Lambing Paddock

The business of the lambing ewes would make me
At times a trifle sick. The strain and quiver
Of life just squeezed past death to stand and shiver
Wet in the cold on wobbly legs would shake me
With pity for these accidents of lust,
Sometimes with mere disgust.

But I would watch the wedge-tailed eagle wheeling
In skies as biting blue as ocean spaces,
Great wing above the messy commonplaces
Of birth and death and the weak sprawl of feeling;

And coolly then would flow through heart and brain
Respect for life again.

The Bush Speaks

I will be your lover
If you keep my ways.
All delights I'll give you:
Gum-tree scented days,
Skies where kestrels hover,
Nights with stars ablaze.

But if you diminish
Care and think me won,
Other gifts I'll give you
Edged with thorn and sun,
And the crows will finish
What I have begun.

The Leave-Taking

She scarcely noticed, that last night,
My hand upon her, nor the light
Shed by my lantern round the stall,
The yellow light transforming all
The straw she stood on into gold.
'You're cozy, girl. The night is cold
With biting wind and stars that throw
Blue sparkles off. You're cozy though
Here in your straw that smells of sun
And summer days and harvest done.'

This was goodbye. Perhaps she knew
The mercy they had planned to do
Next day among the trees where thick
Lay rotting log and stump and stick
Handy for burning things that must
Be speeded on their way to dust.

She did not seem to feel my hand
Upon her in that silent land
Of midnight in the lonely shed;
My shaking fingers at her head
That strove so hard to make her know
My love that could not ward the blow,
So hard to soothe her with the lie
The living tell the soon-to-die.

She did not seem to feel, but oh,
Along my fingers sure and slow
The warmth of her crept into me!
And at her side I turned to see
The dawn with eyes that did not fear
Its golden beauty nor the near
Unhurried heavy step of one
Who came with halter and with gun.

Winter Ploughing

This morning after my plough
Starlings streamed and chattered
Shimmering green, and now
Suddenly gold-bespattered.

And a mud-lark and his mate,
Bright on the winter ground,
Delicate, prim, sedate,
Followed me round on round.

And one black crow was there
Pulling worms from their burrow
With his solemn courtly air
Busy along the furrow.

And joy was mine though I knew
The roots must die that I bared;
And beetle and grub were few
The crow and the starling spared.

For the birds with tug and nod
Dealt death for the need of their lives,
And my coulters in the sod
Were shining and sharp as knives.

Returned Soldier

I put him on the train in Albury
The night he went to take his boat, and he,
Swinging aboard, called gaily, 'Don't forget,
I'll dodge them all and be a farmer yet,
And raise, for every bullet that goes by,
A stalk of wheat, red-gold and shoulder high,
Three hundred acres, lad!' And then the train
Was gone. The night was loud with frogs again.

And five years later, one November day,
I walked with Barry down the stooks of hay
Light yellow in the sun, and on them fluttered
Rosellas red as apples. Barry muttered
Half shyly as we faced the level wheat:
'One good foot left of what was once two feet,
One lung just fair, and one unclouded eye;
But all those years I heard them whining by
And in the mud I chuckled to remember
How wheat turns copper and gold in late November.'
He smiled, and then I knew what charm had brought
Him safely past the 'world's great snare,' uncaught.

A Gnarled Riverina Gum Tree

Knob and hump upon this tree
And the humpy things in me
Have a greeting for each other
And a word I think is 'brother.'

Straighter trees there are that shake
The very heavens wide awake,
And straighter souls, yes, many a one,
Than mine keep threatening the sun.

They speed on without a word
Or the brief rapture of a bird,
Fearful lest the sky might shut
Like iron doors above them. But

I the man and this wried wood,
Hump to hump, as old friends should,
Squat and talk and watch them run
Stretched up thin to catch the sun.

Kookaburras

I've heard the skylark Shelley heard,
The ruffled thrush that Hardy knew,
The English nightingale that stirred
The dying heart of Keats when dew
Silvered the moonlit lawns where he
Had left so little time to be.

I've heard the wren in rocky glades
Darting his silver lance of sound,
And high among the white Cascades
The purple finch pour, round on round,
Fire-music that should swirl and swing
And loose the torrents of the Spring.

And all of these with joy or pain
Were lyrical, as though they wrought
In sunshine or in slanting rain
To free some urgent hidden thought
Whose brightness man at last should see
On the dark brows of Tragedy.

But Kookaburras when the west
Burns red behind the ring-barked trees,
And the dark earth sinks down to rest
And every flower has lost its bees,
Shake the still dusk with sudden mirth
Flung recklessly across the earth.

In gusts of sound their laughter breaks
Against the steepening walls of night
And listening then my spirit takes
Backward through time the wings of flight
And hears among the ghosts at play
The lusty laugh of Rabelais.

At Cross-Streets, Sydney

The bus stopped, and the funeral car; and I
Sat still and wondered which would grab the road;
The car by right of ancient courtesy
The bus for the requirements of its load.

And while they faltered I had time to think
That I should lose a shilling were I late,
And the sad chap below would miss no wink
Of the eternity he had to wait.

The bus went first and I was safe a bob;
But from my high and arrogant seat o'erhead
I leaned, and covered by the engine's throb,
Sent down my brief apology to the dead.

On Reading a Newspaper in the Bush

A honeyeater sang and then
I heard a leather-head,
And I had not the least idea
What either of them said.

Nor would I sentimentalize
By guessing this or that
As the poor human counterpart
Of what their brains were at.

The quiet gum trees may have known
What it was all about;
But I, for all my eagerness,
Was, and remained, shut out.

And so I shook the page to break
The spell of tree and bird,
And read, and read, and understood
No single ugly word.

The Slug

I found him hidden in a clod
When the garden dripped with rain,
Curled in his smooth and clammy cell
Like a wet thought in the brain.

I laid him for the birds to take
(It was high fledgling time),
But the robin would not drive his bill
Into that spin of slime.

When thrush and starling passed him by
Askance, with lifted wing,
I wondered what the gods could find
To love in such a thing.

Then the sun came and shrivelled him
And earth was clean again;
I almost laughed with joy to lose
That wet thought from my brain.

The Swaggy

We worked from dawn to dark those days
Of ripening sun and harvest weather.
The old man said: 'The pace that pays,
The only pace is hell-for-leather.
One wind with rain will lay it flat,
The wheat that's tall this year and thin,
And should that come your Sunday hat
Would do to hold the harvest in.'

One afternoon a swaggy sat
High on the wheat stack in the sun,
Idly surveying this and that
While we went at it on the run
Loading the wagons. Swing and toss,
We threw the heavy bags in place
While the cool swaggy looked across
With a mild interest in his face.

But when I went at last to fill
The pannikin of tea he came
And stood beside me: 'If you will,
I'd like a little of the same.'
I rubbed my eyes and felt them swim
And sting with sweat, and drank, and threw
The grounds away, then looked at him
And noticed that his eyes were blue,

Steady with light, untroubled, clear,
(I felt the murk within my own),
Final as skies that time of year
The warm, life-quirking birds have flown.
And under them his lips were straight
As lean as those that lust not after
The slippery juice of love or hate
Nor drink less absolute than laughter.

'You're heading Wagga way?' I said,
Handing the tea. He thought awhile,
Then tipped his hat and scratched his head
And met my question with a smile
Guileless, I would have thought, and bland
Had irony not thrown a jet there:
'Mister, I'm heading nowhere and
It doesn't matter when I get there!'

Cootamundra Wattles

(Written Abroad)

This I remember
And shall not soon forget,
How in September,
When the low hills were wet
With rain and mornings still were silver-cold,
The wattle loosened wave on wave of gold.

They say the borer
Found out my golden grove,
Death's underscorer,
And took the trees I love;
But come again the silver-cool September
Wave on great wave they live, for I remember.

Red Charlie

Red Charlie had seen wars and sin
And killed his men—he'd tell about them—
'I wonder what their hats,' he'd grin,
'Will do without them.'

We knew him hard and thought him worse,
And often we would tell each other,
'Charlie would tipple in a hearse
Or stab his brother.'

When Toby lost his teeth and grew
So frail even Charlie wouldn't boot him,
One noon we made up lots and drew
To see who'd shoot him.

That lot was Charlie's. With a word
That froze the rising run of laughter,
He turned, and Toby slowly stirred
And trotted after

To live for years blind, deaf, and fat,
With Charlie by to feed and tend him;
Charlie, who'd emptied many a hat,
And couldn't end him.

The Old Racehorse

'Don't let him out,' they always said,
'He'll stumble if he gets his head
And break your neck, or, what's as bad,
His own, so take him easy, lad.'
And always, as I knew I should,
I promised that I never would,
And sober, slow, and most sedate
The Ghost and I went through the gate
And down the hill to where the ewes
Grazed on the flat by threes and twos.

About the business with the sheep
He went obedient, half-asleep,
Jogging when I would have him jog,
Turning a sheep like a trained dog,
Standing stone-still where I would stop him
Until he felt my weight atop him
And nudge of heel that seemed to say
'Wake up, old chap, and on your way!'
Lost deep in dreams of other places,
White rail, curved track, heaped blur of faces,
He did his work like one whose feet
Take without thought the proper street
And miss the ruts while his mind goes
Down arbored walks of vine and rose.

But when the Ghost and I had made
The round of lambing ewes and laid
The poison for the foxes out,
I'd slowly pull his head about,
And take my pipe and gently knock it
Against my toe, and feel each pocket
To see that knife and tar and stuff
Were rightly stowed and safe enough.
And all the while the Ghost would stand
Ears back to catch the quick command
He knew would come. Beneath my knee
I felt him gather quiveringly
His muscles ready for the start,
That old horse with the eager heart.

And then, my own heart dancing free
With a resistless urgency,
Above his withers bending low

I'd barely whisper 'let her go!'
Then came the leap that set the earth
Gliding away beneath his girth
As I'd look down to watch his feet
Strike swift and sure in beat on beat
Faster and faster till the pace
Brought the wind hard against my face.
I'd let him run at his own will
Trailing the field, perhaps, until
The straight-away, when, fierce as flame
He'd rush his phantom rivals tame
And pass them with a surging bound
Gasping and run into the ground.
And always when the post flashed by,
(A ring-barked gum about to die),
He'd wheel and thunder towards the tank
Where brown sheep by dozens drank
And, twisting sideways with delight,
Scatter them out to left and right,
Plunging and wooly dumb with fright.
The Ghost has felt for many a day
No saddle on his back, they say,
Nor will he ever know again
The urging hand, the guiding rein.
Turned out with pet lamb and with cow
He loiters in the paddock now.
And I, though hearty now as then,
Have learned to prize my neck; but when
I light my pipe alone and sit
And speak his name and think of it,
I'd risk that neck most willingly
To feel beneath my hand and knee
The old horse speed to victory!

After the Fire

Walk with me, then, but keep
Your eyes hard as stone;
What has died here will sleep
Better if left alone.

That blackened stump is not
Your tree of pleasant airs;
Pass him, gaunt, grim and squat,
Minding his own affairs.

That burnt heap with a thong
The pet-lamb you called Queen?
Rubbish! but come along,
The rain makes dead bones clean!

Here was your garden—here?
No! but don't look again;
The grass waits spear on spear
The first drums of the rain.

Better come on; this place
Has done with you—it's choice!
Has turned away its face.
And stopped its ears to your voice.

The Hide-Buyer

Each Tuesday, when the drought was hard,
Dan came with horses and a van
For skins that hung about the yard.
He throve that year did greasy Dan,
For every sheep that starved and died
Made him a profit on its hide.

The horses that he drove were thin
And laced across their dusty backs
With lashes that had raised the skin.
Dan used to say, 'Those bloody hacks—
(They were that once)—were lazy jibs,
But they work now—you see their ribs!'

But Dan himself was round and fat
With greasy pants and greasy shirt;
From greasy boots to greasy hat
A lusty lord of stench and dirt.
We said the flies that swarmed his van
Would scorn to touch a cleaner man.

Puffing and quick about his work,
He'd pull the hides from wire and rails
And rip the feet off with a jerk.
Then, having piled them on his scales,
Weigh them with shrewd and squinting look
And write some figures in a book.

The last pile weighed, from a black hole
Under the van seat Dan would bring
A greasy money-bag and roll
The silver out. It had no ring
But fell like a dull shower of lead,
Sealed, even that, with grease, and dead.

And Dan was merry. The long days
Burned on with never a drop of rain;
The distant hills were lost in haze
And heat-waves shook above the plain.
And to the dams, long black and dry,
The sheep came in to stare and die.

I often wished they all would drop
Dead where they stood and be at rest.
With never a blade of grass to crop
And never a rain-cloud in the west,
Peace would come over plain and hill
When the last swollen tongue was still.

And with that wish I hated Dan
Who throve where all was gaunt with pain,
Death's fat and obscene handyman
Merry with grease and stench and gain,
Skilled in a necessary part
Whose wrong was only to the heart.

But most, I think, I hated him
Because his eyes were merchant's eyes
Amid the loss that made ours dim;
And that I heard, with no surprise,
When the first rains came slanting down
That Dan had gone to live in town.

On Watching a Woodchopper

Drive the axe deep!
There is no rub of the yoke
In a clean stroke;

No push and jerk to snarl
Thin nerves of wood and break
The heart of a tree awake.

Again—deep—clean!
He does not even feel
The cleave of the steel.

Only perhaps the faint
Kiss of cool air, lips shut,
On the shining cut;

Only perhaps a strange
Edged thrill at the red core
He thinks of no name for,

But broods deliciously
On what it is, till again,
True, clean and deep—and he's slain.
. . . .
Don't hand the axe to me!
Flesh soft as mine has made
Too many trees afraid.

Desert Country in Summer

There is no tissue left beneath this sun,
No softness to round smoothly for the eye
Earth's gaunt and vastly noble skeleton
That lives with its own life and will not die.

Here is no blood of hope, no nerve of vision,
No pulse-throb of brief hates and loves at play,
Only the old incredible precision
Inhuman, of returning night and day.

Here is no impulse and no hesitation,
No come and go of life; but all things stand
Immobile in their sure and ancient station
Beneath the desert ribs of rock and sand.

And I who dared to offer this intrusion
On what concerned me not, feel here alone
The peace that is when thought sloughs off illusion
Like withered flesh, and leaves the steady bone.

Bottle Swallows

They built beneath the hanging banks
Along the creek. Their nests of brown

Stiff clay in colonies and ranks
Were like rough gourds with necks turned down.

I'd sit and watch the mother birds
Slip in and out; a thousand wings
And a great festival of words
That must have stood for happy things.

But now and then a sparrow came,
Bluff-shouldered pirate, for a nest,
Truculent, without song or shame
Or spot of fear within his breast.

The swallows never drove him off
But seemed to mark, from stone and limb,
Attentively to hear him scoff
At all that they might do to him.

And, seeming pleased to have them there,
Meek victims of his easy sin,
He'd jerk his head with scornful air
And choose his nest and enter in.

Then came what I had known would come:
The swallows left on wings as still,
As soundless as an unbeaten drum
Or sudden shadow on a hill.

And in a moment they were back,
Hundreds with little bits of clay
To seal the robber in and pack
Him down forever from the day.

It took no longer than a minute;
And then the swallows far and near
Said over something that had in it
What seemed like laughter to my ear.

Another tomb among the many
Blind, awful mouths already there!
But thinking pleasant thoughts, if any,
I went about my own affair.

My own affairs I'm bent on still,
But now in me the twitterings run
Where sudden wing and clever bill
Shut something in against the sun.

Blind mouths! Ah God, if I could get
Clear of the accusing memory
That I broke never a nest to let
A single panting sparrow free!

Progress

For fifteen bob a week I ploughed
Daylong for Jennings—fifteen bob!
And every night alone I vowed
To-morrow I'd throw up the job.

But there was sunlight on the furrow
Those days, and white clouds in the sky;
And, every Clydesdale was as thorough
As skill could breed or money buy.

And there was time for quiet smoking
Through sleepy miles behind the team,
And in the brain deft fancies yoking
Sleek horses gently to a dream.

But fifteen bob a week! I gave
Notice, and slung my blanket-roll
Across my back, and went to save
What I was pleased to call my soul.

I must have saved it, too, for now
I could buy Jennings and his land,
House, horses, harvester and plough,
And pay the whole thing out of hand.

And never miss the cash it cost me:
And that is proof enough, 'twould seem—
Could I but only know what lost me
Sleek horses yoking to a dream!

The Crow

You can take a fox with a bait,
A fish with a hidden hook,
A man with a tale of Fate,
A maid with a sigh and a look,
But I knew a bird was smarter than
Fox or fish or maid or man.

He came and went at his will
With an obscene caw and a flap,
Baffling my proudest skill
With rifle and lure and trap;
Aloft he'd sit on the ring-barked tree
And chortle over his joke with me.

But at last I caught him flat,
(And a happy man was I),
With a dainty bit of fat
On a sheep-skin hung to dry;
He pecked and swallowed and cawed and flew
But the laugh was mine, and I think he knew.

For he did not stop to preen
But headed away and away;
And a lonely man I've been
Ah, more than I care to say,
For the bird I knew that was smarter than
Fox or fish or maid or man.

Australian Idyl
(After News of War in Europe)

Ferns uncurl by the stream;
Birds drop to sip and play;
Their mirrored winglets seem
Fairer than they.

Flute-throated magpies cry
Where groves are deep;
I listen where I lie
Almost asleep.

Ten thousand miles from here
Cannon thunder and shake
Men who lie down in fear
And never wake.

Foxes among the Lambs

Each morning there were lambs with bloody mouth,
Their tongues cut out by foxes. Behind trees,
Where they had sheltered from the rainy South,
They'd rise to run, but fall on wobbly knees.

And knowing, though my very heart was sick,
That only death could cure them of their ills,
I'd smash their heads in with a handy stick
And curse the red marauders from the hills.

Each afternoon, safe in a sheltered nook
Behind the smithy, I'd prepare the bait;
And I remember how my fingers shook
With the half-frightened eagerness of hate
Placing the strychnine in the hidden rift
Made with the knife-point in the piece of liver;
And I would pray some fox would take my gift
And eat and feel the pinch and curse the giver.

Each night I'd lie abed sleepless until,
Above the steady patter of the rain,
I'd hear the first sharp yelp below the hill
And listen breathless till it rang again,
Nearer this time; then silence for a minute
While something in me waited for the leap
Of a wild cry with death and terror in it;
And then—it strikes me strange now—I could sleep!

Farm-Hand

Two hundred fallow and three hundred sown;
I call that not half bad
For one who showed no promise as a lad
Of ever calling anything his own.

Of course the land's not mine. Old Grumble mopes
Up there by a warm blaze,
And mumbles to himself and sighs and says
Come summer he'll feel better so he hopes.

Come summer! Well, he hasn't seen his land
For more than half a year,
And mumbles on as though he didn't hear
When I report what's done and what is planned.

There, Topsy, we're all through with drill and plough;
A right near job, I say:
Kick up your heels, old girl, as long's you may—
The grass is good along the creekside now.

I'll draw my wages and be off a while.
It takes a lot of drinks
To square a chap with all the things he thinks
Out there behind his team mile after mile.

But when I've had my fill of Wagga beer
And Nell and Sue and fun,
Our paddock will be waiting in the sun,
Our work, old girl, not Grumble's never fear.

To a Dying Wild Cockatoo
(For Hugh McCrae)

Bird from the sky
Fallen, clenched feet, crushed breast,
Do you remember, as here you die,
Tall hollow gums and a nest
High over the quiet river?
Or, while your wings stiffen and quiver,
Is it all inwardly dark
With the wet ground under, the stubble land round you,
And I who found you,
Seen by your brain's last spark,
A crouching monster of life from whom
You slip, with your heart turned stone and your eyes grown stark,
Into the sheltering gloom?

On Reading a War Poet with a Class

You like this quiet poem that he made
In gratitude because a swallow brought
Down the curved lanes of death a sudden thought
Of autumn sunshine in an English glade
Where cows chewed dreamily and rabbits played

Along a hedgerow where the grass was short—
You like this quiet poem that he wrought
To keep his heart alive and unafraid?

Remember, too, he fell on that same day,
Eyes wild with fear, a bullet in his breast;
And his last sunset, yellow in the west
Saw, as the hot gun-fury cooled away,
Only a corpse with blood upon its mouth
And a few swallows, high and heading south.

On Man

A rat who in his freedom felt the glare
Of hungry eyes in ambush, mused one day,
'Life would be sweet were there a safer way
To win my food'; and as in answer to prayer,
A cage with cheese and safety! —You who care
May find him sitting, gaunt and somewhat gray,
Watching grim phantom cats that crouch and sway,
The bit of cheese untouched beside him there.

A rat, a man! Forgive me, you are young
And merely come to visit at the zoo.
You've even brought your peanuts and a few
Sweet bits of candy for the daintier tongue.
A gaunt, safe rat! God help you when you see
That you and I and all of us are he!

Snares for Beauty

Men set their snares for beauty variously:
Some on clear summits of the tranquil mind
Spread nets of thought to hold her feet confined
If she should pause there on her way to the sea;
And some lay bare their bosoms anxiously,
Hoping the bird will drop there, passion-blind,
But all the same's the luck the hunters find—
Shadows and shadows where no bodies be.

I am too young for wisdom and too old
To think that passion will bring the wild one in;
She slips the knot of even the finest sin,
And goes high-winging where the heights are cold.
I shall believe at last what I've been told:
Where sharp men fail a little child shall win.

One Reason

When in the balance of the mind I throw
Against the eternal cold my little spark,
My glint of light against the eternal dark,
Against the silence the one word I know:
And when I heap my dreams in trust that so
My balance may hold level to the mark,
My last, best dream just fallen there, then hark
A thin satiric Laughter clear and low!

Then, then, O love, hold wide your arms to take
One touched with scorn who yet would reach your side
To spend the warmth he owns before he dies:
And love him not for any other sake
Than that he dared what coward never tried
And comes to you with terror in his eyes.

In Sandstone Country After Rain

Now the sun after rain
Warms the brown stone again,
And trees that have drunk deep
Through root and leaf, sleep.

The birds have sung and are still
As songs that have had their fill
Of sun and sleep beneath
Sound, in a cool sheath.

Even the lizard's ear
Finds only silence here,
Except for the creek that tumbles
And the stone that crumbles.

The Chase

Run, fox! no mincing stride
Timed daintily with scorn
Will save your tawny hide
And keep your throat untorn!

He's on you, toe to heel,
Running without a sound,
His eyes two points of steel,
His belly to the ground.

Ripper his name—you'll know
Its meaning by and by
Unless . . . for God's sake go!—
I would not have you die.

How should he understand
When he has laid you dead
And lifts to meet my hand
His hot and bloody head,

With eyes where pride will flame
Above the crumpled kill
This thing that makes me tame
And loosens all my will?

Then run, fox, run! I say
God curse you if you prove
The cur who would betray
My sin against his love!

Breaking the Colt

Rub of knees and grip of thighs
Cooled the ardor of his eyes;
Heavy hand and dogging heel
Broke his heart and made it kneel.

Once he trusted sky and hill
And his own unbroken will;
Bossed the paddock as he would
In supremacy of blood.

Let no hand bring near him then
Hostile, unclean smell of men!
Let no voice be soft with lies
Husbanding the dark surprise!

There were teeth for that low breed
There were hoofs and there was speed;
There were slanting ears that said,
'Keep away or mind your head.'

Say a thing like that to men?
Poor young fool, we'll teach you then
What the bit and spur can do
To the sullen likes of you.

'Ridden like a man,' they yelled,
From the fences, while I held
All his fire with knee and thigh
Squeezed until I felt it die.

Ridden like a man, no doubt!
But I've still to make it out
How at last it's come to this
That the victory was his.

The Sensualist Replies

You pity me that find
The only good in flesh?
You of the nobler mind
Whose faith is dream-refined,
You pity me that bind
Joy in so frail a mesh?

But if the vision cheat
Your hand, good gentlemen,
And grant you for the sweet
You hoped for, wormy meat,
You'll pocket pity then
And sit with me and eat.

The Snake

I should have been glad, I know, to see
That little river of life that was he;
In a great still paddock, dry as a knife,
That sudden little river of life.

Perhaps he had a mouse in mind
Or such poor game as a snake might find—
Hard-winged beetles under a clod
In a paddock bare as a copper rod.

Room for both! And I should have been glad
To see the speed and the grace he had;
Ripple of life, ah, beautiful,
In a field as dead as a bullock's skull!

But the stick I held flashed up, flashed down,
And the earth turned red where the earth was brown,
'By God,' I said, 'but the ground is dry!'
And I did not wait to see him die.

A Woman's Invitation

Come if you will, but do not look
To read for me the scented book
Fashioned by man of love-conceits
And all the other tarnished sweets
To prove him more than brute; the pretty
Lying book of song and ditty;

Dainty little appetizer
That will leave us none the wiser
If the food be heavenly fare
Or plain beef, a trifle rare.
In your pocket, dear! But say
You came to pass the time of day
And if I'd find 't at all amusing
You'll read a volume of my choosing.
And I'll reply with careless air:
'That plain old volume over there!
By one who never learned to be
The hypocrite of chivalry,
Nor squeezed his voice to pipe hosannas
Nor tricked his lusts in silk of manners;
That honest man—,' but by that time,
You'll be linking rhyme to rhyme,
And I'll declare the day's grown colder
And come to lean against your shoulder.
And if my cheek by chance should touch
Yours, why, do not mind it much
But go on reading till you come
To the word will strike you dumb.
Then I'll have to bend down near
And spell it for you slowly, dear;
And, be you man, you'll learn in time
And match it with the proper rhyme.
Hours later, just to make
Me certain there's been no mistake
Murmur manlike, drowsily,
'Dear, was that really poetry?'

On Cutting a Christmas Tree

If acts could be
Kept strictly celibate,
Each act of mine should have no more of me
Than just his date.

But since I must
Admit the copulation
Of all past things within my helpless dust,
And take my station

To wink and keep
The door against intrusion,
While they, hot-mouthed, do what they will and heap
Pain on confusion;

Therefore this tree
I sought with purpose mild,
Notched at each side and broke against my knee,
Became a child

Awful with pain—
A child I used to know
That jerked his head aside once, but in vain,
Once, from a blow!

Thrift

He loved his horse; and when it died
Grabbed his knife and got its hide.
The cash—consider while you praise—
Kept him drunk for seven days.

Fence-Maker

At less than half a glance 'twas clear
His brain was much like sour beer;
Yet the long miles of fence he'd run
Stood as straight as goes the sun.

At the Grave of a Land-Shark

There was no land, they used to tell,
Old Miller couldn't trade or sell;
A clever man! I wonder how
He'll turn the lot he's stuck with now!

'Guns on Western Front Play Hide-and-Seek'
(A Newspaper Headline)

A pleasant game, of course, and good clean fun
This hide-and-seek of sportive gun and gun;
But when they find each other in their play
It's just as well to look the other way.

In the Garden

These quiet roots will make
Verbenas blue and pink,
And out of these will wake
Delphinium, I think.

I think, but surely these
Unthinking fibres know
Come Spring, as for long centuries,
Delphinium will blow.

Mad Jack

They called him Jack, Mad Jack,
But I think that I often saw
A laugh in the set of his back
As he turned from the kitchen door.

Tucker wrapped up in paper,
Billy well filled with tea,
He walked, I thought, with a caper
That seemed most strange to me.

A frisk every step or two;
In a hurry? But who would wait
For him? And no man knew
Where he went once he shut the gate.

He lived in the hills, they said,
And talked with the wild things there,
With stringybark fluff for his bed
And a sunny rock for his chair.

Mad Jack! But I have ground
Since then at the mill with the rest,
And faltered, and turned and found
Peace in the hills of the West.

And I have learned the drift
Of the laugh in the set of his back
And why his feet were swift
Away on the outbound track.

Aside

Love is good but who could bear
Too long its warm and scented lair;
Or who could live with melancholy
And never heed the beck of folly;
Or feast with plenty and not wish
By and by a plainer dish;

And who could bear to be forever
Virtuous, devout or clever?
Call bluff on our expressed desires;
We're all a sorry lot of liars.

Pastoral

Yesterday I watched a bee
In among the tall white clover,
And each bloom, it seemed to me,
Whispered, 'Ah, my golden lover!'

But I heard another sound
As he set a blossom shaking
And his legs grew pollen-round:
'Ah, what honey for the taking!'

Never mind my laughter, love;
Shut your eyes and let us see
If there's any thought above
Clover-bloom or honey-bee.

Death of an Old Sheep-Dog

With a small boy's solicitude I made
A warm clean bed of straw where she could lie,
Half glad that she was sick and half afraid
My joy would make her die.

And now I had a game to play, in truth
Enough to set my pulses in a whirl,
Better by far than pulling the first tooth
Or kissing the first girl.

For here was one I loved about to go
Forever down into the loveless night,
And mine the splendid duty to say 'No!
Stay! I will hold you tight!'

But she and death had other plans in mind;
And when I laid her gently on the straw,
She staggered up, and though her eyes were blind,
Went sternly out the door.

And all my wheedling words were less to her,
(I see that now), where on the ground she lay,

Than burblings of a vulgar chatterer
When violins, far off, play.

I found her in the morning white with frost,
Dead. And I took it as a reprimand
To my boy's heart, that she had won, I lost,
An ancient game, well-planned.

And with a sense of dark conspiracy
In things beyond my sight, I burned her straw,
And buried her beneath a handy tree,
And shut the useless door.

Natural Economy—in the Garden

A thousand seeds drop out
From this alyssum head,
Yet there'll be room, at very best,
For two or three in this bed.
The eagle broods her eggs,
Just two, or maybe one,
And her's is the whole sky to fill
From Eagle Crags to the sun!

The Man of Parts

These things have kept him still
Alive against my will,
Such trivial things that I
Would give them death hereby:
His one poor borrowed joke
About the 'girl and bloke,'
And the grin that used to sit
As midwife to his wit;
The way he'd pound and twist
The pillow with his fist
Each night of every week
To a hollow for his cheek.
Such trivial things! But then
I was beside him when
His joke, grown dry and slim,
Died at a gasp with him.
And in his last straight bed
The pillow for his head—
I ached to see it—was
Impersonal as glass.

Clearing for the Plough

Through tranquil years they watched the changes
Creep over hill and plain; they saw
The kangaroo go from his ranges,
The clucking emu come no more.

And then the Blacks, with startled faces
Broke off the dance where laughter sprang
Naked and free; and the old places
Forgot the spear and boomerang.

And over plain and hill there drifted
Sheep numberless and meek and brown
That grazed all day in peace and lifted
Low bleatings when the sun went down.

But the great gums watched on, unknowing
What time was saying, could they hear:
'The end has come of bloom and growing,
The blade and the red fire are near.

The round of change is sure and steady:
The kangaroo, the sheep, the plough.
The axe is ground and bright and ready,
The sleeve rolled—and it's your turn now!'
. . . .
The stars, when the long nights close over,
Will miss them in the accustomed spot,
And the great sun who was their lover
Will come each day and find them not.

And winds that laughed to see them shaken
To mighty song, will pause and pass
Half loath, for sorrow, to awaken
The lesser music of the grass.

Sentimentalist

It helped him little that he thought
He set a rose of lovely name;
Some older hand than his had wrought
With a far different aim,

And deep in its eternal plan
Had thinned the bloom and tipped with fire

Each hooked thorn for the flesh of man,
And left it so, a briar.

During Drouth

He said: 'Like flies they die,
Hundreds each day out there
Under the empty sky,
Sprawled in the heat and glare.

On dragging hooves they come
Down to the creek and stand
Staring, black-mouthed and dumb,
At the baked mud and sand

Day after day until
They drop. With lazy cries
The crows, grown dainty, will
Take nothing but their eyes.'

To comfort him I said—
Fearing he felt to blame—
'The beasts have always bled
As their part in the game.

Bitter's the role they play
In the world's dismal plan.'
He spat and looked away:
'It's bitterer to be man!'

To Herrick, on a Windy Day

The wind drives leaves along the gutter
And raggy clouds across the skies,
And causes me to squint and mutter
Harsh imprecations on my eyes.

I lunge, and edge, and squirm, and double,
And flinch at every shove and blow,
And curse the turmoil and the trouble,
And every wind both high and low.

But there a skirt takes fright and dances
Beneath a white, protesting hand,
And were you here, I think the chance is,
Herrick, you'd smile and understand

With me how even a wind like this
Does some things that are not amiss.

Millie

I smile to think of Millie,
So wise, so sure was she:
'I set my heart on Billy
And he'll be true to me.

'His brothers drink their wages,
Joe, Steve, and all the six;
The devil's filled his pages,
I'm certain, with their tricks.

'But Billy's hand is ready,
And Billy's eyes are blue,
And Billy's lips are steady,
And Billy's heart is true.'

They wed in late October
And by next May the First
The brothers had grown sober
And Bill had caught a thirst.

At the Old Crown you'd find him
His whiskers flexed with beer,
Saying to all who'd mind him:
'It's this way, if you'll hear;

'One sober man is leaven
For six that drink and play;
But one to drink for seven
Is mighty work, I say.'

I smile to think of Millie
So innocent of guile,
So wise, so sure of Billy—
Perhaps I shouldn't smile!

A Song for Dark Days, 1939

The madmen have grown noisy in the world,
The liars lift their voices to a shout;
But in deep woods the fern is half uncurled,
And I know where the waratah is out.

Steel falcons scream their anger through the sky,
Nerved with all cunning, eager for the kill;
But there'll be magpies singing by and by
Where the red gums lean coolly to the hill.

Death's busy sharpening up his knife, they say,
And he'll find throats enough to slit, no doubt;
But there'll be wattle blooming, come the day,
By streams where I have business with the trout.

On page and page the hieroglyphics run—
(I've read a new and wilder fling of Joyce)—
But there's my lizard sleeping in the sun,
And who could doubt the Yellow Bob's in voice!

They tell me thought strikes baffled down blind alleys,
Fevered anguished at his little span;
I know the cool green sweep of easy valleys
Older than the brief arrogant years of man.
. . . .
O sad, mad world, you tell me, 'here's good buying:
This for your blood, this you can have for tears,
And this, the best of all, is yours for dying;
Come, gather to your breast the sudden spears!'

No, No! I have a trust more worth the keeping,
That shall be mine when your sick rages pass:
To lead you, broken then, O world, and weeping,
Back to the ancient wisdom of the grass.

'Not Charioted By Bacchus and His Pards'

The body dying,
Who ponders the dark disease
That unsnares from the nerve-net the crying
Wild soul-things and gives them release?

The sick one surely
Cares little enough to mark
How doors are shutting securely
Behind what slips into the dark.

The soul-things steady
Their breasts to the sweet new air,
Glad to be going and ready
For the luck of the otherwhere.

A world dying,
Poet, slip out of him, go
From the nerve-net that held you crying
Against the incurable woe.

I think I am free,
(Though the world may be long ending),
And my luck is a face and a tree,
And wheat in the wind, bending.

Duck Hunters

They shot the ducks last night.
I knew them from the shell,
And they were doing well,
And ready, soon, for flight.

Twelve beauties as would make
Grey water anywhere
Grow of a sudden fair
And bright with many a wake.

Two men of valiant blood
Had ducks to line their bellies,
And two whole broods of Kelleys
Fed well and called life good.

No sin, of course! But sorrow
Will turn bright water grey.
I'll not go round that way
To-day, nor yet to-morrow!

Under Gum Trees at Sunset

Once in ten years, or maybe never again
Shall I see gum trees let the red sun down
As now from branch to branch across the plain.

They ease him by his clinging hands of light
As I have seen a mother slip her own
Child from her bosom to its bed at night.

And what warmth lingers at that quiet breast
I think I know. Ah, softly overhead
The tree-heart opens to the fading west!

There will be other sunsets on this plain,
But what I feel and think were better said
Once in ten years, or maybe never again.

Country Parson

He preached that money was the root
Of evil; with hot eloquence
Paved hell with pounds and crowns and pence
And shod with gold the devil's foot.

And then, his benediction said
Above the green collection platter,
He went to dine quite as a matter
Of course with Mister Dives Sned.

Midsummer-Night's Mood
The Riverina

Speak not at all, or say
Such words now as by day
Would leave you trembling should
You feel them in your blood.

For all is silent here:
Moonlit and far and clear
The voiceless hills arise
To meet the unspeaking skies.

And the Mopoke's cry is a sound
Sheathed in silence, wound
About with the silk of the moon
Like a moth in her cocoon.

No noise of words be made
Unless, through depthless shade,
There come a word that springs
From old and magical things,

Things that have long been shut
In sleep and silence, but
By far and moonlit ways
Quiver across our days

To prove that time is not
Stronger than Camelot,
And that no years destroy
What were the towers of Troy;

That here in Austral night
Tall gum-trees hold the light
Of a moon that rose and fell
Often on Tintagel;

That Helen lives again
On this far southern plain,
Lives and can never die
While there's a moon in the sky.

O speak no word unless
It be, like Lyonesse
Or Troy, spun of the moon
To be a dream's cocoon.

Wind in Summer

The wind is north and hard
And hot with swirling dust
From earth as dry as a shard;
No day for a man to trust!

The gums are grey and thinned,
The sheep lie close to the ground;
Except for the howl of the wind
There's not a living sound.

No day for a man to trust,
With grass in the paddocks dry
As a puff of the whirling dust,
Matted and half knee-high.

No day for a man to sleep
When from the north might be sped
Red bulls of flame to heap
The paddock corners with dead.

Blackened muzzles, ah God,
Burnt and twitching for breath!
No day for a man to nod
With the wind's whip out on death.

Gums

Poplar and elm and pine
Stand fast and may not roam
Far from the ancient line
Of spire and dome.

Each, steadfast in his place,
Rises from roots that heed
Only the mould of race,
The stamp of breed.

But gum trees will not so
Live the old law. By hill
And grassy flat they grow
Each as he will.

One, mottled white and brown,
Stately and clean of girth,
Shafts upward; one leans down
Close to the earth.

One droops in curve and twist
Where sunlight gleams,
Scarred old romanticist
Dreaming his dreams.

One, shade-and-sunshine flecked,
Blue-grey and rose,
Ponders with head erect
Classic repose.

I have gone here and there
Through the wide earth to see
All twisted things and fair—
Life's pageantry;

But here, my journey done,
All forms, all memories,
Look out at me from one
Paddock of trees.

A Dead Magpie

Crumpled on the bare slope
Of earth about the well
He lay dead. The smell
Strangled me like a rope.

By that same well I stood
Only two nights before
To hear the magpies pour
Song in a joyous flood.

I know that wise men keep
Confusion sternly out,
And know beyond a doubt
Why they should laugh or weep.

But I can never tell
The anguish from the hope:
O singer, now on the slope
Rotting beside the well!

To H.S. in Farewell

And so goodbye! I give you back each tree
That was so surely mine this week or two—
They were yours first; I give them back to you.

And every sunset I shall never see
Is yours—may there be many and all fair
Behind the hill and the dead timber there.

And all the birdsong now is yours to hear
That greets the day, that bids the day farewell,
Yours only—and I know you'll listen well.

For all these things were beautiful and dear
To us, but only lent to me; and so
Goodbye, I give them back before I go.

Poems from Brief Waters (1945)

Hold Dear Things Not Too Close

Hold dear things not too close
But touch them lightly so
That when their moment goes
They, too, may go
With never a scar to tell
How once you loved them well.

And let not dear things bide
Too long against your heart;
But wisely all provide
That your parting, when you part,
Be not as flesh from bone
But as water slipping from stone.

A Rabbit-Skinner

A poem mocks me from his eyes
Where he bends at his rabbit-skinning,
Cursing the weather and the flies
And all things born from their beginning
Right to their end—especially these
Dead rabbits heaped about his knees.

His hands are filthy and his slack
Mouth drools disgust as deftly he
Slips the warm pelt from paunch and back
And, where the ears cling, jerks it free
As though some rage were satisfied
By thus divorcing beast from hide.

And yet a poem in his eyes
Haunts me. It is no pretty thing
Such as a poet might surprise
And make quite tame by cherishing:
What mocks me—and the challenge thrills—
Is a red dingo from the hills.

Some shrewder hand than mine must lay
That slinking creature by the heels
And teach him how, in savage play,
The collar of a sonnet feels:

Right royal sport among the blind
Grey mulga thickets of the mind.

I'd like to try. The game so near,
Such cool disdain of trap or blow
In pointed nose and cocky ear!
And I would try, but that I know—
(I learned it from old dogger Porter)—
A dingo's caught with dingo-water!

The Wonder Bird

They laughed to see my bird, laughed till they shook
And scarce could tell each other: "Take a look
At what he's brought home now! Must be a lark—
But no, a parrot, and out of Noah's Ark
So old it is, such a moth-eaten thing
With not a feather left in tail or wing!
Just take a look!" And when at next they saw
My hands the bird had ripped with beak and claw,
They frowned a little and asked me if it hurt
And said, "Don't let the blood get on your shirt!"

How could they guess the glory? And yet how
Dare not to feel it as I do even now?

It happened on a day when the great plain
Lay tense with heat. Like horizontal rain,
(But with the mockery of rain that's dry),
The heat-waves blotted out the lower sky
And left, straight overhead, one spout of blue
For the keen sun to pour his violence through
Right on the head of all things that went out
On such a day. And yet I walked about
The farmyard on such business as a lad
Has when the world has all gone dead or mad,

Such solemn business as to lift a stick
Between the naked toes, or with a flick
Pitch a brown pebble high up on the roof
To show the mile-deep silence was not proof
Against a boy, whose thought ran on a sound;
(The roof was iron, and the pebble round).
What should they think, who turned in quick annoy
In the deep shade, to mutter "Damn that boy!"

And then I saw the bull-oaks in a clump
Way down the paddock, and I knew a stump
Was there might hold a rabbit or a lizard,
Or, if I felt like that, a dry old wizard
Who'd talk just like the one I had in bed
Who nightly mixed the prayers up in my head
Until, though bent on matters stern and sad,
I suddenly was feasting in Baghdad.

How should they know, who kept the shade that day,
How far a stump might lead a boy away!

But there was something more: A story told
One day at breakfast, of a bird all gold,
A parrot such as man had never seen
Before on that wide plain, gold with a green
Crest like a curl of springing wheat. He flew
Among the bull-oaks, and a boy might do
Worse things than see if he could find him there;
"Take salt," the speaker said, "and walk with care."

How should he know, who told the friendly lie,
How hard a boy's heart lets a vision die!

There was no wizard at the stump; too bright
A day for him, of course; nor even a sight
Of rabbit or of lizard did I get.
And then it happened like a sudden jet
Of something through the heart, or like the quick
Metallic challenge of a hammer's click
Brought to the cock: Beside the bull-oak there
The golden bird! I did not see how bare
The wretched thing sat, flightless and afraid,
Hugging the coolness of a bit of shade,
With scarce a feather left in tail or wing
And bleak old head for ever doddering
From side to side in the great stream of heat.
I only saw the glory at my feet.

How should they know, who laughed amid the shade,
How proud a boy's heart, and how unafraid!

A parrot's beak is neither dull nor slow,
And I had more than half a mile to go
With nothing but my hands to keep her in.
But I walked gently, laughing at the thin

Trickle of blood across my wrist that showed
How well she fought, and at my palms that glowed
As though they held, not a bird but living fire.
I would not hurry, and I dared not tire
For fear the gods, who blessed me on that day,
Might see me flinch and snatch the gift away
And leave me in that solitude of heat
Alone with empty hands and naked feet
And never a bird all gold with a green crest
To lie, as now one did, against my breast.

A boy's heart may grow suddenly afraid
Or angry at big laughter in the shade,
And a boy's eyes may know the sting of tears;
But in the twilight, numbering back his years,
The man remembers with what splendid joy
The dream that scarred his fingers as a boy,
The wonder bird all gold with a green crest
No laughter could reach up to in the nest
He made for it, not on, but in his breast!

Song

So I send you like a thief,
Thought, to break the locked and shuttered
Darkened chambers of her grief.

Do not bend above her head
Long, for fear a pulse be fluttered
In the wrist across her bed.

Then come back, your only prize
Something she'd not give to me
Stolen from her sleeping eyes.

And the way past door and stone
Oh, report it faithfully!
She shall lie no more alone.

Early-Morning Train to Sydney

As I sit here and watch the crowds
Stream cityward in train on train,
I think the city must have slept
Well, emptied of all these, her brain;

And now must feel, as wakers do
At dawning, the sharp nibble and thrust
Of many-hungered consciousness
Searching old cupboards for a crust.

Two Friends

I have a friend whose wit can shake
Long buried Caesars wide awake,
Or with a delicate turn and thrust
Spill living Caesars into dust.

There are no stars along the night
His brain-flares cannot put to flight;
There is no miracle by day
He cannot quite explain away.

With smiling lip and narrowed eye
He ushers wonder in to die,
And shows mostly elegantly how
To measure Helen with a bow.

And him I like because I may
Laugh with and at him night or day;
Uncurbed by love or pity, shake
My sides with laughter till I ache.

I have another friend who talks
With roadside grasses when he walks,
And treats to sprightly monologue
The lizard or the drowsing frog.

A bit of broken rock will call
Aeons around him, and the fall
Of one red leaf will let him see
The miracle that is a tree.

And all the dead who ever made
Earth bright, death darker by a shade,
Live in his voice like sound-of-flame
As he recalls them name by name.

And him I like because I may
Let love and wonder have their way
Safe in the shelter of his heart
Where laughter dare not throw a dart.

Two friends I have in the one street,
Two friends—and may they never meet!

Sanctuary

Night-long, rain on the roof,
And in my thought
Something prick-eared and aloof
That would not be caught.

But when morning again
Broke, and the rain was fled,
It ran to my heart—and then
It could not be said.

Land-Buyer

I knew he shouldn't buy the land, invest
The savings of five years, hard-earned at best,
In three bare acres Parramatta way.
But he cared little for what I had to say
Perhaps because he knew full well my heart
Despite my head, was with him from the start.

On the long train-ride, in his knotted hand
He held the brief description of the land
Cut from the paper; and I watched him steal
Glances at it as though to bring the feel
Of the whole prospect freshly back and make
Himself quite sure there wasn't some mistake.

We reached the station and we found the pub
And over beers were told, "The place is scrub.
A garden spot, the paper says? My eye!
A rabbit would take just one look and die.
They shouldn't print such things. I'd stay right here,
If I were you, and have another beer."

We had that beer and started off together
Down the hot road—it was November weather—
And saw the paddocks dry before their time
And covered with a dismal dust like lime;
But he kept saying, "They'll be green again,
You take my word, come one good soaking rain."

The place itself! We leaned upon the gate
That sagged and shuddered underneath our weight
Though we leaned lightly. I but took one look
And then I noticed that his fingers shook
A little on his pipe-bowl, but he said
No single word to show a dream was dead.

We were about to go the way we came,
Wretchedly still with something much like shame,
When he said, "Look!" A dozen magpies flew
Onto that grey flat scar of earth and threw
Their heads back in a song that, sweet as rain,
Made the soul-acres green with dreams again.

I turned my face away, knowing his eyes
Would be on mine to share the glad surprise,
But hear his words I did and hear them still:
"It's mine, by God, and they can sing here till
There isn't any singing to be done
Anywhere in the world beneath the sun!"

And all the beers I bought on the way back,
And all the barman uttered with his slack
Pale mouth that tightened only with disgust
Served less than nothing to waylay and thrust
The traveller from the perilous way he trod,
Yes, less than nothing—oh, thank God! Thank God!

Farm Scene

They come each morning to the gate,
Are milked, and wander off to feed;
Six cows, a calf, and in the lead
A brindled bull, old, fat, sedate.

And every evening they are back,
Loafing along the quarter-mile
Of dusty lane in single file,
The old bull trailing up the track.

I would not load with thought that brings
Meanings deep-conjured in the mind
This quiet scene—but here I find
The rhythm of eternal things,

And envy him who takes his pail
Jingling to meet them at the gate;
Sun-up, sun-down, that constant date
Which neither he nor they will fail.

I envy him whose life allows
Him this cool blessedness: to stand
And simply watch the coming and
Later the going of the cows.

"Blood, Sweat, and Tears"

Now in the battle-womb, the dark place,
His veins knit to the feeding-blood, he lies
Gathering his strength inexorably. Cries
Of victor, vanquished, triumph or disgrace,
Concern him not. He moves at the blood's pace
To the appointed hour when he shall rise
Out of the gates of birth and give our eyes
The hell or the great heaven of his face.

Stand close about her, the mysterious spouse,
And let our hearts be on her with such love
The child must feel it deep amid his drowse
And wake to that. And when the hard pangs move
Ah, do not doubt that from such passioning,
Blood, sweat, and tears, will rise to us a king!

Between Winter and Spring

I doubt if birds know
Now what songs they'll sing
Come peach and cherry-blow,
Come spring.

But winter mediates,
(Winter is wise and old),
Whatever it is that waits
In throats that are cold.

Winter must tell me, then,
And not the shivering bird,
What was it—there again!
What was it I heard?

Godiva's Coventry

I never saw the city of your fame
And shall not see it now the bombs have spoken;
The stone that was the calix for your name
Lies torn apart and broken.

And all the walls are down from gate to gate
That saw you pass while birds forebore to sing,
Ended by one red violence of hate
Their long remembering.

The moss that kept you for a thousand years
Godiva, shall not find you ever again;
Trampled it lies and mixed with blood and tears,
And rotting in the rain.

Your Coventry is gone. Yet in the light
Of flares among its broken walls I see,
In steadfast silent rows young knight on knight
Rising from bended knee,

The men who never thought to let you die,
But lift you to their saddle-bows of steel
To ride with you the pathways of the sky
Until the planets feel

Their passing and that fortitude no less
Than yours before your own black-hearted lord,
Of those who in fire of your own nakedness
Have fashioned them a sword.

The Bargain

The bar was cool that day
When the brown country lay
Like one too tired to beat
The flies off, while the heat
Stitched earth and sky together—
And it was thirsty weather.

I'd nearly filled my skin
When he came sidling in,
A swaggie spent and brown
As trampled thistledown,
And tattered and forlorn
As a rag on a wayside thorn.

The barman knew his kind
And turned stone deaf and blind
Instantly with the skill
That marks the expert still
Whether his trade be beer
Or some less bladdery cheer.

I saw the swagman stop
Half through the door to mop
His brow, and then there ran
A mongrel, black and tan,
Joyous to welcome back
His master to the track.

Let someone else declare
What moved me then and there,
But laughingly I spoke,
(The barman liked my joke).
"Your dog," I said, "for sale?"
And I thought the man grew pale.

"A pound and fleas thrown in,
I offer." Then the thin
Old eyes begged hard of me,
"Not much for such as he,
The best——" I cut him dead:
"It's forty beers," I said.

Let someone else declare
Why day by day I dare
Not meet that mongrel's eye;
And day by day I try
To think a ghost can be laid
By forty beers in the shade!

To a Child at Night in Australia

Did you hear,
Down by the dry creek bed,
The plover?
And the queer
Thing that the mopoke said
Over and Over?

You are afraid, you say?
I am glad, my child:
The wild heart of you answers that way
To the wild!

Sunrise in the Riverina

I watched the sunrise burn itself away
And heard, in the dead gum-tree by the Hut,
The magpies throwing wide such gates of day;
I wondered, come the night, who'd sing them shut!

The Hawthorn-Tree

I wonder what new meanings we should see
Could we be watchers like the hawthorn-tree
That helped the moon so marvelously trace
The passionate beauty of your upturned face?

Would that which moved us be a wind that came
From regions no geographer can name
To bend each branch and set the whole tree swinging
Till every fibre locked in desperate clinging?

Would what we said be what the leaves declare:
We sing but for the weight of him we bear,
And when he goes, as always he is going,
We know a stillness deeper than all knowing?

Would that long after-silence be the pour
Of stars through steady branches, more and more,
Until, like something felt beyond belief,
Eternity lay bright on every leaf?

Only our tree can answer. But I know
He listens, as I listen, for the low
First breath of wind upon his waiting leaves,
And when it comes not, he, as I do, grieves.

Quatrains for a Girl

I

Few could have known your beauty as I know it
And not grown mad or cunning. But I rule
The stars by you; and therefore am I poet,
Wash dishes and most soberly teach school!

II

Why don't you laugh? We should be hurt and bitter
And modern—this is nineteen-forty-one—
And gulp a drink, and with our minds a-jitter
Read, and pretend we understand, John Donne.

III

But silent is the moon's way in the sky,
Silvering the clouds her full breast moves apart;
And silently, let it float silently,
The grave moon of your beauty in my heart.

The Butcher-Bird

Among the box-thorns on a summer day
When earth and sky were deaf with light and heat
And every leaf had turned itself away
From the mad sun, the awful trample of feet,
The song I heard from those gaunt hedges thrown
Was a blue vein across a yellow stone.

And then it was bright water slipping, running
Among dark rocks. And then I seemed to hear
A practice-passage, tentative and cunning,
That steadied on itself and spiraled clear
Up, up and round, and round and over again
To be the dawn-song of the fairy wren.

Now suddenly a thrush; a honeyeater;
And some glad bird whose song I didn't know,
Singing together clearer, faster, sweeter,
Until the song had nowhere left to go
And fell, and was, beside a dying flame,
A lover murmuring his lady's name.

I should have gone home then: the song was done.
But I must find the singer—and I found him:
He sat on a dead thorn-bush in the sun
Vastly content, and on the twigs around him,
Hanging from broken necks like strung-up men,
Were honeyeater, thrush, and fairy wren.

And even as I watched, with dextrous bill
The butcher-bird was stringing on a thorn
A bit left over from his morning's kill,
A bird as soft and secret as the dawn.
I guessed, when it was dangling in the row,
It was the bird whose song I didn't know.

I did go home then, right across a stretch
Terrible with light. But when, so all alone
And fear-beset, I shoved my hand to fetch
Out of my pocket, to comfort me, a stone,
Or, just to close my heart and hand upon,
The yellow stone with the blue vein was gone!

Street Corner

On the street corner I see men stand
As they always have stood
With vacant eye and listless hand
And the chill in their blood.

I, too, some day will take my place
In the dreary row,
With a stone where my heart once had its place,
And not care that it's so.

Some day. But pardon me now, my friend,
For I may not wait:
I still have a wish and a penny to spend,
And the hour grows late!

Bantam Rooster

He used to run like flame
About the yard, till came
Old age and made him tame;
And the fire that had played in flashes
On the brown earth was ashes.

I, being not bird but man,
Watched from my longer span
Of years his down-burning
With tears
And yearning.

On a Piece of Rock from Central Australia

This is the oldest thing
Man's eyes may look upon;
So old that thoughts of it bring
Nineveh, Babylon,
Closer than yesterday:
Blocks that my child at play
Left on the floor when he said
Good night, and went to bed.

Orange and grey and blue
Rainbow in broken stone,
I walk the length of you
Terribly alone
Because I know that I'll find
At the end that my eyes are blind,
And I'll plunge and not ever see
The gulf that yawns for me.

The Gleaner

I am a gleaner where my dreams have run
With swift and shining sickles on before,
But silent are the lands beneath the sun
Where they will reap no more;

Yet all my days I gather broken grain
Content with little when each day is done,
For on the low horizon of the plain
Bright sickles flash the sun.

Brief Waters
(For Charles Cleary)

A puddle not much bigger than your hat
Lay there before me, and I stared at that;
Hunched over on my log, I stared until
I seemed like it, a thing without a will.

Perhaps it was that I was weary: sleep
That night I could not for the rattle and leap
Of wind and rain upon my slab-wood shed
And the cold storm-damp fingering at my bed.

Perhaps it was because I felt the sky
So blue above me that I must not try,
After that night of fury, with pretence
Of thought to prove its baffling innocence.

To left and right of me the empty track,
The forest, a great stillness, at my back,
And at my feet the pool three inches deep
But clear and placid as an infant's sleep.

I stared until the world had shrunk to that
Brief roadside pool no bigger than your hat;
And what I thought was neither less nor more
Than one of the brown pebbles on its floor.

Then suddenly my pool was full of sky
And five black swans that wedged it. With a cry
I bent to see them—but the pool lay still
And empty as a thing without a will!

A puddle not much bigger than your hat;
Yet in my thought I sit and stare at that
And shall for ever till I bring them back,
Black swans—black swans—and from how far a track!

Anthropologist

He sat among the ruins of camp and den
As quiet as the dust in an old house
Or as the ghosts he sought of ancient men,
And came home like himself sometimes; and then
On a good day,
I'd notice in him, even from far away,
The difference that is in a cat's head when
She's got a mouse.

At a Civilian Defence Lecture on Bombs

He lectured with the passion a man uses
Whose heart and mind are fired by romance,
Of TNT precision-wed to fuses
And time-bombs baited terribly with chance.

It was a good performance, but I sickened
Before the thing he fashioned with his breath
And wooed, as Satan Sin, until it quickened
Into a monstrous pregnancy of death.

I wanted no more loving explanations
Of firing-bridges wrought with delicate craft,
Of tail-fine angles for the right gyrations
And nose-caps buttoning the lightning-shaft.

The very figures in my notebook charting
The fine intelligence of each device
Seemed like the sign-boards of man's pathway starting
The shameful way back underneath the ice.

Then through the window swept a jangle of sound
From children come to play outside; their feet
Must have been very sure upon the ground,
Their running very confident and fleet.

I glanced along my figures with new terror
And something else that made me set aright
The note on bombs in which I had the error,
The chart on blasts I hadn't finished quite.

A Muscovy Duck

She was a sour old bag of lusts,
Or so I thought of her when she
Gobbled her food up hungrily
In something like lascivious gusts.

I'd stand and watch her scoop and scoff
Until her neck seemed stiff as wood,
Then, with her eye still on the food,
Hurry for water to the trough.

And what I felt I cannot say:
My mouth grew sickly moist, and yet,
From where she snuffled in the wet
I could not take my eyes away.

Now she has young, a golden lot
With bills milk-white and delicate;
I watch her stretch her neck and wait
While they throng round the breakfast pot.

Her black eyes blink and glare and gloat,
Her breath comes hard in gasp and catch,
But never a morsel will she snatch,
For something has her by the throat,

Something imperious as birth
That turns old lusts to cherishing—
The strongest and the loveliest thing
That I shall see upon the earth.

In Auckland Harbour

A gull trod air, then slipped on stiffened wing
From hover into glide
Above a scum of garbage eddying
Slowly on the slack tide.

And he was beautiful, so that I said
Praise-words, delicious, dim,
For that warm effluence of beauty shed
Round me because of him.

Screaming, he dived, and fished the filth and shook
Fouled wings that climbed from the dart;
And I—(I wish I had not flinched then)—took
The stab of truth in my heart.

An Old Lady

Her spirit raised proud angry pinnacles
Pain-buttressed, far above life's sensuous deep;
Yet on the sheerest crag of that stern soul
Moonlight breathes softly and winds lie down to sleep.

Cleaning Up the Wood-Heap (Between Wars)

Most of these chips were made
By men so long laid
Where axes never ring,
It is a bitter thing
To look upon their names
As the lithe-fingered flames
Write them against the smoulder:
Fred, Allan, Bert and Bill,
The strong of wrist and shoulder,
The great in heart and skill.

Gaza, Gallipoli,
(Only one rakeful more),
Romanie—that makes three—
The Marne, and there's the four!

One has, once in a while
To rake grief up in a pile
And set a match lest the blade
Should falter and grow afraid
And fumble around in chips
As names do on bruised lips.

All clean? The job's done,
And I have ended one
War for another begun.

The Cycle

She had her virtue some three lovers ago,
But she's grown fat, and fatter still will grow,
Until—the simplest logic makes it plain—
Grown fat enough, she'll have her virtue again.

Ewe with Twin Lambs

A good strong ewe; but when her twins
Were born a strangely evil stir
Like squirm of old remembered sins
Moved in the simple heart of her.

One lamb she nursed most eagerly
Daylong. And one she jabbed and struck
With hoof and head whenever he
Came wanly in to kneel and suck.

All day she battered him until
When evening came I watched him grope,
An almost disembodied will,
Far, far behind her up the slope.

And there was much I would have done
To change her heart, but that I knew
I might as well command the sun
Stand still as bid her love anew.

I could have wept—my eyes were dim.
But weep?—And man—And so instead
I grabbed a stick and followed him
And deftly knocked him on the head.

Gunnamatta Bay, Cronulla

Between two walls of hill
The sea hugged its delight
As lovers who, at night,
Turn once and then are still,
Poised on the crest of the flood
Of joy within their blood.

That was three hours ago,
But now the bay is slack;
And greasy, dull, and black,
The dreary mud-banks show;
And stalking grimly there
I see the scavenger.

Foot petal-soft and bill
Steel hard and keenly cleft,
For what the sea has left
He probes and eats his fill,
A hungry gull, no doubt
Glad that the tide is out.

Love, love, the ocean calls
Its waters home, though we
Thought we had trapped the sea
In safe unbreachable walls!
And to our desolate eyes
Slowly the mud-banks rise.

But think on what is gone
As though you did not care,
And watch the mind-flats where
Lone thought feeds grimly. On
Upturned and rotting hull
See, beautiful, the gull!

A Suicide

Young Stephen was a lover of the sun,
But something got him into dark corners;
Before the feast was more than well begun
He left, and so became a theme for mourners.

And many wept; but I could only wonder
What gripping thighs had mothered his first doubt,

Or what magnificence of blue-sweet thunder
Made life so flat a thing he spat it out.

A Pause

I did not know how proudly man could die
Until I watched him shut his eyes; the day
Hung like a frightened gull in the wide sky
For all her power of flight he took away.

Black Woman
(On the platform at Redfern)

A mound of slattern flesh, old, drunk, and black,
She stood beside the train and shook her fist
And cursed all men by piecemeal, front and back,
Until they fled their mad anatomist.
And when the cars moved on with a sliding twist
She shouted curses at the empty track.

Forgive me, pity, that I laughed at her:
That heaving belly, those agitated hips,
And all the people running like a blur
Of frightened sheep beneath a storm of whips;
Running to save their cleanness from those lips
That sprayed pollution hotly everywhere!

Forgive me, pity! Something hard has grown
Suddenly at my heart and presses me:
I think it is my laughter turned to stone.
And who than you, pity, should better see
That, could I clutch that stone and wrench it free,
Never at her, not at her, would it be thrown!

Instructions to a Boy on Digging Rabbits

Shove your arm in till you feel
One hind leg—then grab it.
Let him twist and squirm and squeal,
You have got your rabbit!

Let him hang head down until
He no longer veers there.
Here's your waddy—with a will
Right behind the ears there!

Good! Now here's another trick:
With my hand, see, Andy?
You can't always find a stick
The right size, and handy.

One thing more before I go—
You've the knack already;
Yes, you're right, that one's a doe;
Wait now! Hold her steady!

What thing more?—Now, keep your hold!
There's a leg—quick, grab it!
What?—The tenderest tale I told
You before you were so old
Was about a rabbit!

A Great and Tragic Australian Poet

His lusts were great, and great, too, was his vision,
And when they locked most fearful was the fight
That dropped through heaven from that fierce collision
Star-agonies, his poems, on the night.

He loved the show, and fed his lusts to keen them,
And lashed his vision with a bitter rod
To make it battle-angry, for between them
The clash, he knew, it was that made him god.

God—mighty god—but for how brief a season!
The silence of his after-time records
How with the old inevitable treason
The armies of his soul flung down their swords,

And he was merest man with unclean gashes
That throbbed his flesh and spirit with the long pain
Of fire guessed only by its corpse of ashes,
Of kingship marred, like Lear's, by the rain.

Man? Less than man! I may say so, his mourner,
Where there I see him kneeling on the floor,
A toper fumbling in a dusty corner
To find his bottle—drained the night before!

Happiness

You're cold without there in the wintry weather
And I'm all warm within;
With quiet hand I shake the logs together
And watch the fire-sprites spin.

I'm but a guest, by special invitation,
And bidden to come alone;
You're cold out there, you gaunt and terrible nation
Of eyes that watch through stone.

Fishing in the Australian Alps

He said, I am a parson, but I take
My stand with modern thought,
And I love science deeply for the sake
Of that great truth all science still has taught
(He cocked an eye along his fishing rod),
The love and the omnipotence of God.

Now take these hills—the oldest hills on earth.
Millions of years, they say,
And yet the Lord was present at their birth
And there was joy in heaven on that day
And—don't you think a white fly, white and thin
(He cocked his eye again), will bring them in?

An ant and bee were struggling in the grass,
And soon the bee was out.
I wondered idly just how old God was
And where that love my friend was sure about,
And turning from his quick sagacious eye,
Picked out with care my darkest fattest fly.

Brinsley Town[14]

On Sabbath morn in Brinsley Town
The people wear their Sunday shoes
And creak to church and kneel them down
With foreheads pressed against the pews.

The drowsy elders kneel before—
For prayers are long in Brinsley Town,
While from the cherry at the door
God's laughter shakes the blossoms down.

---

[14] First appeared in *Sedge Fire*. Lines 3 and 4 were reversed in *Brief Waters* and in *Poems 1940-1955*. This appears to be an error for reasons of both narrative and rhyme scheme, so they have been switched back to the *Sedge Fire* version in this edition.

Seven O'Clock Tram

Well, tousle-head,
Just out of bed, I think,
And nearly missed your tram?
Damn!
Why couldn't you turn on your side and sleep,
Mustering your dreams like sheep,
For you, sweet tumble-head, must have
Dreams to keep.
And better were it that you kept them well
Than rush away from them like this to sell
(While who knows what the wild dogs will be at)
To some dry female thing a guinea hat.

The Nameless One*

Though not the merest minnow of a lust
Would nose me now, yet there were other days
Before the world pronounced me stale and thrust
Me where I should no more offend its gaze—
Days—or nights rather—when I took my penny
In London streets with as good luck as any.

Yes, I'm the woman Francis Thompson lost.
And, since you question with a civil tongue
And no sick whine of pity for the cost
We paid to let those songs of his be sung,
And since he's dead in Kensal Green, you say,
Ask what you will, I'll answer as I may.

How did we meet? The fog was thick that night
And he stood by the lamp-post like a child
Afraid to lose the comfort of its light.
I don't know why I stopped—perhaps he smiled,
Or turned his head—however that may be,
He took my hand, simply, and came with me.

Home, home of course! And there I made a fire
By which he squatted warming both his hands
That trembled as though shaken with desire
To gather in the warmth of summer lands
Locked in the coal, lands lying more than south
Of London—and a smile was on his mouth.

You've seen that smile, you say? Well, then you know
Something of what I saw, but only part:
You have not felt the pavement's ceaseless flow
Of footsteps thudding dully through your heart;
You have not slept in archways where the stone
Sends the morgue-damp through wasted flesh and bone;

The opium-gnaw caught in the hunger-squeeze
Like a pinched rat—his smile knew this and more:
The awful strength of unreluctant knees
Bleeding their way to that last holy door
Through which Love looks—or so he used to tell—
Looks unabashed at God straight out of hell.

I fed him, yes, and laid him in my bed.
How strange he seemed there with his thin black beard
And the white pillows propping up his head!
But he would never sleep till dawning neared;
Something about the stars—I'm still in doubt—
Kept him awake until the stars went out.

Sometimes he read to me from a small book—
Its name was Blake, I think—but all I cared
Was for the way his voice caught fire and shook
At some tremendous deed his spirit dared
That filled my simple harlot's room with things
Unnumbered in the treasuries of kings.

He kept a sheaf of papers where his hand
Could find them, scrawled with poems he had made,
And I would watch him take them out and stand
Swaying a little, and pale as one afraid,
Until his own thought lifted him and he
Stood robed in power and crowned incredibly.

Why did I fly when friends and fortune came?
I knew you'd ask, but so I answer you:
Love having won the glory from the shame,
What was there more for even love to do?
More would be less, I lost him but to keep,
And shall even through the longest, darkest sleep.

You say his friends laid roses at his heart,
And violets, in his coffin? That is well.
They will not woo his quiet lids apart,
Nor break the seal God sanctified in hell,

Nor help the world and you and time to unsing—
Go, read, "O brave, sad, lovingest, tender thing!"

*The prostitute who befriended Francis Thompson in London.

Mary Shelley to Trelawny on His Proposal of Marriage, 1831

Marriage, Trelawny? I would laugh at you
But for the graves between us and the eyes
—How can you face them boldly as you do?—
Of all our dead, your dead and mine, who rise
Now at your bridegroom's knocking. My mouth tries
To laugh, but oh, they save you, for they lay
Hot lips on mine with little quivering cries
That will not let my laughter have its prey;
And you, Trelawny, you would kiss them all away?

No! I will keep them, as indeed I must:
I am the anchor of their dreamless sleep,
I am the burnt-out sun that was their trust,
But faithful to them more than graves are deep.
And you, Trelawny, with one quiet sweep
Of your majestic arm embracing me
Would break all that, however I might weep,
That grave-bond wherein for all eternity
I hold him now at the last—and he no more is free,

Not free to follow the bright sea-ways more,
Forgetting me; not Shelley of the sail
I watched so often from an empty shore
Moving far out to taunt the sulking gale
Into quick fury of lightning, wind and hail,
But taunting as men tease a lazy lover
Until, with burning eyes and cheeks drawn pale,
A proud love-falcon stooping from the hover,
She strikes with passion's strength, fiercely, and whelms then over.

That night before I owned the name of wife
—(I had to wait for that till Harriet died)—
When fear looked at me like a pointed knife
And the sick pain was twisting in my side,
The storm upon us, gently Shelley tried
To comfort me, my head between his knees,
But even then I guessed that darker bride
Who whispered him death-amorous mysteries
And kissed his mouth to joy as mine could never please.

Now she has had her absolute way with him,
As he with her, and he no more will roam
In search of her; her eyes, not mine, are dim:
"And I return to thee, my own heart's home."
You helped him back, Trelawny, from the foam,
And you—don't flinch—laid sadly at my breast
All that of him which does not sleep in Rome,
And you should know, ah better than the rest,
There is no room for you or any other guest!

Or do you think, your life-strength being such
A god-like thing, you may lift up again,
Gently and firmly, touch by delicate touch,
All that is fallen, and in flesh and brain
Of widowhood revive the delirious pain
Of Memory's yielding to young Hope new-wed?
Or if not that, what is it you would attain
By warm incredible magic in my bed
With me whose bosom yearns, but only for the dead?

And there are other words to say, Trelawny:
The rose you offer me, as fate commands
—"Who can control his fate?"—is somewhat thorny,
And faded from the suns of many lands,
And bruised by fingering of forgotten hands
Long crossed in sleep to what low requiem
Your heart remembers, as mine understands
That should I take the gift once given them
I still might learn to hate the blood upon the stem.

You are for womankind—let it rest there!
Did I not give my youth, my all, to one
Whose mistress was the sea and the blue air
Filled with the golden trumpets of the sun,
And others that dark Epipsychidion
Names over with a fervour of wild singing,
Splendours for him, and loving powers that spun
The clouds where he, like his own lark, went winging,
But hands that jostled mine upon his warm hands clinging!

He found a vision in a trick of mouth,
—(It was that, Claire!)—and in a pallid smile,
Emelia, oh, more fair than any South
The roads of heaven opening mile on mile;
And I, who, being woman, saw the guile,

—(In you, too, Jane!)—grew part of the "world's wrong"
To him and he went from me as erewhile
He had sprung to me, panting, when too long
The Harriet lips had sealed the fountain of his song.

The song, the song! There was no other way;
And I bore children like a hunted thing
Before the storm that blew us day by day
Across the world. But always he would sing
Among the lightnings where I saw him fling
His pale head back—his eyes I could not see—
But in that song all evil lost its sting,
And in that song together I and he
Found—there alone—"Life, Joy, Empire and Victory!"

Where is your song, Trelawny? But forgive
That bitter jest out of my hollow shell!
For I am tired, and tiredly would live
Now at the last after that dizzying swell
And leap of life; forgive, and all is well:
For you it was who brought his dead heart home
To my unliving breast where now we dwell
In peace you must not break till, past the foam,
You fill that grave of yours beside his grave in Rome!

Parrot-Shooting

It was soon after I had learned to shoot
I sat with rifle balanced on my knee
And watched the lorikeets that hung like fruit
Low in the branches of a grey-box tree;

Fruit for a boy to knock down at his leisure
With sure and eager bullets for a stick
And no one by to portion-out his pleasure
And say which one he should or shouldn't pick.

The sun was warm on me; there was no hurry,
The blossom-drunken birds were everywhere,
And it was sweet to feel the hunter's flurry
Subside and turn into the hunter's care.

My finger took the slack up on the trigger,
But when the target slipped behind a limb
I cursed and chose another, brighter, bigger,
And cautiously lined up the sights on him.

There was a moment for the quick decision
Whether to shoot him through the head or breast,
To try the very utmost of precision
Or send the bullet certain of its quest.

I don't know which I did, but he came down
As cleanly as an apple over-mellow
That frost had loosened high up in the crown
Of a tall tree whose leaves are turning yellow.

His feet were like the stone feet of a griffin,
But small and black. And then I saw his eye,
While every feather seemed to fade and stiffen,
Suddenly lose its hold upon the sky.

That moved me with compassion for a minute;
But knowing this would surely spoil my day,
I broke the breech and shoved a bullet in it,
And aimed again, and bravely blazed away!

The Poet

I'm gambling so much, so much
For nothing a man can touch
And nothing a man can drink,
And little a man can think.
I'm off on the poet's track,
And I carry a sword, not a crutch,
And I laugh when 'twere wiser to shrink.

And it's not at my breast but my back
I fear the counter-attack!

Campfires

Singing sometimes, and sometimes half afraid
Because the night around us gleamed with eyes
Of ancient angers; sometimes with surprise
At some cool by-way to a quiet shade,
We walked the road together. Now is stayed
The forward footing, and the wrung hand tries,
In mute assay for mintable memories,
The ashes of the campfires that we made.

Their fuel was our lives, oh you my dearest,
Gathered with hands that did not fear the burning;
Their death, when they went out, was of our dying.
But thank you God with me for stars the clearest
That ever shone upon the unreturning;
For stone grown sweeter where the ash is lying.

Thrush in Winter

He looks into my window every day,
And I speak to him, foolish words and gay,
Certain he doesn't know a thing I say.

And sometimes there's a little song that blinks
Like a small star in a great wind. He winks
As though he knew I don't know what he thinks.

And then he arrows off across the rain,
While I sit still and ponder it again,
And hope the daffodil will make it plain.

Big Fred

I laughed at Fred, perhaps with more of joy
Because he was so stern a man: a boy
Laughs best at what was once too high a rafter
For him to hang from by the heels of laughter
When something legs him up and lets be
The too-high thing within the clutch of his glee.

Fred had a paddock to mark out in lands
With his six-furrow plough: to lay bands
Of brown across a hill now autumn-green,
Two hundred acres in one slope as clean
And gently tilted as a slate, where he
Should write his skill for all the world to see.

And skill he had: we knew how year by year
He'd mark the lands out with no flags to steer
His team by. Standing upright on his plough
He'd cut a line as straight as does the bow
Of a proud ship that hurries from afar
To keep her set appointment with a star.

But beer was bright in Albury town on Sunday
Behind shut friendly doors—and this was Monday;

And walking out to look around the sheep
I found Fred sitting on his plough asleep
While the big team went wandering at its will
Majestically free about the hill.

I have thought since how well it might have been
An awful thing to see the mad, obscene
Scrawl the plough made all over the green lands.
But then I only glanced at Fred's limp hands,
I used to fear, awake, the brow bent down
That would from now be careful when to frown.

And holding in as best I could the laughter
That was sweet then, and would be sweeter after
A score of eyes, squinting against the sun,
Should stare amazed to see what Fred had done,
I set the plough a good two notches deeper
And left it up to God to wake the sleeper.

After Hearing a Lecture on the Poetic Mind

His word is law, being science; so I heed him.
But here's my question: when you've got him caught,
Your winged horse, how then to house and feed him—
But that's a problem of another sort!

Let's grant that solved; you've got the stall and shut it,
The horse inside; you know the proper care.
Then here's the rub—as Campbell didn't put it—
He's all a stallion, and—well, where's the mare?

A Mother

You were stained with the dust of the road
When first I saw you;
You were strapped with a weary load,
Little son, when I bore you.

For your father's feet were light
On the highway ever;
He left one winter's night
And comes back never.

Your father's eyes were deep
With gipsy passion;
To lie, and kiss, and sleep,
Was not his fashion.

Your father's eyes were wild
With storm-clouds drumming—
You are your father's child
And summer's coming.

At the Post-Office

She said, "I've written John—
(You mustn't scold me)—
To come as quick as the sun
To warm and fold me."

I said, "I've written May—
(Don't look your scorning)—
That my night waits her day,
My lark her morning.

The clerk with eye judicial
And inky fingernails
Stamped on both letters official
Acceptance for the mails.

Bees by Proxy

It was the natural thing to call for Jim
When I discovered a great swarm of bees
Hung like a golden pudding from a limb
That swept low down among the apple-trees,

For Jim, I knew, was surely not the one
To stand and scratch his head and figure out
Cautiously just what risks were to be run
By naked hands when there were bees about.

I got a box; he scooped the bees inside,
Cursing whenever one drove home a sting—
And there were lots—into his withered hide.
And, the job done, said this surprising thing,

First having turned his old dry eyes away:
"You'll learn yet, son—unless you grow too proud—
There's hotter stings than these of mine: I say,
You must have hollered plenty bloody loud!"

Pruning Roses

Here will I cut, and here,
Hard, deep, and clean;
Lop the dead wood and shear
Back to the green.

There the young cane must go;
Though straight and sound,
Too lush he grew, and so
Slash to the ground!

And this tall branch, the bees
Loved it. I cut
What summer memories
As the blades shut!

For pity now no room
In brain or blood;
Is spring to have her bloom
Lay steel to wood.

Finished at last! But whence
That thin cold sound,
Malicious eloquence
Netting me round?

"Gardener, well done, and well,
Poet, well said:
Have back a parable
Aimed at your head!"

Opening the Cage

Then stand and watch with me our love go flying
Outbound, the grey gull, level to the sun;
He spurned the cage we fashioned of our sighing
For him the joyous one.

Nearly we maimed him with our desperate clinging,
Hoping our hands and words would tame him so;
Thank God he still has strength left for the winging,
Thank God—and let him go!

Slaughter-House Idyl

At dawn in their warm camp beneath the trees
I used to watch the bullocks greet the day,
Hollowing their backs, unstiffening their knees,
And moving off then, slowly, two by two,
The white, the black, the red, the brindle-blue,
To where their yokes, dew-wet and waiting, lay.

So had they done through years of comradeship
In the great wagons carting wheat and wool,
Twenty as one, needing nor word nor whip,
Their shoulders constant to the rolling load
Down mile on mile of bushland track and road,
Faithful and strong—and greatly beautiful.

At dawn the bird-song called them to their toil,
At mopoke-dusk the bird-song set them free
To graze the sweet young grass of unploughed soil
And later chew the cud and take their rest,
With clean earth warming under flank and breast;
And all the stars of night were theirs to see.

But iron hands have yoked the world in, steel
And swept the slow and splendid teams away
That made men proud to watch them and to feel
Something more dear than pride at the heart's core:
At Homebush, in the slaughter-pens, I saw
My last sad team of bullocks yesterday.

They stood in twos, ten long on that bleak ground,
Shoulder to shoulder, heads down for the weight
Of yokes that were not there, in mateship bound
Unto this last in this blood-tainted place,
The red, the black, with one blank door to face—
It was past seven—the door would open at eight.

Mouse-Plague

The mice were on the land
So densely packed, they seemed
Like a soft and clammy hand
One grasps at, having dreamed,
And, waking, still may trace
Its pressure on his face.

By day they hid beneath
Chance wood or trampled hay
Till earth seemed but a sheath
Between them and the day,
And boards beneath our tread
Were soft as carpets spread.

By night they whispered out
Like a returning tide;
We watched them move about
The farmyard near and wide
Where the moon served to show
Their masses ebb and flow.

The earth grew sick, and we,
Even as sheep and steer,
Loathed what was ours to see
And smell and taste and hear;
The weary horses stood
And would not touch their food.

So for a month, and then,
As a wind falls, came peace.
Emptied was every den
In one night's quick release;
Lifted the unclean hand
From off the tortured land.

I went about for days
Heaping all tainted stuff
That turned, in many a blaze,
To ashes soon enough.
My joy was keen as pain
To feel earth clean again.

Then came the oaten stack
Last summer's pride, but ripped,
Riddled, and foul, and black;
And where a sheaf had slipped
Two mice sat close together
Shivering in that bright weather.

Sick, sick they sat in the sun
Nodding weak head by head,
Last of ten million,
And they soon to be dead!

—I waited till next day
To burn the reeking hay.

On an Amoeba

I, who in spite of my unworthiness,
Have touched the garment's hem of sage and seer,
Tomorrow may be swept out with the mess,
Or emptied like a schooner of stale beer.

And this wet thing my eye can't see until
A lens has made it big enough will be
Lord of the ages, indestructible
In protozoan immortality.

The Twisted Tree

It was not wind that turned this tree into
A Laocoön of wood,
For there was never on earth a wind that blew
Could muster strength and malice to subdue
His stubborn hardihood.

Nor was it frost nor flood, for these things are
Strong only for their hour,
And fall away and leave at most a scar
By which the initiate can tell how far
As last they failed in power.

This is no work of sculptor's thumb on clay,
Nor birth of chisel or file.
Deep in the earth, listen! (What mouths at play
At what dark breast!) And as you turn away,
Risk one more look at their smile!

Poems from *Beware the Cuckoo* (1947)

Beware the Cuckoo

Beware the cuckoo, though she bring
Authentic tidings of the spring,
And though her voice among the trees
Transport you to the Hebrides!

I saw her come one sunny day,
And pause awhile and fly away,
And I knew where she took her rest
There was a honeyeater's nest.

Later I came again and found
Three dead fledgelings on the ground,
And red ants busy in a throng
At throats that had been made for song.

But in the low nest in the tree
The cuckoo chick sat cosily,
And seemed, to my unhappy sight,
A grey and monstrous appetite.

Beware the cuckoo! By what name
You call her, she is still the same.
And, if you must admire her art,
Keep a wing over your heart.

Draught-Horse and Tractor

Dying he was, and yet he would
Totter around to that bleak shed
Where, squat and black, the tractor stood.
And there, with gaunt and sunken head,
Muse on a thing that made his eyes
Indifferent to the swarming flies.

Is it a fancy that he came
Stubbornly there to lay his curse
Upon this thing of steel and flame
That robbed him of his universe,
His youth, his strength, his place at plough,
And sat to watch him dying now?

Fancy! Well, then it must have been
Fancy again that made me hear
The iron laughter, loud, obscene,
That day, the stillest of the year,
Jack died and the tractor bustled round
To drag him to the burning-ground.

By the Fireside

I blew upon the smoke,
At my hearth bent double,
But no quick flame awoke
For all my trouble.

You blew one breath, how light,
Careless and fleeting!
And the fire-heart shook the night
With its red beating.

And now you say you must
Be up and going;
But I'll be warm, you trust,
By the fire's glowing.

Figure in Clay
(A village blacksmith)

He was in most respects like Chaucer's Miller,
But add to that he was a lady-killer,
Who served one half the town and set sighing
The other half for the heaven of such dying.
No sickly lecher, but a great thrust
Of a man whose laugh went level with his lust.
No setter of snares and about-the-bush beater,
But a forthright hunter and a good eater
Of all the game he got. No Dapper Dan
But a great, deep-chested, bearded, blue-eyed man,
Whose clothes smelled of the forge-smoke and the rust
Of iron, and the mingled earth-sweat dust
Of horses and the shavings of bright steel.
Whose fingers knew the hammer and the feel
Of an iron tire snug against the wood
Of a wagon-wheel. A laughing man, who stood
So proudly and so strongly on his feet,
Women, in this Harem of the Incomplete,
Could not but find his theirward bending sweet.

And I who knew him could have let it go
At that, and mightily enjoyed the show
Of so much force-of-life, so clean a spurt
Of being, like a hose turned on the dirt
That drifts on walks and cushions down the sound
Of footsteps till the whole world is drowned
In one great silence though a thousand walk.
I could have thought of him as the tough stalk
Of what might be a nettle or a rose,
As God would have him, or as just I chose;
Or let him be a modern Chaucer's Miller
Promoted one step to a lady-killer.
But then I learned the thing that would not fit
My pattern of him, though I'd fashioned it
With what I thought was wisdom, moulding clay
Into his image, and feeling that the day
Was coming when I'd know him to the bone
And dare to cut the figure out in stone.

Once every month, always a Saturday,
The blacksmith shop was closed with "Gone away,
Be back on Monday", scrawled across the door.
The wise ones winked, "You know what he's gone for
Two hundred miles to Melbourne. She must be
A wonder."
            That was good enough for me,
That easy comment of the easy mind,
Until I heard this thing that struck me blind:

A local lad, the son of butcher Snell,
Went off to Melbourne for a little spell
And some chance education on the side.
The city left him scared and stupefied
And he sought out, as country people do,
The blessed sanctuary of the zoo,
But had the wrong car number in his head
And landed in a cemetery instead.

He didn't mind at all. The funeral-goers
Stood here and there in groups, heads bent like sowers
In Bible pictures. Their unhindered tears
Put out the burning of his city-fears,
And joining them, although too gay his dress,
He lost in theirs his own great loneliness,
Sang hymns with them, and prayed, and took his share

Of all their hearts, for grief has love to spare
For what is lonely, beaten and afraid.
The last hymn sung, the final prayer prayed,
He thanked his childhood's God for this good bread
Though eaten at the table of the dead,
And turned away with courage bright and new
To find the tram that did go to the zoo.

That's when he saw the blacksmith standing there
Watching the coffin lowered with a stare
Awful in those blue eyes, a stare almost
As if he looked upon the Holy Ghost
Or saw some devil rising out of hell—
Though which it was a fellow couldn't tell.
Right by the grave he stood, erect, alone,
As though his flesh were turned to very stone
And he would never move from there. Wait,
Thought David Snell, or meet him at the gate;
One respects grief like that.

       There was no meeting
At any gate, no hand-clasp and no greeting.
For suddenly the blacksmith seemed to shake
Free of his trance, and David saw him take
A handful of fresh earth and let it fall
Gently, and then, as though he heard a call,
Turn and walk briskly twenty yards to where
Another funeral group stood hushed in prayer.

A country lad will never fail to pry
Into a log although a snake may lie
Coiled in that darkness. David joined the crowd.
The blacksmith stood beside the grave unbowed,
The great stare in his eyes and in his hand
A bit of earth.

       So David saw him stand
Beside four graves, and, far as David knew,
He went on funeralling the whole day through;
For David had seen all that he cared to see
And felt right then like sandwiches and tea,
And after that, if he could only find
The tram, there was the zoo.

       That made me blind,
That story, where I saw so clearly then

When he was simply one of Chaucer's men,
The heavy-shouldered, armour-headed, Miller
Became a blacksmith and a lady-killer,
A luster and a laugher—but who gave
Or found—what was it?—only in a grave.

He was so nearly ready for the stone,
But since I seek his truth, and that alone,
And since his truth is not for me to say,
I'd better throw more water on my clay.

In Praise of *Cactoblastis*

Ten thousand prosperous men
Will live where once the pear
Grew in such mass a wren
Could find no trackway there,
Nor man nor beast could dwell
In that green silent hell.

Children will joy to find
All golden fruits to eat,
Young men will go to bind,
Singing, the golden wheat;
Old men will pledge in beer
The Eden that is here.

And all because you came,
And were content to be
One great and hungry flame
To drink that evil sea;
And, all that sea drunk dry,
You were content to die.

The Praying Mantis
(Mantis religiosa)

His folded hands upraised,
   His reverent air,
I thought the mantis was
   Ever at prayer,

And moved him from the road,
   (Childhood's sweet blindness!)
And felt as though I had
   Done God a kindness.

And though I've learned that he
  Sits thus to take
Some insect guilty of
  Just my mistake,

Some fly that will come near,
  Trusting him quite,
And find death swifter than
  The stab of light,

I'll move him from the road
  Always, if given
That happy chance to make
  My bow to heaven.

On Growing Old
(For Roxie)

Joy is not any more
The stuff I knew,
When there was such a store
One spilled it from the cup,
And laughed to see it drop
And shine on the grass like dew.

Now miserly the hand,
Narrow the eye.
Too well we understand
That, should one drop be spilled
From the cup not nearly filled,
For that small loss we die.

The Turkeys
(Shortly before market day)

When I gathered walnuts jangling into my pail
On an autumn morning as soft as a wood-dove's cooing,
My turkeys heard, and came across in a gale
Of wings to see what it was I might be doing.

They craned their necks and their bodies made a wall,
A warm, dark wall—there were twelve of them—around me,
And the friendly question that gleamed in the eyes of all,
(Strange it is how the thing has power to hound me!)

Was a simple one as to what I might be doing
Hunched there over a bucket at my task,
And not the one whose answer is still pursuing
Me—the question they never thought to ask!

Clearing Out the Rabbits

I may not well pretend
Love I don't feel, or list
Myself as their good friend
Or even apologist.

I have seen poison work,
And know what traps will do;
I've seen a rabbit jerk
When the quick aim was true,

And felt no slightest touch
Of pity or remorse;
Content to let all such
Things be just matter-of-course.

The world has grief enough
For each to have his part,
And man must wear a tough
Or else a broken heart.

And further, there's no doubt
One can't have rabbits and sheep.
Then lay the poison out
And set the traps to reap

Their harvest come nightfall.
But—please don't look my way—
You'll never get them all,
Not ever all, I say.

"Invitation" to the God of War

Let him be seated in that extra chair
At table with us, and, his supper done,
Draw up before the fire—(there's room for one
Everywhere in this house now, everywhere)—
I have some pictures for him, should he care
To look at pictures of who was my son;
(He'll know him). And, a friendly evening run,

Upstairs a bed's all ready for him there.

    I'll turn the covers back, sir. Here you are!
    He used to say it was a cosy bed
    On nights like this, when rain came down in streams.
    D'you think that window's up a little far?
    And would you like two pillows for your head?
    And now good night, good sir, and pleasant dreams.

Atlantis

(Written for a group of young and brilliant students)

Atlantis may be lost. No man can say
It if lies somewhere hidden in the West
Or sleeps beneath the sea. But we are they
Who neither can, nor will, give up the quest.
The centuries have watched our sails go by
Ghost-like on silent ways. The years unborn
Shall see our masts come up along the sky,
Certain as time and confident as morn.

    You are the young. Oh, fleeter than are we,
    And fearless of the night, the wind that roars,
    Sail on past distant headlands and far shores,
    On to that harbour which at last must be,
    When dawn will lift Atlantis from the sea
    Blue-pinnacled against white sails like yours.

The Pet Rosella

I found him under a tree
With ants already on him,
And he shivered wretchedly
When I laid my hands upon him.

A naked thing he lay,
Fallen helpless from the nest,
And I loved him well that day
For the sorrow in his breast.

I loved him well for a week,
And well for a month till he,
His bill against my cheek,
Gave up his heart to me.

And lovelier he grew
Hour after happy hour,

Green, yellow, red, and blue,
And his breast like a poppy-flower.

Lovely and keenly glad,
He played with me day by day,
And I laughed for the joy he had
In giving his heart away.

And I laughed for the joy I knew
In this thing my love brought tame,
When he came at my call and flew
To my hand like a hurtless flame.

But the butcher-bird in the yard
Was watching quietly,
And making his heart as hard
As his beak is known to be.

Watching and waiting near,
And chuckling to his fellow
Of how one stroke would shear
Right through the red and the yellow.

The stroke was sure and clean
On a still cool morning hour,
And he lay where the grass was green,
Breast up, like a poppy-flower.

And the heart I had made tame
When happily we played
Together, now became
A heart I had betrayed.

And it helped no one at all
When a neighbour brought me word,
"I saw your parrot fall,
And I shot the butcher-bird."

Romanticist's Problem

Since what he saw in woman's eyes
Was his torch for paradise,
And what he noticed of her legs
Stirred his being to its dregs,
The hardest thing he had to do
Was to be one man, not two.

An Undertaker's Advertisement

Why pay more for your funeral when
We've put away far better men,
Coffin and all, for twelve pounds ten?

And this about your friends? Their pride?
Because the coffin's only dyed
To look like maple? You inside

May rest secure—our guarantee—
That no man ever made so free
As to scratch a coffin's lid to see.

Postscript to *Paradise Lost*

He heard them shut the gate and lock it,
He felt the heat of Michael's sword;
But one—it must have been the Lord—
Said, "Here's an apple for your pocket."

He slipped it in and stole away.
And now I take much pleasure thinking
That Michael stands there still unblinking,
And has not guessed it to this day

How there has grown a tree so tall,
Outside, that even a youngster might
Climb it and, safely in the night,
Drop gently over Eden Wall.

The Drayman

"It all depends," he would declare,
"On what a man is married to."
And here he'd wink with extreme care
To let us know he knew we knew
The nagging wife who made his home
A first-rate place from which to roam.

And he'd explain, "I mean by that,
The thing that makes a man feel good
All through inside from boot to hat,
And wakes a singing in the blood;
Not what he lies with in his bed,
But what he lives with in his head.

"With me it's been the road. I've kept
My eighty miles with horse and dray
As tidy as a floor new-swept.
And every tree along the way
Has seen me pass or stop and tarry
And never feared the axe I carry.

"I keep the metal in its place,
I fill the ruts and smooth the ridges.
I laugh to see the waters race
In winter underneath my bridges,
Because I know the timbers would
Withstand a prouder, angrier flood.

"I do my work in rain and shine,
The horse and dray and I together,
Until the road seems only mine,
I know it so in every weather,
Mine more than theirs who pay the rates
And have their names up on the gates.

"It's queer," he'd look as though ashamed
Of what he was about to say,
"You get a road like that all tamed
Through thirty years, day after day,
The thing becomes like something human
You live with as you would with a woman."

We'd laugh at that. But when at last,
The Council bought a great machine
To take the drayman's place and blast
The stillness where his dreams had been,
The talk of his became for me
A sad and bitter prophecy.

I stood with him the day they brought
The big machine to scrape the road,
And saw the whip-lash of his thought
Strike him to shuddering, like a goad,
While people cheered with mouths agape
The grunting thing that did the rape.

Elegy for a Farmer
(In memoriam C.W.M.)

Your team
Stands now a-dream
In the still evenings, wondering why another
Unyokes them, bit and rein,
And you come not again,
Low-voiced and gentle-handed as a mother
To stroke them as they turn
Stableward. Ah, they yearn,
And guess at last that you are dead, my brother.

Your field
Lies ripe to yield
The harvest you and it conspired to raise;
The golden plain of wheat,
Level and straight and sweet
With the pure sunshine of the summer days.
But in another's hand
It must go from the land,
And never know the bounty of your praise.

From sleep
Your quiet sheep
In little groups beneath the wide gum-trees
Will turn no more to know
If it be you, and go
Back to their rest with underfolded knees.
Another shepherd will
Come to them from the hill
And make them sad for olden memories.

Your place
Is merely space
Now, and all things that seek you shall not find.
Your hand is from the plough,
And in the harvest now
There is no golden grain for you to bind.
But earth remembers you,
Her servant tried and true,
Your earth remembers you and is not blind.

And you
Who with me sue
All gentle things for comfort, your eyes wet,

Though in this hollow day
My faith has dried away,
And with the bite of pain my mouth is set,
I tell you for my part,
I tell you from my heart,
Whom earth remembers God will not forget.

[Editor's Note—The poem above is laid out centered in the original.]

The Dark Guest

Just once or twice a year he came
At meal-time, and they said,
"Come in", but I could tell their eyes
Begged, "Keep away", instead.

He was a very dirty man—
A child could see as much—
And dirt was bound to be on all
His greasy hands might touch.

The silent men at table moved
To give him lots of room;
But he was brisk and merry as
A cricket in a tomb.

He had a joke for every man
And banter for the maid,
But they all sat as though they were
Grown suddenly afraid.

He ate with hearty appetite,
He drank with right good will,
And then he got up and took his way
Outdoors and down the hill.

And then they scrubbed his cup, as if
It had been lipped by sin,
And said the dark things that their eyes
Had looked when he came in.

But I was not allowed to hear,
"There's time enough for that
When you've grown up," they always said,
And gave my head a pat,

And pushed me from the kitchen door
To run along and play,
And never guessed what thing they made
My playfellow that day.

After Listening to a War-Enthusiast

The world, you say, is great with sound
Of life exultant over death,
Earth, sky, and the wide oceans bound
In syllables of valiant breath
By the proud hero where he stands
And crumbles empires with his hands.

But I, who think upon the dead,
So silent in their silent places,
Would call you wiser had you said
The world is full of upturned faces
That hear nothing, not even the rain
Crumbling the portals of the brain.

At the Pool

I saw the way the butterfly
Came to my lily pool to die:
He sat with all his glories spread
Upon a golden seedum head
And acted all the world like one,
Whose beauty could delay the sun.
Then leapt my bullfrog from the water,
As black as Ethiopian's daughter
And like what might be her desire,
He took in one quick tongue of fire
The butterfly. And that was all,
Except that close beside the wall
I later saw a bulgy eye
Watching for the next butterfly.

Sheep-Killer

I should have known, when I undid his chain,
That darkness had been busy at his brain
As at an anvil, sharpening a fang.
I should have known it by the glint that sprang
Into his eyes when the chain fell and he

Stood stiffly there, as though to let me see
That he had all the time in the world to spare,
If I so felt, to match me stare for stare,
His heart being innocent.

                        I watched him go
Out through the gate with just the slightest show
Of hurry in his trot, as though he kept
His body back from where his thoughts leapt
Ahead to the red kill; that holding back
A dog will never show unless the track
He follows is a secret he would keep
From men whose fingers smell of lambs and sheep.

I should have known, had I but had the eye,
That strain in hip and curving flank and thigh
For what must happen in a hawk's neck when
He spots the quail way down there, but with men
Too near in yard or paddock to make safe
The whistling lunge; the tension of that chafe
That is when lust has the red tongue on fire
But cunning is the muzzle on desire.

So he went slowly till I lost him quite
In the thick fog that made another night
Over the paddocks where beneath the trees
The lambs would be hard at it on their knees
Draining the heavy udders. In that fog
A lamb would learn the coming of a dog
Too late even to get upon its feet,
Or in one wild and lost and desperate bleat
To say that death was hard and life was sweet.

He got his fifty in a mile that day,
Crunched through the shoulders in the killer's way,
Ribs broken in to crush the leaping heart.
Though great my loss, I recognized the art
With which the thing was done. What speed, what power,
He must have known for that one breathless hour,
When long restraint was straw before the urge
Of instinct, the red longing, the hot surge
That leapt and thundered and would not be still
Till fifty lambs lay dead about the hill!

He always liked to work the sheep close in,
Sniffing the blood, no doubt, beneath the skin

He dared not tear because of watching eyes.
Why did I trust that shifty compromise!
Why must sheep stand, by fear together drifted,
Helpless as flowers when the scythe is lifted!
Who was at fault, the dog, or I, or the sheep?

But since a farmer needs must have his sleep,
That night I put a bullet in his head,
Gave the world back to God, and went to bed.

The Bower-Bird[15]

Blue of her eyes he found
In bluebells on his quest
To build his pleasure-ground
Before the time of the nest,
And golden-brown of her wings
In fronds by hidden springs,
And in a shell—this best—
Grey of her breast.

And these he gathered in
Day after happy day,
And placed to help him spin
The pattern of his play,
The dancing and the posing,
The pause when, bright eyes closing,
He sees in a wisp of grey
Her who's away.

---

15   The following appeared before the poem in the original. "The male bower-bird does not pluck any highly-coloured object simply because it catches his eye, but makes a definite selection, within a certain range of colours, because he experiences a specific feeling of pleasure in doing so, and not because of inherent incapacity to perceive the reds in the spectrum. The bower-bird eats reddish-coloured fruits—raspberries—as readily as any other, and has no difficulty in finding them. His selection of certain colours, then, is certainly not due to physical limitation, but to a sensuous pleasure derived from them, since they are associated with the object of his love.

...Neville Cayley was the first to detect the parallel in the colours of the female and those of the objects collected by the male, and to Nubling goes the honour of interpreting the parallel, thus enabling us to glimpse the psychological and physiological phenomena involved in the male's selection of the adornments for his bower." -- Tarlton Rayment: *Walkabout*, 1st June, 1943.

All colours were for him
To choose from, every tone
Of sad and gay, bright, dim,
In feather, flower, and stone,
But, with her image blowing
Through all the ways of his going,
He took but these alone
That are her own.

So in a frond, a flower
(Wiser than man is wise),
He sees with splendid power
The breast of love, and flies,
Ah, with what swift precision
Out of the bower of vision
Straight to the heaven that lies
In her two eyes!

Robbing the Tree-Hive

They leaned a good stout rail against the tree
And then the Old Man said, "It's up you go,
Sonny, and you blokes hold the dogs and see
That all is out of harm's way here below.

"It's that big limb you're after—have a look—
The hive is half-way out there on the right.
Cut near the trunk, and if the bees go crook,
Hang on for life and let the beggars bite."

"They sting, not bite," said Fred. The Old Man frowned.
"And what's the difference? Ready, lad? Take hold!"
One spurt of climbing took me from the ground
Up to the great smooth trunk whose bark felt cold

Under my fingers after the dry wood.
And when I reached the fork the whole tree stirred
Against my flesh as though it understood
Who touched it now was neither bee nor bird.

That made me half afraid; but I looked down
And saw the Old Man watching there below,
And felt the spur-prick of his warning frown,
And braced and swung my axe for the first blow.

That set all right, and soon my thought was running
Only upon my task, and I was proud
To feel in wrist and hand the axeman's cunning
That sent the chips down in a whirring crowd.

I knew the bees were pouring from their spout,
But kept on with my chopping, left and right,
And left again, until I heard the shout,
"She's coming! Drop your axe and hang on tight!"

The trunk seemed going over with the weight
Of the sprung limb, but stopped and twisted free,
And shuddered like a man, and jerked back straight
The broken half of what had been a tree.

Below, the men were running in to smoke
The bees with burning rags. I laughed aloud
To hear their voices stutter to a choke,
And see them come out gasping from their cloud.

But overhead the sky was very still—
The sky I'd made then when my axe went home—
And I but sat and stared at that until
The Old Man called me down to taste the comb.

Barren Country

I know the lands that burgeon with the good
Life-sap engendered by the sun's embraces;
The fertile lands that bring forth in their places
In every season the expected brood
Meekly and surely; the mild sisterhood
Pliant, complacent in their matron graces;
The fruitful women with the tranquil faces;
And, being man, I praise them as I should.

But not the fat lands swelling one by one
With all their milk of harvests can compare
In beauty with the desert when the sun
Bends down upon her and she takes him there
Laughing, and stays, for all that he has done,
As virginal as the surrounding air.

To the Modern University

It may be the new Prospero will lift
Yet fairer towers than he raised of old,
A purer flight of line, a lovelier drift
Of marble skyward. But, his heart grown cold,
Or, like blind Samson, drunk with rage and power,
He may put on his cunning and his might
To topple every palace, every tower,
Himself beneath them dying in the night.

> You are the keeper of his wand, his book,
> The mistress of his magic; be you then
> The mistress of his heart, and should his look
> Grow hard and loveless on the lives of men,
> Bury his book, his wand, and let him be
> Cursed, old and helpless by an indifferent sea.

Bush Psychologist

"After long drought," he said "you've seen a bush
With the first rain burst wildly into bloom,
As though the plant were making one great push
Away from death, having come near the tomb,
Away from death and into life again
With red mouth open for the kiss of the rain?

"Well, Nettie was like that. Her years had been—
She was past forty—uniformly dry
Of that which keeps a woman fresh and green,
And full of promise to the knowing eye.
Yet if men smiled to see her wither so,
There was a thing or two they didn't know.

"You've seen the bush? When months drag into years
With the sun hotter and no rain in sight,
It shuts itself up like a pair of shears
With the spring rammed down hard and fastened tight,
Until a touch sets all that power free,
And then you really have a thing to see.

"She had her dreams, I reckon, when the blind
Thing inside her struggled with despair,
And, struggling so, grew stronger but could find
No way out to the rain that wasn't there.
Perhaps she prayed, for sure as I stand here
At last the rains came. Have another beer?

"Jim was a big, slow, easy-going cove,
A farmer and a good one, so they say,
If there was someone handy just to shove
Him on about his business day by day;
For left alone, they say, to his own will
He simply chewed a straw and stood stock-still.

"He, too, was in his forties, but in all
Those years his manhood slept—you get my drift?
No blood in him to answer to the call
That strikes the dullest even and makes them lift
Their heads and make their eyes flash more than human,
Although the calling thing be just a woman.

"Well, he woke up all right, you take my word!
I saw the wedding. There was lots of beer,
And Nettie was as happy as a bird,
And Jim looked frightened and a trifle queer.
But this I saw, and saw it good and plain:
She was the drought-lean bush, he was the rain.

"From that day on she blossomed high and wide.
But what we noticed was the change in Jim:
The sudden quickening of his lazy stride,
The look of worry that came over him
As though the man was striving, so to speak,
To lift a weight and found himself too weak.

"Whatever it was—don't mind me if I wink!—
It changed him so that in a year or two,
Not knowing him, you'd take a look and think
Him twice his age. A thing like that will do
A man in quicker far than work or booze—
And Jim, poor devil, had no chance to choose.

"How it all ended I don't know; I went
Away from there. But one thing is as clear
To me as that my bottom shilling's spent
And that you've got a fly there in your beer,
If Jim's alive, then Nettie's still in flower,
If dead, she's looking for another shower."

The speaker stopped. The bar was very still.
Then someone sighed and cleared his throat and said,
"It takes all sorts of people, don't it, Will,

To make a world?" He sighed and scratched his head.
"And yet, by cripes, she must have been a wonder
To take a man like that and plough him under."

On Wordsworth's "Daffodils"

Your memory of daffodils was sure
For happiness, but in what cell were set,
What vision-chamber, holy, still and pure,
The eyes and lips and brow that were Annette?

Or must I learn the sadder, wiser thing?
Only the human fails us; would we be
Won back to heaven by remembering,
Look only on a flower, a lake, a tree.

In the Garden

She murmured, "Hear the heather! Don't you hear it?"
And there was sudden light behind her brow,
"One must be lying, oh, so very near it,
As we are lying now,

"To catch the memories of old caresses
Of bees by day and hovering moths by night,
And all that which the listening heart confesses
And may not utter quite."

But he beside her in the bed of heather,
Whose bloom had long since fallen, only heard
The dry sound of the seed-cups rubbed together
When the light twigs were stirred,

And thought the sound, the cups were drained and hollow,
As desolate as a discarded shoe
That has no longer any road to follow
And nothing more to do.

Again she whispered, "Hear it! Oh, the glory
Of life and love!" But he with sunken head
Was making up a very different story
Of what the heather said.

A Visionary

He made a harem of his dreams and sat
Like a rich prince among them, grave and mild;
And though in time they all grew very fat,
Not one of them produced a healthy child.

An Old Light-Horseman Comments on the War, 1940

"They'll never make a war of this," he said,
"In spite of Hitler and the other forces."
And then reprovingly he shook his head,
"The bloody fools don't even have no horses!"

Freeman

The parson died today—you didn't hear?
Well, he and my old woman kept me straight,
And she's dead, too—so have another beer;
They're safe enough behind the pearly gate.

Stream and Rock

What conflict here beyond imagining!
But something speaks to me in fold and curve
Of just enough resistance, enough reserve
To make surrender a strong and lovely thing.

On a Lady's Man, Recently Dead

How darkly hot he was, how very wise
In amorous undertakings! Now he lies
As white as were the women he lusted after,
And as cold as was their laughter.

After Reading a Book on Abnormal Psychology

Now all desires—even unknown ones—I had
Stand stript before me with their names writ under.
And will this make me really sane, I wonder,
Or only more intelligently mad?

Jane Williams (After Her Marriage to Hogg)

I'm drowsy too, but I will sit
Here by the fire, dear Hogg, and fit

Myself into your cosy dreaming.
But listen how the rain is streaming
Against that window! Let it beat!
I'll tuck this rug about your feet;
Like this? That pillow for your head?
Really, you should run off to bed,
But you must sit before the blaze
You say, because of other days
When you sat by your fire with him
In Oxford till the stars were dim
Outside with morning coming on.
And you have much to think upon;
Unfinished business you two had
Concerning God and man, though mad,
A little mad he was for sure.
I've often thought, Hogg, how the pure
Must seem like that to us who know
So many things that are not so.
You smile, "My dear, you're always right,
By day, by dark, by candlelight,
Being fair." I pardon you the jest.
Another pillow? And now rest
Before you wake enough to say
In your inimitable way
How Shelley might have learned from you
To know the false thing from the true,
The rush-light from Promethean spark,
The dormer-pigeon from the lark,
The star from its reflex in water,
And Juno from a mortal's daughter,
If only—but you're sound asleep,
And it is well you are.

Deep

The sleep that binds him now, the sleep
That has not even eyes to close
Nor any bed for its repose.
Not like his Adonais laid
In the still earth, in the deep shade,
But spent and vanished like the breath
One uses speaking the word death.

What should a spirit leave behind
For eyes to look on and grow blind
With tears? The Psyche chrysalis,
Empty, so slight a remnant is,

179

It makes no shadow in the sun.
Round him the fleshly web was spun
Lightly as that, and fallen away,
It leaves no blot upon the day.
"Ariel to Miranda," so
Went his song five years ago.
"Spirit to Phantom," Hogg translates.
Yet there in the dark corner waits
The instrument his hand and eye
Gave me to help him not to die,
The instrument I played for him
Until his eyes, like stars, grew dim
In some far morning of the soul.
Spirit? Ah, yes; but only whole
When lulled by earthly hands on strings
That sang the love of earthly things,
Sunsets and winds and flowers growing,
And lovers coming, lovers going
Through sunny meadows loud with bees
To some glad heaven among the trees.
That gave him strength again to go
Into the world to seek his foe,
Evil, by each and every name;
And that sustained him when he came
Home from the battle to rehearse
In the great pageantry of verse
The joy, the glory that should be
When men at last, equal and free,
Should prove that not in vain was the loss
Of blood on Caucasus and Cross.

That was the spirit part. I knew
Little of that; but what to do
When he came home with aching heart,
That seemed to me a woman's part
Much simpler, Mary, than your Greek.
The drooping head, the faded cheek,
The eyes all dark with weariness,
Oh, Mary, how a hand could press
Healing upon them! This I know.
"Sing softly, Jane, and low—and low!"
You failed to let your hands betray
As only hands of women may
The sleepless man-soul to the sleep
Warm and long and close and deep
Only a woman's breast can give.

And so you made him fugitive;
And blame me that I bade him live?
You were his wife, and did not know
Where he went when you would not go,
Because your children or a page
Of Latin sealed you in your cage,
Or something subtler far than these
Made you declare, "Today I please
To stay at home." And home you stayed.
You did not know where Shelley strayed,
But this—it needs not me to tell—
You knew, 'twas either heaven or hell
Where his feet went, no lesser place;
You must have seen it in his face!
Were you not woman enough to take
Hell and heaven for his sake?
But I think wildly. There, alone,
I saw you change your heart to stone,
And wanly turn away to seek
An opiate for pain in Greek.
He found that stone against his breast;
I saw the bruise.

        And for the rest,
I felt you scrutinize my smile
For the strung arrow of its guile,
The arrow that was never there.
Even though my hand was on his hair,
And my lips very near his face,
His soul and mine kept each its place.

You loved this spirit, be this said,
But in your arms the man lay dead;
And since he was all yours to hold,
Oh, Mary! …

      But the room grows cold
And Hogg will chill there where he sits.
Dear Hogg, with all his nimble wits
Who thought that liberty was but
His friend's wife's bedroom door unshut,
And was forgiven.

       "Miranda, take
This slave of music for the sake
Of him who is the slave of thee."

Dear Hogg has called that "poesy",
And he is welcome; heaven and I
Can wait to give that smile the lie!

The world asleep for half an hour
Has grown too fair, too like a flower
With dew upon it, dew or tears.
Dear Hogg, awake! Your bedtime nears.
(How he would lie awake all night!)
And if my kiss should please you quite
You'll know that this is only due
(You're waking?) to my love for you,
D'you hear, dear Hogg? My love for you.

To a Prominent Optimist

Shielding the wavering flame
Of hope with your hand and your name
From the winds that blow right out of the gates of hell,
Shielding it well,

Hero and saint they say
You are; but look as I may,
(Be it either the lie in you or the blindness in me)
I only see

You an old man cold in his bed,
Cold almost as the dead,
Fingering your pulse there in terror, alone in the dark,
Gauging the spark.

Dew-Plants

I'm doubtful that he knew how well he taught
The lesson, but I know how well I'd learned it
When the hot cane had finished with its sport
Upon my palm,
And he had dropped his arm
And said, perhaps to block a sudden thought,
"Ah, but you earned it!"

I had come late to school,
Although I knew how he would put his book
Down sharply, and then look
Through me and ask me if I knew the rule,
And then, with all eyes watching, get the cane,

Frown the tense class to silence and explain,
"An hour and over, late;
Six cuts this time; next time I'll make it eight.

To walk to school through paddocks in the spring
Is not the easiest thing
For a boy to do and not be somewhat late:
"Now, shall I climb the fence or take the gate?
Was that a rabbit popped into that log?
I wish I had a dog.
Ducks on the dam? I'd better have a look.
Wood-ducks, all right. Now what was that that shook
The branch up there? It's pretty hard to see…
A nesting soldier-bird? Or it may be…
No, it's a soldier bird. But look at the sun!
It's up a mile! By cripes, I'll have to run!"

But that day I had found a special reason
For loitering. The grassland at that season
Was full of dew-plants, each a tiny hand
Palm up upon the land,
Or trap pressed flat, and baited with a sweet
Drop of bright honey for the unwary feet
Of bee or fly. They never got away.
And I remembered hearing someone say
The plants with cold, unholy appetite
Ate every one—I'd dreamed of it at night.

What joy it was releasing foot and wing
Of every captive thing
From the bright treacherous honey, the sly snare.
Oh, laughing, dancing heart
Of a boy who played his part
Foiling Old Malice with the fly-trap there!

He taught his lesson well with that hot cane;
I've walked across the world and back again,
And seen the dew-traps all along the track,
Each with its victim, yellow, white, and black,
Some struggling with faint will,
Some dead already, and still,
All slipping surely into the cold bite
Of the unnamed, unholy Appetite,
And never veered from the appointed straight
Line of my march, nor been a second late.

Wife to a Second Husband

Take valley, hill and meadows,
They're yours by title clear,
And try to understand
When silently as shadows
The big-eyed gentle deer
Refuse your proffered hand.

The Well and the Star

A well is something like a grave; who
Goes down in either has to go alone;
And I was ever one who liked a few
Companions, and warm sunlight on the stone
In some wide open place with winds blowing,
And birds and bees and such coming and going.

But when he said, "I saw a star by day
From eighty feet down there, and saw it clear;
And you may see it, too, if you'll but pay
The price—and that is nothing but your fear—
You'll try it, lad?" I said, "All right, I'll go,
But careful on the rope, and not too slow!"

Partly for safety, partly that I might
Drink the full terror of the long descent
Past dripping walls into that worse than night,
He gave me rope so slowly that I went
By inches down the eighty feet of well;
And time stood still as time must do in hell.

Twenty feet down I scarcely could remember
How sunshine feels on shoulders and on back
When wheat is tall and yellowing in November
And dust goes up like smoke from every track,
For the harsh cold, so new to me, was shaking
My very blood like drums when fear is waking.

The air grew heavy with the wet-earth smell
That goes with wells and darkness, and I tried
To seal my lungs against it with a spell
Passionately uttered, but in vain I cried,
For, crying, I but sucked in deeper still
The stuff that made a fungus of my will.

I prayed all bright things to come back to me,
Telling them I was still the same lad who
Laughed with them from the crown of many a tree,
But they rejected me as bright things do
All who go down to darkness, though they are
Bent on an errand to a possible star.

Darker and darker, inch by steady inch,
And then I cursed the man who stood up there,
The sly deceiver, by his creaking winch,
With sunlight on his shoulders and his hair
And on his mouth the wicked smile of one
Who has let down his brother from the sun.

Just when it seemed I must reach out and pull
The signal-rope, and rise and face my shame,
Or, still the coward, put my wits to school
And lie about my star by day, there came
A quiver down the well-rope from on top,
And soon my bucket settled to a stop.

Then I looked up. Beyond that awful throat
Of darkness one clear pool of blue, and there,
Much like a white and splendid lily afloat,
A single star. Oh, wonderfully fair
And pulsing with another kind of light
From that one ever sees in stars by night!

It was a light like that which streams from thought
When noble presences are in the mind,
And life lies bathed in a new glory caught
From eyes that have grown suddenly unblind;
A light like that man never sees but when
The god is in him—and but briefly then.

Could I have stayed there but a little longer
I would have found what all the poets say
Is lovelier than any dream and stronger
Than death or love that comes and will not stay;
I would have found—but with a sudden shift
The rope was straining on the upward lift.

I kept my eyes on that bright star until
It faded as I neared the wellhead; then
The old black fear took hold upon my will,
And shook me till I stood on earth again

Up in the sun, and heard the old man say,
"Well, did you see it, lad, the star by day?"

He laughed. "You look as though you'd seen a ghost.
But let me tell you, even a coward may
Look up at night and see the golden host
Of stars, but who would look on one by day
Will never see that star and see it clear
Unless he makes a well-rope of his fear."

On Closing a Learned Book

It is far better to live
In filth than in a house
Swept by philosophy's
Broom, that no fugitive
Black-beetle or brown mouse
Or cricket ever will dare
Come looking for his share
Of sweet philanthropies.

In a Farm Bedroom

He said, "Tomorrow I must kill the ewes
Before their bones come through and spoil the hides;
The bankers tell me they must have their dues,
And it is only plain good sense besides.

"The drought will last; they're done for, that is clear.
And yet, remember when you came to see,
The day I brought them home that happy year,
You said the beer had made no fool of me?

"Perhaps it was a banker said it first,
'To keep his body and his soul together
A man must curb his softness and his thirst
And grow as hard and lonely as the weather.'

"So, if there's any tender thing to do
Tonight, I think we'd better make a start.
Tomorrow night—and I'm not blaming you—
I'd just as soon we sleep a mile apart!"

For —

Such is your power you may control
And lock in frozen silence all
The waters that would in their fall
Be wild Niagaras of the soul.

And such your magic that you may
With one quick smile undo again
The ice-lock clamped on hand and brain,
And let the waters have their way.

For L — with a Twig of Berries[16]

Now what will help me hold you so that never
You will go from me? There's not any thought
I can shut on you and declare, "You're caught
Past any doubt, and you are mine for ever!"

You would by anger or by sorrow break
Such mastery, if it were mine to use;
Free as a bird, and twice as lovely, take
Whatever perch or skyway you might choose.

And yet, just now above a winter spray
Of heart-red berries, I saw you open wide
Your soul as night does to let in the day—
And I—I slipped in softly with the tide.

Now what will help you cast me sternly out?
I meditate your posture and your diction
When, wise to what has happened, you set about
To consummate the inevitable eviction.

Bird's Nest in Winter

The leaves all off the tree,
The limbs stand gaunt and bare,
And plain for me to see
Is one brown nest up there
I searched for time and again

---

16 In the third line of the second quatrain, the word "as" appeared twice in the original, i.e.
"as as lovely" and one was removed as a probable error.

All summer, but in vain.

Look not at youth to find
Where lurks its tenderness,
For the green shoots will blind
Even your shrewdest guess,
And leave you standing there
As empty as your stare.

But, if you would` be wise,
Wait till the leaves are sere;
Then in an old man's eyes
Gaze—if your sight be clear,
You'll find before you part
Enough to break your heart.

The Shout and the Whisper

Shout as loud as you will
Your voice won't carry
Even beyond the hill.
Tom, Dick, and Harry
Have tried it, and grown hoarse
And stopped as a matter of course.

But a whisper runs and grows
Like a wind in wheat,
Till the whole world knows
The bitter of it, the sweet
Till the whole world sickens with dread,
Or lifts, laughing, its head.

The Lesson

A smallish man all made of nerves,
With little brain to compensate
For those inexplicable swerves
Of "mind" that seemed to make his fate,

And yet strong-handed, so that we
When there was graceless work on foot,
Called Bowdy in, knowing that he
Would grin his grin and gladly do't.

So was it when old Topsy grew
The age that called for gun and fire,

And Bowdy smiled to know he'd do
What was not any man's desire.

He came with spring-cart and horse
Half-broken, and he hitched behind
Topsy, who as a matter-of-course
Followed, because her eyes were blind.

I watched them go down the long hill,
He seated high, she stumbling after,
And something kept my heart too still,
Boy as I was, for tears or laughter.

Three hours later he came back
With two wet horse-hides in a roll
That kinked his knees and bent his back,
With a weight he scarcely could control.

I think it was my brother said,
"Where are your spring-cart and your mare?"
He only grinned and bobbed his head
Downhill and said, "They both are there;

"And serves them right! I shot the one
The way you said that I should do,
And then the other up and run
A mile at least or maybe two,

"My horse with my own cart behind her,
And me right after, on and on,
Until at very last I find her—
And then d'you know what she has done?

"She's smashed my cart against a tree
In smithereens, done up for good.
And that was just too much for me,
And so I shot her where she stood.

"And so I've got two hides instead
Of one—and worth five pounds, I'll bet
And she has got inside her head
A lesson she won't soon forget."

Spider-Web across the Path from Town

This grey fellow sits to see
What his web will catch for dinner:
Blunt and mellow honey-bee,
Fly as sweet perhaps, but thinner.

No, I will not brush it down!
Let's be frank with one another;
After what I've done in town,
Spider, you may call me brother.

Budgerigars
(Winter evening in Oregon)

This is the winter-time in Oregon,
And where I live the skies are grey as lead,
And all day long the grey rain beats upon
Leaves that were crimson once, and now are dead.

It is November where I was a boy.
Under blue skies, with summer coming in,
The parrots in the gum-trees, wild with joy,
Raise as they used to do the merry din.

My love-birds have grown restless in their cage,
Stirred by old memories that will not die,
Moved by old needs I neither can assuage
Not yet provide the means to satisfy.

He sings to her of secret nesting-hollows
Worn smooth by feet until the dry wood glistens.
The rain comes down and soon the darkness follows,
I sit and look at one who sits and listens.

On a Man of Wit

His tensities are strung
Upon a bow of wit,
And the arrows of his tongue
Are keen—I've felt them hit.

But, though the arrows sting
And drink a little blood,
I'll think of the taut string
And warmth upon the wood.

Thistles in Winter

I like to look at thistle stalks
On old sheep camps when winter walks
With scythe of frost to shear away
All bright things from the earth in May.

She's cut the zinnias down, I know,
In homestead gardens even though
More than a thousand buds they had
For the sun to make him glad.

And what flowers still live, in fear
Listen while her feet come near,
And their fear is worse to see
Even than their deaths would be.

But the thistles, stem on stem,
Have nothing she can take from them;
Long ago their veins went dry
And they laugh as the hag goes by.

Advice to an Over-Intellectual Young Man

Spirit has her marriage bed
In the brain,
Where she yields her maiden-head
Without pain,

That is, if her spouse have wrought
Instrument
For that purpose, of his thought
Competent.

If he fail her she must lie
There unblest,
Sickening until she die
Unpossessed.

Wait then, youth, for spirit-wiving
Till you find
For that sternly tender striving
Strength of mind.

And meanwhile if you must fashion
For your dust
Something adequate in passion,
Wed your lust.

When the time has come for suing
For divorce,
Spirit then may find your wooing
Worth her course.

Explanation

Let not the angry word
Give, love, offence;
It is the arrow shot
After lost innocence.

Through all our days we seek
The feathered thing
That leapt so long ago
From the stretched string.

And, all in vain our search,
Or high, or low,
Again we fit the shaft
And bend the bow.

A Spray of Daphne

He cut it when the storm was wild
With rain out of the south,
And every blossom seemed a child
With a kiss upon its mouth.

And later, in his quiet room,
He saw with no surprise
A girl take shape from the perfume,
And a kiss was in her eyes.

That changed, and then a woman sat,
A sorrow-shrouded form;
So he got up and took his hat
And went into the storm.

Slaughter of the Ants

An ant desired to go
One way; I thought another
More suitable, and so
I block him; then his brother
Came, stubborn as the first;
Then ants like a great thirst
Thronged on the self-same track;
I tried to turn them back
Till, the question being their will
Or mine, I struck to kill;
But they're on the same track still!

To the Muse, in Lean Days

Hopdance cries in Tom's belly for two white herring.
Croak not, black angel; I have no food for thee.
                    --Edgar

Croak not, black angel, I have no
White herring for you, salt or fresh;
However cunningly I throw
The net, it draws an empty mesh.

I'd like to hush your hungry cry
With some glib story neat and pat:
"I'm sorry, but the sea's gone dry,"
But you would only scoff at that.

So, if you really want a herring,
And I've no herring on the shelf,
Shut up and show a bit of daring
And go and catch some for yourself!

Commemorative Verses
(Donald M. Erb, President of the University of Oregon, 1938-43)

I

When grief seems all the meaning that is left
In the wide world, and darkness everywhere,
And we but think of how a heart is cleft
And feed to sickness on our own despair,
It is his voice that calls on us to know
The truth of him triumphant through our woe.

Look to the hills he loved: they are not bowed
With sorrow; and the streams that knew him well
Still flash their waters, clean, and strong, and proud
Through the green valleys, for what they have to tell
Of him is not a sad thing but the praise
Of one who was a man in all his days.

There is a nook where alders drop a shade
On Mason Bend—it is a place he loved—
And thinking of him there, sorely afraid
Of what my heart will say, I stand reproved
For those great waters sing with one clear voice,
"We gave him joy you must not wrong—rejoice!"

So it is everywhere we follow now
The ways he went: a brightness lingers there
Like the clear light that is upon the brow
Of one who dreams and all his dreams are fair,
Or like the splendour left in heaven afar
Along the pathway of a fallen star.

We see that brightness and our grief is still;
We will not dim it even with our tears,
But, like the streams he loved and every hill,
Be proud and speed him onward through the years
In the full beauty of his stainless fame
And all the goodness that was in his name.

II

But there are other meanings he would make
Us know and not forsake,
Pointing ahead to a bright, distant goal;
Calling us from our sleep
Of grief to rise and keep
Sternly the battle-stations of the soul.

For he was ever a soldier in the fight
For freedom, truth and light,
The war from whose hard stress is no relief.
Fronting the battle-blast
He shook not but stood fast,
Ah, steadfastly, a soldier and our Chief!

A story from the past comes back to me,
And there it is I see
The symbol of his vision and his powers;
The symbol of the goal
He set for his own soul;
The splendid thing that knit his life to ours.

The story of Prometheus who gave
The fire that burns to save
Man from the gloom of ignorance and sin.
Knowledge he gave, and love,
And, mightiest to move
The heart toward heaven, beauty the prize to win.

And Jove, the treacherous and all-evil one,
Chained him where never the sun
Warms the deep frost on bitter Caucasus;
And there he hangs today
Tortured as none can say,
The Good who fights the all-evil One for us.

The Chief, whom we pay tribute to this hour,
Led us with quiet power
To where the awful Hero warms the stone.
"Reach up and set him free."
That was his word. "Let be
Good on the earth, its king, and good alone!"

Clad in his strength he stands beside us now,
Our Chief, with lifted brow,
And chants with us the Eternal Hymn of Light;
The faith that will not break
Though earth's foundations shake,
That rocks the throne of darkness with its might:

III

"Still hangs Prometheus on the bitter stone
Shrouded in cloud so that we cannot see
Even his feet;
Flesh of our flesh they are, bone of our bone,
For we, for we
Are all of us his brothers waiting here
As we have watched and waited year by year
And shall until—oh faith how wildly sweet!
Our hands shall break his chains and set him free.

"We know he hangs there by the blood that drips
Out of the cloud, and by the cruel sound
Ever of wings;
We know the agony upon his lips,
And look around
One to another at what our fingers hold,
Salves for his wounds and waters clean and cold,
And turn away, knowing them useless things,
And stare at the red drops upon the ground.

"He died in Greece thousands of years ago;
In Rome amid the torches and the din.
By sword and flame
He tasted every death that man can know.
And when the thin
Cry of sick children in a later day
Came to him from deep jungles far away,
He woke and rose, and answered to his name,
And bared his arm and let the fever in.

"He died wherever evil called for blood,
Wherever beauty perished in the blaze
Of maddened lust;
Wherever truth, shieldless and lovely, stood
At quiet gaze
Upon the spears that thronged against her breast,
He struck some down and gathered in the rest,
And made her live through all our yesterdays.

"But who shall tell us where today he dies,
Each hour, each minute, smitten to his knees
Yet fighting on!
On all the world's wide lands, in all her skies,
In all her seas
He stands with freemen in the time of fears,
His thousand names one name in all their ears,
And, as they fall and one by one are gone,
He dies—and lives—the one great soul of these.

"Still, still he hangs upon the bitter stone.
Oh, lift your heads up, brothers, and be proud
And unafraid!
Though Jove has wooed him with a golden throne,
And though aloud
The evil sirens have sung songs to him

Of joys in heaven, for each tortured limb
Salves and sweet rest, he hangs there undismayed
And keeps his trust there steadfast in the cloud.

"It is not Hercules will set you free,
Prometheus—can you hear us in the gloom?
Not Hercules
Nor any strong one, but your brothers, we
Who in the womb
Took the same dream that chains you to your stone
And that great faith—oh, terribly alone,
Hear us as now we speak it on our knees—
That all your million graves are not your tomb!"

Growth of a Poet

Forgive me if I arm my sling
(As once with rosebuds), now with pebbles;
And still forgive me should I fling
Yet harder stuff when my age trebles!

Poems from *The Waterhole* (1948)

But wherefore rough, why cold and ill at ease?
Aha, that is a question! Ask, for that,
What knows,—the something over Setebos
That made Him, or He, may be, found and fought,
Worsted, drove off and did to nothing, perchance.
There may be something quiet o'er His head,
Out of His reach, that feels nor joy nor grief,
Since both derive from weakness in some way.
                    —Caliban Upon Setebos

Dedicatory Sonnets

Let this stand first, let this thing first be said,
Love, that who looks on truth without you sees
Beauty, wealth, glory, all the treasuries
Unlocked by power, and, as his sight is fed,
Audaciously at last he lifts his head
To grasp the ultimate vision—by degrees
Revealed beneath its cloudy mysteries,
Lies Proserpina's kingdom of the dead.
    There he must enter, even as must I,
    Into that uncompassionate loveliness,
    The mansions of great death, how coldly fair!
    But I have clasped your hand, Love, and thereby
    Taken a warmth, even truth and death confess,
    That will not leave me when I enter there!

No braver praise than this one bitter thing
So faintly said, when you are all that makes
My heart awaken when each morning wakes—
My heart that else, fast shut at evening,
Would lie a stone in tides of winter and spring,
Indifferent equally that by far lakes
The wattle, wildly golden, swells and breaks,
Or the sedge withers there and no birds sing?
    Love, I whom truth will not again set free
    Of her strong bonds and beauty's, though delight
    Come rarely and the end be cold and stark,
    What braver praise than this, that you should be
    The eyes I look to when the day is bright,
    The hand I feel for when the world is dark?

***Part One:* The Quiet**

Confident in the darkness and the light,
Without equivocal eyes to make It blind,
Kinless, and absolute, and unconfined,
It moves, the calm, unshutterable Sight.
And from earth's centre to the highest height
Of star and planet man may never find
It broods, the Intelligence without a mind,
Sleepless through all the years of day and night.
    Such is the Quiet guessed by Caliban,
    Whom ignorance kept simple and made wise
    So that he glimpsed the last, the awful One,
    The Presence that is neither God nor man,
    Who cracks no whips of anger in his skies
    Nor whispers benediction with his sun.

The Quiet watches how the scales incline
Where Life and Law hang counterpoised, and sees
Without concern the treacherous degrees
By which Life sways the balance till the fine
Beam bends; for then, the Quiet knows, will shine
At once upon the scales, in quick release,
A hand that strikes Life empty and so frees
The shaken beam to its appointed line.
    So, when the lemmings in the frozen north
    Increase until they number a vast host,
    Suddenly maddened with fecundity
    They force their seed and wildly pour it forth
    Till, drawn by some dark instinct to the coast,
    They cast themselves by millions in the sea.

Toy with the Balance, as indeed you must,
Man, with your dreams, your cunning and your will
That brought you high and shall bring higher still,
(Such is the sweet delusion of your trust!)
Toy with the Balance, but should you ever thrust
The beam from off its pedestal, your skill
Will not avail to stop the falling hill
Or save you from your tomb among its dust.
    Oh, when in secret places, in the rock,
    You waken Power and recklessly undo
    The mysteries that bound him, then some noon
    Whisper, "You're free! I've broken chain and lock!"
    The world will know what Hiroshima knew
    And earth lie dead as lies the cratered moon!

The law the Quiet knows is excellent
Can we but see it, not as men who say,
"There lies the buried and the happy day,
And we, the children of long banishment,
Are only tortured by the lost content
Remembered, but for ever passed away,
Tortured by dreams that come and will not stay,
Dreams of the hills and valleys where once we went",
    But like the mountain-climber, who, below
    The perilous rock on which he hangs sees spread
    The earth and gasps, "How far, how fair a thing!"
    Not the less fair because, like him, we know
    That, should a hand slip or a foot mistread,
    We would be done with mountain-wayfaring.

Here where the wide Australian solitude
Once lay upon the oldest hills on earth
And on the oldest men, whose simple mirth
And simple sorrow broke the ancient mood
Of silence only as a pebble would
Disturb the sea, until, miraculous birth,
Sudden and monstrous, the New Age sprang forth
And loosed upon the land her iron brood;
    Here, where the Quiet watched that history grow
    Until alone her eagle in the skies
    Kept his old place, defiant through the years,
    (Her children else the iron had brought low),
    I look at what she looked on, but with eyes
    That know the light of joy, the sting of tears.

Part Two: **The Waterhole**

Men by a mountain-torrent hear the loud
Thunder of speed and power like the sheer
Fall of great drums even a child might hear
And understand and suddenly be proud.
And by broad sea-salt rivers with their crowd
Of ships that come and go, ah, very clear
The speech of pomp and glory to the ear
Of him that listens there, alone, head bowed!
    But of the earth's wide regions there is one
    I know heart-well whose single stream came down
    Through rolling hills to where the land was flat;
    Water all warm and languid with the sun
    That curled in hollows where the banks were brown
    Silent and meditative as a cat.

So long the hills that gave it birth had lain
Under the stars, almost as old as they,
And worn and grim, the stream began its way
Like a slow smile that follows after pain
But will not ever quite trust joy again
And so moves cautiously. Beneath the grey
Limbs of old gums it went, not sad nor gay,
From rock-cleft to the furnace of the plain.
    There was no river conscious of the sea
    Waiting to fold those waters in its breast
    And seek with them the shores of many lands.
    But dwindling still, and ever wearily
    The billabong pushed on toward the west
    To die at last somewhere among the sands.

As one whose life-force shrivels more and more
When sorrows fasten on and drink him dry,
Clutching with hand and mouth and hungry eye
Until it seems his blood is only for
Their nourishing and he must surely pour
The last drop out unless he turn and try
Some way that still may help him not to die,
Goes to his room and firmly locks the door;
    So, turning from the fingers of the heat
    And from the gasping mouth of the parched land,
    The billabong slipped in among the trees
    To brood upon itself in that retreat
    And gather strength to meet the final sand
    That would reach up and pluck it by the knees.

A woman who in sorrow has retired
Out of the hard and hot and bitter race
Into her own inviolable place
Where none, no matter with what hope inspired,
May follow her, wears, like the dawn new-fired,
A far and delicate beauty in her face
That makes her—oh, the unutterable grace!—
Warmly and wonderfully to be desired.
    Such was the beauty of this spot between
    The bitter sky and the wide barren land.
    If one had seen it there not quite past reach
    Amid the sun-glare lying still and green,
    He would have walked toward it with a hand
    Pressing his heart, but softly and without speech.

Alien and hostile to each other, came
Creatures of hill and plain to win a part
In that cool kingdom by what strength or art
Nature had given, the nimble and the lame,
Runners and creepers and birds that shot like flame
Shaped to a falling raindrop; nerves a-start,
Yet, with whatever tremble at the heart,
Each dowered with cunning to support his claim.
    Alien and hostile, kind to different kind,
    Treacherous and eager for the bloody feast,
    The salt that lurks in death's delicious foam,
    But to that place, as only love can bind,
    True as the sun is to the waiting east,
    True as a heart that deeply yearns for home.

Among the reeds the brown snake had grown old
As had his kin before him—those that knew
A kookaburra from a cockatoo
And were soon wise but not too early bold—
Languidly he uncoiled sleek fold on fold
To flow along the pathways where the few
Creatures who did not know him would come through
The reeds to water, and find a drink more cold,
    For ever-and-all-thirst quenching. He was glad
    Of this his kingdom but for one small thing
    That drew him daily to the waterside:
    A frog that squatted on a lily-pad
    To watch his coming with cool eyes and fling
    A word that jabbed a fester in his pride.

Shadowed by beak and talon in the sky,
Watched by the snake, the frog sat very still,
Too wisely indolent to show his skill
On midge and gnat and moth that drifted by,
When over the brown reeds a butterfly
Stooped to the lilies. Tensely for the kill
The great frog crouched, and with a sudden thrill
The snake half coiled with sharp head lifted high.
    Now were the fierce and splendid powers at play!
    The brown wings wavered near the lily-pad
    Close, closer to the blank unblinking eyes;
    The snake a-quiver with the will to stay
    His lunge until this moment that he had
    Should ripen to the full and perfect prize.

The kookaburra watched them from his bough
With meditative eye. Since both had grown
Too big for ministrations of his own
He little cared which one would triumph now;
But when the frog, and just in time, saw how
Death curved at him and plunged like a flung stone,
His laughter was the muted monotone
Of wrinkles on a dry, sardonic brow.
    Then, moved to hunger by the play he'd seen
    Down there below, he thought him of a hill
    Where a brown wood-mouse foraged round a tree
    And found the thought so wonderfully serene,
    So sure and sweet a morsel in his bill,
    It muffled half his laughter lusciously.

Given to sleep and wakefulness like sleep,
The grey goanna on a hollow spout
Wondered what the low laughter was about,
Then dozed again. Dreams took him very deep
Into an ancient fear: there was a leap
Of many voices, a heart-freezing shout,
Black bodies thronging in a terrible rout
Upon him, and nowhere for him to creep.
    He woke and listened to the chuckling bird
    And was himself again. Eggs in the nest,
    He was quite sure, or why the merry note?
    And then a deep and pleasant question stirred
    Within him: steal them now, would that be best,
    Or wait till young would better tickle his throat?

A thousand loves sheltered within the grove
In nest and hole and burrow, sweeter made
By the death that lurked all round them in the shade.
Never more sweetly blooms the flower of love
Than when the sickle hovers close above
And she pours out her bounty, only afraid
She may not quite give all before the blade
Cleaves, and she has not any more to prove.
    Tenderer than aught man's thought can lead him to,
    Though he be gentle-hearted as the dove,
    Was the wren's singing as the dawn grew strong;
    Perched sunward-looking, the small singer who
    Sang goldenly within the shadow of
    The hawk that little cared for golden song.

Where shall we hide us when the hosts of flame
Engulf the world, where is our refuge then?
From plain and hill and every secret den
Streaming in hundreds to the pool they came,
The swift, the slow, the nimble and the lame,
In comradeship of terror, much as when
Doom points his dagger at the throats of men
And the most fierce are suddenly struck tame.
    But when the fury of the flame was spent,
    Though still the ash was warm, with shaken heart
    Each looked at each, and, sickened and aghast,
    All clutched their ancient enmities and went,
    As men take up their luggage and depart,
    Each on his own way when the doom is past.

A spirit moved within the waters, one
Who knew the valley where the stream was born
And the low desolate ridges grim and worn
By countless years of wind and rain and sun,
And knew the plain and all wild things that run,
And all that creep and fly, and was not torn
By love for them, nor pity, hate nor scorn,
Or if night found them prosperous or undone.
    And far out in the centre where the shade
    Lay dark and deepest on the waterhole,
    The water seemed to darken with his breath,
    A living spirit not joyous nor afraid,
    A gathered sentience that was like a soul
    Awake but unconcerned with life or death.

***Part Three*: The Blacks**

For untold summers when the plain was sere
And the low hills were strung against the sky
Like blue-hot steel, the black men had come by.
Where time was still an unconceived idea
Their coming made the unit of a year
As did the seasons of the wet and dry
And the loud mustering of the birds to fly
To some far region suddenly grown dear.
    And the pool knew their coming as it knew
    The time when lorikeets would swarm to suck
    The gum-tree nectar, and when, to make his nest,
    Would come the white and crested cockatoo,
    And when from secret coverts the wild duck
    Would spill her eager brood upon its breast.

The wild duck left the waters and the snake
Hid deeper in the reeds. High in the trees
The cockatoo shrieked angrily at these
Black noisome creatures who had come to make
Day hideous with sound and smoke. Awake
Now at high noon, the possum sniffed the breeze
And found the taint there of his enemies
And crawled into his nest to shiver and shake.
    But passively the waterhole received
    The shock of man-life, children on its shore
    And naked swimmers in the centre stream,
    Aware yet unconcerned, not glad nor grieved,
    Like one who in the city's rush and roar
    Sits quietly apart and dreams his dream.

Boisterous life, like a storm-spirit blown
Out of the north, shook that still place: the flare
Of night-fires lit the dancers; everywhere
By day and night, wildly together thrown,
The song, the shout, the quick laugh and the groan
Hung like a dust of trouble in the air;
And when the camp slept, in the noonday glare
Dogs would rise up to snarl across a bone.
    But sometimes when the moon was very bright
    And the low hills had wonderfully drawn near,
    A youth would leave his lonely camp and creep
    To sit and watch the waters half the night
    Forehead on knee and soul a-stretch to hear
    The voices that had broken through his sleep.

Voices of old men awful as the sound
Of mountains moving hugely in the stark
Hours when heat leaves the rocks and sleepers mark
A sudden living tremble in the ground
Beneath their bodies as though Earth had found
A great sky-spirit near her in the dark
And stirred to blow her fire up from a spark
That he might see and fiercely clasp her round.
    What do they whisper from the secret places
    Where, should a child stray or a woman tread,
    There is a spear in wait to thrust them through,
    The old men with the mystery-graven faces
    In their grim circle head by moveless head,
    That you so tremble? What do they say to you?

"In the eternal dream-time, following
The sun's track day by day the Hero went
Alone. Sometimes a man like us, he sent
His spear to break the soaring eagle's wing
And laughed to see the thunder-smitten thing
Fall through the sky. Sometimes, with travel spent,
He was a great grey kangaroo, content
To graze by hidden soak or mountain spring.
    And only on his pathway is our home,
    His spirit-land and ours; all other ways
    Lead to the kingdoms of cold death and fear.
    O wanderer-born, however far you roam,
    Stray not, in all your sum of nights and days,
    Beyond the friendly shadow of his spear!

"There where the shade in summertime is deep
Under the trees upon a blinding day
Of dust and heat he put his spear away
And dug a hollow till the hill was steep—
You see it yonder—and he felt the creep
Of water through the sand. Then like a grey
Old kangaroo he stretched himself and lay
Below the wind in his cool bed asleep.
    So pleasant were his dreams, so sweet his rest;
    Waking, he looked upon the place with eyes
    A man might bend, lust-sated, slumber-dim,
    Upon the comfort-giving woman's breast,
    And joyously he bade the waters rise
    And fill the hollow level to the brim.

"Then, while the dream still moved deliciously
Within his blood, he stretched his hand to crease
The hills with valleys, saying, 'Here in peace
Shall live the hosts of children made by me,
Kangaroo spirits; here their home shall be
Until they find a mother-womb and cease
From spirit ways and in the quick release
Of birth are clothed with bodies and set free.'
    And to the waterhole he whispered, 'Here
    Shall bide the spirit-children I have made,
    Men-spirits you shall foster every one.
    Ah, let your care of them be close and dear
    Till woman's body fold them in its shade
    The last step on their journey to the sun!'

"Youth, man-aspirant, where the terrible name
Of death is like a wind about the sky,
Where fear will press upon you till your dry
Throat splits with anguish and you choke on flame,
Where all are hunters and where all are game
Hunted by evil, with beseeching eye,
By this our ageless wisdom lifted high,
Look back upon the region whence you came.
    Your father found you in a dream and knew
    What woman you would enter to be clad
    In flesh, death's hostage and your spirit's setting,
    But his you are whose great hand fashioned you
    In the eternal dream-time—oh, be glad!—
    And birth was but a sleep and a forgetting.

"Back to that dream-time will your spirit go
Happily after death; but you must end
Your days where mourning kinsmen may attend
To all the rites of death and lay you low
With proper magic in the grave that so
Your spirit may rise up with might and rend
The earth that covers you and swiftly bend
His steps upon the track that spirits know.
    O wanderer-born, however far you roam,
    Stray not, in all your sum of nights and days,
    Beyond the magic in your brothers' hands,
    For it alone can steer your spirit home
    Across the darkness down the secret ways
    That lead through far and foe-infested lands!

"Enough of birth and death. Your life is one
With Nature. Her best hunter, you will take
The cunning snake with cunning of the snake,
And the red dingo, slyly though he run
His crooked ways, will find himself undone
By one more sly than he; all things that wake
To flee before you swiftly will but make
Your spear sing the more shrilly in the sun.
    But one you shall not slay—the kangaroo,
    Nor ever give him cause to cower and shrink
    From you who are his brother, flesh and soul,
    But woo his spirit to companion you
    On every hunt, and bid him come to drink
    In peace by moonlight at this waterhole.

"And all the fruits of hunting must you share
With your own kinsmen. As the ant brings back
The grass-seed from however far a track
Untouched though hunger tempt him, shall you bear
Proudly your game. Upon the evening air
The campfire smoke will climb above the black
Shade of the hills to prove they do not lack
Faith in your faith who wait your coming there.
 For all are one; and so for all must be
 One hunger and one feast, one life, one death,
 One camp though lit with many a single flame;
 And he who breaks this law will surely see
 All faces turn from him and feel the breath
 Of scorn and die lonely alone with shame.

"Manhood lies opening to you, warriorhood,
Man-slaying, woman-taking; but before
You pass beyond the threshold of that door
You must stand where your fathers all have stood
Reverent in presence of the sacred wood
To learn its hidden language, more and more,
And let your flesh be cut with knives and pour
Your own blood out and drink your brothers' blood.
 Make then your camp far off in lonely places
 And let your heart prepare itself to drink
 The joy, the pain, of all the mysteries;
 And when in sleep grow dim our words and faces
 Go then to listen at the waters' brink
 Alone, with forehead dropped upon your knees."

Naked, and bound upon no splendid quest
More than the hawk is; their wild lusts confined
By law but for survival of the kind,
And love, if known at all, a chance-come guest;
Childen of nature never dispossessed
And compensated with this bitter rind
To chew: the dream that lights the noblest mind
Makes but sad hypocrites of all the rest;
 Such were the beings who with dance and song
 Made the nights loud beneath the tranquil moon
 And daylong played or slept upon the shore.
 But the pool felt them only as a strong
 Hot breath of life from thirsting lips that soon,
 Having drunk deep, would lift and breathe no more.

Then, with the dawning of a summer day
The blacks would rise and go as though the night
Had whispered to them of some new delight
Beyond the hills. Like children off to play
They streamed across the plain and of their stay
They left no token other than a bright
Chance-gathered stone and little mounds of white
Ashes the winds would quickly blow away.
    The snake came out then and the duck once more,
    With sounds as gentle as a lover's word,
    Sat in her favourite place and preened her breast;
    On tree and water and the trampled shore
    The Quiet settled back as does a bird
    Some prying hand had lifted from her nest.

Part Four: Annunciation

"Click-clack" of hooves upon the hard dry ground
Ringing from hillward, strong and sharp and clear!
The very trees seemed hushed and tense to hear
The dark cascading thunder of that sound
And, hearing, seemed to shrink as though they found
Suddenly something in the world to fear
Inexorable, nearer and more near,
Inevitable, bound by steady bound.
    In all its centuries the drowsy pool
    Had never wakened to what now it knew;
    Never a sharper footfall on its brink
    Than, in the evenings when the air was cool,
    The lazy thudding of the kangaroo
    Come quietly by moonlight for his drink.

Still as a clock-hand moveless in the space
Between two hours, one ending, one to be,
The horseman sat. An over-arching tree
Bathed him in shade. Then with an easy grace
He turned his head so that his eyes could trace
Hill-line and plain, and ever eagerly
Back to the water lying at his knee;
And a great light of joy was on his face.
    The Quiet, watching through a hundred eyes,
    Saw him turn east and slowly ride away
    But knew no comfort, for the very earth
    Had felt from that brief shock of hooves arise
    What was the death-pang of the ancient day,
    The life-pang of a new day poised for birth.

***Part Five*: Transition**

Sheep came in autumn like a running tide
From over the horizon, sweeping in
Under a froth of sound, a swirling din
Troubled and shrill in that still countryside
That had known silence only or the wide
Whisper of winds, or, clear as dew and thin
As gossamer, the love-song poured to win
The shy Blue Bird of Happiness a bride.
    And all about the waterhole they swept,
    A violence of trampling feet, a lust
    Two thousand strong but with a single will;
    And from their breathing a light shiver crept
    Across the waters where the muzzles thrust
    Gaspingly in and deep to snatch their fill.

Shores may be fouled and trampled hour on hour,
Their beauty kneaded to an ooze of clay,
Their music stilled, their colour rubbed away,
And all their sweetness horribly turned sour;
Yet do they wear strange beauty like a flower,
That, old and faded, shelters night and day
Something within its heart beyond the sway
Of time and safe beyond destruction's power.
    So, out beyond the trampled banks and where
    The shade lay deepest on the waterhole,
    A living spirit moved and shed its grace
    Over the ravaged scene and made it fair
    As does, when sorrows come, a taintless soul
    Make beautiful a bowed and broken face.

On feet as silent as the morning mist
That shrouded him a boy crept through the trees,
And, as he neared the pool, on hands and knees
Inched himself forward with the hunter's twist.
Topping the bank, with cool and steady wrist
He brought the rifle up. Oh, gently squeeze,
Proud marksman, the curved trigger to release,
True to your aim, your hot evangelist!
    A wild duck is a strangely quiet thing
    Dead on the waters she had once made fair
    With silver wake; but quieter than is
    The final languor of her unstrung wing
    The water doing its last office there,
    Haunted by old and happy memories.

He liked to keep his game as delicate
As was the moonlight, and as finely strung.
No frothing jaws and red and dripping tongue
And slashing fangs that struck as though in hate—
Way of the warrigal. But he could wait
Until the little wooly victim clung
To him as to a comrade happily sprung
From night to be his mother and his mate.
    But dawn and danger loomed above the hill;
    And since all games must end, with one clean bite
    The fox took the lamb's tongue and let him go;
    And then, pleased with his dinner and his skill,
    Turned home but paused to tell the listening night
    That life was good and he was saying so.

His dainty nose between his dainty feet,
The red fox laughed at them down there below,
The men and dogs who wandered to and fro
And could not reach him in his high retreat.
Fools! For the Quiet that had made him fleet
And cunning, made of them an idle show,
The Quiet, mother of all wild things, and so
He laughed again and mockery was sweet.
    But when thick smoke and the maddening breath of flame
    Climbing the hollow poured about his head
    And death was on him sure and suddenly,
    The grim betrayal struck his laughter tame,
    And, twisting wildly round, he plummeted
    Down through the roaring chimney of his tree.

At dark upon the pool the alien light,
A red sword on black velvet, proudly gleamed.
Not, this, the campfire where the black man dreamed
Of hunt and feast; not, this, the wild and bright
Death that had once made terrible the night
When in his hollow tree the possum screamed
And round the brooding dove the hot tongues streamed
And could not make her lift her breast in flight.
    Ash of the camps the winds had blown away
    And after the great fire had sprung again
    A greener life and sweeter throats of song;
    But this red sword, unsheathed, had come to sway
    The world in service to a hand and brain
    More cunning than the Quiet and more strong.

The ridge was close; he might have crossed and been
Safe, but the does were heavy with young, and slow.
He looked down to the plain that lay below
And found the spot where trees were dense and green;
Then, his mild eyes with conscious valour keen,
He turned to meet the unsuspecting foe,
The pack and hunter, who would never know
About the others if he first were seen.
    But when the dogs were fairly on his track,
    The horseman close behind him, cheerily
    The old man set his course and showed his speed,
    And though he felt them gaining at his back,
    He knew that he would reach the pool and be
    Safe there, as always, in his time of need.

A dog swam out to battle where the roo
Stood in the shallows, panting from the chase,
But confident in that so-well-known place,
Instinct awake and every movement true.
Little it was the swimmer ever knew
Beyond the anguish of a quick embrace
And the suffocating plunge that left no trace
More than a stream of bubbles breaking through.
    Then at the surface, as though half perplext,
    The old man held the thing so strangely slacked,
    The foe he had not chosen, limp and dead,
    And raised his eyes to see who would come next;
    A voice on shore cursed and a rifle cracked
    And he went down, a bullet through his head.

It was an autumn evening when they came
To burn the reeds, children shrill-voiced and gay
And men who gave them fire and showed the way
To set it for the wind to spread the flame.
Laughter rang out to speed the happy game,
The whirling, mad, delirious holiday,
With sprites and witches busy in the play
And goblins of the fire without a name.
    The brown snake died there and the little singers
    Who used to love the sunshine in the reeds,
    But on the earth the ash lay clean and sweet,
    A soft grey carpet for the fire-bringers
    Who sweep from out their pathway what impedes
    The full stride of their over-going feet.

Where is our help when all we ever knew
And trusted suddenly becomes a snare
Set for our feet to take and hold us there
Till Death comes with his iron to thrust us through?
How shut our eyes in sleep or ever do
Gladly the old glad things when everywhere
There is a whisper in the winds, "Beware!
Your very soul is traitor and untrue!"
    If one had then stood by the waterhole
    He would have caught the language of that fear
    Spoken more clearly than by any words
    In thirsting things that shrank before their goal,
    Or in, like a dead hand against his ear,
    The sudden silences of all the birds.

For many years, much as a billabong
Withers among the sands and the great heat,
The tribe had come with fewer, slower feet
To dance and fewer voices to make song
Beside the waterhole. Though lingering long,
They were like a sick heart whose faltering beat
Whispers the coming of the last defeat,
The final insult, death, the final wrong.
    At the end had come the wretchedest of men,
    Old, filled with sores and swarmed upon by flies
    And scarcely breathing for the squeeze of pain,
    Who had sat beside the pool awhile and then,
    The lost smokes of his tribe before his eyes,
    Turned west into the furnace of the plain.

Sheep watched him indolently with the wide
Stare of indifference and the well-chewed cud
By which the timid speak their hardihood.
A single bullock, fat and lazy-eyed,
Moved from his path an insolent one stride,
A steer whose grandsire desperately had stood
At bay and choked on his own froth of blood,
    The hot and leeching spears deep in his side.
    Outcast, and scorned by all that once had feared him,
    Naked and shelterless and hawked by fear
    The shade, the whisper, the carnivorous breath
    Moist on his neck as the pursuer neared him,
    Swept from all hope and with no course to steer,
    Sobbing he ran before the winds of death.

O wanderer-born, be glad that your heart, breaking,
Will bear you not beyond the sacred ways
The Hero marked for all your nights and days
To follow to the brink of this leave-taking!
Forsake he will not who was unforsaking,
And, though there is no magic and no praise
Of friends to charm your grave, will he who slays
Have power to lock your eyes against awaking.
    Fall and be dead! The crow has followed long
    From tree to tree announcing happy things
    About to come, whose hour draws close—is here!
    Faith fill your hearing with a tribal song
    And let your sight interpret those black wings
    As the swift shadow of the Hero's spear!

Part Six: The Homestead

"The old man used his head, that's pretty clear,
Picking a place like this you couldn't beat
If you wore out a half a dozen feet
Looking. Yes, put the cook-house over here!
And, Alec, throw a wet bag on that beer
To keep it cool! And you get off your seat,
Tom; lend a hand! You're worn out with the heat?
Well, you'll get hotter yet, just don't you fear!"
    White tents beside the pool; loud talk; the ring
    Of hammers; merry builders come to make
    A homestead. And around them everywhere
    Bright, peering eyes, and cocked ears listening,
    And in the waters Something wide awake
    Though no man saw it looking at him there.

Moonlight upon the hills and on the plain
Making a fairer day of night, a day
With all its parched austerity away
Like a fact become a poem in the brain
And waiting there with hope akin to pain
While memory ponders searching if it may
In all the world's words find the word to say
What beauty lives and will be born again.
    Upon the tents the campfire softly shone
    And there was in the voices of the men
    A clear precision sheathing every word
    As though they knew they did not talk alone
    To men but had another Listener then
    And what they said was being overheard.

"The house is going well. It's queer to think
We've planted something stronger than a tree
That will root deeper, and whose roots will be
Fed by a stuff not water for their drink,
And whose proud growth will arch through time to shrink
The past into one point of memory
No bigger than the star-point that we see
Out yonder there, and just about to sink.
    Now in the present we destroy the past.
    There is no marriage of the new and old
    Possible here, nor even an armistice,
    Since there has been no war. The die is cast.
    And yet it leaves a man a little cold
    Thinking such thoughts upon a night like this.

"Don't weep into your beer—that's if we had
Beer you could weep in!—Blast my blooming eyes,
You take a bloke completely by surprise
With talk like this! I'd reckon you'd be glad
To build a house like that; and let me add,
You're never seen a better, shape and size,
And here you sit like Moses acting wise
When, if the truth were known, you're really mad!
    Come back ten years from now and you will find
    The finest farm you ever saw, my boy:
    Wheat, wool and apples for your hand to pluck—
    (I talk your style)—and then, well, strike me blind,
    If all that doesn't move your heart to joy,
    Go live among the rabbits, and good luck!

"They say the niggers, not so long ago,
Camped on this water. Ever see one, Jack,
With flies in thousand swarming at his back?
And stink! You'd smell him half a mile or so!
They lived like animals, but twice as low,
Since they were men like us, but only black.
Give me a monkey with his fleas to crack
Like one a cove had at the Sydney Show.
    Well, they're all gone. The last one that I saw
    Worked on a station fifty miles from here,
    An old chap rarely more than half awake,
    With eyes the blasted flies had eaten raw;
    But, fill him to the bloody gills with beer,
    You'd laugh until you had the belly-ache!

"Good riddance to bad rubbish, so say I!
They had the country long enough and what
Did they do with it? Now, you take this spot—
As fine a place as ever met the eye,
Land, and a waterhole that's never dry—
And yet the lazy, low and shiftless lot
Simply came here to lie around and rot
And then move on like clouds across the sky.
    You've got no right to what you never use,
    That's what I reckon. But that heap of rock,
    (For all the years they spent here, the one trace
    They left behind), if laid in twos and twos—
    Though some we'll have to hoist with rope and block—
    Will come in handy for the fireplace.

"You take my word, the boss is pretty wise
Grabbing a place like this you'd think was dear
At half a quid an acre: land to clear,
Fences to build, work, dust and heat and flies,
Droughts when the stock dies under a man's eyes,
And all the rest; but, take it year on year,
He'll make it pay all right, and never fear,
He'll leave a lot of money when he dies.
    Now, that's what I call progress: start out poor,
    Work hard and take your chances with a smile,
    And use your brains to make the business pay.
    I'll tell you, boys, of this I'm bloody sure,
    If I can just keep off the booze awhile
    I'll have a place as good as this some day!

"Give me the city where a man can get
A woman when he wants one and a drink
And other things like that to help him think
He's not so old and life's worth living yet.
As least he's always got a chance to bet
There, on the next race. With the cash to sink,
He rules creation with a knowing wink,
And, best of all, he keeps his whistle wet.
    Look at these god-forsaken hills too long,
    You'll grow as old and grim as they; this plain
    Will make a hunk of iron of your soul.
    Wine, women, someone said—I'll pass the song—
    Or this! My God, to feel your very brain
    Go dead and stagnant as this waterhole!"

Moonlight, and the great heavens bowed to hear
The rustling words, the hot and squirming brood
Spawned in the heart and hungering for food;
The blind face with the wet mouth and the leer
Confident at life's counter: "Bring it here,
I've got the money and I'll suit my mood!"
The face lit with a hope not understood;
The face greyed over with a sudden fear.
    "With how sad steps, O Moon, thou climb'st the sky!"
    But never sadlier than, when looking down
    Upon the earth that feels you and grows fair,
    You gaze upon the hot unseeing eye,
    The wrinkled forehead and the puzzled frown
    Where once the children of the Quiet were.

Part Seven: **The Farm**

Now in the unpassionate land began to beat
A heart like one responding to a brain
Fevered by love. The lean flesh of the plain
Throbbed to the strong insistent rhythm of feet
Where great teams drew the ploughs, throbbed and grew sweet
With new and tender passion and felt the grain
Fall, and lay still then dreaming of the rain,
The feeding roots, the soft birth of the wheat.
    What had been free now suddenly became
    Enslaved and acquiescent; what had been
    Wild and austere grew faint with tenderness;
    An eagle land become a dove, and tame;
    Turned common maid who once had been a queen,
    A maid and waiting for the next caress.

And as, when flesh and spirit capitulate
To the no-more-to-be-denied desire
And draw together warmly to conspire
How they may yield all up, and meditate
Ways to be shed of that which would abate
The fever in the blood, the singing fire,
Of all that would dismantle spire by spire
The full surrender at whose door they wait,
    So did the land divest herself of all
    The hard and stubborn things that would not bow
    In acquiescence to her passion's plan;
    And, slyly glad to hear the axes fall
    Upon her trees, and eager for the plough,
    Stretched herself naked to the husbandman.

Wheat is most fair when the spring wind, its lover,
Comes from the hills to woo it. Sweetly breaks
Open each blossom for the seed he shakes
From bloom to bloom, bending the whole field over,
And rising then so that she might recover,
His mistress, and look up to where he takes
His brief rest while anew the passion wakes,
Life's and Love's kestrel poised there at the hover.
    Who walks among the wheat then surely sees
    The shadow of those wings and feels again
    Renascence of the thoughts he once had known,
    Then, when companioned by dear mysteries,
    A youth he walked across the empty plain
    To find two eyes that yearned into his own.

So may an ambush for his heart be laid
Who walks around his wheat-fields but to see
How rich the harvest and the gain will be,
How well his autumn labours will be paid,
And all at once before him stand arrayed
Armies of angels, and half guiltily,
Because his thoughts were low, he bends a knee
And yields himself, shaken but unafraid.
    O glorious captive, you who were before
    Only a freeman counting pounds and pence,
    Copper and gold for thought to finger and shove
    In pile on pile, how they will teach you soar,
    Dizzy with new-born rapture, the immense
    Heavens on splendid heavens of great Love!

If this be error and not ever stays
The man transfigured while on boundless wing
His spirit roams where all the poets sing,
Though he know nothing of their names and days;
If never in the dry and rutted ways
His feet have worn at labour wells a spring
Of wild and sudden waters whispering
And he kneels down to drink and offer praise,
    Then is he nothing but the stronger brute,
    The fiercer, deadlier, madder appetite
    Curbed, mocked by the disease he calls his soul,
    And time has dug the deep pit for his foot
    And taken out the red sword to requite
    His rape of upland, plain and waterhole.

Beneath its ringbarked trees the water lay
Moveless as is a stricken creature when
It hears the hunters close about its den
And may not flee, and knows they will not stay
Their search until they find the hidden way
Into the thicket, loud and laughing men,
Who seek the game out cunningly and then
Send the gaunt greyhounds leaping at their prey.
    But ever in the centre where the shade
    Lay dark and deepest on the waterhole
    A spirit stirred the waters like a breath,
    A spirit never till this day afraid,
    But trembling now, ah, like a sentenced soul
    That hears the coming of the feet of death.

All wild clean-hearted things had long since fled
Or perished when the little bitter smoke
Leapt from the muzzle and the rifle spoke
Its single word. Snake, possum, all were dead.
Only the eagle, fierce and mountain-bred,
And scornful when the death-sound rose and broke,
Bare-taloned as he dreamed the answering stroke,
Hung in the empty heavens overhead.
    The children of the Quiet all were gone,
    Vanished like him, the black man, long before,
    The old man sick at heart and weak with pain,
    Who had come a weary way to look upon
    And sit beside the waterhole once more,
    And then had turned into the burning plain.

Another age had come, another race
Possessed the earth, if nobler than the old,
Time would reveal, but cunning and more bold,
Masters of circumstance and skilled to trace
The roots of profit to their feeding-place
Where the good soil would nourish them and hold
Against the winds of chance. A race controlled
By a god who wore a terribly human face,
    And to the waterhole the newer lord,
    The farm-boy, when the summer nights were fair
    And the dead water lay like polished stone,
    Came with his girl and whispered many a word,
    And when as last she yielded to him there,
    Stallioned his love and knew the world his own.

Part Eight: **The City**

Between the hills and plain a city stared
At heaven with a blind white face of stone
Immobile as its underlying bone
Of steel; a face like a dead prophet's bared
Where men may look to read the dream he dared
On lips turned ashen where the fires had blown,
Dropped eyelids over wild abysses thrown,
Stark brow still haughty with the thing declared.
    And over that stern face the Quiet bends
    Undeathing it, till, fearfully upflung
    From the cold lips, stream love, hope, anguish, joy,
    Lust, fear, Despair with her grim troop of friends,
    The many voices of its single tongue,
    A smoke of words acrid as burning Troy.

At the Racecourse

First Voice:
It's been a tiring day and yet I'm glad
I came to see the old place, and alone,
Though Susan said they'd crush me, flesh and bone,
These milling crowds. Well, Susan never had
More spirit than it takes to keep one sad,
And thinks I should sit by her, stone by stone,
Ninety by eighty years and groan by groan—
And here I'm at the races! Surely mad!
    Ah yes, dear Susan, madder than you know!
    They've called the last race and they'll run it soon,
    My bet's laid—ten to one, the bookie said—
    But, till the barrier springs and lets them go,
    I, by the wan last light of afternoon
    And through this haze of life, look on the dead.

The dead! And can it be that such things die
Or is that but an old man's word for change,
Life moving to an ever wider range
And past things what we measure progress by?
I do not know. But there it used to lie
Where now the Post stands, well-beloved and strange
To a boy's heart, in silent interchange
Of light and shadow with the cloud-strewn sky.
    They filled the waterhole to build the course
    So that the city might look up with pride
    Among her sisters over the wide land

And men might loose their thunder of applause
On winners with the odds on the right side,
Where quietly the heron used to stand.

Down at that end, one morning when the mist
Was on the land, I crept up through the trees
And, as I neared the pool, on hands and knees
Inched myself forward with the hunter's twist.
The ducks were there, two lovers keeping tryst,
And I with fingers closing to the squeeze
Upon the trigger paused awhile to please
The marksman in me ruling eye and wrist.
    A wild duck is a strangely quiet thing
    Dead on the waters she had once made fair
    With silver wake; but with a scornful lip
    At such unmanly thoughts I grabbed her wing
    And hurried home to reap the praises there
    I knew would greet my proof of marksmanship.

And ten years later, when the moonlight made
Deep shadows underneath the trees, who stole
Along the margin of the waterhole
To me? And did I shake like one afraid—
I who had stood so long there in the shade—
Before the wonder of you when the whole
Night reeled with passion and soul leapt into soul
Across the hot moist lips together laid?
    There was a Hunter creeping on from star
    To sheltering star until he found us there
    And took his aim and waited, even as I.
    Oh Jane, how empty all the waters are
    You once made lovely with your eyes and hair
    Now seventy years laid where there is no sky!

An old man's whimsy, Jane—you mustn't frown!
A twisted impulse, but the thing is done.
For when that bookie, sweating in the sun
And mopping at his forehead like a clown
Shouted his offer to the gaping town,
"I'll give you Lady Jane at ten to one,"
Some old mad anger deep within me spun
And I called "Here!" and laid my money down.
    And now one race with you against the field,
    Against the odds as that time when we lost
    And were for ever bankrupt. Hush, my dear!
    Soon will the barrier flash aside and yield

Way for the running feet to the white Post,
Home, bravely home, to find me waiting here!

Second Voice:
I've fought two wars and beat death all the way
And had so many rounds, and won, with syph,
The blokes would say, "Tom's such a lucky stiff
He'd show the devil himself the way to play
Two-up." Well now I wonder what they'd say,
Those same bright lads, had they not died or if
They could stick out their noses for a sniff
Of this same luck that has been mine today.
    One way to change it, maybe. That old bloke
    Went down to place his bet a while ago
    And now acts like a kid with a new tooth.
    I'll ask him what he backed—just for a joke!—
    He must be pretty close to death and so
    It's even odds he'll tell a man the truth.

Third Voice:
Let it be right, please God, let it be right!
They say the widow shall not call in vain.
It has been long, the labour and the pain,
The desperate, the lonely uphill fight.
Only this once! My weakness to your might
Pleads! Only think, should I come home again
With empty hands and sodden from the rain
What eyes they will lift up to mine tonight!
    Let it be Amaranth! And then I swear
    I'll grieve you never again, and all be well.
    But if, O God, you turn away your head,
    I'll pluck the fruit that beckons everywhere
    And show you, though I suffer all of hell,
    A way will grieve you more to earn my bread.

Fourth Voice:
I know a bloke who knows a bloke who knows
The trainer of that gelding Flying Dot,
Who says, in confidence, the owner's got
Dough on that horse today. And so here goes
My fiver—a week's wages. And that shows
If you'd make money fast and make a lot,
Having eyed your ball, you've got to take a shot,
Like Bradman flicking boundaries off his toes.
    Well, mine's a sixer! So that's thirty quid
    I'll pocket in a minute, never fear;

And then the hero homeward bends his way.
But wait! I'd better keep a tenner hid
For future reference and a pot of beer—
The missus grows less reasonable each day.

Fifth Voice:
I prefer men to horses. One can laugh
At men even when embracing them; they make,
Persistent hypocrites, the old mistake:
The bull-man lowing at one like a calf,
Or, if one feeds him, swearing that the chaff
Is purest grain. That's sport. But horses shake
The pulse like thunder. So it's wise to take
Horses and men, let's put it, half and half.
    Archie, I've quite decided: hop along
    And put this tenner on Lord Athelhurst;
    I like his colours. What a man you are,
    Shaking your head at that! Now, don't be long!
    You've almost let me lose my voice from thirst.
    —Don't run! Here's Jim will take me to the bar!

Sixth Voice:
One more race, and a few bob left to send
After the cash I've lost. Give Chance a go
And see if strip-tease Luck at last will show
More than her petticoat, or wisely spend
The solid coin upon the solid friend,
The good companion, beer, who, cool and slow,
Will undo all my loss and let me know
The happy veer and lurch at the day's end;
    That is the question—and time's running short.
    Of all the field the one that takes my eye—
    I like her jockey, too—is Lady Jane.
    No, no! How often will a man get caught
    In the same trap! I'll give the beer a fly
    And, being drunk, at least I'll know I'm sane.

Voice of the Announcer:
They started fast—Amaranth has the lead
Then Robin, San Rafel and Mindanoo
A length behind! Now quickly coming through
Playboy! He's checked! And here comes Malameed
Past Mindanoo, Rafel and Singing Reed,
Past—but there flashes out the white and blue
Into the open with the Post in view—
She's gaining, gaining at tremendous speed!

It's Lady Jane! She's catching—no, she's passed
Malameed! Right on Robin! Gamely there
He challenges but clearly lacks the strength!
Amaranth in the lead is failing fast!
She's caught him! Passed him! Running like a hare
Lady Jane's winning—wins by half a length!

First Voice:
The course lies empty, bruised and foul. About
The darkening stands and on the trampled ground
An autumn of dead papers eddies round,
Hope's fallen leaves. Where rang the urgent shout,
Lifted to frenzy as faith turned to doubt
When spur and whip flashed hungrily and found
But sweat and blood to drink, without a sound
Night's scavengers will soon be coming out.
    And soon the moon will rise upon this place,
    The moon that wrought such water-witchery
    Upon the pool, such glory on your head
    My lips were half afraid to brush your face;
    And where you lay and looked at it with me
    Rats will be fossicking for scraps of bread.

Advance Australia! Wherefore should I pine!
My father pushed the black man out to die
And changed the land into another sky
Clouded with sheep. And when the turn was mine
I tamed the earth to wheat and fruit and vine,
Till others came, the clearer, shrewder eye,
The stronger hand to lift the dream more high
And boldly cap with splendour the design.
    There roars the city where was once the plain
    And silence broken only by the wren.
    My heart should be—my heart is lifted up
    With pride, but yet, forgive an old man's pain—
    Advance Australia!—who grows fearful when
    He sees you drinking from so foul a cup!

In Church

Voice of the Pastor:
Humbly, O God, we offer thanks to thee
For all thy gifts: life and our daily bread;
Our homes, our friends; this noble city spread
Beneath thy smiling heaven tranquilly;
Our land so proudly fair from sea to sea

And all who wrought with heart and hand and head,
The young, the brave, who let their blood be shed
In time's most dreadful hour to keep it free.
    Thine be the glory! O, bend down to hear
    The voices of thy children when they pray
    To thee, their Father, in this holy hour,
    And let their words find favour in thine ear
    That they may go forth blessed upon their way.
    Clad in thy love and mighty in thy power.

First Voice:
I thank thee, Lord, it fell on stony ground,
That seed of sin; had it borne fruit, oh how
Could we have hid the heavy-weighted bough
From these quick eyes so watchful all around
To catch the devil at work. But I have found
In thee the strength, O Lord, not ever now
To kiss below the level of her brow
No matter where my erring thoughts are bound!
    I thank thee for this fear that keeps me clean
    And so shall keep me till the day I wed.
    And let that day come, Lord, on wings of fire,
    When I may turn my hunger loose between
    The holy covers of the marriage-bed
    And feast and feast in sanctified desire!

Second Voice:
I wonder is it that he loves no more,
So cold he seems since that one throbbing night,
So eloquent a spokesman for the "right"—
A term I never heard him use before
We were so madly happy. Has a door
Blown shut between us? Lord, he hadn't quite
Even lifted up the cup of love-delight
And all the wine of me is yet to pour!
    Forgive our sin, if it was sin, but make
    His eyes come pleading as they used to do
    And save us both, O Lord, through one long kiss
    Nothing can cancel—for your own love's sake!—
    Because I know I shall not look on you
    Unless it be with my hand clasped in his!

Third Voice:
Lord, grant me health! It's growing worse and worse,
This hard malignant thing that has my life
Squeezed in a trap—one jaw the doctor's knife

And one the silver bar upon my purse.
Why should your servant wring his hands and curse—
I who have honour, riches, children, wife—
Curse while I slip, in this unequal strife,
Inexorably from hospital to hearse!
    Be merciful! I have your work to do
    In this great world, or, if you have no need
    Of me that way and all that I have wrought,
    You need my praise, O Lord, to honour you,
    And I cry out, yes, even as I bleed,
    How should a sick man praise you as he ought?

Fourth Voice:
Let it not rain! I have broad acres where
The plain lies northward, and the wheat is tall;
So early ripe, one rain would lay it all
Flat as upon his skull that young man's hair
Three pews away. Keep the skies summer-fair
As fits the season. Lord, on thee I call,
The Giver of all increase, that men may fall
Gratefully on their food and have to spare.
    Not for myself I ask it but for those
    Whose cry is bread (albeit the price of wheat
    Is good this year!), the poor who suffer pain,
    To feed even them who were my country's foes
    And prove—a lesson we need oft repeat—
    A Christian's love compatible with gain.

Fifth Voice:
Lord, send us rain! My sheep by hundreds die
Upon the stony hills. Famished and weak
They straggle on like skeletons to seek
A wisp of fodder savourless and dry
While over them the crows about the sky
Wing drunkenly. It chokes me while I speak,
The thing I smelled beside the burnt-out creek,
The thing I heard, O God! the carrion-sigh!
    The fault is mine: I should have sold at least
    Half of them long ago to ease the land.
    Let them not suffer for my fault, I pray.
    Or, if you are indifferent to the beast,
    Look down in pity on me thy child who stand
    To lose a cold two hundred pounds a day!

Sixth Voice:
Dear Lord, I just can't think of anything
Right off the bat like this that you would care
To know about. There's Myrtle over there
With hand well up so we can see the ring
Her William gave her! And there's Betty Fling
Beside that Harold with the slicked-down hair;
It's just a little shocking how they dare,
When all's so still, to go on whispering.
    Good Lord, the time is up! And now there is
    A thing I'd ask—but you will shake your head—
    (That's why I knocked off praying all these years),
    How much did Will pay for that ring of his,
    And what was it that Harold must have said
    Made Betty turn so pink behind the ears?

Seventh Voice:
O Lord, I pray thee, in these days of peace
Let men remember that it was my brain,
The soldier's, found through windrows of the slain
A way to victory and the sweet release
From terror. Teach them wars will never cease
And they in days to come will turn again
Beseeching eyes to me—oh, make that plain
Above the cackle of dream-besotted geese!
    But thee I thank that war, become an art;
    Is beautiful as thy red star in heaven.
    "Euclid alone has looked on beauty bare,"
    So sings a poet, but with beating heart
    I out-soar Euclid and to me is given
    To lay a soldier's hand upon her hair!

Eighth Voice:
I ask no certainties, O Lord, but give
Me courage still to doubt. You will not blind
Eyes that would look on you, nor make the mind,
Your best gift, surely, a poor fugitive
Hunted by faith and driven down to live
In caves! Nor, when the seeker kneels to find
Water of life, will you in mockery bind
His soul to dip it only with a sieve!
    Surely your love is for the warrior-child
    That goes to seek you in the open field!
    Surely!—If this be mortal error, Lord,
    Ah, yet I'll glimpse you striding through the wild
    Heavens of anger and not shame to yield
    My breast up to the lightning of your sword!

Ninth Voice:
Never a question, Lord, and never a doubt
In all my years—now past threescore and ten—
Have I sent up to trouble thee. And when,
Like a great wind of darkness, all about
The world I heard the laughter and the shout
Of the world's creatures shut within the pen
Of sin (O Lord, be merciful to men!),
Thy light burned steadily and went not out.
    For this I thank thee. And, my hand in thine
    (Unworthy as I am!), gladly I face
    The final doorway bathed in tender gloom,
    Because I know your light of love will shine
    Across the dark to lead me from this place
    To where you wait me in the other room!

Tenth Voice:
In gratitude I thank thee for the brain
Thou gavest man, reason and thought and mind,
And one clear aim: above the weak and blind
Passions that cry like beggars in the rain,
And with no thought of pleasure or of pain,
Of good and evil, to seek truth and bind—
Didst thou not say, "Go seek and ye shall find"?—
Her feet that she may never flee again.
    There's Nagasaki, Lord, to witness how
    We sought and found; and nobler fruit by far
    Ripens each day beneath thy gracious sun.
    Thy servant's hand is ready on the bough
    To pluck for thee—what woulds't thou have? A star?
    The world itself, if so thy wishes run!

***Part Nine*: Epilogue**

The Quiet heard the voices as they went
Up from the city to heaven's Magistrate.
These *were* the City and the living State;
These were earth's oldest, gravest continent
Speaking its dreams; these were the World-soul sent
Back to its maker, the Compassionate,
With downcast eyes and a conspicuous plate
For Sunday issue of soul-nourishment.
    And to the Quiet all these voices were
    The single Hunger that stalks gaunt behind
    The urgent hunting-cry of bargain-shoppers

Or drips from heaven when with heavy stir
Of wings a flock of ibis goes to find
Celestial pastures fat with grasshoppers.

It was Man's Farce she saw, enacted thus
With the old cast for scores of centuries,
Hope grown a little threadbare at the knees,
Greed with sagged belly groaning in a truss,
The same old crowd of Virtues in a fuss
About the scene while through torn fineries
Show their bare hides in places that would please
An eye that savours the ridiculous.
    And underneath the stage, to make it all
    More modern and exciting, quietly
    Sleep tens of Krakatoas boxed for use,
    And now and then the players pause to call
    The whole cast over name by name to see
    If one has slipped away to light the fuse.

Indifferently the Quiet turned away
And passed into those realms where sound is not
Nor any breath of life. But to that spot
Rooted, Australia, we for ever stay
Mouthing the words set down for us to say,
Shaping our actions to the ignoble plot,
Ruled by one passion of the polyglot
And babbling passions—to play out the play.
    And in our hands the script is old and rotten
    From use and torn in places where some grip
    Faltered beneath the prompter's angry stare,
    But patched so that no line might be forgotten
    And that no actor, growing bold, might slip
    A sword of language in it unaware.

And yet, who wrote the sorry script, and when,
Curtained by cloud on what stern Sinai
That men might see Him not lest they should die
Before the splendour streaming earthward then?
What awful and ineradicable pen
Shaped act and scene so mockingly awry
The only setting had to be a sty,
The only actors—dare we call them men?
    Never the Quiet, the Intelligence
    Without a mind, the Sight that has no eyes,
    The Life that has no heart to burn or freeze
    But watches with the same indifference

The carrion-bird hung black amid blue skies,
The white-robed worshipper on bended knees!

This is our hope, my country: only we
Wrought the sad thing we look on with sick eyes.
Dear Brutus, hear my whisper, the fault lies
Not in our stars! How is it they should be
Concerned with us who have so beggarly
Flattered the very pavement with our sighs
And called—ah, basest of inequities!—
What is our will's permission, destiny.
    Give back to silence every ugly word
    And tear the page across so foully written!
    And if a dreadful penalty be due
    For the past wrong, resolute, undeterred,
    Stretch forth the unclean right hand to be smitten
    And with the left hand learn to write anew.

The fluency of hate may so be spent
Short of its goal, the hand that lends it force,
The Greed, bewildered where his ancient course
Drops out of sight, and with no instrument
To build anew, may falter where he went
So boldly once, and, reft of aim and source,
Die, and in Man's heart, cleansed by that divorce,
Leave but a high and sacred discontent.
    No other way than this? I only know
    That man or nation never shall see Love
    Across a counter handing out the change,
    And that a Lover—let me call him so,
    The noblest title man has knowledge of—
    Found His cross bitter but not very strange.

Now at the end let this again be said,
Love, that what nation walks without you sees
Beauty, wealth, glory, all the treasuries
Unlocked by power, and as her sight is fed,
Audaciously at last she lifts her head
To grasp her ultimate empire—by degrees
Revealed beneath its cloudy mysteries,
Lies cold and still the kingdom of the dead.
    But who has walked with you, though she must be
    Thrall to that kingdom whither all things go
    Under the warrant of eternal laws,
    Surely your hand will turn her round to see,
    Before she pass the portals, Hope aglow
    On earth she blessed with her name shut in yours!

O Love, your brow shows never tenderer
Than in the dawn above Australian hills
When the crests brighten and each valley fills
With the last sleep of shadows. Slenderer
Is not the wheat, wind-charmed, nor half so fair
The queens of all our gardens, daffodils,
Nor sweeter the wren's singing when he trills
That his shy mate should know he wakes for her.
    Come from your heaven to us who madly press
    The gaunt pain and bitter-mouthed delight
    To hearts grown cold and desperate and stark,
    And be—ah, lovely with all tenderness!—
    The eyes we look to when the day is bright,
    The hand we feel for when the world is dark!

Poems from *The Lifted Spear* (1953)

The Lifted Spear
Delissaville, Northern Australia

Upon the mangrove roots I watched him stand
Above the sea, a naked black man, and
His spear was pointed at the breast of the sea,
The eternal, the illimitable. He,
In that vast atmosphere of time and space,
Poised all his strength and skill upon one place
Where there might flash a silver side, a fin
Out of the deep, then splendidly drove in
His claim to a harvest out of the great sea.
And they were very beautiful to me,
Those dying ones, shining on the black mud.
And there came up a madness in my blood:
Oh, were they silver women that he caught,
Visions from the last hiding-places of thought,
Desires and adorations, flame on flame?
But little knows the fisher of his game,
And best it is in hope and love and fear
To stand beside him with a lifted spear
And plunge it now and then.
                              My luck is here.

Girl Surfing in War-Time

This dragon-ocean, crested dragon, has fed
Immeasurably on the dead,
Nor are the hollows of its hunger stilled,
Dark cavernous belly filled,
Nor is the tongue yet coiled within its head.

Yet, clad in a rag of laughter, you have flung
Your beauty; ah, you have sprung
From my shut fingers with the dragon to lie,
Yielding your pointed breasts up vixenly
To the cold, curved caresses of that tongue.

Now, dared I kiss you, cleaving through the bloom
That is both laughter and spume
Upon your mouth, which is it I should find—
(Being old, you see, I kiss with double mind)—
Your dragon joy the world's hope or its doom?

Verses for a Birthday

Two beings suggest a fitting gift for you
On this your birthday, and they both are true
To truth, and each the very heart of me.
The one — white angel — whispers tenderly:
"She asks for nothing, she is tired, would sleep;
So let her fall on slumber warm and deep
And tiptoe from the room and shut the door,
Nor kiss her eyes nor wonder any more
If, waking, she will miss you. Sleeping so
She has the gift you cannot give her — go!"

And one — dark angel but with flashing eye —
Whispers: "And will you let her beauty lie
Mouldering in sleep, that wrong to heaven and earth
That makes a wretched mockery of birth
And all men strive for? For her own dear sake
Hurt her with kisses, sting her wide awake
Until she sees, athwart a mist of tears
And chasms of dark pain and darker fears,
The crown her brow was made for!"
                           So I stand
Between my warring angels, and my hand, —
Because they both are eloquent, both true —
Has no rich gift, my love to offer you.

Still Interval

Through the black rush of storm,
In the most desperate moment,
A hand on my hand, warm,
Made heavenly comment.

And what it said is this:
"Though shameful in your fear,
Know that your courage is
Near, because love is near.

"And love that may not stay
The storm-winds, yet will give
Strength that be man you may
If you deserve to live."

Deserve? Who earned the blood,
The dear face drawn and pale,
And, sweet on the hard wood,
The hand pierced by a nail?

I live, and now the storm
Stands baulked and hushed a moment
While your hand, pierced and warm,
Makes heavenly comment.

Preparation for a Dark Voyage

When our good saints, the wise old rats,
In grey procession shoreward slip,
Preferring the whole hell of cats
To that which waits the outbound ship,

And the crew, naked suddenly,
Stand leering in a muster-line
With eyes unmasked and comradely
At grinning wolf and goat and swine,

Our seven or seventy deadly sins
That must be all our crew to sail
Us where no vessel ever wins
To where lurks not another gale,

If then should come a pure and fair
Woman aboard, would not a hand
Be reached to grasp her gently there
And set her back upon the land?

Spider
(Fable of a Neurosis)

As spiders go, he was more civilized
Than most, and strung his web a little tighter,
With knot and brace more cunningly devised
To take the strain, because his thread was lighter.

Sportsman by instinct, connoisseur in taste,
He had no interest in the vulgar fly
And shunned the forthright beetle in his haste
To find some dung before it should be dry.

But for the veined ephemera of the night,
The wandering psyches wonderful and pale,
He had a lust as hunger-hammered and bright
As the hard metal of some savage grail.

Hunting was good, but since the victims were
Nearly all wing, there was no juice to press;
The hunter kept on saying, "These I prefer",
And grew the gaunter on his own success.

At last he ate them only with his eyes.
To compensate his belly with the thrill
Their struggling made along the spoke and guys,
He pulled the web a little tighter still.

Just when he'd half convinced himself that soon
The Incomparable would strike his web, it did:
Something fell on him from the capsized moon
And ended dream and web and arachnid.

Yet not quite dead, he lies on the cold ground
Crushed by a butterfly that opens and shuts
Enormous wings and smothers him, bound
By the silver cordage of his very guts.

Invitation to Taste Wild Honeycomb

Taste of the comb but let
Yours be the lizard's tongue,
A listening arrow set
To the brain-bow tensely strung,
And swifter from the string
Than the off-dart of a wing.

You'll see it, never fear.
But know that it will be
Only a moment clear
And never again to see,
A wing, an immanence
In the thickets of your sense.

What is it? Who would dare
To shut a clammy hand
And feel it beating there!
And won't you understand
Why the lizard on the stone
Does his hunting alone!

Turn About

A bee clung in the flower, a zinnia red
As dawn is sometimes, clung there with his head
Buried in sweetness, but I shook him out.
And it was only turn and turn about
That, when I held the flower for you to take,
You gave it yet another cautious shake,
Saying, "There's many and many a sort of bee" —
And I had little better luck than he.

A Coast Idyll

I always took the path along the bluff:
On one hand blue-green hills and on the other
The green-blue sea. There one could hear the surf
And yet not have to listen; there one could
Feel the vast continents of land and water
Around him and yet pay no heed to them.
Even the path asked nothing of my eyes,
Less of my thought.
        Why should an old man walk
Beside the sea in bitterness of heart?
Why choose that spot to rattle in their case
(His withered mind), the leavings of his years,
Making a sound less noble than the bush,
Long dead, that turns the wind to a lament?
Why give the sea that chance to laugh at him?

I always took the path along the bluff.

Today there were dip-net fishers in the surf
And on the rocks below me; so I sat
Among the low sea-daisies in the sun
To watch them and to rest. It might have been
A stirring thing to live in those young bodies
Dipping old death for fishes, but I soon
Tired of them and took my rattle out
And gave my thought to it.
        When the two came
I did not know, nor did I ever see them,
But heard their voices in a nook near by.
I would have gone then, but I told myself
(Annoyed at their intrusion), "They are young
And fools, no doubt, and you are surely old:
What matter what they say or what you hear!"

And true enough, their talk was idle chatter
For half an hour; and then there was a silence
Before she spoke — (I'd come to like her voice
For something in it I suppose love gave
And I'd forgotten women ever have) —
"Let's play a game and say that all those fishers
Are after something that's not really fish."
I heard his laugh, but she went on, "The one
Far out there — farthest out — he must be brave;
So let us say, because he is so brave,
He must be fishing for God." He joined her game,
And with the fine audacity of youth
They fitted every fisher with his quest
As Joy, Truth, Beauty, Power. Love was not
Mentioned by either. Then at last he said,
"There's just one left and what's he fishing for?"

I heard a rustling in what must have been
A bed of sweet dry bracken and I rose
And for the first time in so many days
Saw the green hills and the blue sky and laughed
Joyously with the waves, the ever-young.
But for the lovers hidden in the fern,
(Being a gentleman) I did not look.
A gentleman? An old man grown so happy
All of a sudden, it would have been my death
To find, perhaps, they never had been there!

Escape from Death in the Desert

Dying of thirst, he leaned against a stone
Deep in a gully; utterly alone
Except for crows' heads coolly measuring him,
And the great heat. Then in a strange and dim
Death-whim,
Or call it something heavenly sent to save,
Some angel with her hand across his grave,
Some interdiction on the grim despair
That dragged him terribly downward by the hair,
He dug his fingers deep in earth, and there
Trickled before his glazed and wondering eyes
A stream pure as the skies.
And there he drank and was made strong again,
And went across the plain
Steadfastly to his goal.

And will you think his soul,
All that lived by that one sweet miracle,
Will not remember well —
Now, all the ways up heaven or down hell,
With gods or devils walking, or alone —
That water and that stone?

The Wood-Cutter

For thirty years his axe had bit
Daylong into the shuddering trees,
And, if he ever thought of it,
They were such thoughts as surely please.

A boy with down upon his lip
He'd gone into the bush and made,
After a brief apprenticeship,
Himself a master of his trade,

And would have lived his tranquil span
And died upon some quiet day
And found death nothing harder than
The putting of his axe away;

But someone told of engines that
A clever man far off had wrought
Could lay whole miles of forest flat
With something like the speed of thought.

The story, a dark spore wind-spilled —
(Surely no evil was designed) —
Grew till its fungus-threads had filled
Each cranny of that simple mind.

They burgeoned fiercely day by day,
Great crimson mushroom-caps of fear:
Millions of hungry saws at play
Over the world — and drawing near,

Until earth's forests were but one
Great climbing wave of green that stood
Leaning between him and the sun
Above his hoarded bit of blood.

He called on all the trees he'd killed
To say how stubbornly they died

Even though his hand was strong and skilled,
But they all shuddered terrified.

There was no place where he could go
But that green wave would follow after
And curl above him with a low
Dark hollow sound not unlike laughter;

Until one morning wretchedly
He rose and stumbled from his door
And hanged himself upon a tree
He should have felled a week before.

The Young Lubra

Always on the outer ring
Where the women of the camp
Huddled at the harvesting
Digging yams beside the swamp,
Always where the danger was
Poised and hidden in the grass
Hung Midjanma, lingering.

Eyes intent and hands dropped slack,
She would search among the trees
For a token and a track
Leading on to mysteries,
She would follow where it led
Slyly, slowly with bent head
Till loud voices called her back.

They were old and full of dread;
Shrunken breasts and matted hair
And the scars on cheek and head —
Could they ever have been fair?
They were old and bitter ones
Withered by the winds and suns —
Must she turn and heed them there?

Slowly she would come again
To her place among the rest,
Sickened by the sudden pain
Breaking open in her breast,
Angry at the words would pour
Cold and dismal, more and more,
On the fires of her unrest.

"Child, an evil one has laid
Magic on you that you go
Wandering blindly unafraid
Where lurks many a hidden foe.
You who will be woman soon
With the changing of the moon,
What is there for you to know?

"Woman's lot is what you see;
Take your stick and dig for food.
Look on her and her and me
And drive the madness from your blood.
What we are shall you become;
Do your work then, and be dumb;
Life is neither bad nor good.

"Nearly woman! Is it then
That worst fever is alight?
You will know the ways of men
All your days and every night
At the changing of the moon
Soon enough, too soon, too soon,
Neither good, nor bad, but right.

"Life is law: then set your heart
Firmly where the law will give
Shelter and your proper part
In the life that all must live,
And, at ending of your days,
Your just meed of tears and praise —
This, oh only this, believe!"

Always on the outer ring
Where the women of the camp
Huddled at their harvesting
Digging yams beside the swamp,
Always where the danger was
Poised and hidden in the grass
Hung Midjanma, lingering.

Farm Day

The magpie's meditation is
Mother of mourning melodies;
The kookaburra's laugh at night

Remembers some obscene delight;
And I between the two have done
A good day's work beneath the sun,
Just pausing by the stable fence
To applaud the magpie's eloquence,
And at the other's merry din
To smile at a remembered sin.

Angle-Shot of Farmer Brown

"Lazy," they'd say, and lift a brow
To show that words could not express
The measure of his laziness,
Then hurry on to mention how,
When others' crops were up and growing,
He'd start to think about the sowing.

And how, when other men had got
Their harvests in, he'd sit and wait
Till storms had ruined half his lot,
Then with a slow and easy gait
Roll out his rusted old machine
To harvest where the wheat had been.

Lazy! But I who saw each day
This marvel of indifference
In wasted fields beyond our fence
Saw also — do I dare to say? —
A sort of glory where he trod
Gleaning behind the wrath of God.

Invitation to Help Make a Better World

Dead hopes leave tendrils clinging where they grew,
Like vines that fall in winter, and as we go
About our gardening, and the spring is slow,
The wind makes voices of them. Never do
They fall and rot unless we cut them through
And strip them down — (a gardener should do so) —
And never are they still while the winds blow,
Persistent talkers though their themes be few.

> I have been troubled knowing that out there
> The garden waits the hard thrust of my spade
> And will not blossom till my hands have made
> The magic that compels it to be fair,

Yet at the window here I stand and stare
And am — God, that this should be so! — afraid.

Sun-Healing

Don't ask the moon for peace; far off and dim
She'll show a headland and a single light
Beyond a Hellespont you cannot swim
Nor ever turn from, night by desperate night.
Nor ask the stars. How should the wake that swings
Behind brave ships ever pass from their gaze
Who knew Cook, Flinders, and the voyagings
Of men like them in other, greater days!

    But, sick at heart and all disquieted,
    Stretch your frail, naked body in the sun
    And let him seal the portals of your head
    Against all thought, all longing, one by one,
    Against all dreams of headlands and wide seas,
    All hope, all fear, all love, all memories.

How and What the Corals Built
For a College Teacher on his Retirement

They hurled no trumpet-challenge at the sea,
But in the wandering, vast, subaqueous night,
Linked cell to cell, and building silently,
They plumed and turreted towards the light,
Till on a day the heavy surface stirred,
Heaved sullenly a moment, and then broke,
And the sea stopped before a mightier word
Than ever throat of battle-trumpet spoke.

    So knowledge breasts the wave. Behind her, curled
    Warm at the quiet bosom of the land,
    Lies the lagoon upon whose level sand
    Visions and Powers and Loves with bright wings furled
    Saunter like laughing children hand in hand
    In hearing of the thunder of the world.

On Having Grown Old

Now are those peaks unscalable sierras
Against a darkening sky. I may not climb
Sure of my skill, contemptuous of errors,
Their crags as gaily once upon a time.

To reach those heights now, even were I able,
Were but to push a faltering heart too far
And be laid out at last on a stone table
Bare to the gaze of a mortician star.

      No, never again! But from the dull plain counting
      Before dark blot them, every hazardous peak,
      I'll let my eyes leap in a swift up-mounting
      To what I knew, and having known, still seek;
      Then, on my slab, while stars put on their white
      Uniforms, yield myself to absolute night.

A Scientist Writes from Bikini

Yes, I may tell you what it is we learn
Poking among the wreckage day by day:
Measuring Force by what he did in play
We estimate (granted that he should turn
Serious some day), how clean the world will burn;
And thus I'll summarize it if I may:
For men well grouped — a million, let us say —
A thimble will be a sufficient urn.

      PS. We notice, even where the flare
      Of death was hottest, both on land and sea,
      Myriads of living things how merrily
      About their business, sporting, coupling there!
      I never dreamed such hosts of birds could be,
      Nor have I seen such greenness anywhere.

Marguerite[17]
(After Reading "The Terrace at Berne")

The old companion still is at your side,
The Interdiction with the cruel brow
You called your soul, but that I knew to be
A barren, bitter angel with a sword.
You said she was Salvation, that through her
We should see God; but I saw only her,
A faint wraith in the hollows of your eyes,
Mocking me there, a winter in your voice,
A frost upon your lips.
                She deck for us

---

17   Extensive notes regarding the original Matthew Arnold poem and Moll's intentions have
       not been included.

A bridal couch? She draw the shadows down
To hide us from the world, breast against breast
And mouth to mouth pressed hotly? She? And yet
You would trust none but her! Take her gift, then,
A bed of marble colder than a tomb,
And her sword laid between us that all men
May know her faithful in her ministry.

Ten years! And still, you see, the river runs
Through the green fields, the river that we loved,
And still the Jungfrau snows look faint and far,
And even — how should this be? — through the tall hedge
Of oleanders, rushing joyously,
You see me come, crying, " 'Tis thou! 'Tis thou!"
And dash my heart on yours. Had you stopped there,
That vision had saved us for eternity;
For, though my lips could never touch yours more,
Nor my hands hold you, in that dream we'd lie
Close-held till death, and death would only make
The dream go on for ever.
                    Had you stopped there!
But the malicious one must have her say,
Pushing you back, a too-impetuous child,
And chiding you: "Your love has walked the streets
Of shame in France; her smile has died within
The dens of lust and laughter; on her cheek —"
Ah, God, I'll hear no more! Is this the heart
That long ago treasured the memory
Of hair and lips and eyes you said were mine,
Only to stamp that memory in the dust
As now you do?
                    A god our severance ruled?
Who is it, then, comes now to bury me
With ceremony fitting to a whore,
Dropping on me a flower of sick contempt?
A god? That had been noble; tears, perhaps,
And the long grey and desolate waste ahead,
But courage in the heart, and clean grief.
But now, dishonoured in your elegy —
No god, I think, had stooped so very low
To bury me. Your hand and yours alone,
O love, I loved so, heaps this dust of shame
Over my eyes, and heart that beat for you.

There was a day we walked beside the Aar
Upward towards the two lakes. Your spirit slept,

Or so I read your eyes, and quietly
You took my hand and held it as we went.
We could not see the Jungfrau. I was glad
Of that because that far white monitor,
When we could see it, always drew your glance
And something in you to it that made stern
Your silence, that was warm and friendly now.
I drew you to a nook where gentians grew
And there in sunshine and below the wind
You lay beside me while I stroked your brow.

The mountains were a music playing softly
Our souls together, and you did not resist,
Till suddenly my lips were hard on yours
And all my flesh ached for you. Then you broke
Roughly away, as though you had been wronged,
And left me in my tears. Next day you brought
The poem that I hate, about the Voice
That blew such thrilling summons to your will
But could not shake it and that drained the life
Your full heart had to spill yet could not break it.
There spoke the lover! No, the cruel thing
You called your soul, the cold and selfish one
That made you — brave you were in all things else —
A coward to the eyes of love. Her boast,
This, that she saved you, snatched you from my arms
And the red shame of passion; kept you pure
And dead and lonely as the Jungfrau snows.

Strange how you loved the watered sylvan valleys
Yet in your heart were always stretched against
Black, overleaning, frightful cliffs of thought;
For ever running from your own desire,
For ever beating up against the stars
Because the one who sang along our valley
Valley of laughing waters, how you loved them!
You soul had named a siren.
                          So you fled,
And still are fleeing after ten years,
And so shall flee until the weary foot
Strikes on the dark, last threshold.
                          But you came
Often again to me in those lost days,
Seeking me in your dreams to hear me say
"My love! Why sufferest thou!" to feel my hands
Upon your hair, my cheek against your cheek

In love and pity laid. For in your dreams
She could not rule you, the all-hateful one!

And sometimes in sad fancy you would tell
Our story of the merman and the maid
Who left him sad for ever, but even there
You would not say why she deserted him,
You could not be quite true to truth who were
Untrue to love. And sometimes you would come
Weary and shadowed into quietness,
Like a lost pool somewhere among dark trees.
And then it seemed I moved you — but that was
As when a wind, toward night, upon still water
Would seem to make it stir and rise and flow
Though it lie locked deep in its walls of stone.
And sometimes — since you loved bright water so —
I thought my heart a pool, and you stooped there
But always as your lips came down they met
The cold and scornful lips of your own soul
Opening to claim your kiss, and you would turn
Shuddering away, as once among the gentians,
To leave me with my tears.
                              Pitiful one,
With what deep longing did you turn to them,
The death-marked lovers in old Brittany,
To find your own heart dying against mine,
But she, the mocker, watchful even there,
Twisted your thought and made your story of them
A harsh and bitter sermon on desire!

So all things failed you who had failed yourself
And love and me. So let it rest. But while
The last light lingers on the Jungfrau's snow
And the dear river murmurs as of old
Below my window; let me turn the page
And cast the bitter words out of my mind —
(The words you made long after you were dead) —
And let me think of you my last thought,
Unless death be not sleep. Not in my arms
Now, and unhappy; but I see you move,
Your dark head bowed, through avenues of pines
Up a far mountain slope. I think you must
Feel the trees round you in still comradeship,
The cool unmating trees, and feel the earth
Opening her heart to take you. Slowly up —
(I miss no step, beloved!) — till on the crest

Against the flaming sunset rises one
Out of the earth to meet you. Hand in hand,
After a long look earthward, ah, you turn,
To plunge in Etna with Empedocles!

Jonah at Nineveh

Part One: The Journey South

Jonah trudged south from Galilee, against
The frown of Jahweh and the lifted hand
Pointing him north. A wind from beyond Jordan
Struck on his left cheek like a blow that would
Turn the most stubborn ass; the gritty sands
Drove deep into his eyes and made him weep;
Under his beard his mouth was stiff with dust.
Yet Jonah moved on southward. Along the way
Travellers about to greet him turned aside
Abruptly at his hot and angry eyes
Like men stumbling on danger unawares
And seeing it just in time. He did not mark
From under shaggy brows the shrink of them
Out of his path, for all his sight was filled
With the great brow of Jahweh and the frown
He lunged into as one might dare a flame
Lifted to stop him or to overwhelm.
Stride upon stride he went, south, south, and south,
Though all the winds of heaven shrieked, "Turn north",
And all the winds of heaven were of God.
And sometimes from the darkness of his beard
His voice came harshly, flung against the wind,
And fierce as it:
     "What have you done to me,
The prophet and the sword in your right hand,
Your sword of justice and your tongue of fire
To burn out sin, setting a trap for me
In distant Nineveh? Must I be quenched
In those dark waters of iniquity
Because you would betray me to the thing
You call your love, that is no part of you
But only a sick dream that clots your brain?
How is it law and mercy should be one!
And you are law, or so you used to be
Then when I was your prophet and could trust
Justice, law, truth. Now I trust none of them,
Nor you because of this vile trap you set.

How should I stand in far-off Nineveh
And say to them, 'In forty days my God
Will strike you dead and lay your city flat,
Your city one of the greatest of the earth',
And then have you, when they were frightened quite
And most repentant, breathe like a soft wind
Of spring above them, 'I forgive your sins,
Live on in peace; Jonah was partly right,
But partly fool, and an imperfect prophet.'
How should I —"
                    But the wind choked out his words.
And one with water in great skins, going by
And seeing the gaunt man, spoke to his beast
And stopped and said, "Friend, here is drink for you,
If so your need be." And the prophet of God
Stared at him wildly for a second and said,
"Drink? In the desert? Friend, I thank my —" but
The word "God" choked him and he said instead
Quietly, "I would drink, have you to spare."

A little water hung upon his beard
After his draught, and Jonah raised a hand
To let his fingers taste it. On his eyes
Peace for a moment laid a gentle shadow
As a cloud might on hot and bitter stone.
But quickly with a gesture of denial
Casting his weakness from him, Jonah spoke,
Staring sun-up against the barren hills,
"Water of life that have become for me
A draught of death! Jahweh, I speak your name
But not in thankfulness. My feet are set
Against your pointing and my heart is turned
A stone to cast upon you. From my land
You drive me, but not north, not ever north,
In spite of all your wrath shall my steps take me,
But south and away from you. Even as Jordan
Plunges into the hollows of the sea
And is not seen again, so I from you
Plunge and am lost — am lost!"
                    The traveller
Spoke sharply to his beast, "Let us be gone!
I've heard hyenas laughing at the moon,
And that meant death and corpses."
                    Jonah watched
Them go as one on waking sees a dream
Pass on into the nothing beyond sleep,

And then turned south again.
                        The second night,
As on the first, he lay among bare hills,
Letting the dew fall on him while his flesh
Ached with the cold. But in the dark he said,
"Tomorrow I reach Japho and take ship
And heap the silence of the sea upon
The voice of Jahweh. It will never reach me
In far-off Tarshish where men have not heard
His name and shall not hear from lips of mine.
And as sweet Jordan sleeps in the salt sea
So I among those barbarous ones shall rest,
Uncouth Phoenicians, and grow like to them,
Letting my anger die as love has died."

And then the morning broke upon the hills,
Red on the bare marl summits, purple where
Their folds made shadows. Jonah, rising, stood
And saw the sea far off and a rich plain
Below him, field and groves and gardens fresh
In the new light, and close against the sea
White buildings, and a smile was on his face
(The first for many days). "Oh, beautiful,
Japho, so means your name, the beautiful!
Out of the desert and the wrath of God
I come to you."
                     He took a single stride
Down hill and suddenly cried out in pain
And fell upon the ground. A thorn had pierced
His foot and stood an inch above the bone.
Slowly with shaking hand he drew it out
And stared at it. "The last of Jahweh's gifts,"
He muttered; "so let men beware,
Lest, loving him, they find a crown of thorn."
And rising in his pain he started down
To Japho and the ships upon the sea.

Part Two: Japho

Along the streets of Japho Jonah limped,
With stubborn will hiding his pain as best
He could from curious eyes. The pain shot up
With every step and lingered in his brain
Filling a pool of anguish till he reeled
And all that met him gave him a wide berth.
But Jonah was not drunk; beyond his pain

He saw the green trees and the watered gardens,
Cool, shadowed doorways, and deep courts of peace
Asleep beneath the noonday sun. A name
Buzzed in his memory like a summer fly,
And there was the description of a street:
"A large house on your right and then a garden,
And after that a small house almost lost
In greenery and then — and then — and then —"
And then a voice was saying: "Come with me,
Your foot is bleeding and you walk with pain.
How did it happen?" Jonah braced himself
Against the calm regard of the black eyes
Measuring him, but measuring as a shepherd
Would do a lamb he must bear long miles home,
A lamb hurt in the wilderness. "I need
Neither your help nor pity," Jonah said,
"But if you would direct me —" The man laughed.
"From Galilee, I take it, and as proud
As the sharp thorn that went clear through your foot!
But this is Japho and I bid you welcome.
I'm a Phoenician trader and my house,
If you should deign to look, is right behind you,
And only fifty feet away. Come, friend;
Were you not ill I never would have seen you,
For I'm a busy man." Again Jonah
Tried to brush off the haze upon his eyes
That pain made there. "I'm given to understand,"
He said a bit uncertainly, "there is
One of your race has ships that ply to Tarshish,
And him I seek." Again the brown man laughed:
"That's a long way. But he? I know him well.
And when your walk is, shall I say, more steady
(This is a small town, friend), I'll take you to him.
But Tarshish, did you say? That's a long way,
And hardly worth the seeing when you get there."
"Never," said Jonah, "far enough from him,
Even should I drop from off the edge of the world!"
"Him?" said the brown man. "But, my friend, you'll drop
Right in the middle of a common street
Unless you come with me. The edge of the world?
That's an heroic matter, and you seem
Right now quite incommoded by a thorn
No better than the very poorest get
Between their toes. But come, I'm in a hurry;
This is the way, friend." Jonah, faint with pain,
Followed the brown man through an iron gate

In a low wall of stone. A quiet garden
Lay spread before him, like a thought one thinks
Somewhere within the very heart of storm,
Placid and full of ease. A rough stone bench
Stood in the shadow of an olive-tree,
And to that Jonah went. "Forgive my weakness,"
He said half grudgingly, "and I will rest
Here, if I may, while you go on your business,
And soon I will rise up and go on mine."

"A stubborn lot, you Israelites," his host
Said with a smile, "I've bargained with you and lost
Most of the time, and yet had my reward
In something like amusement at your pride.
You walk as though a god held your right hand,
You talk as though his words were on your tongue,
As, as though caught in a great condescension,
You beat us to the profits." Jonah laughed,
A thin dry laugh there in that pleasant garden
"Look at my foot," he said, "that's Jahweh's gift,
The God I grew to as a cedar grows
Against the shoulder of proud Lebanon,
Or plume upon his crest. It's swollen now,
Tomorrow it will fester, like as not,
And next day it will turn a rotten green.
You may laugh at our pride and I will join you,
Laugh, laugh, and laugh! But go about your business,
And in good time I'll go about my own."
"You should serve kindlier gods," the man replied,
And went into the house and came again
With food and wine. "Eat, friend, and be at peace!"

And peace did steal on Jonah while the sun
Slept in the tree-tops and a score of doves
Cooed drowsily, and from the house there came
The sound of women's voices. Peace crept in
To still the angry heart and Jonah stayed
Some days in that cool house until his wound
Was almost healed and he had found a ship
Readying for Tarshish. Jahweh seemed far off,
A thunder-cloud sinking on the horizon
And never to threaten more. His passage sure,
And only a few lazy days to wait,
Jonah walked much beneath the olive-trees
Or sat on the stone bench and heard the doves
And women's voices, and a song came up

From deep with him, gently, and he said:

"No more your prophet, Jahweh, now I fill
My blood with coolness and my lips with song.
What now to me the strife of good and ill!
The nights are gentle and the days are long
And lovely in the shadows of this hill.

"Somewhere the desert sickens with its heat
And men drive on beset by doubt and fear,
But I have heaped the shadows on my feet
And lie by waters musical and clear
And slumber, and my dreams are very sweet.

"Somewhere you sit upon your burning throne
And mock your prophets — but no longer me,
For I have slipped your bondage and alone
In these deep gardens wonderfully free
Let the great peace seep in through flesh and bone.

"Somewhere the waves on Galilee are blue,
But what care I who have nor God nor race,
From them I turn as I have turned from you
And let the sweet sleep fall upon my face
And tender darkness pierce me through and through."

Part Three: Outbound for Tarshish

The breeze was off-shore and the sea was calm
When the bireme lifted her delicate prow,
Outbound from Japho, into the long swells.
Jonah stood on a platform at the stern
Close to the master, but his eyes were on
The roofs of Japho and the hills beyond
Just visible through a light haze. He stood,
Not like a sailor easy in the swing,
The rise and fall of the sea, but stiffly braced,
A landsman suffering the indignity
Of dip and heave, as best a landsman could;
And if he heard the striking of the oars
And the low flute that timed them, or even saw
The creaming wake, none could have guessed, for all
His gaze clung to the falling land. The master,
A slim bronze man, glanced at him now and then
Uneasily because of the unknown
In the man's bearing and his yearning eyes.

At last the land was gone. Then Jonah turned
To gaze along the ship and watch the oars
Flash in the sunlight, and he felt the ship
Alive upon that sea as a dancer lives
(A memory of his youth) in some great music,
Or as a bird lives in the living air.
"A noble ship," he said, "a splendid goer,
Lean, swift and strong. Surely there is no sea
Could baffle her, nor any port so far
She could not reach it and move queenly in."
That pleased the master. "Yes, a good stout ship;
No easy mark for pirates when she hears
The urging flute and feels her pulses leap
To the wild thrill of flight. No easy mark.
And since we carry cargo and not arms,
It's well to have her swift." "Yes," Jonah said,
"The dove needs all her wing when the brown hawk
Tilts for the lunge." It's queer I'd think of it
Just now," the master said, "but isn't Jonah,
Your name, the word for dove?" A bitter smile
Twisted the mouth of Jonah, "You know much!
And for your greater knowledge I will tell you
There was a hawk somewhere amid the sky.
But hawks," he said more quietly, "do never
Hunt far at sea, not ever far at sea!"
"That's true," the man said, puzzled, "but you speak
Half angrily, and I meant no offence."
"Nor I," said Jonah; "let it rest at that.
And now I would go down into the ship
And sleep, for I am weary, strangely weary,
And I would sleep though it is not yet night."

He turned and found the aft companionway,
Telling himself the weariness upon him
Was from his wound, a last remembrancer
Of Jahweh that a little sleep would heal;
Telling himself the strangeness in his mind
Was nothing but a sea-change that would pass
Tomorrow with the sunrise; telling himself
That he was free at last, a whole man,
With voice, and brain, and will, and hand and heart
To use in his own service. And all the while,
In spite of what he told himself, a fear
That had nor name nor feature pressed against
His side, and when he lay stretched out to sleep,

Bedded beside him.
                    Then it came, a blast
Straight down from heaven. It was less a storm
Than a vast hand that struck into the sea
And hurled the waters madly. Wind and wave
Followed no law that any sailor knew,
But leapt and shrieked, one hurl of violence,
Chaos of insane force. The rain slashed in
On twisting gusts, and towering through the rain,
The water-mountains rose to have their crests
Torn into streamers by the blast. Stunned,
The ship spun dizzily, not answering
Oarsmen nor helm, but like a smitten thing
Some hunter has brought low that strives to rise
And cannot, and would flee but every nerve
Unstrung, refuses duty, dizzily
She spun and wallowed helpless in that sea.

The cry was "Lighten ship!" and staggering men
Flung cargo overboard. Vessels of bronze
Gleamed as they fell, and now and then a man,
Some delicate vase clutched in his shaking hands,
Gasped, "God, the pity!" as he cast it forth.
Rich cloths of Tyrian dye, purple and red,
Floated like petals on the grey-green sea,
Until the weight of waters dragged them down.
But all that sacrifice proved vain.
                              Then men
With haggard eyes and streaming beards and hair
Fell to their knees upon the plunging deck
And prayed their gods. "What is it we have done
To anger you? Lo, we have cast away
Our treasures from us into the wild sea,
And heavy are our hearts. If sacrifice
Neglected thus have moved you, we will make
Atonement, or if one of us has sinned
Against you tell us but his name and he
Shall die." But the winds shrieked and a great wave
Came up and almost swept them from the deck.

The master said, "Where is the Israelite,
Jonah?" "Below and sound asleep," a sailor shouted,
"Or was an hour ago." "His god must love him
To let him sleep through this. I will awake
This sleeper that he pray for us, for night
Comes on and we must perish."

Two-score eyes

Followed the master where through sheets of spray
He clutched and crawled and stumbled down the deck;
Then voices harsh as storm-blown sea-birds' cries
Darted among the huddled mariners:
"Jonah's a madman with a curse upon him
And fleeing" — "No, there's blood upon his hand
And he fears vengeance" — "No again! I say
Offended — gods — filthy abominations —
A Hebrew devil." Then a creaming wave
Choked every throat to silence. When it passed
One in the lull that followed laughed and said:
"You be right or wrong, but at the best
He's an unprosperous cargo. Let's cast lots,
And if the guilt be on him —"

With numb hand

One brought out dice and cast them. All pressed in
As closely as they could to watch, and when
A sea struck, clung together like a mass
Of floating weed. At last the word went up
"Jonah is guilty! guilty!" And all turned
As by one impulse to stare hollow-eyed
At Jonah and the master drawing near.
And as they came it was as though a hand
Stilled the wild ocean, and the winds were still;
But such a calm it was as falls between
Two crests of anger, one gone by, the other
Boiling and climbing upward to the burst.
And in that stillness he who cast the lots,
Looking at Jonah, said: "What man are you?
What occupation have you? What your country?
And last" — he glanced aside upon his fellows —
"For whose cause has this evil come on us?"

Then a great light came upon Jonah's face
Out of his soul, but also out of heaven,
And he spoke proudly and with haughty eyes
Bent on the master and the mariners.
"I am a Hebrew and the prophet of God,
Jahweh, who made the sea and the dry land,
And whom I fear. Out of his presence I fled,
Thinking his heart had grown untrue to justice,
And lo! his presence is upon the sea,
And all the earth is his, and I am his" —
The voice rose up exultingly — "And he is just.
Because of me has he done this to you."

Then were they all afraid and said to him,
"What shall we do to make the sea be calm?"
And he said softly, "Cast me in the sea."

But the master said, "Behold, the winds are still.
Take up the oars and bring the ship to land."

But when the oars bit deep into the sea
It was as though one with an axe had struck
The roots of the hills and brought them crashing down;
So crashed those water-mountains on the ship,
And the winds tore at her and the rain struck
All into darkness.
               Then a cry went up:
"God of this stranger, lay not innocent blood
Upon us, nor let us for this man's life
Perish!" But Jonah smiled, "He is not mocked;
Come, cast me forth!" And they took Jonah up,
And with their eyes averted cast him forth.
And in a little while the sea was calm.

Part Four: The End of Flight

Somewhere just south of Tyre, in a grey dawn,
As grey almost as birth or death, Jonah
Lay face down on the sand. Waves now and then
Nuzzled against him, but his ashen face,
Half lost in the black beard and fallen hair,
Rested above their farthest venturing.
High over the slim beach a mountain loomed,
Holding the day back, and rocks piled on rocks
Gave to the spot a gloomy privacy
Not without grandeur.
              With a shuddering sigh
The man awoke, then got upon his knees,
Then to his feet, and stared with haggard eyes
Upon the mountain and upon the sea.
At last he staggered to a sheltered nook
Among the rocks and dropped down wearily.
But soon life moved within him and a song
Rose to his lips.

"The womb has opened and cast me forth!
Out of the belly of hell and the grim darkness
I am come out to the light.
The land is around me and under, the sky is above,

And the waters are bound in their shores.
To an old familiar world I have come forth,
The steady hills and the heavens,
A child born of what darkness, what terror!
"Let me remember that place of fears!

"I was a sword grown false to your hand, Jahweh,
Therefore you broke me;
A blade that turned in your hand that your foes, laughing,
Said, 'Lo! how it mocks its master,
Breaking the flesh of his palm!
Now with a reed shall we pierce him' Against your knee
You broke me and hurled me back to the fire and the hammers!

"I was the voice of your law and the glory of Israel,
But my tongue grew forked like a serpent's to hiss against you.
My tongue was a dog's that licked the festers of pride
Till the gorge broke. Then it lapped the vomit.
You saw the abomination and with your foot
On me, plucked out my tongue by the roots.

"My heart was your temple;
There were you shrined, my Lord and the God of Israel.
But vanity, covered with vermin, crept through the portals,
Filth that spawned in your sight.
Fouler my heart than the places of Baal,
Or the temples reeking with Babylonian whoredoms.
Then did you strike!
One blow and my heart was dust.

"Why did you not destroy me utterly?

"Let me remember the place you prepared for me,
The womb of rebirth.
Its walls were the roots of the mountains under the sea.
I tore with my fingers against them, the cold slime
Baffled my grip.
Darkness was all about me. I thrust with my eyes
To pierce it and saw only a blacker darkness.
A terrible sighing
Was in my ears, the sound of the streams of the sea
Far down from light. I cried aloud in my fear
But my mouth was stiff with silence.

"Then I did lie in that womb
Drinking the terror of God, the fear of you, Jahweh,

Out of the dark veins drinking.
And life moved in me again and I saw your temple
And cried to be there.
                    "You heard my cry, O God!

"The womb has opened and cast me forth!
Out of the belly of hell and the grim darkness
I am come out to the light.
The land is around me and under, the sky is above,
And the waters are bound in their shores.
To an old familiar world I have come forth,
The steady hills and the heavens,
A child born of what darkness, what terror!

"Now has the sun come up upon the hill
And I, new-born, will rise, oh joyously,
And go to Nineveh and do your will."

Part Five: To Nineveh

Like one who wakes at dawn in the half-light
And moves about still burdened with a dream
That had oppressed his slumber, Jonah turned
Into the lower spurs of Lebanon
Eastward towards Damascus. The cold fog
Of morning had drawn off in little clouds
That hung about the sky until the sun
Had caught them all and there was only blue
Over the hills. Through his sea-wearied flesh,
Beaten and sodden, Jonah felt the warmth
Spread like the benediction when soft hands
Press against pain until it is no more.
Even thus he thought of it; his mother's hands
Then when he was a boy in Galilee
And in the dark night cried aloud with fear
Because of some wild dream. The tender thought,
So strange and sweet after the iron years,
Made gentle the worn face and the deep eyes,
And Jonah smiled.
                    Then gradually his mood
Changed as he saw the cedars all about him,
The dark proud trees, the cedars of his God,
And the great mountains rising in the north
Where Jahweh's voice was thunder and his rod
The naked lightning; and his heart swelled
With glory of God and Israel, battles fought

258

And battles yet to be against the hordes
Of vile barbarians, and himself the sword
In Jahweh's hand soon to be raised above
The reeking temples of far Nineveh.

And now there was no smile on Jonah's face.

At dark, just when he thought that he must sleep
Hungry beside the roadway, Jonah saw
A lake and a small stream that entered it
And by the stream a camp-fire burning brightly.
Dark figures moved about the flames and voices
Rolled on the still air, harsh and boisterous,
Or broke in gusts of laughter. Jonah paused
For all the ways were filled with thieves and worse;
But, thinking on the few poor rags that were
His worldly riches, and remembering
The hunger-pinch, with a wry smile he walked
Straight to the fire.
                        Two men who saw him leapt
To him and grasped him fiercely by the wrists
And jerked him to the light. A lazy voice
Said, "Bring him here! A gift from Baal is he,
With money in his pouch? But no, ah no!
A walking skeleton a wretched thing
No better than a straw! A thief, perhaps?"
Jonah looked down and saw lying there,
Propped on one elbow a great mass of flesh
Scantily clad, and an uplifted head,
Gross, heavy-jowled; and lizard-lidded eyes
Surveying him. "I am a traveller
Whom night has overtaken and I would
Eat, have you food to spare." The fat man laughed.
"To spare? We've food enough for every dog
In the whole land. As long as there are goats
Untended, and as long as fowl at night
Sleep with their heads beneath a wing, there'll be
Food at our sitting down. Sit, then, and eat."

They gave him meat and watched in silence while
He ate. A dozen wild and ragged men
Studied each morsel as he lifted it
And proffered more when the first bone was clean
With that deep satisfaction which alone
Those know who starve more often than they feast.

"Now, having filled your belly, fill our ears,"
The fat man said, "with news of the great world.
You come from Tyre, I take it?" "Not from Tyre."
Jonah replied, "Nor does it matter where
I come from, whither I go." The fat man laughed,
Scratching the hair upon his chin. "I've seen
Your kind before. But let me tell you, friend,
The road you came by is the road to Tyre,
And whence you come, why, is your own affair.
They still have virgins, so I'm told, in Tyre:
Damascus has not seen one in an age
Except, of course, in the soft beds of princes,
And I'm no prince. A man grows old apace
Unless he have a virgin now and then
To gasp and cry his strength. The practised ones" —
He heaved a slobbery sigh — "the cunning ones
Have grown too much for me. So I'm for Tyre
To try my luck, and pay the tribute due
To Baal and Astoreth. I'm a Phoenician — "
"I know your people," Jonah interrupted,
"And have found kindness at their hands, but you
Honor them little and your gods even less
(Though they are false and worthy of no honor),
Proclaiming here your kinship with the beasts,
The goat and the wild boar." "False, say you, false?
Ah well, I leave such questions to the priests.
But tell me, friend, out of that beard of yours,
Are there no gods to serve by copulation,
No altars to make spicy with our lust,
None for the belly? Are we men that live
On good fat meat, such as you ate just now,
Or ghosts that feed on prayers and the thin air?
That's been your diet, friend, I would surmise,
Judging by those poor withered shanks of yours.
A ghost," he laughed, "we have for company;
My comrades, let's do honour to a ghost!
Hand me the wine there!"
                But another man,
Marking the scorn on Jonah's angry face,
Touched him and whispered, "Lay your anger by.
He's a great eater, as his belly shows,
And had a woman once and can't forget
The glory of it, and is drunk besides.
Yet is his heart of gold."
                A voice was saying
Across the fire, "What do you know of gods,

You who have never stood in Nineveh
In the great temples and beheld the gods
Who rule the heaven and earth, Anu and Bêl,
Ea, Sin, Shamash, Ninib —" "Spare us the rest!"
The gross man shouted, "Names, and names, and names!
Braying of asses on most barren hills,
And listen while I tell you of a god.
It was in Sidon by a summer sea
In the high place of Baal. The people thronged
About an altar. (From a broken wall
I had a better view than most.) Then when
The hush was deepest came a wedge of priests
Stern in red robes and in their midst a maid
White as a lily. Silently they walked
Through the deep stillness to the altar. There,
While the great host seemed not to breathe, brown hands
Were laid upon the maiden lifting her
High to the altar. Then a song broke forth
From all the priests, standing with upraised hands,
A deep and hollow chant echoing death
And fear and supplication, and the chief
Of all the priests lifted his knife and struck.
Ah, then a sigh went up, a shuddering sigh,
Such as men heave when love has had its way
Or they have drunken deep; and they had drunk
A cup of blood to Baal, a royal cup.
That night," he ended, "by the summer sea
The women of Sidon had an added warmth,
The gift of Baal or maybe Astoreth,
And I —" But Jonah had sprung to his feet
And stood, the firelight flashing in his eyes,
Fists clenched and mouth knotted with rage and scorn.
"Abominable!" he thundered, "Must I see
The loathsome adder and not hurl a stone
To crush it? Must I let the slime of lust
Be spewed upon me and not lift a hand
To strike the offending mouth? And yet not I;
Jahweh, my God, will rise in terrible wrath
To smite the evil; in tremendous flames
Melt the fat hearts of priests and men like you
And with wild terror make your eyeballs burst.
Into your bellies will he set the worm
To twist and gnaw until you cry the hills
To fall upon you, and they will not fall,
Until you sob for mercy and find none.
He that made earth and man and all that is,

The only God, almighty and all-just,
Will not be mocked. A little while your mouths
Will suck the poisoned milk of Babylon,
The unclean breasts of Tyre, and then his hand
Will hurl you and your mothers in the dust,
The vile and haughty cities that you love,
Their temples and their kings and all their priests.
And Israel, his own people, will rise up
Like a great wave and sweep you from the earth.
And where your dens were shall his temples rise,
And where your gods babbled will be his voice,
And where your fat dripped will lie bare his sword
Beside the book of law." He paused and said
More quietly, "Now, even now, I go
To cast his doom on far-off Nineveh,
I, Jonah, prophet of God!"

                                   The fat man laughed.
"Jonah? Did you say Jonah? That means dove;
But sure your mother must have been a raven
So dismally you croak." But when he turned
To look at Jonah, by the sinking fire
Was none but his old friends who sat head bowed,
And in the darkness, going quickly away,
He heard the sounds of footsteps.

                                        Now, like one
Who carries coals across a wide wet field
And fears they may be dead before he reach
His destination, Jonah pushed ahead
Daylong, through twenty days, towards Nineveh.
He passed Damascus with her gleaming spires
Rising above ten thousand trees and saw
Her myriad roofs and briefly thought of all
The stories of her glory, but his heart
Was set against her. What was all the world
But vanity, the pomp of futile kings,
The babbling of mad priests, the delicate
Iniquity of heathen crafts that wrought
Wood, steel, and stone in honour of false gods?
The coals were hungering for Nineveh,
There in his hand, the sleeping fires of God,
And he must hurry.

                            Crossing the Euphrates,
He thought of Babylon, far off downstream,
The wicked city, and half hoped that when
Nineveh lay in ruins God would say,
"Go down and do the like to Babylon."
And his heart laughed within him.

                                    On the plain

Of Syria he passed a hundred cities,
Each in its miles of gardens, till at last,
Beyond the Tigris, veiled in a light haze,
He saw the palaces of Nineveh.

Part Six: Nineveh

Above the press of people in the street
The word "Jonah" hovered like a wild bird
With nowhere to alight. Temple and palace
For days had echoed to the voice declaring
"You all shall die", and now the rumour was
The strange and terrible man would speak once more
This day, for the last time in Nineveh.

Deep in the crowd, locked firmly arm in arm,
Moved three men like a little island floating
Down a wild stream, and on the face of each
Thought brooded in the lines of mouth and brow:
"He is a madman surely, such a one
As now and then the wilderness spews forth,
Who, having eaten his own heart, would tear
The hearts of others with his cry of 'Death'.
They say his garment has been rent by thorns
And the brown flesh shows through it, that his cheeks
Are hollows of grim famine and his eyes
Fever aflame. How could he be a priest
And lack the fine robe and the well-lined belly,
Or how a prophet and so miserable?"
"You count too much on outward circumstance.
My wife said — and she heard him yesterday
While I was busy with that sale of bronze
(Damn those Phoenicians and their bargaining!) —
That every word he spoke was a bright dagger
Poised at her heart. She cried out in the night,
Feeling his eyes upon her, that I woke
And had to soothe her and then soothe myself
With a cold wing of fowl and sup of wine.
But, as I said, there's something in the man
Not altogether comfortable." "I'm struck
Most by his courage. Out of Galilee
They say he came, that long and dangerous way,
With neither man nor beast for company
And among people he could hardly call
Friends of the Hebrews. Such a man must walk
Clad on with something we know nothing of,

Some faith, some knowledge, or, as you suggest,
Mere madness." "Say you? When did madmen ever
Conquer a city with a blast of words?
And Nineveh lies vanquished. Look on these
Who push against us thronging all one way,
Look on their faces, that man's, his and hers,
Intense, pale, empty of everything but that
Which draws them, hope or fear, I cannot tell,
But draws them irresistibly to where
He waits to tell them, what? — That they must die!"
"I think you take all this too seriously.
Our gods have grown so numerous that men
Become bewildered: bend your knee to one,
You seem to turn your back upon another;
Offer a prayer to this one and you find
You should have started lower down. The priests,
Of course, will set you right — at a small fee.
All this you know. But it is very strange
That, when a man stands up, no matter who,
With the right flash of eye and hollow voice
Thundering, 'There is but one true God', men
Should pause to hear him?" "Do you call this 'pause',
These straining bodies, this wild fire of souls,
This vast intoxication? — Here's our turning,
Into the side door there, and let us hold
Firmly together."
                         Within the temple walls
The three were but as drops of water cast
Into a pool already full. So close
The people stood, there was not any movement,
So hushed, not any sound. Far at one end,
Beside the highest altar stood a form
Straight as a spear and dark and ominous,
One with the stillness that filled all the place.
It was a feeding silence such as lies
On earth and heaven before the break of storm,
Or just before the night turns into day,
Or, happiest known, when spring is at the verge.
And he who towered above it, was he spring,
Or daybreak, or red lightning? — Hear his voice.

"Jahweh has spoken!
A trumpet pierces the ears of the city,
A cloud has covered the sun;
In far places the winds of anger are filling
Their arms with dust to cast on the doomed city.

"In his foul den
The jackal has aroused from sleep and licks his paw;
In the heavens the vultures have drawn darkly together
In convocation over the doomed city.

"In my own country
Did Jahweh, Lord of the earth and God of Israel,
Give me a seed of death to plant afar off?
I have borne it safely the long ways and the bitter:
Open your hearts, for the seed is in my hand.

"Behold where I stand!
Is it the altar of Anu? Of Bêl? Of Asshur?
Where is he, then, to bid me stand farther off?
Nor even a priest to pluck me by the garment!

"Fools that you are!
Look on your god there, the black and towering idol,
A bull with his engines of lust and on his shoulders
The head of a man!
Out of sick dreams, the filth of your hearts have you
          made him,
Man-beast who lives alone in the filth of your hearts.

"Jahweh is God
Mighty and to be feared where he rules in heaven
Or plants his feet in thunder upon the hills
Or lifts the sea with his breath.
Height cannot measure him, depth cannot fathom,
Nor can time tell the number of his days.
Before him is strength but the crying of little children
And the pride of man a straw cast into the fire.
Mighty is Jahweh and just;
This above all.
Evil can find no hole to hide from him.
Under the hills, under the waves of the sea,
In the deepest caverns the red sword of his justice
Probes for the cowering game.

"Run then not from him, but stand and die.
For your shame is naked before him and all your evil,
And his word is a net cast on you: 'In forty days
Shall Nineveh be dust.'

"Jahweh has spoken!
A trumpet pierces the ears of the city,

A cloud has covered the sun;
In far places the winds of anger are filling
Their arms with dust to cast on the doomed city,
In the heavens the vultures have drawn darkly together
In convocation over the doomed city."

Part Seven: Vigil

Only some children watched while Jonah built
A hut of palm fronds on a little hill
Outside the city. Why not live below
In one of the cool houses with thick walls
That keep the hot winds out? they asked of him,
And he with eyes suddenly sorrowful
Answered evasively he liked the wind
To blow upon him, and they laughed, it would.

There, on the ground beside the opening
That served as doorway, daylong Jonah sat
Watching the city. Bitterly the sun
Pressed down upon him, but he rarely moved;
And, though the hot winds cracked his lips and filled
His beard with dust, he never turned his face
Away from them for comfort. Like a stone
He would have seemed but for the sombre eyes
Staring upon the city and an air
Of watchfulness about the lifted head.
The friendly children, curious and amused
In the first days, had grown afraid or tired
Of the unknowable man and came no more
To question him. Only a wretched dog,
A city scavenger, lean, mangy, scarred
From many a battle, trotted up the hill
Each day at noon, licked the brown hands and then,
A habit honoured or a duty done,
Went back the way he came.
                                        Nineveh seemed
Asleep within her walls — asleep or dead.
Jonah could see into the streets below him,
And there no people moved; and in the courts
Before the temples was no stir of life.
There was no sound of voices, call of gongs,
No smoke of fires, no torches in the night,
But every day and every night there rose
A sound of sighing borne upon the wind.
And Jonah heard and clenched his fists and struck

The earth and bit his lips.
                    In forty days,
Then twenty, ten — now five.
And still the city stood and still the sound
Of sighing swelled stronger each night, each day.

At noon in the full sun-glare Jonah saw
The punctual dog and would have turned away
His glance as always, but a woman walked
Behind the creature in the narrow path.
Bent lightly to the hill, she had the grace
Of one long used to pathways winding high
Over uneven ground, and her brown robe,
Caught up a little in one hand, seemed less
A garment than a part of her. Had one
Looked with unclouded eyes, he would have known
Her beautiful, a woman neither young
Nor old but in the summer of her days,
And moving with that easy confidence
Only those have whose flesh and spirit are
Parts of a single rhythm. This Jonah saw,
But not with friendly eyes, and would have fled
But anger held him and he set his frown
Against her like a spear poised at her breast.

The dog came bounding joyously, assured
This day was not as other days for when
The stranger joined him was there not a bowl
In the crook of her arm and the good smell of food
Trailing behind her? And his tongue was wet
With more than friendliness on Jonah's hand.

The woman laughed "He likes you; is he yours?"
"Nothing that lives is mine, but I had thought
My privacy at least —" He had arisen
And seemed about to go, but quietly
She laid a hand upon his arm. "No, stay!
Six score thousand in the city wait
But on the day of Jahweh's grace to pour
Their thanks upon you. There will come a host
Out through the gates to this poor shed of yours,
And the brown hill will shake beneath their tread,
And the blue sky will open to their song
Lifted to God in gratitude, your God,
Whose mercy is upon them. On that day,
So soon to be now, like the waves of the sea

Dancing in joy around a little island,
Will they press all about you, singing, singing,
And their hands yearning but to touch your robe,
But, since there are so many, none will touch you.
Therefore, have I come early that my eyes
May look on yours and know that they have seen me
Before the glory of God in awful light
Shuts you for ever from me.
                                              Jonah stood,
Her hand unnoticed on his arm, and stared
Into her upturned face. "What do you speak
Of Jahweh's mercy? Lord of all the world,
He still is not your God but Israel's,
Hers only, and when others hear his voice
It is the voice of anger, not of mercy,
And all his words are doom." "So did you say"
She answered gently, "in the temple there
That strange and terrible day when first you came,
That day whose fruit has grown so sweet. Tell me,"
Her dark eyes held him with their quiet strength,
"When on the darkness there comes up a light,
When out of silence there is born a song,
When the grim desert laughs in bloom, how say I!
When through the reeking chambers of the heart
Moves a sweet wind and every heart is cleansed
And where corruption spawned her filthy brood
Of lusts and fears and pleasures worse than fears
Is peace unutterable and only love
Musing upon her own dear mysteries,
Shall we not say that these things are of God?"
But Jonah answered, "Go! You are a fool!"
"Happier so," her voice shook with the thought,
"Than wise as I was wise, and lost — lost!
And you, Jonah, have saved my soul alive,
And all the thousands in great Nineveh.
What greater glory —" He struck her hand away
Roughly, "Do you tell me of God, who was
His prophet in the great time when his word
Was law and justice, when he spoke with swords
And fire from heaven and his enemies
Fell down before him crying, and in vain?
The warrior God who led his people forth
To slay the wicked and bring low the proud
With their great cities crashing on their heads?
So Nineveh —" She dared his angry eyes,
"Who but a sinner such as I can speak

Of God? Does a child know its father by
The frown that strikes with terror or the hand
Laid soothingly upon its troubled brow,
Quieting pain? I who have felt that hand
Speak what I know. And look on Nineveh:
After the wild delirium she lies
Like a pale child asleep — ah, Jonah, look! —
A child that sinned, was punished, and crept to bed
Sobbing, and fell asleep, but in her dreams
Feels not the anger but the loving hand
And smiles content." Her voice was very low,
"Have you, Jonah, not ever loved a child?"

He did not answer that but turned away
From her and the white city at her back
And went into his hut. She paused to lift
A gourd vine that swung down from the low roof
And looked upon it wonderingly: who set
It here and how on this dry stony hill
Should it have grown so green? She put her bowl
Inside the doorway, "I have brought you food."
She said in gentle tones, "and now I go.
But where I am will you live in my thought,
And in my prayers, lifted by night and day,
Will your name rise beside the name of God."

Jonah sat dully listening to the sounds
Of her departure and with indifferent eyes
Watched the dog gulp the food. Then gradually
His head sank on his breast and while the flies
Made a low buzzing in the stifling hut
He uttered words that were less words than sighs
Out of a heart heavy with weariness
And pain and grief and anger, broken sounds
Like the dull mutter of a spent sea.

Part Eight: The Gourd

On the last day before the fortieth
Jonah moved restlessly about the hut.
He would not let his glance stray to the doorway
And the fierce sunlight that he knew would be
Shimmering on dome and tower and the white walls
Of Nineveh though habit called him forth
To sit and shaft his anger on the place.
Nor would his thought, in its old bed of pain,

Lie straightened and half dead as it had lain
Day after day, but struggled futilely
To go it knew not where. At last Jonah,
Still for a moment, found his maddening cage
Of restlessness flung open. Then he felt
How strangely cool the hut was and how dark
With not a crack to let the sunlight through
Though walls and roof had gaped the day before,
And, wondering how this should be, felt a presence
About him never known before and heard
Himself called though there was no voice. Quickly
He went outside and lo! a miracle:
Where the brown hut had rattled in the wind,
Its palm-fronds shrunk by the long withering,
A shelter even a dog would scarcely pause at,
Was a smooth mound of green like a small wave
Arrested and held still and yet alive
With the light movement of a thousand leaves.
Under the sun-glare Jonah looked at it,
A marvel of leaves and twining brilliant stems,
More wonderful than eye had ever seen,
More pleasant than the nest of any bird,
And Jonah knew that this thing was of God
And went inside to pray.

"I lifted my eyes to the heavens but the fire of the heavens
Filled them and burnt them black;
I turned my eyes to the earth, but the dust of the earth
Smote them with darkness;
On a proud and evil city I hurled the spear
Of Jahweh and it struck and the walls gave back
A tinkling sound of laughter;
For my heart had forsaken the Lord and its trust in the Lord.

"What is the man whose heart has forsaken the Lord?
He is a lion caught out on the plains and wounded
And the hills that would shelter him lie far off,
The well-loved hills beyond the circle of spearman.

"He is the eagle a hunter has long sought after
Struck in the wing at last and he sees the club
Lifted to crush his head and beyond that shadow,
Wide and free, the familiar impossible heavens.

"He is the swimmer whose strength has failed him
Even in sight of the shore and the sound of voices

And who opens his mouth to call but the water closes
Over his head, sealing him in with silence.

"I had forsaken the Lord and my trust in the Lord
For I thought in my pride he had turned away from Israel
And me his prophet and would strip me bare to the laughter
Of all the wicked, the wet red mouths waiting.

"Then was I as the lion, the eagle, the swimmer.
Now have you lifted up your hand to shelter me,
Between my fainting head and the hot sun
Put forth your hand, Jahweh, to shelter me!

"Now is your love a vine
Green, wonderful, out of the stony earth
Come up to shelter me!

"The lion is home in the hills,
Screaming, the eagle soars,
The swimmer laughs by the sea.

"You have given a sign as of old, and I hail it, God!
As your love lies cool on me shall your anger pour
Flame on your foes and mine.
Under the vine of your love I await the day,
Tomorrow, Lord, when the word you spoke through me
Will be an angel of death in the halls of the proud,
And I shall turn homeward to far-off Galilee
With a story of falling towers and breaking walls
For your children, Lord, who await with hungering hearts
The wheels of your victor's chariot drawing home."

Part Nine: The Fortieth Day

Hours before daylight Jonah watched the East.
He sat beside his hut with the black ridge
Before him where the stars began and saw
The stars at last grow dim. A turn of the head
And there lay Nineveh, her towers like ghosts
In the dim light but all the lower mass
Still hidden in darkness. This was her last sleep
And day the executioner drawing near
To wake her with "Arise, your hour has come!"
And Jonah watched them both, the growing light,
The city ever more distinct, and seemed,
So still he was, only another stone

Among the stones of the hill.
                     Just when the red
Began to flood the upper heavens there came
A sound of wind harsh like the rasp of fronds
On palm-trees heard from far and a dark shade
Rose from behind the hill and climbed the sky
Like a great smoke that towered and spread until
All of the East was black, a terrible wave
Of darkness curved and leaning to the fall.
And now the wind struck Jonah's face, a blast
Hot as live breath, and filled with stinging sand,
And a sound half hiss, half thunder filled his ears.
Then did the gaunt man rise to front the storm,
His hair blown back, his garment wildly tossed,
And in a voice breaking with fear and joy
Shouted, "You come! Oh Jahweh, you are here!"
But the wind tore at him so that he clutched
The hut to hold by. There a moment he swayed,
His fingers twisted in the gourd-vine stems,
Steadying himself until a shudder crept
Up through his arms and frightful ghastness fell
Upon his face: the vine beneath his hand
Was dry and dead — dead!

                    Under the shock
Jonah fell to his knees and a great sob
Broke from him, "God why have you done this thing?
The vine that was your love and that I loved
Have you struck dead. The covenant that stood
Between us have you broken and I am
Cast naked out to laughter. I would die.
Let me not live dishonoured among men,
Discredited. You that have taken all
That was my life, crush now the empty shell,
Even with your foot that spurns me!"
                    Then a voice
Stronger than the wind's fury yet not loud
Spoke: "Are you angry, Jonah, that I sent
A worm to kill the vine, because you loved it?
And would you have me lift on Nineveh
My awful hand of death, her six score thousand
Men, women, children who have life like you,
And who from darkness came into the light,
And from my justice have appealed to love?
Nor is there justice, Jonah, without love!"

But Jonah staggered to his feet: "There is
Nothing but darkness left in all the world,
And I would die and pull the deeper darkness
Upon me and have peace. And I will die
Even on this the day of your great mercy
To Nineveh the wicked, for my heart
No longer knows your ways. Let me not live,
Lost as I am, but let the wilderness
Swallow me and not ever give me back
As once you made the sea do, why? oh why?"

Then, while the storm seemed lulled to let him pass,
Jonah went up the hill and from the ridge
Dropped down into the empty wilderness.

Poems from *The Rainbow Serpent* (1962)

The Rainbow Serpent

Summer Noon

The Rainbow Serpent slid between
The hills that lay with open thighs,
(For so he saw them curving through
The lens of lust behind his eyes).

The sun he had not seen nor felt
Through aeons of black loneliness
Pressed on his moving back like hands
In the twin rhythm of a caress

But could not make him pause where he,
Pulsating light in many a hue,
Slid on between the straining hills
To a more urgent rendezvous.

The Serpent's Pool: Morning of the same day

Serpent:
What joy I had in making all these things:
Earth, sea and sky, foot, claw and balanced wings
To lift the eagle! Yes, what joy I had
Making myself a world to drive me mad!

I should have known that, when I'd made the sun
And set the stars in courses they must run,
Hung bloom upon the bough and taught the bee
To make sweet-scented honey from the tree,

And taught man how to find the honeycomb,
I'd nought to do but make myself a home,
Put on the form it pleased me best to keep
Of all that I might wear, and fall asleep.

I'll be a Rainbow Serpent, so I said,
And in this pool prepare my secret bed,
Should any creature call me, I will hear,
Change to his form, and thus to him appear.

And, coiling down deep in this hidden pool,
I proved myself eternally a fool.

My sleep was very pleasant, but it broke,
And, rested from my labours, I awoke
And listened to the voices drifting down
Into my chamber where the light was brown
And made all things seem dim and far away.
I heard a thousand birds up in the day
Talking together and I smiled to hear
Them say what I had taught them. Very clear
The smallest voices came to me, and then
With special joy I heard the words of men
Praising me and my works — a pleasant sound.

The centuries wheeled in their steady round
As I had said they should, and then there came
Upon me a slow nibble of slow flame
That pierced my outer shell and gradually
Ate me to madness. What is this I see
More than a lily floating overhead?
My world a vast, unravished maidenhead,
And I impotent? Where the serpents twine
The deepest copulation should be mine,
Mine and another's — but I lie alone,
A thing that only I myself have known.

The centuries brought madness, but they brought
Another, not less sad, but calmer thought:
I, the one source of all fecundity,
Have none to pour myself into and be
Multiplied past belief. I who prepared
The joys of flesh and — was it rashly? — dared
Loose passion on the world, myself not least
Of passionate things, now stare upon that feast
And, since none ever eats that feast alone,
My passion gnaws me as a dog a bone.

I cannot answer if no one will call
Though I would rush to meet them, one or all,
Any one of my creatures, and consume
Him utterly and in my hunger's tomb
Lock him for ever. But none ever calls,
And the brown light sleeps on my cavern walls
Unshaken by — unshaken? — look again!
Somewhere, far off, upon a grassy plain
Beyond the hills one beckons, the light shakes,
Turns into sound! I hear! the water breaks

Open above me and upon my eyes
Blazes the light of centuries of skies!

Two women, sisters, lying under a tree, talking.

First:
Sister, why can't you be still?
It's cool here and pleasant for sleeping
Stretched out at ease. On the hill
Far off our husband is keeping
Watch for the euro and stalking
Shadow-like, close for the kill.
When we may rest as we will,
Must you keep talking?

Second:
Sprawled like a dog in the dust
Sleep if you must!

First:
Anger? But why? All is well:
There are the yams that we sought,
There lie the lizards we caught,
Here the grass-seed in a shell.
Didn't we talk as we wrought?
Are there more stories to tell?

Second (*tossing down a handful of grass she has been plucking*):
Stories are not for the dead.
Here is more grass for your bed!

First (*rising on an elbow*):
Sister, you always were a little fool;
Crying for summer when the days are cool,
And when the heat comes down upon the plain
Crying your eyes out for the winter rain.
If you could have your wish all things would be
Changed to their opposites continually.

Second:
Have it your way and let the matter pass,
And go to sleep. Another bit of grass?

First (*angrily*):
A digging stick across your shoulders laid —

Second (*scornfully*):
Well, there's your stick and here's my back! Afraid?

First (*after a pause*):
Afraid? Yes, afraid!
Come, leap back from the brink
Our mad anger has made!
Leap back lest we sink
Down from the sunlight for ever
Into that terrible shade!

Second (*shuddering*):
Into that terrible shade!

First (*soothingly*):
Tell me now, sister, what was troubling you
When my unkindness brought this anger on,
And let us laugh the way we used to do,
The happier for a sorrow that is gone.

Second (*eagerly*):
Heart to heart, then! And as I fire the grass
You watch my foolish troubles as they pass
Scurrying for shelter, watch and hurry after
Each one to pierce him with your spear of laughter.
Daylong and nightlong, with a whispering,
Hot and lascivious, a formless thing
Presses my breasts and coils about my thighs
And throngs my blood with little gasping cries.

It speaks to me of things so dark that night
Would be as day beside them, things so bright
That day beside them would be darkness, and
It tries to press them all into my hand.

I cannot hide from it, I cannot shake
Its touch from off my shuddering flesh nor make
Its whispers cease nor still the cries that spring
Out of my blood in horrible answering.

I hurl myself upon the lusts of men.
A moment's respite, then they come again,
The nuzzling and the weight upon my thighs,
The whispers and the terrible answering cries.

Until — until — an hour ago, alone,
There where the sunlight shines upon the stone,
Shuddering with fear and every lust awake,
In agony I called the Rainbow Snake!

The Rainbow Serpent slid between
The hills that lay with open thighs,
(For so he saw them curving through
The lens of lust behind his eyes).

The sun he had not seen nor felt
Through aeons of black loneliness
Pressed on his moving back like hands
In the twin rhythm of a caress

But could not make him pause where he,
Pulsating light in many a hue,
Slid on between the straining hills
To a more urgent rendezvous.

First:
Tortured one! Yet do not fear,
Though you call, he cannot hear,
For the Serpent sleeps by day.
Only when the stars are bright
On the black boughs of the night
Does he wake, and then he may
Hear a call and find his way.

Second:
Never will I call him then!
But, when by our fires we sleep,
Should I stir them till they leap
Bright as day, and angry men
Scold me, say you, too, are chill
And would build them higher still.

First:
That I promise!

Second:
          Sleep then; I
Will keep watch.

First:
       And, watching, try
To forget the Rainbow Snake.
Should he grasp you he would break
The frail vessel of your lust —
Break and crush you into dust.

Second:
Yet to feel all of it, just for an hour,
All the wild surges of power beyond power,
Strength of the hunter, the strength and the cunning,
Speed of the runner and joy of the running,
Rage of the eagle and cry of the plover,
All in the arms —

First (*earnestly*):
       Oh hush! Be still!
Look yonder in the shadow of the hill
One comes towards us at a hunter's speed,
Our husband, surely, and I'm glad indeed!

Second (*excitedly*):
No, not our husband! See how tall and strong
He is and with what power he strides along!

First (*sadly*):
A stranger, then.

Second:
A stranger, but not one
Who hides his face from daylight and the sun.
Sister, if he demand of us, shall we
Grant him the traveller's ancient courtesy?

First (*wearily*):
If he demand, it is the law, we must.
But do not spread your charms abroad and thrust
Yourself upon him.

Second (*eagerly*):
See, he waves in greeting!

Stranger (*coming up*):
Who could have dreamt of such a pleasant meeting!
I saw you from far off and thought I would
Make myself known as every traveller should

In a strange country. Do not be afraid
But give me drink and let me share the shade
Here with you for a moment.

First (*in dull tones, as she rises and walks slowly to far side of the tree*):
                I will get
Some water and some food for you — and yet —

Stranger (*in a low, tense voice to Second*):
You are the fairest woman on the earth,
Fairer than day's red dying and red birth,
Fairer than moonlight or the brightest star,
And dearer than all these to me you are.
Out of the shadows of a distant place
I have come far to look upon your face.

Second (*as in a trance*):
You are the voice that cried within my blood
Until I called the —

First (*her voice hard but with overtones of fear*):
                Stranger, here is food —
Eat! and here water — drink! Then, if your way
Be long, there is but little left of day.

[*The man leaps up and dashes water and food from her hand.*]

Stranger:
Water and food! My hunger and my thirst
Are not for these!

First (*shrieking wildly*):
                Then may you be accurst!

[*The man gathers the entranced woman in his arms and runs swiftly off with her.
Her sister, her voice dropping to a hoarse whisper, sinks to the ground.*]

First:
                It is the Snake, the Snake! In pity spare! —
But no — his flashing eyes, his floating hair!
There is no pity there!

In a Yackandandah Garden

Sultry Evening

The sky is swollen with thunder ripe to break,
And every bud's importunate to make,
Tomorrow, in the drift of gentle showers,
The other, lovelier lightning of the flowers.

Storm

The storm has set the willows in a stir;
They toss their branches, and they all are hair
Blown wildly, Maenad-like, as only woman
Can use a storm to magnify the human.

Iceland Poppies

How queenly in the wind they toss and sway,
Their stage the pomp of each November day,
But I most love them when toward night the bees
Have brought them at least partway to their knees.

To a Blackbird

Best stop your talk about "Where are you working?"
Because I'm not; and, if I should be shirking
The woodheap and the axes and the saws,
It may well be that you are half the cause.

Cicadas in February

What subtle gearing
Moves this sound
Through cool tree-ducts above hot ground,
What subtle gearing
And how profound!

One need not love it,
The hot, dry, shrill
Song that ties valley to neighbouring hill,
One need not love it
But ah! the skill.

A thousand singers
All drunk with heat

Say how the summer is hot and sweet;
A thousand singers,
A single beat!

A thousand singers
With fife and gong
Say how the summer is hot and strong,
A thousand singers,
A single song!

What subtle gearing
Moves this sound
Through cool tree-ducts above hot ground,
What subtle gearing
And how profound!

One Way to Fame

He was an actor always off the stage
Arguing with the prompter; thus he got
A reputation as a mighty sage
With those who paid to see, and saw him not.

The End of Eloquence[18]

His words that once, like Moses' wrath, made blind
The sun with a massed arrogance of wings,
Now straggle down the flyways of the mind,
So very few, and such bewildered things.

Cemetery at Yackandandah

You, whose mouths scorned, the dry Australian way,
To speak of beauty or confess her charms,
Now sleep — you had no choice — all night, all day,
Locked in the deep enchantment of her arms.

Lizard

You must know lots and lots about the sun;
And you would tell me, were I only one
With soul enough, throughout the changing year,
To bend to you, and sense enough to hear.

---

18   An earlier version published in the Summer, 1959 issue of *Northwest Review* read "Now
      falter down the flyways..." and "So very few and such pathetic things."

Magpies in the Rain

My eyes were gloomy at the rain
Because I had a patch to weed
Where grass and nettle walked again
Sowing their dragon-teeth of seed.

My eyes were gloomy at the rain,
But then two magpies sang together
And suddenly my heart and brain
Laughed Jason-like at the foul weather.

Kookaburras at Evening

The kookaburra laughs a tree
Into the sky when day is done
And leaves it there for all to see,
Anchored against the setting sun.

The kookaburra's very clever:
Have you or I
Lifted a tree — now tell me — ever,
By hoists of laughter to the sky?

Morning[19]

Magpies unlock the day;
Then it's for me to say
What track I'll follow.
The wren's no help at all
With his gay harem call,
Nor, from his pulpit-wall,
The parson-swallow.

I have, myself, to choose;
And, if I win or lose,
Have luck or sorrow,
The kookaburra will
Lock up my day until
The magpies on the hill
Unlock tomorrow.

---

19   Originally appeared in the *Bulletin* (Sydney) under the title "Riverina Morning" on Dec.
21, 1955.

Summer Evening

Now let the evening fold us gently in,
Children of grace, and certainly of sin:
Let be for all the one grave, deep delight,
Man knows alone at coming in of night.

The magpie has a hundred things to say
He quite forgot through the long drowsy day;
Or he was wise to keep his last and sheer
Music until a star should come to hear.

And may this music and this listening star
And this delight be with us still when far
From the safe harbors of the day we creep
Across the lonely oceans of our sleep.

Two Ships to Mitylene
(Based on Toynbee's translation of Thucydides, Book III, Chapters 35-50)
For Professor John La Nauze

The black ship and the white, a sea apart,
Moved toward the dawn and Lesbos. "Let the dawn
Be rosy-fingered over Mitylene,
Not red with blood," Diodotus had ended
The hot debate in Athens; by a vote
Favouring him, as thin as a sword's edge,
His plea for mercy sent the white ship out
One night and one long day behind the other.

War, the deep cancer, long had flourished in
The body of the Empire, pushing up
Protuberant generals and the lesser lumps,
Orators, politicians, patriots,
And breaking the fair skin with open sores
Of treachery and sour vindictiveness,
And wracking all the haemorrhages of hate.
Athens was sick, yet the strong heart beat on
Nourishing Plato, itself nourished by
The blood of Socrates, the unspent power
Of Homer and the cauterizing wit
Of Aristophanes.

Now Mitylene,
Wedded to Athens, played whore with Lacedaemonia
And, caught as Aphrodite had been caught

By her lame spouse, lay naked, waiting judgment.
But this was not Olympus and no gods
Thronged round the bed to leer at her ripe beauty
And laugh at and half envy the red Ares
Locked with her in the net. Here were no quips
Such as gods make, the laughter-loving ones,
But, with all Athens hanging on his words,
Cleon, in full address: "What empire is
I should not need remind you, but I fear,
Drunk with the wine dispensed by orators
In golden chalices of words, you have
Fallen into a soft forgetfulness
Of everything but wine, wine, wine, more wine.
Empire is power, the power that holds in chains
All that is weaker than itself; it asks
No pity and gives none; self-interest,
Tempered by justice, is its only law —
Justice, not mercy. Do you think allies,
Won by the sword and held but by the sword,
Are such for love of you? Self-interest sways
Their lives and yours. Would you cut off a hand
Because your neighbour, who pretends he loves you,
Asks you to do it? Quickly you would hear
His mocking laughter on your no-hand side
And, on the same side, pointed at your throat
See poised his bright unsentimental sword.
Empire is power, and power is but for him
Who knows the way to wield it. Have you known,
Simpletons that you are, of any man
Choosing to be a slave, of any nation
Choosing to serve another when it might
Have ruled instead? The perverse spirit of man
Keeps him a rebel. Who would govern men
Must note the head that's lifted up too high
And lop it off.

      "And now for Mitylene.
She was our ally and we trusted her
And pampered her until contempt drove out
Her fear of us, and seeing us beset
By enemies, she leapt to join their ranks.
With no compulsion other than her own
Evil desires she struck the dastard blow
Against us. Do you think that had she won
She would have drooled in pity over us?
But Paches our good general saw to that;

He hurled her to the dust and there she lies
Writhing like the crushed serpent that she is.
Glib orators, drunk with their own importance,
Will charm your ears with words: 'Humanity',
'Pity', 'good nature' — the stock-in-trade of weakness!
It was our softness that begot her crime,
And so the crime is ours; and shall we now
Forgive her and thus sin a second time?
Pity her and you teach all our allies —
Those we have left — the way to follow her:
'Why not revolt with freedom as the prize,
No punishment to fear if we should fail?'

"Let this assembly take the wiser course,
The course of strength, not weakness, of self-interest
Which is the only good for Athens. Feel
As then you felt when first the knife was plunged
Between your shoulders; let retaliation
Be swift and sure. All men in Mitylene
The leaders and the led, the high, the low,
Must die at once, all women and all children
Be sold as slaves."
              And Athens voted "aye".

Then in the evening a black galley slipped
Out through Piraeus to the open sea,
Moved southward for a while, then turned north-east
Towards Lesbos. And the captain, Phides, spoke
When the first rollers lifted the curved prow:
"Row as you like, you bastards, as you like!
I've sent this ship to war a score of times;
Then, if you'd miss a stroke, the lash would bite you
Across the shoulders and I'd lay it on
Hard, for the work was work for men. But now,
Row as you like, for we are turned to butchers
By the command of Cleon. Here it is —
You see this parchment? — half a hundred words
Will set the blood frothing in Mitylene
Down all the streets, or will we line them up,
The young men and the old, the high and the low,
Where the dry sands will drink the slaughter up?
That Paches will decide, for ours is but
To bear the mandate and help out a little
Should he lack swords and executioners.
I have a captain's office and this ship
Must on to Mitylene, but how fast

I leave to your own hands or to your hearts,
If you still have such." "Well, I'm damned!" a rower
Said, slumping on his oar, "Girls, what a picnic!
D'you bring your fish-line, Chloe, and a cushion
To put beneath your bum? It's warm in Athens
And the sea air is just the thing we need.
Now, Heracles, don't dip so bloody deep!
You heard the captain — or you'll scare the fish."
"Cut out the chatter," someone growled. "I've killed
My men but never one with empty hands
And neck stretched out like a damned fowl's—God damn you,
Cut out the chatter!" And the first replied
With a low cackle, "Grown a little edgy,
Now ain't he, boys? Can't take a little joke
The way it's meant. But when it comes to necks,
I'd sooner slit than be slit, that's the truth.
And what's the use of worrying? Cleon said,
'Kill the damn' lot' — now ain't that what he said?
'Kill the damn' lot'? So here we go, me boys.
He didn't ask us one way or another
And if he had I s'pose I might have said,
Feeling important, 'Kill the bloody lot',
Or 'Let 'em go, poor bastards.' Anyway,
It's nothing to get edgy at." "You beast,"
A tense voice said, "You worse than any beast,
To talk of life as though it were the slops
Tipped by a chambermaid, to talk of death
As though it were a little harmless joke
Played by an urchin on his grandfather
Asleep before the fire. There will be
Lined up at Mitylene wife and man,
The one to watch the other die and then
Feel round her waist the arms of such as you
Comforting her, you'd call it, with your hands
Red and lascivious. Have the decency
To keep your lusts in their own secret sty
And let us go the terrible way we must
At least unfilthied by such dung." "Well now,"
A new voice said, for night was on the sea
And men were only voices in the dark,
"Praise be the gods there are the gods,
And under them the statesmen such as Cleon
Who tell us what to do and what to think.
They are our conscience, and our actions are
Only our muscle doing what their brain
Tells us to do. This thing in Mitylene

Is not our making. Doubtless they are guilty
And should be punished, but I hope my oar
Rots in the sea before I make a step
Firmly on shore and heave the dry sword up
To drink their blood — be that reserved for Cleon.
Meanwhile, the sea is easy, and I'll sleep."
"Upon my soul," one muttered, "there must be
Virgins in Mitylene, ripe to pluck,
And Athens keeps them from us behind walls
High, of respectability; the conqueror
Takes as he chooses — where's that oar of mine!
Wake up, Dardanius, you beside me here,
Let us be on our way!" And then the captain,
His supper done, stood on the rowers' deck
And called out loudly: "Rest upon your oars.
The ship is on her course to Mitylene —
That's all I care. After the night the dawn,
And then another day and then a night
And after that a dawn not rosy-fingered
But dripping all with blood. Rest on your oars."

That night men strolling in the streets of Athens
Exchanged the usual greetings, but instead
Of passing on, drew into little groups
Eagerly as though fleeing solitude.
Some had come forth from homes where women's eyes
In wordless inquisition forced them to
Answers they dared not make; some from lone rooms
Where the old comfortable silence had
Turned to a Nessus' shirt. All were abroad
By some compulsion that made faces tense
Under the torchlight, and from not a group
(Where must have lingered many a merry man)
Came the least sound of laughter. What the night
Heard were the words of Cleon dropped like swords
On the rough stones, dull swords flung down by men
Who, as they talked, looked anxiously north-east
To where the stars hung golden over Lesbos.

Dawn found the restless mutterings of night
Settled into a clear and strong demand
That Athens think again on Mitylene.
At noon the Assembly met, and angry Cleon,
His mouth a-twitch with scorn but his voice cold,
Opened debate: "At last I see why Empire
Is not for Athens; how should Athens grasp

The naked sword-blade pointed at her breast
And snap it when her hands are soft as women's
Or milk-fed babes'! Statesmen you call yourselves
Importantly, and yesterday you passed
Statesman-like judgment on your enemy.
But you had dreams last night and now you cry
Like frightened children and would fain undo
What would have made you honoured among men.
The wrong you suffered still remains a wrong,
And justice still is justice, power power,
And man is man as he is strong and just.
Be men then, and do not undo yourselves
With idle words and by this vile debate
Cast Athens to the laughter of your foes!"

Then rose Diodotus, so quiet a rising
That, till he spoke, none knew that he was there:
"Who scorns debate is either knave or fool.
Raw haste and passion, natural as they are
To man, are fatal to all statesmanship,
Whose very soul is policy, not force.
Grant Mitylene wrong and make her crime
As heinous as you wish, it still behooves us
As statesmen to think not on what she did
But how it profits us to deal with her.

"Ten thousand corpses heaped upon the earth
Will testify, no doubt, to our revenge;
Ten thousand women bear the lesson on
Through the next score of years for men to read
Stamped in their hollow eyes. And how shall this
Profit us here in Athens? Will it bring
Gold to our coffers? Will it bind our friends
Closer to us and warn our enemies
'Beware the power of Athens'? Gold comes not
From rotting flesh nor from the ash of cities
Laid waste by fire, and friends are hardly won
By reckless pouring out of blood. Our foes,
What will they learn from this? Here let us pause.
Empire is power, as Cleon has informed you,
And, as he said, no man submits to power,
No man or nation willingly. Revolt
Is natural to man as it is natural
For the penned bull to try with slashing horns
To gut his keeper. Be the keeper wise,
He'll crop the impulse with his whip and so

Prevent the act, not first be mauled and then,
In spendthrift anger, strike the herd's sire dead.
Slaughter the Mityleneans and we teach
All the penned cattle that we call our Empire,
'Lift but a horn and you shall feel — the whip? —
No, not the whip, but death. Better then let
Your instinct launch you boldly at our breast
With all your savage power, for if you fail
You can have only death!' And this we call
Policy, we the men of subtle Athens!
This were an act of weakness and not strength,
Weakness driven mad by fear.
       "Let us be just:
Punish the leaders, let the led go free;
For the first task of justice is to make
That grave distinction. Hers the scales and not
Only the unsheathed sword.
       "I say no more.
And what I urge springs out of no such pity
As Cleon laughs at but the clear self-interest
Alone of Athens. Yet in after-days —
I do not urge this on you, but I'll say it —
Should men behold that Athens was not only
Strong, and not only just, but merciful,
This might not be so very bad a thing."

Thus ended the debate, and by a vote
Favouring him, as thin as a sword's edge,
Diodotus prevailed.
       The afternoon
Was half spent when a long white galley slipped
Out through Piraeus to the open sea,
Moved southward for a while, then turned north-east
Up towards Lesbos. At the straining oars
Sat the best rowers in Athens, such a crew
As would have made Odysseus' heart leap up
With pride or won Alcinous' praise. A wind
Blew to the north, a wind that made the sea
Buoyant beneath the sliding keel and carried
To every ear the shrill sound of the pipe
Setting the rhythm for the flashing oars.
And now the captain spoke: "Travel the crests
My lads, and never mind about the hollows.
Make the sea smoke beneath you. There is wine
To drink whenever you will and there are cakes
Of barley for a ten times longer voyage.

Row till you feel your strength at ebb, then eat
And sleep while fresh men row. You are the ones
Chosen by Athens to keep bright her name
Before the world. For you it is to write
The words upon this parchment into action
With your strong sweep of oars. Make the sea smoke,
And I shall watch you with unsleeping eyes
And proud heart till we touch at Mitylene.
The black ship will go slowly, that I know.
I stood by Phides when they ordered him
To take her out, and saw his cheek grow pale
And the quick frown that came upon his brow.
He shot a lost look at me and went off
With slow step and bent head. However great
The odds against us, greater is the prize
We strive for in the name of Athens. Think
This ship an arrow and yourselves the hands
That speed it from the bow. Then, if the gods
Favour us, we shall touch at Mitylene
Before the swords are out. Lift up your prayers
To them and know that they have ever honoured
Courage and strength and skill."
      "Trust us," a voice
Called cheerily, "good Menos, and we'll show you
A wake that will be white still at Piraeus
When we have run her up upon the sands
There where we're going!"
      Then the ship became
As taut with power as is a strong bow bent
And silent as an arrow in mid flight.

A night, a day, another night they shot
Their strength out through the oars, and when that strength
Could scarcely answer to the captain's pipe,
Dawn showed their bloodshot eyes the dusky hills
That sheltered Mitylene. They drove in
With one last surge of power that lifted them
High on the beach. Then every man stood up
In the white ship and stared with haggard eyes
At a black galley on the sands beside them
With not a man in her. "Too late," they sighed
And sank back wearily upon their benches.
But Menos leapt ashore. "No, not too late!"
He shouted, "Look up there — that open space
On the hillside! Those are the men and youths
Being herded in to die. Those herding them —

See there the glint of arms! — are Paches' men
Turned executioners. Stay with the ship
While I try what these legs of mine can do
In this short race with death!"
            He sped away
And in the stillness every man could hear
A sound that seemed to hang above the city
More like a cloud than sound, and one man said,
"It is the cry of women", and another,
"It is the cry of women."
            On the hill
Menos found all things ready for the slaughter:
The victims in their thousands, very quiet,
Drawn up in long thin lines; in front of them,
And still as they, the soldiers with bared swords.
And on an eminence commanding all
Stood Paches regal in his robes of power
About to give the signal with raised hand
But waiting till the dawn should fire the sky
With colour, for he'd said the night before,
"At rosy-fingered dawn it is you die."

Nearing him, Menos called, "I come from Athens
With orders for her general — you are he?"
"I have that honor, but the orders must
Wait till I have the time —" "The time is now,"
Menos said boldly, "Read!" Then Paches took
The parchment like a man disturbed at business
He'd given his heart to, read, then frowned, glanced up,
Then read again, then shifted on his feet,
Then read again. At last he turned to one
Resplendent almost as himself, but with
The difference that shows master from factotum,
And snapped: "Here, read this out! It comes from Athens —
Athens who seems to like to foul her nest
With dung of weakness! Read it out, I say
And, while you're at it, read it with some warmth,
As though it came from me — curse the damn' fools!"

The reading was not long. And then the dawn
Was rosy-fingered over Mitylene
While Menos, arm-in-arm with Phides, walked
(Simple Athenians a long way from home)
To find a jug of wine, and Paches stared
With angry eyes upon a laughing sea.

Dear Coleridge
Dorothy Wordsworth on the night before William's marriage

Not even God! Only a lidless eye
You could not hide from since it had no sight,
The omnipresent sea. And on the deck

Those uncapped vials with their precipitate
(The Curse), where Death played chemist — Death or you.
Fear is, so William says, for noble minds
The ear that catches whisperings of God
That swell the heart with power. What did you hear
That turned your heart to dust, O Coleridge,
Alone, alone, upon a wide, wide sea!
She must have helped you, softly going up,
As here tonight she swims above the hill,
Our moon — and do you see her? You have been
Her nursling ever and she helped you then,
Loosening the clutch of horror at your heart
Until the spring of love gushed clear once more.
Bright, bright she is as when we walked together
And the sea lay below us big and white,
Swelled to the very shores, but round and high
In the middle, and you spoke the lines again,
Drawing me deep and breathless to your fear.
I think I took your hand, for I remember,
Later, on parting, how cold your fingers were,
As though you had been holding hands with Death
Before I half-surprised you.
        Had that been true
I could have warmed them, but your voice betrayed
A previous commitment, let us say,
And not to Death. He moved not in your voice
Nor could you find a word — not even you —
To bring him up beside us. No, not Death!
But how you trembled when you spoke her name,
Trembled with fear that was half tenderness
And all an ecstasy! Her yellow locks,
Her bold eyes and her red alluring lips,
And the — O God! — the whiteness of her skin!
It was her kiss that froze your very blood,
And I, who could have mastered Death for you,
Had to let go your hand. We parted where
The wood shut out the moonlight; in the dark
Took, chill and wordless, each his own way home.

Long, long ago — or was it yesterday?
You parted from us and the house was still
As memory itself. Your lost voice made
A yearning in my blood; your vanished eyes
Haunted me with their sorrows and wild dreams,
Till I could bear no more and wept aloud.
"But hush, my dear, your nervous blubberings,"
William said gently, smiling his old smile.
It was not so! I could have hated him
For that hard lie. O Coleridge, you twist
My heart too much; you wring the poison out
And make it visible. Had he but known
Who waited for you just beyond my sight
He would have laid a hand upon my head
And spoke no word.
        I fought devils for him,
And not in vain. "She gave me eyes": to see
The sparrow's egg, daisy and celandine,
Mountain and lake and star. "She gave me ears":
To hear the skylark singing heaven down
Upon his nest on earth; "and humble cares":
Twigs gathered in the woods that yet could make
Our hearth a blaze of living Presences.
"And delicate fears": ah yes, I would not brush
The dust from off, and was it Psyche's wings?
"A heart, the fountain of sweet tears": but there
How can a brother know? "And love, and thought,
And joy"! He *is* my brother, Coleridge!

She is a sham that holds you! From the wreck
Of Revolution and the more difficult dust
Of love gone dead, I raised a poet up.
How should you think I could not then lift you?

Sara was but a punctuation mark,
Part of the grammar of Pantisocracy;
A peg to hang a dream on, and the dream
Blown off, she sticks out naked from the wall.
You could have loved her well and made her live
But that you love your visions and her eyes
Are sealed to all the far ways of your seeing,
And that her feet will never let the moonlight
Show how blue-veined they are.
        The last red leaf
And did you see it first, or was it I?
What matter, so we made of that poor thing,

That bit of soon-to-be-returned-to-earth,
A fluttering pennant of unearthliness!
A leaf does have its part in the wind's song,
And I in yours. Does the moon know herself
Fairer than when she finds a lake to show
Herself her golden beauty? That last moon,
The one that held the old moon in her arms
And was encircled by a silver thread;
The one by whose pale light you sang the dirge,
August and splendid, for a poet dead,
Even that moon was mine! I gave her to you
Who threw a brightness on your going out,
A last grave splendour on your fallen brow.

"The Ballads are not liked at all by any."
She who made that a letter's afterthought,
Wielding her postscript like a household broom
To sweep the Quantock stardust from her floors —
(You didn't ever learn to wipe your feet) —
She would not, could not, push me from your side,
For only spirit can behold a spirit
And to her eyes I was invisible.

Who gave you honey-dew to feed upon,
Offering it on her lips that you might live
Only by kisses? Milk of Paradise
Sweet with the sleeping poison of wild dream?
Who drew the temperate blood from out your veins
And thronged them with hot tongues, O Coleridge,
Until your heart was fevered into dust
Stirred only be her whisper and you lay
Alone? Alone? — Would God it had been so! —
Terribly companioned on the wide, wide sea.

I could have won you from her, for I have
Something of her own beauty and strange power;
And your sick loathing of her would have helped,
And the great hills and the clean winds of heaven,
The lakes and streams, and every flower and bird,
As once they helped me lead a poet back
Into the sunlight. How I fought, and with —
Now they lie broken — what sad instruments!
I did not pray the stars to help me, but
Gathered them like sweet apples for your food,
Bold at the branch of heaven. I made the winds
Speak to your ear intelligible things,

Bright challenges to the proud lists of song,
And when you roused and took their gauntlet up,
You were my knight. And is this then a tale
Woven by fancy to pleasure sick desire?
So, let me speak more humbly. On a day
When the clear winter sunlight slept upon
Meadow and hill as only winter sunlight,
Having no work to do, lies tranquilly,
I saw the hips red-ripe upon the briars
How beautiful they were! And there I stood
Waiting till William and the rest had gone
And I was quite alone. Breathlessly then
I snatched the fruit and ate, whispering your name!
Humbly, my heart? But God will have the truth:
The Journal you and William chuckled over
Wears never a sacrament upon its sleeve!

But she who is as close to you as flame
Is to the wood that feeds it; she who lies
Waiting for you in every cursed bed
With yellow hair and red lips opening
(Ah, God, not that! Let me be blind…be blind!)
She would not lose you lightly. Even I
May come to admire her cunning when she plucked
Your eyes from me and sent them hungering after
A woman innocent as children are,
Who would but think of her as a grim fiction
Lost somewhere in a poem.
          Coleridge,
When Sara with her naive eyes looks up
Blankly into the anguish of your own
And with a smile snaps all your strings of passion,
Leaving you mute and safe, I see that harp,
A dead man stretched face-up upon a deck
With staring eyes that look but on themselves,
The empty sky and the wide stagnant sea.
And you will never hear my feet beside you
Pacing that deck. She will take care of that,
The jealous Bride — she will take care of that!
"The blessing of my future years" … so God
Keeps madness from me. A great poet's need
Accepts the sister-poet thankfully.
Deep in that grove of love are tranquil places,
Green shades and quiet thoughts and I must win
So far, so deep into those solitudes
That never from wild shores again will reach me,

Is it my own voice or another's wailing,
A woman wailing for her demon lover!

Indoors with me! William is surely waiting,
And wondering where I am. How dark it is!
The moon is down and I have missed the path.
William will laugh at me, my dearest William,
Who knows this path so well or any path
Once he has walked upon it. The hour is late,
And I'd not blame him should he chide a little …
Tomorrow is my brother's marriage-day!

Elegy for a Teacher
In Memory of Howard Rice Taylor

In a Sicilian valley, long ago,
The shepherds rose to find the stars grown dim
And dawn already leaning from the low
Familiar summit of the eastern rim.

And when they went to drop the sheep-fold bars
And drive the flocks to pasture on the height,
One whispered to his fellows, "See the stars!
Surely they have known trouble in the night."

And one said, "Listen to the wind go by,
That used to sport with us at break of day;
Its voice has fallen to a listless sigh
And it would seem to have no words to say.

"And look upon the hills that used to tilt
Their heads to drink the light as at a cup;
Like flowers the worm has found they gloom and wilt,
Their heads are bowed, their faces muffled up."

Then eyes sought eyes, and hands were clasped in hands,
And, speaking very softly, someone said,
"He has gone out from the familiar lands
To a far place — Daphnis our friend is dead.

"Come let us seek the spot that knew him best
And there, remembering all his works and days,
Weave them in words and send him to his rest
Garlanded with our sorrow and our praise."

In a Sicilian valley, long ago,
Thus did the shepherds; and Theocritus
Gave their lament to time, and the deep flow
Of centuries has brought the song to us.

For there was never a valley, plain or hill
Whose stars have not known trouble in the night,
And never a wind that has not fallen still
Because the dawn was emptied of its light.

And though men sing a thousand songs that tell
Of love and laughter, and the end must be
Heard, like the tolling of a distant bell,
The song the shepherd sang in Sicily.

He whom we mourn
Was one who rejoiced in his strength,
Who loved the ardour of dawn
And the height and the length
Of mountains against the sky,
And who set his foot and his hand
Bold on the uphill land
To follow the track of his eye.
And the mountains were glad
As a man when the arms of his son
Clutch hard on his shoulders in play;
And they told him the joy that they had
When the difficult summit was won
By the beauty they cast on his way.

Rivers that leap
From the heights where the tree-line is passed
And the glaciers dream in their sleep
Of the seas that shall fold them at last,
He sought, not the placid, the tame,
And he strove in a happy strife
With their speed and their strength and their life
For no prize save the joy of the game.

No prize? But the kind gods sent,
Unasked, what was more than a prize:
It was clear in his voice, in the bent
Of his brow, in the light of his eyes.

All that is man
He looked on with eager gaze

In the hope to discover the plan,
The rhythm and dance of our days;
And, whatever it was that he saw,
He followed his own heart's law
Less ready to blame than to praise.
Yet, in the rush and the swing
Of the turbulent dance of the years,
Even the littlest thing
Caught at his love and his fears —
A bird just beginning to sing,
A child first acquainted with tears.
His heart beat warm
And his mind went paired with his heart
Through the calm and the storm
Of his days, the joy and the sorrow,
For he held all these in his vision but as a part
Of the vast, the unknowable whole,
Where one day's end is the pledge of another morrow
For man, and a life's best goal
Is the strong, the compassionate soul.

That goal he won,
High-hearted, with force unspent.
And, or ever the race was run,
Be glad that we saw it, the prize,
In the tones of his voice, in the bent
Of his brow, in the light of his eyes.

In a Sicilian valley, long ago,
The shepherds mourned for Daphnis. Grief is young
For ever, and lives on, but even so
Lives the good fame that never can be sung.

In Memoriam E. C. A. Lesch

He whom I speak of was a crag-like man,
Firm in his standing and deliberate-paced
In all his goings, and the strength of stone
Was in his brow and face. Storm-driven ones
Found shelter in his lee as by a cliff
Travellers take rest and smile at the loud storm.
Those who, plumed-up for strife, struck hard upon
His steady front felt the deep granite-bruise
The hurl had cost them and could still be proud
To have matched their strength with his.
            A crag-like man!

Yet, as the crag nurtures the tenderness
Of moss and lichen and the wispy fern,
So he in thought and word and action wrought
A gentleness upon himself and all
Who sought for gentleness.
                    Since memory
Garners one blossom from a teeming garden,
One color from a score of rainbows, one
Star from a thousand nights of stars, I take
These single things to speak my thought of him:

His fingers loved the frost within the earth
And then the thawing and the breathing roots —
Loved them and knew their ways. The talk that trees
Have with each other in the quiet hills
Was as well known to him as speech of friends
Living or poets dead. At earliest dawn
He sought his farmyard with a word for all
The animals, joyous this side of night,
That looked to him for food; a good gruff word;
Perhaps, his morning's lecture in his mind,
A salt Shakespearean quip, then on his way
To wonder, audibly, at eight o'clock,
While the class sat expectant, if a dog
Had not, maybe, a better comprehension
Of Shakespeare than most sophomores had. The smile
With which he said it made it very clear
That he cared much for sophomores *and* for dogs.

Teacher we called him but in fact he was
Rather a co-creator who made live
The poet's vision with an eloquence
That matched the poet's own. With equal power
He trod the comic and the tragic stage,
Held the most fragile poem that the light
Might wake its opal meanings, boisterously
Roared Bottom's lion or stood hushed with awe
At the cathedral grandeur of a thought
Risen from the dust of half a thousand years.
That was his greatness. Lower in the scale,
He knew and used and loved the teacher's tools:
The startling question, the quick jest, the rope
Payed out to let a dullard hang himself,
The stinging comment, the quick word of praise.
He was a teacher, take him all in all,
We shall not look upon his like again.

He loved the forum when debate ran high
And all the stratagems of argument
Were on the move. Rock-fast to principles,
He still enjoyed the skirmish where his wit
Flashed like sword-lightning in the smoke of words.
Stubborn at times he was, but never dull.
Not always right, but never meanly wrong.

Now at the last I see him with his books
That were as dear to him as any thing
A man may turn to in the deep of night
In search of his own soul. A poet's book,
That poet Wordsworth and that poet's truth
The one we mourn held sacred: "I have felt
A presence that disturbs me with the joy
Of elevated thoughts; a sense sublime
Of something far more deeply interfused
Whose dwelling is the light of setting suns,
And the round ocean and the living air,
And the blue sky, and in the mind of man;
A motion and a spirit, that impels
All thinking things, all objects of all thought,
And rolls through all things."

The Lightless Ferry

Introductory Note

I do not want to be in the position of an author reviewing his own book or attempting to tell his hoped-for reader what he should find in it. However, my subject is capable of so many different treatments and interpretations that I feel it not improper for me to comment briefly on my materials and my handling of them.

The idea for the poem came to me when I had returned to America after a trip through Central Australia and a short stay on the Aborigine Reservation at Delissaville, and, in the University of Oregon Library, was rereading Sir Baldwin Spencer's *Wanderings in Wild Australia*. There, in Volume Two, I was most forcibly struck by a series of pictures of the death and burial rites of a Central Australian tribe. I soon found myself constructing a poetic text for these pictures.

Inevitably I had to rush in where angels fear to tread and anthropologists walk with caution; for I had to decide what beliefs to use as the animating spirit of the rites depicted. I had to cross the quicksands of interpretation.

My bridge — if I may call it that — is as follows: Death is not a product of natural forces, but of magic directed upon the individual by an enemy, often a member of a distant or a hostile tribe. By magic this man introduces into the body of his victim an object — a bone, a lump of wood, a stone — which, unless speedily removed, will cause his death. The tribal medicine men gather round the stricken one, locate and identify the foreign substance, and, by magic of their own and various physical manipulations, attempt to draw it out of him.

At his death man's spirit leaves the body and starts upon his journey into the Dream-time, or, as we think of it, eternity, sometimes taking the form of a bird or other living thing. The spirit of the murderer lurks near by, anxious to do more evil.

However, possibly because it fears the long journey, the spirit of the dead may try to slip into the body of a living person. Should this happen, the unfortunate host will sicken and die. To prevent such an occurrence and to send the spirit confidently on its way, the tribe must carry out ceremonies, a knowledge of which — though the meanings of many of these practices are not understood by the performers — has been transmitted through uncounted centuries from some point lost in "the dark backward and abysm of time".

Though death and life are for ever locked in conflict, they achieve a mysterious union in that which is both "destroyer and preserver". This union is expressed in symbols and actions powerfully sexual in their nature.

So much for the bridge — or plank.

The Aborigines of the poem are conceived as having significance, not as individuals marked by distinct traits of character and temperament, but as members of a tribe made sharply aware of tribal unity by the death of one of its members. The old men, speaking in dialogue and chanting in chorus, voice the tribal beliefs concerning death and direct the tribe in ceremonies related to death and burial.

The narrator and commentator are men of the modern world, the first used to describe the action, the second to comment on it. The word "commentator" may be misleading, for I thought of this person's responses as those of a lyric poet rather than as those of a philosopher or social scientist.

With great pleasure I here thank my friend, the American artist David McCosh, for the illustrations he made from Sir Baldwin Spencer's pictures, and which enrich the verses in ways I am sure it will be a pleasure for the reader to discover.

E.G.M. *Yackandandah, Victoria*

Editor's Note: The illustrations are not included in this collection.

The Lightless Ferry

I

Charon is on the job, and Styx
Flows by the mansion, camp or hut
Where death has entered to unfix
Hands from the hands on which they shut
And start upon his journey there
One more unwilling passenger.

Earth's oldest taxi-man, at call
He finds the number-on-request,
Noses his boat in to the wall
That flanks the landing, lays at rest
His oars and twitches into place
The hood that covers head and face.

Slowly the passenger steps down
And takes a seat. There is no word
Of greeting, be he white, black, brown,
But suddenly the dark is stirred
And there's a sound of dipping oars
And the dim loom of distant shores.

While life endures in time and space
There will be Charon and his boat
And straining eyes that try to trace
His journeyings and only note
That, howsoever dark the night,
His ferry never shows a light.

Narrator:
At Yackandandah, when the sun goes down,
The valleys brim with bird-song; one by one
The hills are snuffed like candles; then night,
The greater Prospero, speaks Benediction:
"Our revels now are ended", and the world
Is suddenly a soft enormous flower
Closing itself into a curl of sleep.

This is a different land — one whose corolla
Of hill and valley long since fell away
And left a calyx withered into stone.
And in this cirque, come night, the desert children

303

Will huddle, as in far and savage days,
In the arena when the lions were out,
Men crouched and waited. For they will be out,
This night, the lions of fear, the terrible shadows
Unloosed by death to pad the shifting sands
And breathe about the darkness. Everywhere
Will be their presence, worse than hungry eyes,
Because no man can see then. Even the cry,
So well known, of the warrigal will clench
Nerves like a muzzle's wet and sudden touch,
Cold on a careless hand.
        So night will be.
But now the sunset fills the sky, a froth
Of colour sweeping in before the wave
Of darkness. On the sand a dying man,
Lies staring face-up while about him hunch
The wise ones skilled in magic, and near by,
Watching with furtive eyes, the old men sit
Muttering low so that no spirit may hear.

Commentator:
Fear is the cling to a cliff — so Hopkins found —
Fear turns the hanged man's heath to holy ground —
Thus Wordsworth — and Odysseus for his part
Found fear adrenalin to the tired heart.

But on that cliff one clutched a rope to God,
One saw a path to beauty on that sod,
And he, the Wanderer, loved Charybdis for
The crushing power that made his strength the more.
And how shall these, with no such rope, nor strength
To hurl at danger, nor a path the length
From fear to beauty, meet the desperate hour
When all the manes of terror are in flower!

Old Men Speaking:
First. My eyes are old — do they still press on him
With hands that hunt the evil in his flesh
To force it out and let him breathe again?
Second: Their hands are only hands!
First.   You say?
Second. Their hands are dogs that lost the game and droop
Ashamed among the shadows. He must die!
First. My ears are dull or I would hear the song
They sing to draw the magic out of him
As women pull a lizard from its hole.

Second. Their songs have failed; they will not try again.
Their lips are stiff with nothing as the branch is
From which the eaglehawk has taken flight.
First. But do they blow their breath into his mouth?
Second. His mouth is a wide cave in a grim land,
Hollow and filled with darkness.
First.   He must die?
Second. Must die!
Third.   The sun is falling; when the light
Strikes on that withered tree his spirit will
Start out upon its journey. Yesterday,
Just at this hour, a bird I did not know
Perched there a moment and was gone. His soul
Will be in it tonight. Watch, you will see
Him clear against the sunset.

Commentator:
Death, from a dying mouth's strategic centre
Blows a bubble of unimaginable stuff,
Inviolable kingdom that none may enter —
Oh no, there is not any strong enough
In love or hate to pierce that wall and dare
Intrude upon the operator there!

From the outside they stare into the hollow,
The watchers, till themselves are changed into
So many bubbles ranged around a shallow
Saucer of time, with nothing left to do
But cling together till the Blower goes home
Tired of the iridescences of foam.

He does. And bubble drifts apart from bubble.
Night falls, and ninety million miles away
A star comes out to ask about the trouble
But finds the saucer lying hushed and grey
And empty but for his own image at
The centre, so he sits and stares at that.

Chorus of Old Men:
He was a great hunter
And a man for women.
In the dry hills among the rocks he was
In silence a lizard, in speed a spear flung,
And the euro, one moment quietly feeding,
The next lay limp, broken across his shoulders,
Bleeding,
And with dust on its tongue.

Hunter and taker of women;
And the hunting is over!
But the women are crouched in their camp.
Come, let us call them to cover
His flesh growing cold, with their thighs,
And his eyes with the heat of their eyes.
Let them arch themselves over him,
Cover him, cover him
From whatever looks down from the skies!

Narrator:
From the low mulga scrub the women come
Running at the loud summons. In a light
Almost as brown as are their naked flanks
They dart like shades out of some underworld
Where a god rages or a devil leers
Lasciviously. Now, where the sick man lies,
They swirl into a circle, lifting up
Their arms in supplication and their voices
In a shrill wail that beats across the plain
Like something wounded that can find no den
In rock or thicket and must wander on
As it has wandered for ten thousand years,
Anguished, defeated, terribly afraid.
And some fall down upon the prostrate man
With thighs wide-spread to cover him, their flesh
Not flesh now but with a burning magma poured
Out of that chaos where the elements
Of life and death writhe, knotted each in each.

Commentator:
For this marriage now begun
Sing a prothalamion.

Stretched face-up the bridegroom lies
With slack mouth and staring eyes

And hands unstrung that cannot do
The rites of lovers when they woo.

Hurry, women, you his bride!
Make the woman of you wide

To lay upon him all you can
Woman's flesh on flesh of man,

On loins and thighs and hands and feet,
Cold and dying, woman's heat,

Woman's grief and fear and lust.
Press upon him, writhe and thrust

Till in his last living nerve
He feel the spasm and then the swerve

And the long arching plunge to death.
And with your mouths then drain his breath

And from the rifled corpse arise
And lock your lips and lock your thighs

And slip away into the dim
Shadows whence you came to him,

Leaving him alone and dead
On his wide, trampled marriage-bed.

Narrator:
A shaft of light has struck the withered tree.
The mounded bodies cease to strain, and now
With a slight shudder break and move apart,
As lovers move when the deep spasm is done.
The dead man lies like a rag doll that children
Fought over and then roughly cast aside.

Commentator:
Instantly in this play without rehearsal
The private thing becomes the universal;
What was no more mysterious than a tree
Is filled with whispers of eternity;
What was bound in by time is timeless made;
What hands could clutch is turned into a shade;
He who submitted to the tribal rule
Has been transported to a higher school,
And, since he sits with the great spirits of night,
He may learn more of darkness than of light.

Old Men Speaking:
Second. They have got up from him.
First.   He is dead then.
Third.   Dead!

First. Did you watch the tree? My eyes are very old.
Did a bird show there?
Third.   Yes, an eaglehawk.
First. Our totem and our god; that's well.
Second.   Well?
It may be just a trick to make us think
His spirit's on its way when it is here
Waiting when dark comes to steal into us
Chased by the spirit of the man who killed him
With magic from far off.
Third.   It is so! It is so!
He will find our ears in the dark, our open mouths,
And enter; then some one of us will die
Because his spirit will break out again,
Rending our flesh, to go the way it must.
First. Don't look! He'll follow our eyes into us
(Fearing the hollow ways that wait for him),
And we will die as he has died. The charm
That killed him is hovering in the air
Ready to dart on us. Thwart the darkness
And all the spirits that walk then with a noise
Of lamentation; wall the darkness out
With living voices; make the night loud
With sounds no spirit will dare plunge against.

Chorus of Old Men:
The night is dark and the goers who make no sound
More than the rustle of wind in tufts of grasses
Will stalk at will on the death-polluted ground
And the sleeper will turn and moan as a gaunt hand passes
Over his chest and head.
Heap wood on the fires till the light
From fire to fire is spread
An island in the night
Unfriendly to the dead.

A wind breaks over the trees and the sand begins
To move, or is it the sound of boneless feet
Coming from where, far off, the darkness thins
At that grim line where earth and heaven meet?
Cry out in grief and fear,
Shout, till the sound is made
A sharp and lifted spear
Against whatever shade
Lurks ready to come near!

Narrator:
The fires are close together; not as when
The tribe in scattered groups sits down to cook
The evening meal with jest and laughter flung
From camp to camp, but gathered in a knot
Drawn tight by fear. And in that lighted space
The naked figures crouch or move about
From fire to fire, their staring eyes upon
The black walls or else lifted up to seek
The longed-for dawn. They have no being now
Distinct each from the other, but are one —
A smitten tribe. Harshly upon the night,
In savage tones they shout the words of fear
And grief and supplication while the sparks
Swirl up towards the far and quiet stars.
Hour upon maddening hour the voices climb
In the one desperate chant, hour upon hour
Unceasing, while the darkened continent
Turns to the east, how slowly! and the dawn.

II
Dawn of the next day
Narrator:
In this flat land where the horizon is
As level as a saucer's rim, the dawn
Comes out of nowhere; suddenly the night
Is gone; day is; and soon the sun will wipe
All softness from the sky and it will be
A steel-grey pressure on the shimmering land.
In the parched scrub the rhythmic trumpeting
Of zebra finches is the only sound
In miles of silence, and the only movement,
High there! the lone drift of an eaglehawk.
The campfires have burned down to heaps of ash
With here and there a smoldering stick that sends
A wisp of blue smoke into the still air.
But no one stirs the coals; the night of fear
Is ended, and there is no food to cook.
Like a dark tree when a great gust of wind
Has shaken it and passed and it awaits
A second blow, the tribe droops silently,
Heads bent and eyes half shut. A space apart
The old men talk together.

Old Men Speaking:
First. We live! Has no one sickened in the night?
Second. No one. We held them off.
First.   I felt them near
Then when the warrigal, who scented death,
Howled and was still; they call the whole night long
If spirits do not scare them.
Third.   They were here.
I felt one touch my shoulder, but a light
Rushed out of heaven and he leapt away.
Fourth. I felt a lump rise in my side, but see,
It is not here; our magic was too strong.
First. Beware of boasting! They will try again.
Even now the dead one walks among the fires
Seeking a home, and he that murdered him
Hunts a new victim.
Second.   Call the women to mourn,
And the young men to gash their thighs in grief!

Chorus of Old Men:
Strike with the fire-hard wood
Your bodies, women, till
Your sides stream with blood;
Strike till the anguish spill
Out of your bursting eyes
Upon your breasts and thighs.

Strike, strike! Again, again!
His spirit will drink the sweet
Wild torrents of your pain
And go with happy feet
Into the far, the dim,
Because you mourn for him.

Break open brow and head
(The agony is brief!)
Till he be fully fed
With the honey of your grief,
And turn at last aside
As a bridegroom from his bride.

Fill him that he may go
Bravely to where he must;
Fill him with blow on blow,
Grief, fear, and pain and lust;
Strike till the great release
Flood all our hearts with peace.

Narrator:
Their yam-sticks clutched in hands as beautiful
As any Raphael dreamed or Angelo,
The women rush together. With loud cries
And eyes that glare they brace their legs to launch
The blows with power. Blow follows blow until
The flanks are washed with blood, and over all,
Rising and falling like the sound of the sea,
Shrills the lament. The sun, now fairly risen,
Stares at the blank land that stares back at him.

Stirred by the hurl and thrust of many feet,
The dry earth billows up in dust; it swirls
Over the bent knees and the straining thighs
Till the black torsos seem to writhe upon it,
Medusa serpents maddened by a fire
In the dark, mothering brain. Higher it climbs
Over the gaping mouths, the desperate eyes,
Hiding the group from sight, while from the cloud
Where is no Sinai stream the terrible cries.

As suddenly as a star drops the sound
Has ceased. The wind of morning blows the dust
Into the nowhere. Crouched on the bare ground
The women press together till they form
Mounds of bruised bodies with arms interlocked
And heads bent down. Silent and motionless
They sit as though, under the glaring sun,
A single touch has turned them into stone.

Commentator:
This handful of white sand
Once played a royal part
Helping a mountain stand —
Was once a mountain's heart.

These stones, lying one by one,
Were once a shining horn
That rubbed against the sun
An hour before morn.

The storm of time has laid
All high things low and wrought
A silence without shade
For a thinker without thought.

The wind of time has blown
Until this lost world lies
A grim, sardonic bone,
Under sardonic skies.

Now, as a memory
Moves in their troubled brain,
Earth's oldest men set free
Those winds of storm again,

Or, like a harsher lyre,
(Not sweet Aeolian),
They turn to shapes the fire
That is the spirit of man,

As pines transmute the breeze,
Invisible, to sound
As veined and sharp as these
Red stones upon the ground.

And what the wind that blows,
And what the memory,
Not any of these knows,
But knows its power to be.

The paradox is this:
That life must die to live,
And the hot struggle is
Strangely restorative.

Dark daughters of the sun,
Let droop each bleeding head;
Your awful course is done
And what can speed is sped.

The storm is over-blown,
The ancient angers fed;
In quietness like stone,
Dream, and be comforted.

Chorus of Old Men:
All that can be has been done;
Carry him without a sound
From the death-polluted ground
To his platform in the sun.

He is well upon the track
To the far, appointed place;
Hurry, lest he turn his face,
And behold us, and come back.

On the shoulder of a hill
Pausing, far across the plain
He may see his camp again
And his women sitting still.

Hurry, that an end may be;
Lift him up and let him lie
Guarded by the watching sky
On his platform in the tree.

Narrator:
The warriors lift the gaunt thing to its place
Quickly, and turn away like men who fear
To wake a sleeper or alert a foe.
One, having paused to lay a bough across
The upturned face, drops to the ground and runs
Hard to outspeed his fellows to the camp
Where the tribe waits in readiness to move.
Like a small outbound ship they start across
The glaring plain, a small dark ship of flesh,
Silent upon the wide sun-smitten land.
Beyond them, where at dawn the horizon was,
Looms a mirage, grey waters in the sky
And cloud-like trees where death has never hung
His grisly fruit. This they have seen before
(How many times, through what long centuries!)
And are not fooled by it; but surely must
There come some little coolness on their eyes
From those impossible waters and that shade,
Their eyes the sun stares into as they go!

Commentator:
Lullaby, oh, lullaby!
Watched by ravens in the sky,
Sleep while silence gently locks you
At her hollow breast and rocks you
Sweet and low and sweet and high;
Lullaby!

Lullaby, oh, lullaby!
Sun that watched the mountains die,
Wind that gathered up the sand,
These will hold you in their hand,
Swing you low and swing you high;
Lullaby!

Lullaby, oh, lullaby!
Have but one dream where you lie:
How the sand that once was stone
Will reject not flesh and bone.
Soft and low and sweet and high,
Lullaby!

Sing the sharp heads in the sky
"Lulla-lulla-lullaby!"

III
The same place, a year later

Old Men Speaking:
First. The bones have fallen.
Second.   He is safely home
In the Dream-time and with the heroes makes
His camp and hunts with them among the hills.
Third. We need not fear him now for he has known
The better hunting and the women who are
For ever young. He will not see our fires
With longing eyes nor try to steal into
This flesh of ours; his long journey is done,
And he is safely home.
First.   The bones have dropped.
The sun has eaten the flesh and the winds have drunk
The blood, but the bones remain — we must gather the bones.
Third. Gather the bones!

Chorus of Old Men:
Warriors, bending quietly
At your task beneath the tree,
Gather from among the stones
All the white, sun-sweetened bones,
And lay them where the ants have made
Homes of silence and deep shade,
Hills within whose secret breast
They shall sleep as in a nest.

But the arm that poised the spear
In ambush when the game drew near
And, when the fight was surging high,
Hurled the great shaft joyously,
Arm that curbed the bride until
Hungry flesh had had its fill —
This keep reverently and well
For a better burial.

Women, yours the sacred bone!
In a secret place, alone,
When no eyes of men may see,
Do the ancient mystery
That will make your lover glad
Of the woman that he had,
That will make your lover proud
Where the heroes laugh aloud!

Commentator:
Time, do you carry
A basket for your fruit:
Janet the fair and Harry
So little more than brute;

The slow, the swift, the clever,
The crooked and the true,
The learned and who never
So much as thought of you?

If so, with gentle fingers
Drop in each sweetened bone
About whose whiteness lingers
An essence like your own.

Narrator:
Like one who sleeps yet has about his mouth
The creep and drift of a sagacious smile,
Born of some ultimate knowledge, the still earth
Lies in the sun-glare. Her dark children make
Ready the rites that shall return to her
The dead for whom she waits. They will not fail
In any part, as they have never failed
Through the long centuries, for all their skill
She taught them.
      In a hidden place the men
With clay and blood and eagle-down adorn

Each other, chest and back, till each one stands
Clad in the sacred symbols of the tribe.
Sheathed in god's mystery, the upper man
Passes from sight, but all the lower parts —
The sheer man-flesh — stay naked. And as on
The shore-line between time and eternity
Breathes a dark rhythm, so that mortal flesh,
Below the symbols of immortality,
Stirs and grows tense.
        Upon a level space
The sacred totem of the tribe is laid
In stones and clay and feathers, and near by
One scoops a burial-hole.
        In a hushed group
The women wrap the bone with bark and hair,
Then press it to their bodies. Let no man
Intrude upon these mysteries of love!
Enough that when the magic strikes him down
He, too, will lie a moment at the breasts
Of women and be comforted.
        Now rise
The old men's voices on the heated air,
Cicada-shrill, and, moving to the chant,
The tribe performs a sacrament whose wine
Tastes of no grapes that ever knew the sun.

Chorus of Old Men (*to the women*):
Through the groove of earth that lies
Underneath the arch of thighs
Move like water when the cloud
Is a god who laughs aloud
In the fullness of his lust
While the earth awaits his thrust.

Move like water that will make
Every hidden seed awake;
Move like water that will bring
Every plant to blossoming,
That the birds may come from far
To feast where the sweet blossoms are
While kangaroo and emu pass
Within spear-throw on the grass.
Move like water that will bring
All the earth to blossoming.

With the cloud above you bent
In a curve of ravishment,
Let your bodies answer to
The strong lover come to woo:
God through man would pour his power
And earth through you receive the shower.

Narrator:
All have crept through the living arch but one
Who bears the arm-bone in its case of bark,
And waits until the old men speak again.

Chorus of Old Men (*to the women*):
You through whom the living earth
Brought her spirit-child to birth
Letting him awhile abide
Hidden in your hollow side
Till his feet were shaped to run
Anywhere beneath the sun
And his eyes were straight and bold
And his fingers curved to hold
Spear and woomera and he
Broke you open with his knee,
Back to the great mother give
Her own longed-for fugitive.

(*To the men*)
You who with your flesh prepared
The path on which the spirit fared
To fill the woman's hollow side,
Press with power upon the bride
And open for the child the way
Shall lead him downward from the day
To a greater day than earth
Knows, and a second, greater birth:

(*To the woman with the bone*)
Now the flesh quivers, arched, astrain,
Creep you through and pass you under,
For the flesh would fall and have peace again
As the sky goes slack at the break of thunder —
Pass you under.

Narrator:
Slowly she creeps beneath the thighs that are
God manifest in man-flesh lifted to

The crest of some wild utterance, but she
Moves with her burden under the poised storm
Still as a thought among the dragons of sleep.
Now she has made the passage. Quickly one,
A warrior, takes the bone and thrusts it deep
Into the hole beside the totem. At once,
As though a band has snapped, the ordered groups
Fall silently apart and men and women
Drift to the thickets near by on the plain.
Until the sunset and the homing hour
Only the drowsy voices of the old
And the shrill cries of children at their games
Will break the sun-drenched silence of the camp.

Commentator:
Now the manes of terror all
Have unbloomed and Charon's boat,
On its desert-Styx afloat,
Bobbles idly by the wall
Waiting for another call.

Once again has been expressed
What no word has power to say,
Symbolled forth in blood and clay,
Eagle-down and ochre pressed
On taut back and heaving breast.

Flesh has spoken what no word
Ever compassed, and afar,
Heroes sitting near a star
Felt their ear-lobes gently stirred
And rejoiced in what they heard.

For they heard what the great sun
Always knew: how single men
Enter Man's true kingdom when,
All their petty courses run,
Fear and love have made them one.

And how in death's deepest gloom
When all hearts are sore oppressed,
Man and woman, breast to breast,
In the re-enkindled womb
Forge an answer to the tomb.

This they will no longer hear
For below them on the plain
Now not even bones remain
Of the tribe that once was dear,
Bound to them in love and fear.

And new tracks are on the sand,
Monstrous, and the ancient air
Heaves with monstrous noises where,
Dark upon the shimmering land,
Lies what woomera for what hand!

Poems from *Briseis* (1965)

Editor's Note: Moll's chosen spellings of such names as Patroklos, Hektor, Kleitemnestra and others are retained. I am not sufficiently familiar with the *Iliad* and other works relating to the Trojan wars to know whether Moll's repetition of certain lines and groups of lines in the earlier and later portions of the sonnet series has any particular basis or purpose.

PART 1

1

Literates in war and lust, the heroes write
On our clean flesh their tale of victories,
Smutting those tablets over by the light
Of burning towns stared at by blood-blind seas.
Our breasts are towers they mastered, our sick thighs
Gates broken wide to let the live bronze in,
And even the hate and fear behind our eyes
Are for them only further heights to win.

Deep in my loins the ravisher's hard thrust
Throbbed with the triumph of my husband slain,
My brothers dead, our fields laid waste and bare,
Lyrnessos the fair city ground to dust:
Deep in my loins, again and yet again,
Hairy Achilles wrote his victory there.

2

I am glad it was brute rape without a word
Pulped with apology for beauty thrown
By fate as to a hungry dog a bone
Who needs must snatch the meal by fate prepared;
No lying talk of a great pity dared
Full in the onrush of war's lion, grown
Mad from the sting of bronze, the bruise of stone;
Or, last and worst, of amorous pleasure shared.

This would have soured the vintage. But the feet
That crushed my grapes at least were hard and clean
And unapologetic as old fate;
And from their trampling there rose up the sweet
Aroma of the ferment that would mean,
In its due time, the good strong wine of hate.

3

Day-long I sipped that wine so that I lay
At night quite ready for the rough caresses
That tapered into whispered tendernesses
And little quirks and frolics of love-play
For whose small strategies I made a way
Into—he thought—my woman's wildernesses,
And whispered to him, "How your ardor presses
Out of my grapes sweet wine to sip all day!"

Sweet wine of memories! I coaxed him up
The path from lust to passion until love
Lifted him higher than his own belief.
And I was ready then to drain my cup
And brace my hands upon him for the shove
Would hurl him down the chasm of my grief.

4

We left Lyrnessos on the rutted track
That led towards Troy. Achilles had me ride
In his own chariot, bolstered either side
With robes I knew too well, and at my back
The shields of my dead kinsmen spotted black
With spatter of their dying. But a bride
Amid her dower must lift her head with pride
And never let that new-kissed mouth go slack.

And I did lift my head and curl a smile
Under the spin of his solicitude
Which clung to me as soft as silk of the moon;
And I fed fat with honey of my guile
Grey, monstrous grubs, that, winged and armored, would
Someday swarm on him out of that cocoon.

5

My father knew Troy well: He used to bear
Gifts for great Priam (that was long before
Paris returned from Sparta with his whore)
And we, his children, huddled round to share
The trinkets he brought home and breathe the air
Of court and temple and tremble to the roar
That welcomed heroes from some distant shore.—
My father told his stories with a flair.

I saw her first from the Achaian camp,
Looming not far away through a light rain,
Ghostly as dead Lyrnessos; then a voice
Was saying, "Come, the morn is cold and damp;
Unclench those fingers from your throat of pain—
The gods have given you no other choice."

6

And was it, then, the gods? In what sick hour,
Palsied by fever or driven mad by wine,
Would they come down to root the earth like swine?
Ah, not to woo some Danae in a shower
Of gold, but, gods only in lust and power,
Immortal, and in only that divine,
To heap their thunders on this head of mine,
Yes, hurl down mountains but to crush a flower?

Achilles said it was so; and he spoke
Solemnly out of deep, and laboring thought
That first cold morning, and a shiver went
Through me: are we, then, sharers in a yoke?
Both in a dark and monstrous pattern caught?—
Is he, almost as I am, innocent?

7

My brothers stole a falcon from the nest
And gave him to me, a soft downy thing
But with a beak that even then could bring
Blood to the too-bold finger. And I pressed
Warmth, food, and love upon him. So caressed,
I told my heart, he'd stop remembering
The death-lunge of his falcon-father's wing,
Nor heed the savage pulses in his breast.

A day came when I freed him from his cage,
A day when my white doves were in the sky.
He flashed among them and the heavens shed
Like snow-flakes the small victims of his rage.
Then he came back to me, and, weeping, I
Smoothed down the bloodied feathers of his head.

8

Tears for the doves, and my half-amorous hand
Stroking their slayer in a sort of trance!
By such equivocation circumstance
Baffles our wills until we understand
That to the gods we are no more than sand
For their foot-printing, and that the wheel of chance
Turns only with gyrations of their dance,
Steadies and stops alone at their command.

I told this to Achilles. He looked up
From cinching a dark belt upon his hips
And said, "Then you forgive me, saying this?"
And then I drank him as men drain a cup
Gasping because their hearts are at their lips—
Lyrnessos died again in that wild kiss.

9

Two apples on one branch, desirable
Equally, so it seemed, until he said,
Patroklos, with his hand upon my head:
"I read your thought, Briseis: heaven or hell
For him and you; Oh, may the future tell
How you, though hate's ripe apple hung so red,
Plucked for his hungry mouth love's fruit instead."—
I kissed his hand to say that all was well.

And it was he who led me through the din
Of voices horneting the wrath-choked air
And said goodbye and left me standing there
With Agamemnon's men, fated to be
A woman who, without fair Helen's sin,
Would slay almost as many men as she.

PART II

10

I grew accustomed to the warrior-smell
That clings to hands and hair, compounded of
Dust, sweat, blood, bronze—of everything but love—
And by quick stolen glances learned to tell
If that day's fighting had gone ill or well;
How many he had spared—but just to prove

If they could stand another, harder shove;
How many he had sent outright to hell.

But when the dogs of war were chained and sprawled
Twitching in night's dark kennel, I sent out
Such troops as only woman could deploy
Against his breathing flesh, however walled,
And then he knew surrender and a rout
Such as he would not live to see for Troy.

11

Lyrnessos—dead Lyrnessos! Can a ghost—
And such Achilles made you—fade to less
Than an uncertain memory in the press
Of living day by dreary day? Almost
Your ashes are like snow on a far coast
Where I have never been; a sort of guess
I must have made at a white tenderness
In fields no mortal feet have ever crossed.

Now leave me utterly! Why should the grave's
Eyes ever hunger at the wedding feast?
Its bony fingers skitter for the least
Crumb that might fall? Tonight the storm-wind raves.
Let go my hand! The lover in my bed,
Having killed you, knows right well that you are dead.

12

He would turn over drowsily at dawn
Like a small child fumbling its way from sleep
And seem to listen to the pulse and leap
Within my body, hour by hour borne
Closer to his and longing for the drawn
Bow of his mating; but, with a light sweep
Of his hand across my breast, he'd say, " 'Twill keep,
As will not, if I linger, Hektor's scorn."

A hot day later, at the set of sun,
He would come back to where I knelt to pour
The cleansing water, tweak my ear and then
Cast the bronze trappings from him one by one
And bend above me, naked as before
But taller by the height of three dead men.

13

She had grown old staring at unbreached Troy.
An early prize of war, when first she came,
They said, her lover lapped her like a flame
Stolen from Venus' altar. A mere boy,
He took the toss and pitch of war, a toy
For friend and foe in that hilarious game;
And so his end was sudden, and quite tame:
A chariot crushed his chest and all its joy.

I saw her at a small tub one bright day
Trying to bathe her body, a livid, thin
Leer of a thing in that warm sun-washed air;
And when a lad came by upon his way
She raised her breasts—buttons on strings of skin—
And tilted withered buttocks at his stare.

14

And is her end the promised one for me?
Patroklos laughed in his quick way: "You make
Too much of pain. Achilles will forsake
You never, but in Phthia by the sea
Will wed you and his Myrmidons will be
Your shield as he is theirs and you will wake
Forever from this nightmare war and take
Gently his fair-haired children on your knee."

Did he not know Achilles must go down
Clutching the dust before some bitter gate?
Had he not read it in the brooding eye
That darkened thoughtfully beneath the frown
That knew it could not turn the spear of fate?
And yet—and yet, I thanked him for that lie.

15

If, like a snake that spits upon the feet
That crush it, I should curse the gods and take
All heaven and earth to witness how they slake
Their lusts on all things holy, all things sweet,
Like swine that dung and trample the good wheat
Man would be nourished by but for their sake,
Would they not laugh upon their thrones and make
My woman's curse spice to their wine and meat?

Better to laugh as they do: We are dust—
The fillip of your jest when you would move
Your guests to merriment; but our estate
Is not quite unlike yours when even Zeus must
Squirm on his belly after fruits of love
And glorious Venus squat to urinate.

16

Poor, vulgar, futile anger, wretched thing
Crawling about upon the sodden ground,
A lion-rage but making never a sound,
A hornet-fury but without a sting!
Yet live—yet live! And I myself will bring
You pain to batten on; and scattered round
Lie rotting sorrows such as you have found
And will find worthy of your scavenging.

My thought has but two chambers: one a den
For you to writhe and knot in; one a place
Made royal by a footstep and a face
The boldest and the fairest among men.
And when the gods pluck him from my embrace
I'll let them crush you, too—but not till then!

17

Achilles came home angry one hot night
While I was watching how the stars begin
To take their place in heaven. With a grin
He held his helmet to the fading light:
The slashed bronze let the stars through on my sight
Dreadfully, but he smiled, "You always win:
You wished a pot to plant some flowers in—
You'll find this one almost exactly right."

And I did plant a flower that I knew,
In childhood wanderings over the green plain
Outside Lyrnessos, before summer flamed;
He stopped to see it on a day of rain:
"You call it—what?" And when I answered "rue,"
He seemed like one grown suddenly ashamed.

18

He was not given to laughter and much less
To lovers' talk, and yet I found a way
To tease him into laughter day by day
And after laughter into tenderness
And back again to laughter lest he should guess
Too soon how I had made his heart betray
Its dearest secret; and I made amorous play
Confess for him what he could not confess.

Yes, even in that iron cage of war
On which the gods pound till they drive men mad
Who know that fate has locked the only door
And sealed them from the light forever, glad
For even such privacy, oh, more and more
We laughed together for the joy we had.

19

Then the plague struck. Men heard the silver bow
Clash terribly as from his angry hand
Apollo sped his arrows till the sand
Around the ships was foul with corpses; low,
Mules, dogs and men lay row on rotting row,
Oozing pollution till there was no land
Left clean where the unsmitten ones might stand—
How many died Hades alone could know.

Mules, dogs and common men; no heroes died,
No kings or captains, for the god would make
The mighty look on dying that should be
Only a bursting of the rotted side,
A blur of fingers in the palsy-shake,
An unheroic crumbling of the knee.

20

Nine days nine nights the corpse-fires burned. The air
Was fetid with the fumes of charring flesh,
And men, like insects tangled in a mesh
Of horror, formed in clots as though just there
Someone had sniffed a breeze all hoped to share.
And some beat on the fires as though to thresh
A harvest from them and the logs afresh
Burst into flame and smoke was everywhere.

With streaming eyes we stared at Troy. She rose
Regal and fair beyond our pit of shame,
Fair in the day and fairer still at night,
And knew that she, untroubled by her foes,
Watched as we gasped amidst the smoke and flame
And laughed from her clean towers at the sight.

21

Like one who darkly broods upon an ill
Spawned in his flesh by lust, or pride, or greed,
And does not bare the fester since the seed
Was sown by the permission of his will,
But, vainly loathing, keeps it hidden still,
(However inwardly he rot and bleed),
From that which might avail him in his need,
The priest's hot mouth, the surgeon's colder skill,

So the Achaians brooded on the thing
That slimed their blood and kept them ashen-lipped,
The evil known and named but unconfessed
Even in their most guarded whispering,
Till with an angry word Achilles ripped
The royal rags from Agamemnon's breast.

22

Patroklos told me, when that day was done
And the assembly over, "Thus he said:
'An evil thing o'erwhelms us, hand and head,
And shuts us out from the life-giving sun,
Apollo, who is angry. Let us run
To him for mercy. Let our sin be shed
Even though fostered in a royal bed
And Agamemnon be the guilty one.

"Speak, Kalchas, from the shelter of my shield,
And say the truth'; and the affrighted seer
Bent on the king a stern yet pleading eye:
'When a god speaks it is for man to yield.
Great king, however fair she is and dear,
Give back Chryseis or we all must die!' "

23

Agamemnon:
        "So be it, even though Chryseis lay
        Softer than Kleitemnestra at my side,
        Afraid, perhaps, and therefore still a bride
        And virginal in that delicious way
        That pays a debt and leaves a debt to pay.
        I babble—let the god be satisfied;
        King that I am, his is the greater pride,
        King that I am, his is the greater sway.

        "But this I tell you: Let another prize
        Fair as Chryseis now be given me
        That I, your king, lie not disgraced, alone;
        Some maiden who will gladden my sad eyes
        And in a happier day than ours would be
        The ornament, and footstool, of my throne."

24

Achilles:
        "Greediest of men behind that royal mask!
        We've stripped the vineyards of the Troad bare
        In almost ten long years; not anywhere
        Is there a city left to sack. The flask
        Of victory is stoppered, yet you ask
        More wine to swill! Oh, did you only dare
        Point us the way, we'd find you wine to spare
        Nor count the getting all too hard a task!

        "When Troy has fallen you shall have your choice
        Of women, treasure, anything you will,
        Granted by us, your servants, dutiful
        And all-submissive to your hand and voice;
        And I have heard—be this not taken ill—
        Cassandra is a maid and beautiful."

25

Agamemnon:
        "An ill-aimed jest, Achilles—when Troy falls!
        Or do you think that Atreus begat
        A fool to serve your cunning as a mat
        To wipe its dirty feet on when the squalls
        Of fortune foul the road your honor crawls?
        When Troy shall yield! Let me remind you that,

You and your friends, we still are staring at,
After ten years, the outside of her walls!

"Give me a prize, and now, or I will take
One to my liking—possibly your own
Or that of Aias or Odysseus there!
Yet, let us pause for thought nor rashly make
That choice till rage and spite have overblown
And left us, for our thinking, cleaner air."

26

Achilles:

"Have I then laboured only to feed swine?
I came to Troy unwillingly, but now
I'll make the water smoke beneath my prow
Returning home to Phthia. While your fine
Orator's tongue licks flat the mocking line
Of walls and towers, I shall be 'homeward-ho',
And in my curved black ships with me shall go
My Myrmidons and all things that are mine!"

Agamemnon:

"Run, by all means, and fast as cowards alone
Know how to run! To speed you in your flight
I think it well that you should travel light
And with no curse upon you but my own—
And even that may turn a blessing, bred
Upon fair-cheeked Briseis in my bed."

27

Patroklos dropped his voice: "I fear to tell
How then black rage knotted Achilles' face
While his right hand moved quickly to the place
Where hung the sword his fingers knew too well
And clutched the hilt. I saw his knuckles swell
And whiten and before him half a pace
Pale Agamemnon rooted to his place
Only two little breaths this side of hell.

"Then something snapt: as though a goddess had
Struck down his hand, Achilles turned: 'I'll fight
Neither against you nor proud Troy, but stand
And watch grim Hektor, suddenly grown glad,
Drive you like sheep in shameful headlong flight
Till for your running there is no more land!' "

28

That night we lay cold-silent, side by side
Each frozen in the ice of his own thought.
I only know what mine was: how the taut
Bow of our joy was broken, and how pride,
by love, rage, loathing terribly multiplied,
Had lost for both of us that which he sought
To save—my sad, unwise Achilles! brought
Thus to where rage alone must be his bride.

I hoped he'd touch me before day, but when
Dawn broke at last he stared at his bright shield,
Then dressed himself in clothes not made for war,
And muttered: "When the gods and god-like men
Speak we must heed them, but, Briseis, yield
Never to be vile Agamemnon's whore!"

29

Was it his pride or love said that? (There would
Be hours enough to let that question dart
Like a trapped bird through my bewildered heart).
The heralds came at noon; I saw the flood
Of anger sweep Achilles, but he stood
To greet them courteously, then called apart
Patroklos and gave orders that he start
The term of our god-fostered widowhood.

It was Patroklos brought me through the din
Of voices horneting the wrath-choked air,
And said goodbye, and left me standing there
With Agamemnon's men, fated to be
A woman who, without fair Helen's sin,
Would slay almost as many men as she.

30

I saw Achilles sitting by the sea
Staring far out when I was led away
From his strong shelter. All around me lay
Piles of bright armor thrown down carelessly;
The Myrmidons bent angry eyes on me
As though I were the thief of their bright day
And symbol of an awful debt to pay,
A sorrow come, a greater yet to be.

I only saw his back, the shoulders down
But the proud head shaft-straight with rage, and then,
(So dark he was against the glittering waves),
I knew that underneath that terrible frown,
(Seen only by no-longer-living men),
His thoughts were filling up a thousand graves.

PART III

31

I doubt that Agamemnon thought his prize
Worth looking at: it was enough to know
That he had caught Achilles with a blow,
Clever and quick, between the haughty eyes
And, as he staggered blinded by surprise,
Snatched from his hand a pretty thing to show
Who was the stronger. Valued only so,
I knew myself a piece of merchandise.

I herded with the females, who would snicker:
"Don't grieve, for he will call you to his bed.
Were there no others he might love instead
Of you, be sure he would be somewhat quicker!"
And there I saw the double insult flicker
Like a snake's tongue at foiled Achilles' head.

32

Those days I rarely looked at Troy but stood
Often at dawn to scan the darkened huts
Where Myrmidons slept late beside the sluts
Who drained them of a dearer thing than blood;
And my black thoughts were on me like a hood
That seals the brain and every sense and shuts
The heart in a self-prison where it gluts
Its hunger with the loathesomest of food:

Were there white hands feeling along his thighs
In that half-light when men turn from their rest
To fumble at love's portals drowsily?
Slept he bewitched in the warm valley that lies
Midway the soft division of a breast,
And all forgetful of his gods and me?

33

The Trojans, who, like men grown satiate
With lust, had shrunk from further hot embraces,
Now seemed to feel again the power that races
Through quickening loins. They streamed from every gate
And I laughed seeing the Achaians wait
The clutching shock as helpless in their places
As women lying with averted faces
When the bared phallos arches up elate.

I, having known such waiting, was right glad
To see how pale tall Agamemnon grew;
And even greater was the joy I had
For that which I and every man there knew:
How nearby lay Achilles' camp, as black
And indifferent as a wart on a hog's back.

34

Oh, not to music rose the walls we built
Between the ships and Troy. With grunt and groan
Quite unheroic the heroes heaved the stone
And wood and muck together. I saw them wilt
Under the angry sun and felt no guilt
When laughter shook me where I stood alone
To watch the taming of that flesh and bone
That once had been so proud upon the hilt.

Ever the eyes of Agamemnon were
Darting about from face to anxious face
And up to heaven as though to ask a grace
Of the high gods. Had he a child to spare,
Doubtless an altar would have risen apace
And we'd have seen a second Aulis there.

35

It was the current mistress of the king,
(A creature with brains only in her hips,
Heart only in her moist, lascivious lips;
A venomed tongue, but all too dull to sting),
Who came one day among us twittering
Like a demented bird that slides and slips,
Catches its singing-pose, yet ever trips
Over the song it has in mind to sing:

" 'Odysseus, Phoenix, go to him; say I
Will give Briseis back untouched, and more
Treasure than would outweigh a better whore.
Plead with him: take her or we all must die!'
These were the words great Agamemnon said—
I heard them as I waited in his bed."

36

The women said I swooned; and this I know:
My opening eyes beheld the sneering face
Of her who had just spoken, and the place
There by the looms spun dizzily. "The blow,"
One kneeling by me said, "was just as low
As her own viper-heart. I, who by grace
Of the kind gods, once had the king's embrace,
Swear Agamemnon never called you so!"

O women, have you never felt the swirl
Of wild love-longing fill you like a cloud
Gathering up from every fevered cell
Until you prayed, hot-mouthed, for Love to hurl
His shafted lightning through you, and when loud
The thunder broke, you were the heavens that fell?

37

That wildness still was on me when they went,
Odysseus, Phoenix, Aias on their way
To parley with Achilles. Almost gay
Their going seemed, such hope the gods had sent
Into their hearts. And I, who never meant
To trust the gods again, found words to say:
'Oh, grant them fortune on this fateful day,
And let him even for love of me relent.'

For love of me! What laughter runs on high
When a crazed woman lifts her frail hands up
Beseeching—no, demanding—the bright cup
Whose draught alone can make her not to die:
I see a god lean over from his place
And dash the wine into her upturned face!

38

Odysseus weeping, "This Achilles said:
'Tell Atreus' son that, mad with greed and pride,
He took away from me my own heart's bride;
So, let him lie beside her in his bed.
And that fine proffered treasure he had spread
before me, with my kinsmen at my side,
I won it for him, and thus well supplied,
He is most free with that for which we bled!

'Tell him—and this make sure he understand—
I came unwillingly to Troy, and now
I'll make the water smoke beneath my prow
Returning home to Phthia, while with hand
Untrammeled Hektor smite him thigh and brow
Till for his running there is no more land.' "

39

That night I should have felt the battering
Of love and hate in wild confusion thrown
Against my heart. Surely the winds had blown
Waves high enough for any shattering!
Not even that was granted me to bring
Strength back into the will, but, like a stone
Forgotten by the sea, I lay alone
And muttered through dry lips this idle thing:

'Where will I stand to watch the black ships go
Come dawn, and will I see Achilles there?'
Words without substance in an endless flow
Through a heart dead and empty as the air
Except for words like grains of wind-blown sand
In a dull iterance, 'Where will I stand!'

40

How quiet would the going of the ships
Have been compared with what that morning brought!
It was as though the mighty gods had sought
To crush the earth with thunder. Blown like chips
Before a blast that splits the sea and rips
Trees from their roots were the Achaians, caught
In the storm-rage of Troy. So near they fought,
We women could taste blood upon our lips.

Then to the shelter the sore-wounded came:
Strong Diomedes with his foot pierced through;
Odysseus with his ribs laid horribly bare;
The king himself with one arm hanging lame.
Yet over it all we heard a shout and knew
That Aias lived and still was fighting there.

41

The voice of Aias by the shattered wall,
The voice of Aias where the beached ships lay
Like beetles turned upon their backs, the prey
Of who should reach them first. Then a black pall
Of smoke rolled through our shelter. One and all
We gasped, "The ships are burning! Nought can stay
The hand of death, with night so far away
That will not hasten, loud though we may call."

"Achilles fights! Achilles!" Even now
My heart bursts with that glory. "See, they run
Like hares between the wind-rows of their dead!"
Diomedes shook the anguish from his brow,
Odysseus flashed like a new-risen sun,
And Agamemnon lifted up his head.

42

Never did wind drive back the writhing sea
Upon itself to leave the beaches dry
With strength like his. We saw the Trojans fly
Like shredded foam until they seemed to be
Piled at the base of Troy's own walls, and we,
Even we women lifted up a cry:
"Smite them, Achilles! Teach them how to die!
Smite and spare not even the earth-kissing knee!"

Then a spent runner reached us, gasping out:
"They who yet live are safe behind their gates,
But Hektor struck one blow to leave no doubt
That Zeus still rules all heroes and their fates—
Achilles lies with cleft and bloodied head
Hard by the walls of Troy—Achilles is dead!"

43

Before my grief could break from smoke to flame
Out of the horrible smother in my heart
A woman touched me where I sat apart—
One I had liked—and called me by my name:
"Be comforted! A second runner came
Gasping it was Patroklos felt the dart
Of death; Achilles lives. So now you start
Up with the wheel again in this mad game!"

Always to win by losing, water joy
With tears and see the hoped-for flower spring
Brighter, but only for the rotting thing
That feeds its roots! Such gifts the gods employ—
Just enough gold to plate the dark alloy—
That we may thank them for their cherishing!

44

His joy was like a dog just off the thong
That ran before him, tripping up his voice:
"Achilles has forgiven me—rejoice!
Speed to him with my gifts! Hurry along
The women and Briseis and the strong
Fleet-footed horses, and tell them that I swear
In all these days and nights I touched no hair
Of her who brought upon us all this wrong!"

I heard him and felt nothing. "Brought upon?"
Let Helen's be such honor, and let the lie
Smile on its god-like father. Meanwhile I
Go to my lover who would cast me on
The camp's dunghill if by so doing he could
Unfreeze the current of Patroklos' blood.

45

He sat beside the dead man in the gloom
Of the hushed shelter. I could dimly see
The shaggy head drooped almost to his knee
Like a stone effigy's upon a tomb.
They two so filled that place, as bride and groom
Fill up the world wherever they may be,
The terrible knowledge smote me sickeningly
That here there was for me not any room.

Yet there was worse to learn, for when he raised
His head and saw me, first a hollow stare
Transfixed me, then, harsh as a knife on stone,
His voice rasped while his eyes with anger blazed
Through the black tangle of his matted hair:
"Woman, behold this thing that you have done!"

46

A flame shot through me, anger in part, and part
Grief, and that final, utter desperation
That seizes one who has nor tribe nor nation
Nor even an honored place in his own heart,
But stands from all of life and death apart
Like a loathed leper in his lonely station;
And it was but a pauper's compensation
To count my wealth of tears about to start.

Imperious flame that knows not law nor schooling,
Captain nor priest, that will not fade nor shrink
Until the last twig ashens into rest,
I cast myself and you for that last cooling
Over and down from life's terrific brink
Upon the cold slab of Patroklos' breast.

47

I woke to see Achilles bending low,
Naked, above his armor; in that place
Where death alone seemed to have any grace
He was most graceful as, deliberate, slow,
He donned each piece, then stretched to feel the flow
Of power through the bronze ducts. With kingly pace
He left the shelter and I turned my face
To watch if dead Patroklos saw him go.

Then a shout rose above the din of strife
"Achilles! Strong Achilles!" And it sped
Even down to Thetis deep beneath the sea;
But I, a woman, though not quite a wife,
Harkened to hear its mortal thunder tread
The listening chambers of Andromache.

48

The names of dead and dying dropped like rain
Upon us in the shelter. Far away
Under the walls I watched the masses sway,
Break, scatter, and like waves rise up again
While round me women sobbed. I felt no pain
Over the dead because for me that day
Of all who would be slain or live to slay
Only two mattered somewhere on that plain.

In the hot evening, just at set of sun,
Achilles strode to where I knelt to pour
The cleansing water, softly spoke my name,
Cast the bronze trappings from him one by one
And bent above me, naked as before,
But taller by the height of Hektor's fame.

49

It is not for even the gods to speak
Such passion as I knew in those next hours,
For all their loves are but the chance-sown flowers
Among the many pleasures that they seek,
And pluck in passing. Not for them to try
The perilous heights above the grim abyss,
The heights man reaches only by a kiss,
The gulf he must drop into by and by.

O women, have you never felt the swirl
Of wild love-longing fill you like a cloud
Gathering up from every fevered cell
Until you prayed, hot-mouthed, for Love to hurl
His shafted lightning through you, and when loud
The thunder broke, you were the heavens that fell?

50

A feast of heroes—(incidentally,
The funeral of Patroklos!)—As men should,
They bathed his honor fresh in sweat and blood
And in their giving were not niggardly
But hurled the spear and lashed the horses mad
In chariot races, laid each other low
At wrestling, boxing, that all men might know
The glory of the thing that made them sad.

The clamor reached me where I sat alone
Deep in the shelter, but I scarcely heard
Because another sound was moving there,
A voice with love and pity in its tone;
And while my heart sprang open to each word
I felt a spirit-hand upon my hair.

51

"Briseis, all your grief is known to me,
Your grief thorned-round with anger; but you make
Too much of pain. Achilles will forsake
You never, but in Phthia by the sea
Will wed you and his Myrmidons will be
Your shield as he is theirs and you will wake
Forever from the nightmare war and take
Gently his fair-haired children on your knee."

Friend—friend! You know Achilles must go down
Under the bronze before some bitter gate!
The gods have spoken, and his brooding eye,
Hollow beneath the death-defying frown,
Knows that no strength can turn the spear of fate.—
And yet—and yet I love you for that lie!

52

Still Hektor lay unburied. In the dark
Hours of night Achilles smote his breast
In grief and could not turn him to his rest
But writhed and wept and rose up often to mark
How far the stars had paled, until a lark,
High in the heavens, and spying from the west,
Announced the dawn that would show unpossessed
Great Hektor's body lying stiff and stark.

Then, like a wild bull maddened by the sight
Of an old foe, on horns of rage he hurled
The naked corpse in the polluting dust.
Oh, horrible to see the hell's-delight
With which Achilles let himself by curled
In the thick folds of his own python-lust!

53

Then came old Priam, he my father loved,
Pale as the moon, and stately, and as calm.
I saw Achilles take him by the arm
Courteously, and watched them as they moved
To where dead Hektor lay. On desperate knee
I prayed the gods to let sweet pity flow
Into Achilles' heart and bring him so,
Forgiving and forgiven, back to me.

Upon our couch he kissed me with new lips:
"Hektor goes home," he said, "and I shall soon
Lie in that place where every debt is paid.
Look, love, above the sea, the silver moon!
Eleven days beside the hollow ships
Are ours for love as simple man and maid."

54

The eleventh day has passed; Achilles shakes
The dust out of his armor, hefts the spear
From Pelios and sorts out his battle-gear
And lays it where a man when he awakes
Will find it ready. So the cursed wheel makes
Another turn, and I, half-sick with fear,
Clutch at a thing my heart will hold most dear
Even in the moment just before it breaks:

Less than an hour ago he took my hand
And we went from the shelter side by side
Into the stillness of the dying day
And he stooped low and lifted from the sand
A potted plant and smiled with tender pride:
"I cared for it what time you were away."

55

When we are dead carve crudely on my tomb
A phallos and a sword to signify
What I clutched nightly between thigh and thigh—
The sower and the reaper of the womb.
And let, beyond the corpse-encumbered plain,
White and far-off, the walls of Troy be seen,
And, where Skamander's banks are newly green,
Men marshalling for battle once again.

And, if there still be left upon the earth
A heart not scornful of love's mystery,
A hand whose gentleness is all its power,
Let him carve something of far greater worth
Than sword or phallos, for gods and men to see—
A broken helmet and a withered flower.

Poems from *The Road to Cactus-Land* (1971)

Part One

I

Shoveling manure in the big stable,
My head filled with visions that rose to me out of books
Read often by candle light but relived
Daylong and through all tasks, I used to say
Boastfully to a phantom, non-shovelling companion,
Boastfully, a boy's way:

"Yes, I have been in those places:
Walked with Alcinous in his garden
Under the ever-bearing trees,
Blossom, green fruit and ripe
Spicing the air that held only
The warmth of eternal summer.

"In Eden I saw
Eve naked among her roses,
And when our eyes met
Mine fell before her glance and a strange warmth flowed,
Strange and delicious, all through me,
And I quickly turned away.

"And another place,
Much like Alcinous' garden and much like Eden,
I chanced on.
There was a blossom-starred bower
Filtering the sunlight that played
On the form of a sleeping maiden
Naked as Eve and as fair; one hand
Under her cheek, she was unaware that her breasts
Flickered with shadows and lights
As though Nature herself were breathing.

"And yes, oh yes, I have seen many battles;
Ridden with Launcelot, Bedivere, Gawain,
Slain many evil ones,
Rescued fair maidens,
Stood on the flaming decks, facing the galleons,
Stood beside Drake, stood beside Grenville,
Stood beside — stood beside —"

And there it ended:
The first horses came
With thudding hooves and hungry eyes,
From the harvest fields, sweat
Caked on their shoulders
And muzzles twitching to be at the sun-sweet chaff.

And then my non-shovelling companion
Left me, and I
Put shovel and barrow aside
And gave mind to filling the mangers.

II

It is the privilege of youth to dress
In flesh of romance the unsightly bone
Time will reveal, for how should young lips press
The humps and hollows of a skeleton!

And when the mouth craves honey it seems right
Youth should employ a stratagem to thrive
And, having set a twist of rags alight,
Blow smoke to numb the bees within the hive.

For only time can harden so the hand
That it may reach through swarms of unnumbed bees,
Hardened and cunning from long practice, and
Take thence whatever honeycomb it please.

III

I did not always sit at Arthur's table
Or make brave talk to phantoms. There were men,
Brothers, strong-hearted, heavy-handed men,
Who tamed the land with axe and horse and plough
And would have laughed or sickened at my visions.
Their love I had and their companionship
Proven in ways romancer never dreamed of,
Ways redolent of sun and wind and soil
And spiced with earthy humour.

Summer nights,
After the sliced cold mutton had gone down
Dust-weary throats into uneager bellies,
And after the old papers had been read,

We "men-folk" executed the pre-bed
Manoeuvre with our mumbled joke about
A last look at the weather;
And then we stood together
Under a sky that arched towards the west
Star-diamonded as a rich woman's breast
In which the milk has long since turned to gall,
And someone always said in a half-drawl
Much like the singsong of a benediction:
"O Lord, whatever our blessings or affliction,
Surely, we thank Thee, standing here, for this —
We still can piss!"

Should we, grown old now, ever be together,
After the sliced cold mutton and the rest
I know we'd use our pre-bed stratagem
And, facing solemnly into the west,
Repeat our benediction on the weather.

IV

A dropped match and the world is all ablaze,
The brown lands summer-ready for the fire:
So was it with me on that day of days
When I learned, not the meaning of desire,
But what the grass-lands and the forests know,
The power of its ways.

Her father talked of horses and the wheat,
Her mother and mine, across the dinner-table
Exchanged their recipes for sour and sweet
Pickles and such, but clear above that babel,
I saw a splendid tower leap at heaven
Up from her slender feet.

I saw her blue eyes through that haze of talk
Alive with all my Edens, and I saw
Nausicaa in her secluded walk,
Eve by a drift of roses, and even more
Distinct, Acrasia like a woman-flower
Asleep upon its stalk.

And then I had a secret worth the care
I used in after days to keep it hidden
From those I knew too well would surely dare
Enter my shrine, the unwashed, the unbidden,

To strip my votive wreaths with lusty hands
And leave it foul and bare.

This was a holy thing, to breathe her name
Into the sunset and a flush of dawn
And feed with prayer and worship the clear flame
On which I saw her image nightly borne
From that new Eden that involved the old —
So different, yet the same.

A holy thing to dream of lips and brow
Reverently as a saint might dream of heaven,
Accepting with full heart nor asking how
Such gifts can be to struggling mortals given,
Accepting with a faith beyond all doubt
Heaven in the here and now.

V

It was the time of mating:
The mares, the beautiful Clydesdales,
Loitered in the paddock nearest the stallion's yard
Their white-blazed faces turned all one way
Their eyes forgetful of the green grass
And the oaten hay piled in the outdoor manger.

And the stallion,
Massive shoulders pressed to the yard-rails,
The sun hot on his mounded and shining buttocks,
Stood in that focus of eyes,
Squirmed under the burning-glass of those glances
And felt the maleness creep out of him, slide and stiffen
And strain towards that sheath in the paddock
Where it might plunge and be spent
And fall upon peace and creep back
Fold upon fold
Into the darkness again.

Only men could open a way through the fences.

Noon was the favoured time:
Far off in the tree-blind house the women
Were safe, up to their elbows in dishes.
The women were safe, but knowing the time of year,
And hearing a new string in the harp of Spring playing,
And having noted the men

Quick at their meals and their eyes furtive,
They worked in silence and laid the dishes down gently.

A stallion worth five hundred guineas,
A mare worth a hundred:
And out of these might be born
Not a king, but a champion of champions,
A foal to beget more champions
And be worth a round thousand guineas.

Carefully, then!
Lead the mare to the trying rail,
Set the stallion beside her;
The rail between, let them stand there head to tail
And sniff and wrinkle their lips and stamp and squeal
Till the shudder of flesh and the throb and the drip reveal
The male-thing primed for the seeding
And the primed womb pleading.

Now, having gauged the temperature of lust,
Lighting their pipes, the ministrants declare
That all is ready and the omens fair
For a safe, deep, and profitable thrust.

It was as though two hills,
Alive and violent with the lava heaving,
Should mount the one the other
And with a slow, tremendous agitation
Strive to beget a world.

The spasm fell
Into the wrench and shuffle of uncoupling;
The coin had clinked, the register snapt shut,
The two, tremendous in the thrust of mating,
Were suddenly mere unstrung draggles of flesh
With dull eyes hunting for a blade of grass.
The men knocked out their pipes.
In a tree-hidden house
The dishes were all done and laid away.

But I
Turned from my peep-hole in a shed
With hot eyes, sweating brow and gasp of breath,
Turned to the distant hills beyond which She
Lived, and I felt a hand I've never touched
Laid on me and her presence

About me like a presence come from heaven
To still the waves; and they were still and I
Was free again and in the sunshine spoke
Softly her name in blessing.

VI

Moonlight, as only in the Riverina
The moon makes summer nights a tenderer day;
We two alone. A scant five miles away,
Looming above the intervening plain,
The Tabletops, majestic in that light,
And round us the deep mystery of night.

Sometimes one knows the night as his true friend,
And this I felt as falteringly I said:
"That is a mopoke calling from the bend
Of the dry creek there where the red-gums stand,
And that's a curlew; — that —"

But suddenly her hand
Slid into mine and in a moment more
I felt her hard against me, breasts and thighs
Urgent as the strange light within her eyes;
And when I tried to kiss her reverently,
As in my dreams, she crushed her mouth on mine
And her hot gasped-out breath shot into me.

Mine was a boy's strong body uncorroded
By care or passion though I'd known each night
That stretching of the flesh, that rising up
As of a pointing to some distant goal,
But distant and so vague thought did not try
To find a way to reach it. In my branches
A pre-dawn bird sang of well-being and joy,
And went to sleep again. What wars there were
Between my flesh and spirit were quickly done,
Squalls that but made the ensuing sunshine brighter.

Her hot mouth in an instant changed all that:
I held the fallen Eve, I held Acrasia,
Awake, with outstretched arms and heaving breast.
Trembling, I felt my male-flesh stiffening,
Eager to consummate itself in her
And celebrate the death of all my visions
In one embrace. Desperate with shame and fear

I twisted sideways that she might not feel
My lust against her thighs. Then suddenly
She dropped her arms and laughed: "Tomorrow maybe
You will have better manners. Let's go home."

VII

Having sown no wind, why should I reap the whirlwind!
Choked in its snaky spirals through the nights
I longed for the sane, steadying light of day
And dreaded daybreak and the waiting eyes
Like spiders poised in the spun web of laughter
To which I'd be the fly.

       Through the long hours
Of daytime and its one-time sobering tasks
The inner chaos raged. No boyish talk
Then, with my friendly phantoms, but tight-lipped
Endurance of a wrong I could not name,
A kind of rape by some amorphous thing
Only my eyes could see and my weak hands
Strive as they might, could not push from me.

A man may match his devil wile for wile
Or banish him with a stern "apage"
But a mere lad knows nothing of such skill
And has not heard that word and so lies helpless
For all his devil-ants to feast on him
Until his very tongue is eaten out
And he can cry no more.

VIII

Into my den of anguish then there came
One, the charred, stub-end ember where a flame
Had once played brightly. Had he known my trouble
He would have pricked the whole thing like a bubble
With the dull knife-point of a smutty joke
And the goings-on of "girl and bloke".
I was spared that. He only came to say
He'd like to take me hunting some fine day
And it was time I'd learned the manly art
Of sending bullets cleanly to the heart.

From that time on, through hours of rain and sun,
He was my guide and mentor. Knife and gun

Were the choice instruments by which he taught
Me how to tame the dragons of my thought
By turning my young heart into a stone
Warmed by the hunter's lust, and that alone;
So I, with nothing left to love or feel,
Punished my ruined Eden with cold steel
Levelled with grim and calculating care
Against all things that once had made it fair.

He stood by me when I had learned to shoot
And sat with rifle balanced on my knee
To watch the lorikeets that hung like fruit
Low in the branches of a grey-box tree;

Fruit for a lad to knock down at his leisure
With sure and eager bullets for a stick
And no one by to portion out his pleasure
And say which one he should or shouldn't pick.

The sun was warm on me; there was no hurry;
The blossom-drunken birds were everywhere,
And it was sweet to feel the hunter's flurry
Subside and turn into the hunter's care.

My finger took the slack up on the trigger,
But when the target slipped behind a limb
I cursed and chose another, brighter, bigger,
And cautiously lined up the sights on him.

There was a moment for the quick decision
Whether to shoot him through the head or breast,
To try the very utmost of precision
To send the bullet certain of its quest.

I don't know which I did, but he came down
As cleanly as an apple over-mellow
That frost has loosened high up in the crown
Of a tall tree whose leaves are turning yellow.

His feet were like the stone feet of a griffin,
But small and black. And then I saw his eye,
While every feather seemed to fade and stiffen,
Suddenly lose its hold upon the sky.

That moved me with compassion for a minute;
But knowing this would surely spoil my day,

I broke the breech and shoved a bullet in it,
And aimed again, and coldly blazed away.

Day after day after day
That bloody business. Even now in sleep
I see the bright birds falling and the leap
Of death-struck rabbits. Strange,
Savage and pitiful that a killer's rage,
And yet it was the only strength I had.
So I had moved from bad
To was it worse? Until there came a change
And I could turn that death-polluted page,
And though remembering, write in blood no more.

IX

Always I shall remember.
It was a day
Surely not made for death;
A Riverina day in late September,
A day for the deep drawing-in of breath
And heart as light as birdsong in the branches
And blood as golden-warm as the gold wattle
Blooming along the creek.

We did not speak
But walked, true hunters, with the stealthy going
That brings quite sudden death to the unknowing.

He was a big man, hard of hand and heart
Who had come to us with a history
We could but guess at from the mocking mouth,
Harsh laughter and the lines on cheek and brow
Like cracks in stone. He said he had killed men
In Africa, black men, for the mere sport,
And we believed him. Sometimes when strong beer
Breached the stark dykes of his long reticence
He spoke of "home" somewhere in distant Europe
And of a wife and children parted from
Years since and never to be seen again.
He was the sort of man one does not question
And so we had no answers.
                              In a shed
Equipped with forge and anvil, his domain,
He wrought the farm its thews of steel and iron,
Plough-share and coulter, binder-knife and all

The implements for sowing and for reaping,
But never laid his hand upon a horse.

So we went out each Sunday to strike dead
With shotgun blast and bullet bird and beast;
Before us a sweet wilderness of singing,
Behind us silence.

                      I had often watched
Galahs in flight on stormy days. They loved
To let the great wind sweep them past a tree,
Wheel, and drive back in madcap revelry
And perch, crests up, defiant of the blast,
Then launch again and do the whole thing over.
To prove the storm had found his finest lover.

They came at us across an open space
Wing-tip to wing-tip at eye level height,
A mated pair. Their rose-breasts in the sun
Glowed under slate-grey wings. "They're yours," I yelled,
And crouched to give my friend a clearer shot.
The gun crashed; one bird hurtled to the ground
The other swerved away and circled back
With wild shrill cries, fluttered as though to land
Then rose again but would not go from there.

"They mate for life," I said, "best bring her down.
Those cries will drive us mad; best bring her down,
Or let me have your gun." He had picked up
The bleeding broken thing and stared at it
As though amazed or horror-struck, and then
His heavy shoulders hunched and shook, and tears
Spilled down those stone-hard cheeks. I did not dare
Look long at him: half-sick and cold with fear
Of him, of everything, I turned away.
And soon he walked beside me bent for home
In the dark silence of some stern arrest.

Arrest it was. From that hour never again
Did gun and rifle run like ravening dogs
In deadly fellowship. He had not said
"Don't tell them what I did:" perhaps he knew
Out of some deeper insight that my lips
Were sealed. We put our guns away uncleaned,
Mine, and I think his too, uncleaned forever.

X

There was an ending and there a beginning.
Feebly I groped for meanings as a child
Plucks at a flower, head bent, with serious eyes
Scanning the parts it has not learned to name.
Feebly at first but ever more urgently
I strove to think — for not to think was death —
Think out beyond myself to God and man,
Good, evil, life itself, and found no help
More than a faith that somewhere help must be
Waiting, and I must find it. Paradise,
Long lost, must be regained and I was ready,
Young, ignorant, but with the eager heart
Of one who fronts some Everest of the soul
And does not fear the climb.

Part Two

A farmer lad, these many years ago,
I saw her first, the City of the South,
Part ringed by hills and bright with almond trees.
My father walked beside me through her streets,
His hand half shyly feeling down for mine
As I myself had often stroked a foal
When weaning time had come and it must pass
From the close sanctuary of its mother's eye
To wind-swept paddock and hawk-lonely sky.

And this was weaning time: ahead lay doubt,
Hope, loneliness, a vast bewilderment;
Behind me the sharp clicking-shut of gates.
An Eden lost, perhaps one to be gained,
So ran my thought.

                  Even yet I see that place,
The sandstone cloister-prison in the charmed city,
As, and I speak with loathing and with pity,
A yellow rotting tooth in a fair face.

Five years I festered in that cavity
Absorbing and imparting poison till,
The place and I both having had our fill,
I was extruded unceremoniously.

I brought with me a vision of life, a boy's
Patch-quilt of many readings, bright and warm
To cover me and make endurable
The pangs of homeward longing and secure
A secret place for musings in the night.
Had they stripped me of that I might have stood
Naked and desperate a little while
But soon, like a lopped tree, sent out new growth
Robust and eager for the wind and sun.

There was no wind, no sun. Nothing was taken
From me and nothing added. Never
"The still, sad music of humanity"
Struck on my dulling ears, but always
That other music of "Concordia",
That concord of sweet sounds — and what were they?

How simple it all was! In Hebrew, then
In Greek, God spoke — his favourite languages
And what He said, and only that, was truth.
But after many years the Anti-Christs
Throned in the Eternal City (next to Hell
The cesspool of creation) had so fouled
The holy text with their own lusts and lies
And the dark perversions that God spoke again
Now for the third and last time, and in German,
And the Triune had proved himself tri-lingual.

So was the temple raised, the concord reached:
God, Prophets, the Apostles, Martin Luther,
Learned professors (Lutheran, of course),
Parsons and students, all in one great bond
To lift the heavenward beacon, God's own light,
Above the desperate hordes that swarm upon
"The plain where ignorant armies clash by night."

To me it was no temple but a ladder
Up which one had to kiss his way, no concord
But that of lips to foot or parts up higher;
And seeing this, I lost all taste for climbing.

I think I came to find the glory of God,
And found instead a shackle and a rod:
Shackle upon the runner who would run
With violent love towards the very sun;
Rod laid upon the young defiant back

To keep the traveller on the beaten track
Of stale theology that had no worth
For anything upon the well-loved earth
But promised, if obedience were given,
A sure way into a stale Lutheran heaven.

 I came to find that Luther whose proud name
Was to the Western world Olympic flame,
A running torch. My teachers showed a man
Pompous, in the worst sense Olympian,
Whose one concession to mere man's estate
Was that a man should cherish his good mate
And, in the sight of God and man thought proper,
Just twice a week should top her.

(Of course, that worthy bit of news I had
In private from a somewhat older lad.)

One with no more to learn has little to teach,
To show, beyond the grasp, forever the reach.
What was it they could learn?
Were they not Doctors of Divinity
And teachers by a sort of right divine?
Were not all texts established long ago,
All scholia long since in?
Were not all questions answered, chapter and verse?
And who thought otherwise, surely the curse
Of Pride was on him, and her bastard, Sin,
Intransigence, and at the Last Inspection
He would be paid for that brash intellection
In the hottest flames of a hot Lutheran hell.

Ah. well!

As one Joanna, after months of rumour,
Died not of a Messiah but a tumour,
So out of my dim spiritual blastema
Their husbandry brought forth in its due season,
(They gave my own perverseness as the reason),
An itching rash of spiritual eczema.

What was the manner of it? All as simple
As to squeeze out the substance of a pimple
Or, with perversion of Socratic wiles,
Scratch the new crop of intellectual piles —
For piles and pimples surely best express

That state our masters called true saintliness —
And theirs the holy duty to keep hatching
Increasing hordes for squeezing and for scratching.

I have known rooms serene with lamplit talk
Of men and manners, things far off and near,
The ways that Christ and Plato used to walk,
And all the business of the changing year;
And other rooms, foul dens where lust and passion
Held dialogue on Sin's most recent fashion.
From heaven to hell the difference, yet in each,
Since life moved there, there was a truth to reach
For the attentive mind.
                      The room we sat in
Was dank and dismal as a hollow nut
Long since abandoned by the wiser worms.
And there we did our academic squirms,
Mouths open, and our minds securely shut,
Rows of small desks severely bolted down,
Each with a chair as rigid as a frown,
Filled the whole space except for the raised throne
No bum dared press except the master's own.
Miserable desks that would not hide within
Their one cramped shelf even the smallest sin
Nor give fair sanctuary to a lollie
One might suck on in secret praise of folly.

There was no trace of beauty anywhere:
The floors were scrub-dead boards, the walls as bare;
Hungering for beauty, one had done as well
To seek for her in Dante's deepest Hell —
I jest! For in that place God frowns upon,
Passion is one tremendous Laocoön
Whose agony can feed the heart and mind.
We stared at nothing and our eyes were blind.

And, as the furnishings, so the instruction:
In thought the syllogism ruled; induction,
(The glory of modern mind), was held to be
The very highway into heresy
And heresy the highway into hell.
Thus all was God-ordained and ordered well,
And ours the duty but to stay at heel
With lolling tongues and firm sequacious zeal.

We read some Latin — Cicero and Caesar,
But not Lucretius, that Satan-pleaser;
Some Greek — New Testament, and nothing more;
For how should fledgling saints endure the roar,
The roll and thunder of the Odyssey?
Or how should eyes like ours unblasted see
A mighty king with eyes gouged from his head
For taking his own mother in his bed?
And what — I feel a shaking in my knees,
Stiff though they are now fifty-odd years after —
What would our buds have done beneath the laughter,
The sleety gales of Aristophanes!

And we read much in Luther's mother-tongue.
Muffled, of course, was the great bell he swung
Alaruming a drowsy world awake:
We read him only for his dogma's sake
And learned to make that dogma more emphatic
By crude perversion into the dogmatic.

The sage of Weimar passed in quick review,
Puppeted just to show us how the true
Could lie so far beyond the reach of knowledge;
(And may the Lord preserve our humble college
From ever teaching that the two are one!
Witness how Goethe's intellectual sun
Gained him a world and lost him heaven. Alas,
Behold the mighty wither like the grass!
Sadly, oh sadly, let us pause and think
How "apage" had saved him from that brink,
And he'd have been a wiser, happier man
Had he but held to doctrines Lutheran!)

And we read Hebrew — just enough to scan
Exactly how and when It all began.

History — the names and dates of kings and battles —
We treasured much as children do their rattles,
And hailed as champions, as best and proudest,
Those who could shake the longest and the loudest
In memory-boxes pebbles gathered on
Time's highway through Victoria back to John.

Philosophy? What wisdom could be known
Beyond the trust in faith and faith alone?
And that we had by grace. Why listen to

The mouthings of that sad ungodly crew
Who walked in darkness? Let them not be heard!
But, if our ears had caught a single word,
Let the good Lord shame us into forgetting
As though we had been guilty of bed-wetting.

All literature was but the vernal breeze
Tempered to the young lamb with wobbly knees,
Breeze soft as touch of fern-fronds half uncurled,
Not the great wind that roars across the world
Ripping all veils to shreds, all masks to tatters.
How should the soul be served by that which batters
All sheltering decencies aside and lays
Man stretched obscenely naked to the gaze?
God covered him — be His the thanks and praise!

This was the daily food on which we fed,
The manna, milk and honey, and the bread.
"Give us this day our daily bread."
They did
By way of hour-long dreary catechism
To test rote memory and probe for schism.

As men catch fish with neither bait nor hooks,
We caught our learning without aid of books:
Our teachers were our only library.
From them we learned the truth that makes men free —
Free to come in as "stirks and go out asses",
Gravely transmogrified by college classes.

Ah, Darwin, how, though we had never read
A word of yours, we split you loin to head
With the sharp sword of Genesis, and then
Dragged you, vile Hector, where the mouths of men
Could void their spit upon you! Hip and thigh
Smiting you, we proved Science all a lie.

After the drench of classes came the hour
For what faint life was left in us to flower
In games or low-voiced, closely guarded talk
Sprinkled with words that urchins scrawl with chalk
On latrine walls — pitiful whisperings
Out of the young blood poisoned at its springs
By teachings that made filth of all desire
And pointed to the far-off marriage-bed
Where, burning with his hoarded, holy fire,

Man be loosed upon a maidenhead —
The promised paradise where he shall revel
Approved by Paul, and fearless of the devil.

But till that time the devil had his way
Where taut and helpless the young bodies lay
In shaking beds — which I hear creaking still —
Where the hot hand proved mightier than the will,
And threats of pimply cheeks and softened brains,
Dull, watery eyes, and finally hell-pains
Could not arrest the fall of barren rains;
And when dawn quenched night's agony and heat,
The guilty hand hiding the guilt-stained sheet!

And all the while, each in his double bed,
Our masters did as Paul and Luther said
To teach their spouses beyond any question
Just what it means to be a true-born Christian.

The tutelary spirit of that place
Was a big lad with virtue for a face
And learning for a shield. So virtuous,
He had the drop on every one of us
For smoking, swearing, drinking, and he had
The Master's ear to keep him far from sad;
So studious that he could almost speak
In Latin and, the rumour went, in Greek;
So cautious that he never once displayed
His strength and courage in the games we played
Where hip to hip we clashed and let take all,
The saints or devil, so we had the ball.
A raw-boned pasty lad with a limp penis
Shaped like the tear-drop of a weeping Venus,
Who later on, or so I've heard it said,
Begot twelve children in his marriage-bed,
All, like himself, in holiness begotten,
And all as rotten.

Enough of that vile chapter. There were hours
Smiled on by other and far happier powers
When, friend to friend, we spun our yarns of home:
The paddocks, dogs at heel, we used to roam
Hunting the hare; wild gallops on the hack
Who carried only princes on his back
(For none could feel those shoulders at his knees
And not be made a prince); robbing the bees

When the keen axe had brought the full hive down
And then, our fingers sticky with the brown
Honey, we gorged upon the honey-cake;
And then — and then — alas! the bellyache!
The fledgling magpie slyly taught to speak
A language that would blanch a parson's cheek.
A thousand lost, loved, trivial, boyish things
Remembered from the days when we were kings.

And there were nobler memories to impart
When, school forgotten, heart spoke out to heart:
Buoyed by a sort of mental hand-in-hand,
We travelled into the forbidden land
Where I had found my Edens. Fearfully
We stalked enchanted gardens, tree to tree,
In deadly terror of the dragon's hold.
And so we felt the very realms of gold
Beneath our feet, to our rapt eyes revealed —
And then — the evening study-summons pealed,
And we sat down to porridge stale and cold.

There were hours when — and still the memory blesses —
We tried to fit the hawks of thought with jesses
That they might serve us in our falconry
With truth the prize and Time's wide heaven free
For our bold hunting; truth brought wild and clean
Down from the skyways, not the stuffed, obscene
Carcass, shown daily to our weary eyes,
Of something that had never known the skies.

I think I hunted boldly, but my winning
Turned out to be the ultimate of sinning;
For sins born of the flesh could be corrected,
But never those of mind (or faith). "Rejected,
Now let him be rejected utterly,
Unworthy of our teaching; let him be
A farmer among farmers, where the harm
He'll do will be restricted to the farm,
(And may that prosper!) After absolution
He may in cash make us a contribution
To show the Lord has set him in a path
At least not head-on into heaven's wrath."

There is no Paradiso in my story
And very little even of Purgatory,
But now, years after, it is sweet to tell
How on that day I was delivered from Hell.

Part Three

I

A poet once described a poet's thought
As "soul in sense", and that will guide me now
As I survey, but briefly, the great years
At Lawrence first, then Harvard, where my mind
First knew its strength, spread wing and faced into
The lifting gales of Spring. Those winds of thought
Were like the storms that hurled my wild galahs
Past tossing tree-tops and, I blown like them,
Turned, fought my way back, perched, launched out again
And did the whole tempestuous passage over
To prove the gale had found a worthy lover.

Here was a world of books and famous men,
Scholars and teachers each of whom had lit
Lamps on the paths of learning to make bright
The way for future travellers such as I.
Their names are in the roster of the great:
McPheeters, Golder, Kitteredge, Robinson,
Perry and Lowes. These were my friends by day
And my companions in the studious nights
Who stood unseen beside me and spoke words,
Sometimes of praise, sometimes of reprimand,
But last and always of the aspiration
That points the way to beauty and to truth
And whispers that the ultimate prize will be
To find the two are one.

          They all have passed
Out of this partial into the great light
That Shelley saw beyond our dome of life,
"The still, white radiance of eternity."
By doing deathless things while still Time's slaves,
In lecture, friendly word and learned book,
They added to that radiance which itself
Is a becoming, is a crescent brightness
Fed by the thoughts and deeds of noble men,
Who thus inherit what they helped to make.

Could they have read these words, I hear them say:
"A bit sententious; better read more Pope
To keep your thought in manageable scope."
And then a smile.

         I thank them as one may
Thank the great sun for giving him a day
More wonderful than even his dearest hope.

II

Those were the days when Volstead's bony hand
Was like a plague of locusts on the land
Chewing it dry. The W.C.T.U.
Smiled its big-bosomed blessing on the crew
Of low inquisitors whose hands could throttle
By law both merrymaker and his bottle,
And men of spirit rose up everywhere
To show the world our banner was still there,
And millions who had never touched a drop
Grew very fond of barley and the hop.

Drinking became a sort of ritual
For the elect, those who could find a well
At which to fill their crock; an act designed
To keep oneself and all men else in mind
That laws, like customs born of finger-shaking,
Are honoured best by laughter and law-breaking.

Our well was Doctor Mash on Harvard Square.
A running nose or cough would take one there,
No question asked, for the good doctor loathed
A wolf-cough in a lamb-cough meekly clothed
And reached for pen at once to serve eviction
Notice by way of medical prescription:
"One pint of whiskey taken in small doses
As remedy for coughs and running noses."

We caught our pulmonary ills by turn
And stored our bottles with a due concern
For the next feast night when the right amount
Was credited our corporate account
And we could plan to have a few friends in
To meditate on whisky, love and sin.

And so we did our happy duty; read
Aloud from books grown dear to heart and head,
From serious to the increasing light
In tempo with the spirit of the night
And the warm ministrations of the cup;

And as dawn neared we always ended up
With a fond look at Burns' "Jolly Beggars"
Housed in their barns where all the girls were leggers,
And where the men, with doxies in the hay
Pursued the even tenor of their way,
Then rose to sing, like angels new-ejected
From heaven, "Liberty's a glorious feast
And our proud standard, here on earth erected,
In what it says is honest at the least."

We sang that chorus loud and lustily
And for the next week lived on bread and tea.

III

Classroom and library were the twin springs
From which there flowed a stream of lively talk
Brightened by glancing wit. Our minds were stripped
Like athletes for a race in which the swimming,
The simple joy of it, was the chief prize;
That, and the acclaim of all one's student peers.
We plunged like boys that on hot summer days
Cast off their clothes on banks of well-loved rivers
And dive and splash each other and are glad
Of the hot day, the river and the surge
Of strength in their young bodies. No one feared
The water or the buffets of the game,
And, if one lagged, he set his mind to learn
A new and better stroke.

Concordia

Had tried to teach me passive-mindedness,
The sponge recipient of the water poured
From the teacher's jug and ready to give back
At slightest squeeze the liquid drop by drop.
Or I was taught to be the gape-mouthed goldfish
Decorous in his bowl and waiting for
Crumbs to be sifted to him one by one.
Or I was taught to be the memory-box
In which professors dropped their daily penny
That I should empty on examination
And be accorded fitting rank and station —
Said Simple Simon. "Sir, I haven't any".

Whatever else, I'd not been tamed, and now
Could fly my wild galahs' way, loose my hawks

On what bright game might wing across the sky,
And bring the kill home proudly. Best of all,
And proof the child is father of the man
And all his story an unbroken thread,
I lived my boyhood fantasies,
Roused fair Acrasia sleeping on her bed,
Was bold with Eve and, walking by the creek,
Kissed One on something warmer than her cheek.
For I had learned, through many indecisions,
That one who never had his boyish visions,
Grown man, is rarely likely to see more
Than lies before him on his plate for dinner.
Having come to count the sins of blank omission
More damnable than those done by commission,
I was right glad I'd not been such a sinner.

IV

And gladly would he learn and gladly teach.

So Chaucer said of the shy Oxford Scholar
More than five hundred years ago. I pause
To think of all the teachers throughout time
Who lived by that ideal and to record
Gratitude that for nearly fifty years
I travelled in their goodly company.

And travelling so, we stayed in many a place
Famous in history, saw many a face:
The ghastly ones that throng in Dante's Hell,
The Juliets our boyhood loved so well,
The emperors with slightly tilted crown
Who strove to master kingdoms with a frown
And found their boasts of glory choked in sand
Heaped over them by a bold poet's hand.

Men, times and manners passed in long review,
Always familiar and forever new.
Through the clear text imagination caught
The glowing forms of beauty, passion, thought,
Loved for themselves; but also we could see
Mirrored in them the shapes of things to be,
And by the falling towers of Ilium
Felt the cold shadows of the days to come
And reached for wisdom that alone might save
Our Troy from Ilium's ash-covered grave.

V

The Dean taps lightly on one's shoulder when
It's time to close the classroom, drop the pen,
And go on acting like most other men.
So let me tap as lightly as the Dean
On laughing memories of what has been:
The sly up-creeping of a mini-skirt
That kept the eye expectantly alert
And made the mind exert its shrewdest force
To keep the lecture running on its course;
And here and there a long-haired lad who'd sit
Stroking his beard to stimulate the wit
Or with raised hand and heavenward rolling eye
Pose like a man about to prophesy
Or just to call my lectures one damn lie;
The girl who took notes so assiduously
In preparation, so she said, to be
A teacher — heaven bless us! just like me.

Lawyers and doctors, statesmen, many more
First moored their boats against my friendly shore
And sailed each day to many a far horizon
On which I had myself not ever laid eyes on
And brought me back great tidings, brilliant pieces
That would provide the backbone of a thesis.

You've written your theses as I've written mine.
Hail and farewell, and may the sun long shine
On you and all your ways, and may there be,
As I of you, a happy thought of me.

VI

Time and the Dean have bid this prince goodnight,
And I am very sure that both are right
Social Security, Retirement Pension
In pocket — these I would not fail to mention —
And faithful Eve beside, hand in hand,
I set my destined course for Cactus-land.

Part Four

I

The way stretched over and between
Hills taut and knobby as arthritic hands
Clenched on a core of pain.

The skyline stood out clear
With humps and hollows sharp against the west;
Some like the contours of a withered breast
That blossomed once and will not bud again.

And I had speculated
Concerning the geology,
Zoology, ecology
Of those far hills, debated
A thousand questions idly while the hills
Waited,

And waited patiently because they knew
What only an old master understands,
That he who reads the alphabet right through
Must end in theirs, the Omega of lands.

The approach was easy and I travelled light
Shedding impedimenta on the way:
Old aspirations and old fears that might
Persuade the foot to profitless delay.

And when I felt a sharpening in the air
And a new heat upon me from the sun
And a new brightness on all objects there,
Rock, thorn and sand, I knew my journey done.

There were no paths, no flowers to reproach
The trampling foot, no sound of streams to wake
In the charmed ear the knowledge that their song
But elegized their destined perishing;
There were no wind-stirred, shimmering leaves to broach
Questions of autumn and a desolate lake
That broods on some old mystery of wrong
And on whose withered sedges no birds sing.

It was like passing from a crowded room
Heaving with gay confusions whose loud talk

Settles a leprous mildew on the brain
At one stride through a blast of cleansing air
Into the august silence of a tomb
(Without its shadows) where lone pilgrims walk
Head-bowed in meditation to regain
The souls they lost in some far Otherwhere.

II

I have my visitors, who come for reasons
As various as the changing hours and seasons.

Some come to Cactus-land
With that half-secret air and hurried step
With which shy women seek the door marked "Ladies",
And I have thought, and counted it no treason,
That, as the manner of their coming is
Like theirs, so is their reason.

They seem to find unburdening here a pleasure:
Unthreatened privacy and lots of leisure
For no one's near half-angrily to "scat" them
Or shake a monitory finger at them;
And the absorbent sand and sun-baked rubble
Erase all evidence and thus save trouble.

. . . . .

On holidays I often see them come,
Blobs on the low horizon, with the dust
Swirling behind their eighty-miles-per thrust
Into this Nowhere. Then the falling hum
Of power breathing to a stop: a car,
Pulsing with wealth, exuding the attar
Of cities, stands before me; "Lost, I think",
The driver says and tosses me a wink,
And I reply, "Too goddamn right you are!"

That startles him and almost startles me
Into a spasm of better manners, "We",
I hasten on, "are solitary folk;
I should have paused to think before I spoke."
"That's quite alright; my wife has heard before —
Haven't you dear? — such words and many more,
Some, should I say, of quite a stronger flavour;
But may I ask of you a little favour
Before the kids grow desperate for a Coke?"

I answer briefly, "That won't be amiss."
And he goes on, "My question, then, is this —
But first let me explain: we take a ride
Each Sunday through the neighbouring countryside
To give the kids a little touch of nature;
But I, being born and bred a business creature,
Keep an eye peeled for bargains on the way,
And, well — the place you've got here, may I say,
Has possibilities. Imagination
Unfolds it all: attractive filling-station,
Restaurant, cocktail lounge with souvenirs
To sell to those who've had too many beers,
And for all those who can no longer roam
A cozy place we'll call 'The Sunset Home'.
I see it all! How much a freehold acre,
That is, good friend, if you could find a taker?"

"The price is seventy years and everyone
Has lease-hold on all things beneath the sun."
"And what the yearly taxes that you pay?"
"What one has lost the day before today."
"How as investment, should one want to buy in?"
"No better place on earth, young man, to die in;
But let me add, to keep the record true,
You can't buy here even though you're in Who's Who."
"Well, thanks a lot; I see the evening growing;
And what's the best road out? We need be going."
"All roads are better, friend, on the way back,
And I am sure you'll burn the bloody track."
                . . . . .
Such trivia are cross-garters to the mind
That hold the socks up but provoke unkind
Throbbings and jabs in the constricted blood;
But even a saint might falter when he should
Spread wide his arms and shower ripe civilities
Even upon the worst of imbecilities.
                . . . . .
There are the graver hours when talk is free
About the busy corners of the world
And words seek for the truths that they have sought for
Since the first word man ever spoke. They are
The embodiment of thought, and tentative
As thought must be, and truth, until both find
"A local habitation and a name", eternal form —
Itself the final truth — in stone or colour
Or sound or in utterance of a poet
When he is breathed on by eternity.

Such forms my guests and I cannot create,
However we strive to. So we re-arrange
Our glittering fragments of the world much as
Children might try to reconstruct a flower
From shattered sepals, petals, stamens, pistil,
And turn at last to the one perfect thing,
That flower itself, its name "The Second Coming",
That says for us all that we cannot say.

So, with the setting sun ends many a day.
The guests, departed, leave in the still air
Sweet evidences of their presence where
I stand alone to watch the sun go down:
The Herrick rustle of a silken gown,
The hand I shut a moment in my own,
The glance that leaves me never again alone.

And sometimes then
When all have gone and given my desert back
To the night wind, the stars and me,
And every sense has fallen released and slack,
A sly insidious fever wakes and climbs
Up through my being till aghast I see
The ape, desire, astraddle on my breast
Grinning like one possessed.

III

Were it not broad day
This could be dingoes crying;
Were it not dead calm
It could be blown sand shirring
Through dry thorn-bushes. Heat —
And it is hot — could make a sound like this.

Thus would the drowsy ear
Interpret, and the half-awakened sense
Drop back into a dull indifference
Appropriate to the place and time of year.

But multi-coloured spirals in my blood
Climb to an apex in the startled brain
And steady there into a pointed bud
Whose sepals curl back instantly to free
Petals, each one a woman and to me
Dear once, long lost, and now twice dear again.

And I rush madly off through Cactus-land
Gasping and calling,
And fall and have my mouth stopped up with sand
And rise and stumble on
While the great sun above me stares upon
A Satyr-lust
With cloven hooves and tongue besmeared with dust.

They call, I follow till
A huge rock fronts me. Did it open and shut,
And are the Mi Mi women safe within?
All Cactus-land is still
And all its mocking eyes are watching there
To see me naked in the heat and glare
With sweat and sand like goat's hair on my skin.

The kookaburra loosens up his breast
With an apologetic cough or two
As prelude to his customary jest;
The butcher-bird, uncertain what to do,
Pecks at the newest corpse beside his nest.

The Mi Mi women are figures in a legend of a tribe of Australian aborigines. They are invisible, but with seductive calls lure male wayfarers to go in pursuit of them. When the pursuit grows hot, they slip into the sanctuary of some large rock that conveniently opens to let them in. An old, old story. --EGM

IV

In Cactus-land all forms are as precise
As winter shadows on a field of ice
Or summer shadows where long-dead trees stand
Up to their gaping armpits in the sand,
Patterns unblurred by any compromise.

All things are absolute: by day the heat
Allows no coolness to the veins that beat
With thin and rapid blood; by night the cold
Is the white covering stretched without a fold
Over the dead from moveless head to feet.

Here laughter has no genial fat to shake
With joy made visible until there wake

A bright contagion in another's breast,
But rumbled in its bone-cage, self-possessed,
Loving the loveless sounds for their own sake.

All thoughts and passions, naked, here but see
Essential self, and monstrous though that be,
Glance not aside nor seek to twist about
The shameful or the ulcerous part a clout
To hide the bitter, sad deformity.

The plants that root beneath the crumbling sherds
Have never worn a diadem of words
Strung for their beauty, but they hear the song
Of butcher-bird and kookaburra, long
The Villon and the Rabelais of birds.

The one sends up in spirals to the sky
The songs he gleaned from all the birds that die
Upon the altar he has wrought for death.
He floats them up like iridescent breath —
Bubbles a child might blow half-wonderingly.

The other, with his foot upon a snake,
With clashing laughter brings the world awake
To that fine jest he newly brought to pass
Upon the cunning slitherer in the grass,
Partly for breakfast, part for the jest's sake.

These are the master voices of the day,
The tragic and the comic muse, who say
The whole of knowledge in disparate song;
And even they fall silent when the long
Night closes and the moon is far away.

V

As the hand withers with the failing blood
It seeks for things with a texture like its own,
Things scarred by graspings and much letting go,
Departings, fallings-off;
Not velvet of the bud
But rasp of sand-pocked stone.

As the eye fades
It sets its rest on knobbed, arthritic hills,
And is at ease,
Not with the sprightly dance of daffodils
Sunlit beneath old trees,
But with dead stones and ever deepening shades.

And, as the rods of sense
Shrink back from contact with ephemera,
The watchful mind at last discovers whence
The leaf, becoming thorn, wins competence
To thrive in arid earth and parching air,

And learns, like it, to store
In darkened cells the rain that long ago
Brought quickening and may return no more,
And, in due season, when the spring winds blow,
To dip desire in that Promethean source
And light a candle on this desolate shore.

VI

After the winter nights in Cactus-land
Have hung white robes of fog upon the hills
And things long said or done
Have drifted through the mind like autumn leaves
Blown by the winds of memory, I rise
To greet the dawn
And watch the sun disrobe the nearest hill.

This is no boy
Fumbling at buttons in a darkened car,
Nor is it an old lecher with the skills
Learned in hotels,
Nor bridegroom who may press
A lawful claim even though he rip the dress.

And well it suits my mood
To hear this troubadour sing fold on fold
His lady's garment to him in the sky
And be content in gentle brotherhood
To call on all things living to behold
And praise her beauty and his mastery.

Poems from *The Well & The Star* (1983)

The title for this privately printed collection of poems is taken from a poem I had written several years before it was published in 1947. I was then in my late forties. Now, in my early eighties, I am happy to have that poem serve as a preface to the present volume. E.G.M.

.   .   .

A well is something like a grave; who
Goes down in either has to go alone;
And I was ever one who liked a few
Companions, and warm sunlight on the stone
In some wide open place with winds blowing,
And birds and bees and such coming and going.

But when he said, "I saw a star by day
From eighty feet down there, and saw it clear;
And you may see it, too, if you'll but pay
The price—and that is nothing but your fear—
You'll try it, lad?" I said, "All right, I'll go,
But careful on the rope, and not too slow!"

Partly for safety, partly that I might
Drink the full terror of the long descent
Past dripping walls into that worse than night,
He gave me rope so slowly that I went
By inches down the eighty feet of well;
And time stood still as time must do in hell.

Twenty feet down I scarcely could remember
How sunshine feels on shoulders and on back
When wheat is tall and yellowing in November
And dust goes up like smoke from every track,
For the harsh cold, so new to me, was shaking
My very blood like drums when fear is waking.

The air grew heavy with the wet-earth smell
That goes with wells and darkness, and I tried
To seal my lungs against it with a spell
Passionately uttered, but in vain I cried,
For, crying, I but sucked in deeper still
The stuff that made a fungus of my will.

I prayed all bright things to come back to me,
Telling them I was still the same lad who

Laughed with them from the crown of many a tree,
But they rejected me as bright things do
All who go down to darkness, though they are
Bent on an errand to a possible star.

Darker and darker, inch by steady inch,
And then I cursed the man who stood up there,
The sly deceiver, by his creaking winch,
With sunlight on his shoulders and his hair
And on his mouth the wicked smile of one
Who has let down his brother from the sun.

Just when it seemed I must reach out and pull
The signal-rope, and rise and face my shame,
Or, still the coward, put my wits to school
And lie about my star by day, there came
A quiver down the well-rope from on top,
And soon my bucket settled to a stop.

Then I looked up. Beyond that awful throat
Of darkness one clear pool of blue, and there,
Much like a white and splendid lily afloat,
A single star. Oh, wonderfully fair
And pulsing with another kind of light
From that one ever sees in stars by night!

It was a light like that which streams from thought
When noble presences are in the mind,
And life lies bathed in a new glory caught
From eyes that have grown suddenly unblind;
A light like that man never sees but when
The god is in him—and but briefly then.

Could I have stayed there but a little longer
I would have found what all the poets say
Is lovelier than any dream and stronger
Than death or love that comes and will not stay;
I would have found—but with a sudden shift
The rope was straining on the upward lift.

I kept my eyes on that bright star until
It faded as I neared the wellhead; then
The old black fear took hold upon my will,
And shook me till I stood on earth again
Up in the sun, and heard the old man say,
"Well, did you see it, lad, the star by day?"

He laughed. "You look as though you'd seen a ghost.
But let me tell you, even a coward may
Look up at night and see the golden host
Of stars, but who would look on one by day
Will never see that star and see it clear
Unless he makes a well-rope of his fear."

Part I - Twigs for a Winter Garland for Old Men

Twigs for a Winter Garland for Old Men

From my own garden and from many others
Where dead flowers hang and tendrils of the vine
Cling in their death-grip on the tree that smothers
In fallen leaves the grass where came to dine
The birds of summer, these dry twigs with care
I fashion for a garland such may wear
Who love all things that bloom and sing, and share
With me the joy of gardens such as mine,
And, leaving them by edict of old age,
Accept that edict with no thought of rage,
Content to know that that same law will bring
Its royal singers to the Court of Spring
And gardeners, standing still, will hear them sing.

A Reading of Earth

I chipped some lichen from a crumbling cliff
For an old man to study at his leisure;
His hand will clutch his magnifying glass,
His heart leap up to meet the promised pleasure:

His ruse to trick the hunter closing in,
Not as men play at dominoes or cards
Nor as they fashion epics hoped to be
Their monuments when empires fall to shards,

But from his Omega of days to read
Life's Alpha etched in living hues on stone.
What matter then what talon-fingered shadow
Loom up behind him where he sits alone!

Old Men Sowing Seeds in Late Autumn

We old men till, in the decreasing light
In our deep valley of departed years,
The little soil eroded from the height,
The uplands we once ploughed. That solstice nears,
Angel of darkness and the shortest day,
That bids all growing cease, and yet we break
Feebly the soil and hide some seeds away.

Forgive us, you, with your slight chance of growing,
Sown by us out of our vast need of sowing,
Hostages promised their release in Spring:
For our old hearts and old brains tired of knowing
How Winter scoffs at such fond bargaining,
This act of hope is not a little thing!

A Senior Citizen Muses

Senior? Well, now, we're all a little wacky
From wrenching of the years;
As with my car, the upholstery is tacky
And there's an ominous rattle in the gears,
And from the long, rough roads of grace and sin
The tires are eggshell thin.

We crawl past wrecking-yards along the way—
Those where the grass is green
Forever and some flowers bloom every day—
When the new models thunder and careen
Past us unenvied, for we surely know
The road they have to go.

We wish them well. and when the resplendent cop
Whistles and waves us down
For slowing traffic, after a brief stop,
We give up our fool journey to the town
And take the sleepy back roads as directed,
Homeward, but not dejected.

Intimation of Senility

I talk and talk and my unmarshaled words
Dart hither and yon blown by wild gusts of thought,
Thousands of lovely tempest-scattered birds
Off base, off target, with black fear distraught

And their one hope against the fall and dying
Is but to keep on flying.

Many a noble phalanx cleaves my sky,
Each wing of hundreds beating strongly on
In unison and swift as visions fly
To the one goal all hearts are set upon;
And my eyes lift to watch them as they pass
High over this sere grass.

Autumn and time for the last long migration!
But all my winged ones swirl about my head,
Chaos of motion that is but stagnation
Above Charybdis and the final bed,
Still beating where they cannot choose but stay,
The goal not lost, but the way!

Winter Sunset

Our trees against the sunset quietly
Put on a beauty they had never shown
In naked branches by the light of day
Or even, when in leaf, like a wild sea
They claimed the kingdom of the storm their own
And sent what bloom they had aloft like spray.

Two moments in the passing of the years:
The tumult, power, the glory and the grace,
The wild unleashing of pent up desire.
But better now to watch, as darkness nears,
With the last warmth of evening on my face,
Our trees, how still! against the sunset's fire.

In the Garden

I'm an old bumbling man
Tending my garden
And conscious of the shrinking of life's span
As arteries harden.

A robust, bouncing lad
Pushes my barrow,
Whistling some strange wild tune that never had
Chill at its marrow.

He wields my one good hoe
With fine abandon
As though no plants have any right to grow
In land they stand on.

He pulls the weed, the flower,
With equal gusto
And thinks, in the young innocence of power,
Things should be just so.

He goes his jocund way
And leaves my garden
Half ruined, as receipt for what's to pay
When arteries harden.

Sixty Years After First Reading Tennyson's "Ulysses"

Dreams, old men's last resource against despair,
Throng in the darkening chambers of their minds,
Present most then when Autumn's in the air
And the heart, seeking much, but little finds.

There's no Ulysses' way to grasp an oar
And call the old companions to the sea
And with them push out stoutly from the shore
To seek what fabled treasure still may be

Won in such isles as Circe ruled. That call
Can speed now only to the long-since dead
Who lie behind a sound-impervious wall
Above which none has ever lifted head.

The wine of Circe, sweet upon the tongue,
Drink for the youthful, godlike and the bold!
Ah, that enchantress is forever young,
And you and I, Ulysses, have grown old!

Departure of a Guest

Where will it go? It's only God who knows,
But why it goes is quite a simple matter:
It does not like the smell of crumbling houses
That groan and sigh with every wind that blows;
It hates and fears the loud heart-chilling clatter
That every footstep on loose boards arouses.

It's not the dread of ghosts, for long ago
As men and women these came through the doors
Of the warm house to join in wine and song.
But now there's only silence and the slow
Movement of shadows on the sinking floors—
It is the spent house does us all this wrong.

Go, untamed spirit, since this brain no more
(Though listening from first dawning till all's dark)
Transforms your song into the living word;
Go while the wind moans through the sagging door
And take elsewhere your bright Promethean spark—
I hear the goat the lonely old man heard.

Of Grass and Men

The meadow grass that hears the storm-wind near,
Lies down in cunning masquerade of fear;
Then, in the hush that shows the storm's gone by,
Rises refreshed to claim its share of sky.

But we, that other grass, by suffering schooled,
Know other storms not quite so neatly fooled,
And, lie we flat or proudly stand erect,
The end's the same, whichever we elect,
And leaves us envying, for what's come to pass,
The luck or cunning of the meadow grass.

A Fancy in Drought-Time

These devastated trees
Breathe their last breath in flowers
When drought is on the land.
My sad-sweet fancy sees
Each in its dying hours
As a white, lifted hand.

The sun, a Judas-friend,
Blights with its kiss of gold
Life to the very root,
But the betrayed ones send,
Here, of their thousandfold,
To Life, this last salute.

On My Seventy-Sixth Birthday, 1976
For Neiva

Love is the "many-splendored" thing
Whose protean forms and colors
Make mockery of the questioning
Of seers and priests and scholars.

A boy, in Riverina skies
I watched the sunset flame
And strove in childish-eager wise
To give each hue a name.

My elders smiled at my despair:
"You'll know, when you grow old,
It is the dust from earth up there
The setting sun turns gold."

The dust of earth, the light of heaven,
The alchemy of hurtless flame:
Today I know why love is given
Its many-splendored name.

Verses for a Fiftieth Anniversary

"Nature's first green is gold,
Her hardest hue to hold.
.   .   .
Nothing gold can stay."
> *Robert Frost*

The gold went as it must.
We learned to prize the leaf
That, often dull with dust
And scarred by many a thief,

Bright-winged, moth-lovely some,
And others fat, obscene,
A caterpillar-scum,
Moving upon the green.

Still rode the tides of air
Till Autumn's torch-fire came;
Then April's gold sang there,
A phoenix in the flame.

Part II - The Wreath

A Wreath
In Memoriam N.C.M.

"What else is love, but remembering."
Robert Nathan, *The River Journey*

Garlands turn into wreaths
For everyone who breathes
The sun-warmed air
And looks, and finds that one
Who was his heaven's sun
Will never again shine there.

With Heavy Heart, Cold Hand

With heavy heart, cold hand,
I gather these few sprays
From death's own tree, the yew,
And weave them in with rue
From meadows where her days
Made happy all the land.

For every day its night
As silence falls on song,
As sleep on those who grieve,
Who, waking, half believe
A dream has done them wrong
Then find their dream was right.

To all the loves that cling,
Bees in the honeyed sheath
Of flesh, there comes an end
Of what's to take or spend,
The blossom fell—this wreath
Is my remembering.

Dirge in Early Spring
(Oroville - March 1979)

Grief, why must you use
Our dearest memories to heighten pain
By making them a worse than hangman's noose
To choke us with what cannot be again!

Now the rathe primrose lifts
Its swelling buds to greet the morning sun
And soon the iceland poppies in bright drifts
Will flash like dancing rivulets as they run.

Soon, well I know,
The birds she loved will come to mate and sing,
And I will hear her call, her eyes aglow,
"Come to the window; listen, it is spring."

I dreamt spring-song would be
Not what it is this turning of the year:
We bloom as always but she cannot see;
We sing as always but she cannot hear.

Matin of the Awakened Spirit [20]

"For I have learned
To look on nature, not as in the hour
Of thoughtless youth; but hearing oftentimes
The still, sad music of humanity,
Nor harsh nor grating, though of ample power
To chasten and subdue. And I have felt
A presence that disturbs me with the joy
Of elevated thoughts; a sense sublime
Of something far more deeply interfused,
Whose dwelling is the light of setting suns,
And the round ocean and the living air,
And the blue sky, and in the mind of man;
A motion and a spirit, that impels
All thinking things, all objects of all thought,
And rolls through all things."
Wordsworth, *Lines Composed a Few Miles above Tintern Abbey*

Her Faith

Her faith was simple as a walk in spring
From the loved house and slowly back again
With eyes alert to catch the thrush a-wing
And foot that left the path so as not to harm
The firstlings of the rain.

---

[20] The Wordsworth poem is placed here with an italicized title in the original. Although extensive notes of a literary history nature are included at the end of the original volume, none say anything about this inclusion, other than a brief definition of "matin." — Ed.

She knew the world of "struggle and alarm"
But turned from it into this better world
To stand with me, her hand upon my arm,
All questions stilled, all earthly sorrows shed,
To see the ferns uncurled.

She stooped to touch the violets in their bed
Among the moss, Wood-Reveler, Knight's-Plume;
With light, love's effluence, on hand and head,
That made the place where silently we stood
A hushed, yes, holy room.

That hush be mine through all my widowerhood;
My pain, my hope, my good.

White Violets

This spring the white violets
Came early and everywhere
Greet me with their white, expectant faces.
For years I'd kept them sternly in their places:
A rock-bowl here, a thin, neat border there.
They've broken lines and every boundary
A gardener sets for such;
Even the lawn, still winter-brown, 's a sea
Foamed over by them and the warming air,
Filled with their scent, proclaims their empery.

Why did they come so early? Did they know
That one was on the way to still the hand
That bestowed blessings on them with its touch?
And why such masses? Did they fear
She might not see them with her pain-dimmed eyes,
Or, hastening on the way she had to go,
Would miss them at this turning of the year?

Grief to these questions asks for no replies.

Bedside Moment

I saw, with an awakening memory,
A light I'd seen far out upon the sea
Rising from the still deep mysteriously.

Her brow, that sometimes clouded with the pain
Of body and spirit, was now clear again
As skies that flood with sunshine after rain.

I spoke my joy. Her smile was soft and slow
And like that light I'd seen so long ago
Rising from depths not given me to know.

Mysterious Though the Alembic of Our Being

Mysterious though the alembic of our being
Is, yet we feel the beauty and the power
Of thought distilled from petals of a flower,
The child of sense born in each act of seeing,
The soul of sense in every fleeting hour.

She did not think such thoughts. Content to be
Fed at their source by her quick senses and
The life in books she loved, that other land,
The "realms of gold", that set her spirit free
In ways she did not try to understand.

No, not for her cold reason's chilly strife
Against the angel singing deep within
Of that one beauty where all truths begin.
She pressed her heart against the heart of life—
What better goal for her was there to win!

Beside her urn I whisper, "Never fear,
I'll know your call in all the birds that sing,
The scent of violets and the winds that bring
Fall's red and gold to deck the dying year.
Cor Cordium, await my answering."

Death Keeps His Bond of Silence with the Dead

Death keeps his bond of silence with the dead,
But grief, to those who mourn, has much to say;
And part of that 'twere better left unsaid
Lest words should turn the golden thought to clay.

A hundred faiths may ease the laboring heart,
Philosophies lock passion in a chain,
But what shall help when two hands fall apart,
Never to clasp, as hands, in love again!

I ask no oil be poured to calm the beat
Of rising waves on my small, desolate shore;
Above them looms a form, a paraclete,
A light I shall see clearly more and more.

That form is like her form, changed into light,
Or like a curl of cloud that drifts apart
And moves across the moon at dead of night,
And a voice speaks, heard only by my heart:

"You shall come to, and be a part of me,
As I of you, when your last race is run;
Beauty without its pain our empery,
Spirit in spirit, and forever one."

Death, You that Quenched the Light

Death, you that quenched the light that was her eyes,
And turned to ashes all her nerves of sense,
And sealed her lips to questions and replies,
And made of silence her last eloquence;

You wrote "ad infinitum" on her brow,
Your "ave" and my "vale"; I must be
Your acolyte and you must teach me how,
With eyes gone blind, I still may learn to see,

See with the eyes of memory and dream
That which has been and that which lies before;
My heart a pebble in a rolling stream,
My mind a child by a mysterious shore.

Let "vale" be my "ave": I shall meld
My spirit in her spirit, both to be,
As once in flesh, but then as spirit held,
Spirit in spirit, for eternity.

The light I saw upon her brow and hand,
And once, at night-time, rising from the sea,
These are the promise, help me to understand,
The dawn-light of the full epiphany.

Vesper & Epiphany [21]

"The One remains, the many change and pass;
Heaven's light forever shines, Earth's shadows fly;
Life, like a dome of many-coloured glass,
Stains the white radiance of Eternity,
Until Death tramples it to fragments."
       Shelley, *Adonais*

"He is made one with nature: there is heard
His voice in all her music, from the moan
Of thunder, to the song of night's sweet bird;
He is a presence to be felt and known
In darkness and in light, from herb and stone,
Spreading itself where'er that Power may move
Which has withdrawn his being to its own;
Which wields the world with never-wearied love,
Sustains it from beneath, it kindles it above."
       Shelley, *Adonais*

"Lamp of Earth! Where'er thou movest
Its dim shapes are clad with brightness
And the souls of whom thou lovest
Walk upon the winds with lightness."
       Shelley, *Hymn to the Spirit of Nature*

Spirit in Spirit, but Never Hand in Hand

Spirit in spirit, but never hand in hand
Along the well-worn, well-loved garden walk;
Never, when darkness lies upon the land,
Books laid aside, the lamplit drift of talk;
Never again the lingering goodnight kiss.
By her shut eyes and moveless brow all this
Death bids me to accept—and understand.

I understand. There is no other way.
For, musing by her shattered dome of glass,
I lift the fragments to the light of day
And watch the colors glow and fade and pass,
Knowing these were the colors of her love
Lit by the eternal radiance from above;
That these, in all her gracious ways, she was:

---

21 This set of quotations has an italicized title in the original. An extensive commentary on
Shelley is included in an appendix to the original. Moll states that The One is beauty, as
distinguished from transient things, but says nothing about the choice to place these
quotations here. –Ed.

Rose-light of love and gentleness and grace,
Heart's-red compassion and the April green
Of hope; and here, once queenly in its place,
The royal blue of beauty. I have seen,
With heart and eyes, for more than fifty years,
Through all the joys of earth and all its tears,
These make my heaven the beauty of her face.

The Colors of Her Life

The colors of her life, warm shadows thrown
Upon me as I lived my ways and days,
Are blent with that white radiance surely known
Though, by its brightness, hidden from my gaze;
The light of truth no mortal eye can see
Till death turns hope and faith to certainty
And Love claims all who loved her for her own.

I lay these sacred fragments gently down
With her own gentleness. Serene and slow
I take my way back to the populous town;
Serene, because in heart and spirit I know
That, when I have looked my last upon the sun,
To where she with the ineffable is one,
I with uplifted, pilgrim soul, shall go.

But till death choose to bridge this chasm of loss
By which I stand in darkness and but hear
Cassandra's voice rising where nations toss
In Hate's delirium that brings terribly near
Man's final lemming-madness, dearest, come
Back to me in this place that was our home,
Back on the bridge you were the first to cross.

Our garden, whence you took your quiet way,
With primrose and white violet breathes of spring.
I speak your name who loved them, day by day,
And greet the birds that have begun to sing.
From realms not made for living eyes to see,
Look homeward, and for Love's sake grant to me
Love's answer to this prayer that now I pray:

> "Come: not in watches of the night,
> But where the sunbeam broodeth warm,
> Come, beauteous in thine after form,

And like a finer light in light."
Tennyson, *In Memoriam*, XCI

A Vision of Grief
...earth with heavy grief so overplussed.

.   .   .   .   .   .

      Ah! must—
      Designer infinite!—
Ah! must Thou char the wood ere Thou
canst limn with it?
Francis Thompson, *The Hound of Heaven*

Soul's canker or soul's grace,
Common, not commonplace,
Grief, whose massed power's the bar
To utterance, yours the eyes
Of a tiger dreaming far
Where caged he lies.

In eyes that once burned bright
Through forests of the night,
The canker-worm! Within,
Dark, save for that flash thrown
When the keeper from his bin
Flings insult's bone.

In a mist-shrouded lake
One cups a hand to slake
Fever of some dread spell.
Yours, grief, the mouth which he
Twists wide to sigh "La belle
Dame sans merci."

Locked in this ring whose fire
Is the heart's betrayed desire,
The way for him can be
But one: With failing breath
Through scorpion-agony
To scorpion-death.

Eden-inspired, one wove
Roses to crown his love,
But when, sly, unabashed,
She told of sin's proud birth,
Yours, grief, the hand that dashed
The wreath to earth.

388

The shattered wreath, turned brown,
The hand that struck it down
Brushed the spent bloom aside
To leave a bed of thorn,
Where, as a phantom died,
A man was born.

One, with grief turned to rage,
Built hell, grim page by page;
Then, to that vision true,
Wrote, choked with pity and fear:
"All hope abandon you
Who enter here."

A mountain-freshness crept
To where Hell's poet slept.
Waking as from a kiss,
He saw from a veiled land—
Ah God! The awe, the bliss!
The down-stretched beckoning hand
of Beatrice!

Note: The original book contains many pages of notes, poetic reprints from Shelley, Keats et al. and explications intended to assist the reader in tracking Moll's allusions and meanings. These "Notes & Definitions for the Convenience of the Reader" are not reprinted here, except for a couple that are removed to footnotes or the Glossary at the end of the collection.

Poems from *The View From A Ninetieth Birthday* (1991)

Lyrical Poems of Old Age

Some of the poems included here are reprints from *The Well and the Star*. They are included in order to show the poet's vision for the collection. – Ed.

Preface

> *"Only stay quiet while my mind remembers*
> *the beauty of fire from the beauty of embers."*
>> From *On Growing Old*
>> by John Masefield

In their widely various levels of intensity of feeling and weight of thought, these poems are the stuff of moods lived and relived in old age. A few date back to my seventies and the rest, in singles and small groups, through my eighties and into my ninth decade.

Over that span of years aging brought me the to-be-expected physical disabilities which take from one much that had been part of the meaning and good of living. Sometimes that happens with the suddenness and force of the fall of leaves from a tree at the first wind after frost. But often, and happily, also after the first frost there is a short mild season, a sort of pensive hesitation, before the weather turns from summer into full autumn on the way to winter, which in some areas of North America is called Indian Summer.

In my life that season lingered unusually long, and during it my bodily deterioration was gradual and there was time between the more significant episodes to regain balance and momentum for pleasant on-going. It also happened that mental disability in the form of lapses of memory and weakening of concentration came gradually. This means that I have had a remarkably long time for getting acquainted with aging and for writing poems of it.

I said these poems are the stuff of moods lived and relived in old age. In that statement the word relived may need elucidation.

Imagination, in the form possessed and constantly used by normal people, is "the faculty of reproducing copies of originals once experienced but not present." The copies exist as memories which correspond fairly closely to their originals, often come to mind uninvited and sometimes from the depths of the unconscious; and when they are called up at will make possible such human functions as recognizing and learning. Whenever a person says, "I remember," it is 'on the job.'

But remembering is only the first step in reliving moods as they become embodied in poems, paintings, musical compositions and other art forms. There the imagination goes beyond the production of copies to the creation of originals.

During the centuries of human experience of it, the process by which this is done has been a subject of self-renewing inquiry; that is, what is discovered reveals how much remains unknown. To the still growing number of books and articles on the creative imagination, with specific reference to its functioning in the making of poems, I contributed my pennyworth in a book published fifty-eight years ago (1933). The memory of what went into that undertaking impresses on me the impossibility of saying anything really meaningful in a few sentences on the subject. However, in the same memory there are two passages in the nature of a summing up which I would very much like to know are in the minds of readers who may chance upon the present poems:

"Building relationships between units of experience disparate by difference in the experiences themselves, the creative imagination is the force which imposes forms and order upon the chaos of sensations, feelings and ideas which collectively we call life. Reason, analytical in its method and therefore acutely aware of differences, can bring together various parts of experience only on the basis of logical appropriateness. This imposes a limitation upon reason which does not exist for the imagination.

"To bring order out of chaos, form out of shapelessness, is perhaps the most fundamental of human desires. Were every experience to remain unrelated to every other experience, life would be no more than a going from event to event in a meaningless progression. Under such conditions not even a sense of our own identity could exist, for we know ourselves only as we find in the present shadows of the past, in one experience qualities of other experiences already our own. It is by fusing the past with the present that all parts of experience with all other parts that the creative imagination, through its best product, art, imposes a pattern on the formless materials of living and brings to man, as Lascelles Abercrombie put it, 'a raised and delighted consciousness of self.'"

That this be true, even if only now and then, for anyone who pauses over these pages, it is my hope; and that in the delight be fulfilled what the poet who wrote the two lines that head this preface asked in the first line of his poem, "Be with me beauty, for the fire is dying."

Indian Summer

I can't believe I'm old,
Although I'm more than sure,
However far from pure,
My heart is growing cold.

Within my dulling head
If something stirs by day,
By night I'm bound to say
That something, too, is dead.

A fiddle without strings!
Yet be it understood
That, when I tap the wood,
Remembering, it sings!

In Search of Self

   And long we try in vain to speak and act
   Our hidden self."
     Matthew Arnold: *The Buried Life* (1852).

At my first twinge of age
I thought it well to pay
A visit to myself
On some unscheduled day,

And knocking on his door,
By virtue of surprise
And child-eyed questions gain
Unedited replies;

To play the loving spy
On what his plans may be
For time disposable,
And then, eternity,

So that when he starts off
For some far Otherwhere,
I'll know the way he went
And how to track him there.

  .   .   .   .

So I approached the house
On a conspirer's feet.
Through a gate sagging out
From flower-beds drab but neat;

The house itself sat firm
Behind its peeling paint,
And by that firmness seemed
To lessen my restraint,

So that my knock was loud
On the long-faded door,
While my heart ran to meet
The sounds I listened for.

But after waiting long
In vain for sound or stir,
It seemed an insolence
Longer to loiter there.

And so I turned, but Ah!
In its accustomed place,
Was it a curtain moved?
And did I glimpse a face?

To a Goldfinch

In youth, through joy I knew
What caused you thus to sing
When skies had cleared to blue,
And winter changed to spring.

I shared the rapture then,
As now in age I try
To share your silence when
A hawk is in the sky.

Sweet singer on your bough,
Through knowledge of its cause,
Locked in your silence now,
My heart is doubly yours.

Winter Sunset

Our trees against the sunset quietly
Put on a beauty they had never shown
In naked branches by the light of day
Or even, when in leaf, like a wild sea
They claimed the kingdom of the storm their own
And sent what bloom they had aloft like spray.

Two moments in the passing of the years:
The tumult, power, the glory and the grace,
The wild unleashing of pent up desire.
But better now to watch, as darkness nears,
With the last warmth of evening on my face,
Our trees, how still! against the sunset's fire.

Sometime After Viewing the Summer Olympics of 1988

Drawn by a quenchless flame
Placed high in Glory's name,
The young, the brave, the bold
Came venturing for gold

In trials of strength and skill,
And unrelenting will
Fed by the heart's desire,
Warmed at ambition's fire.

I watched them hour by hour,
With beauty matching power,
In deeds make half-divine
Flesh once as frail as mine;

While, as to make heaven proud,
From an adoring crowd
Each hero's praise flared out
In thunderous shout on shout.

.   .   .   .   .

In images that fade,
Each contest is replayed;
But one, I know, will be
Not soon to go from me:

After the failed attack,
A vaulter on his back
Staring with empty eye
Up at an empty sky,
While in the distance rolled
The roar for one more Gold.

In the Season of Migrations

I talk and talk and my unmarshalled words
Dart hither and yon blown by wild gusts of thought,
Thousands of lovely tempest-scattered birds
Off base, by fear bewildered and distraught,
And their one hope against the fall and dying
Is but to keep on flying.

Many a noble phalanx cleaves my sky,
Each wing of hundreds beating strongly on
In unison and swift as visions fly
To the one goal all hearts are set upon;
And my eyes lift to watch them as they pass
High over this dead grass.

Autumn and time for the last long migration!
But all my winged ones swirl about my head,
Chaos of motion that is but stagnation
Above the wide sea and a final bed,
Still beating where they cannot choose but stay,
The goal not lost, but the way.

The Pre-Dawn Breeze

I

I know it in the pre-dawn breeze
As Nature's great imperative,
That everything endowed with life
Shall break from sleep's cocoon, and live.

It is a reaching out from rest,
A pulse that quickens with the light,
And falls, and rises up again
Like something readying for flight.

Then comes the leap, the lift, the surge
Of power in turn, and dive, and swing;
And though hawks keep no armistice,
Heaven's for joyous journeying.

. . . . . .

II

Swallow, I hear you at your nest
Above the window near my bed,
Preparing for your daylong quest
A moment, and then you have sped.

And matching-up with yours my fate,
Too weak to act, too dull to plan,
From my bed's edge I contemplate
What seems the sorry lot of man.

And then, O Joy! the sun breaks through
From brightening heavens where you fly,
And on its beam I rise to you
Where you await me in the sky.

And there the dizzying lift, the surge
Of power in turn, and dive, and swing
As every motion fires the urge
To swifter, wilder venturing.

For you this is the daily round,
The commonplace from birth your right;
For me, a broken thing earth-bound,
The strength, the beauty, the delight.

Of Beauty

Beauty, though shy, is proud
And does not heed the loud
Summons to bend her knee
To what each day may be
The thing to celebrate:
Some idol of the crowd,
Some glory of the State.

But where a lighted door
Tells she is waited for,
How glad to enter there
She is, and warmly share,
With all who come to dine,
A loaf of bread and pour
A festive glass of wine!

For Dreams That Come Too Late

We old ones till, by the decreasing light
In our deep valley of departed years,
The little soil eroded from the height,
The uplands we once ploughed. That solstice nears,
Bringer of winter and the shortest day,
That bids all growing cease, and yet we break
Feebly the soil and hide some seeds away.

Forgive us, you who have small chance of growing,
Sown by us out of our vast need of sowing,
Dreams that may never feel the touch of Spring;
For our old hearts and old brains tired of knowing
How Winter scoffs at such fond bargaining,
This act of hope is not a little thing.

Two Metaphors

I

*"That even the weariest river
Winds somewhere safe to sea."*
         Swinburne; *The Garden of Proserpine*

As truth beyond mere fact,
In an old metaphor
Self is a river which
Looks seaward from a shore.

The banks that hemmed it in
Are now no longer there
As it is drawn into
The one-shored Otherwhere:

And thus at last from time
And all its bonds set free,
Its little life grows one
With the eternal sea.

II

*"Life like a dome of many-coloured glass
Stains the white radiance of eternity,
Until death tramples it to fragments."*
         Shelley, in *Adonais*

But when a sunset breathes
Its life into my blood,
I live a metaphor
Of things not understood.

As, beyond knowledge and
Reason and thought's control,
In friendly conference,
Soul speaks with oversoul.

Our talk is of that dome
Beneath which rise and pass
Forms glowing as they wear
The colors of the glass.

They are my spirit-selves
Set for this moment free
To love their loveliness
Before eternity,

Which has no place for pride,
Will gently call them hence
To put those colors by
For its white radiance.

   .   .   .   .   .

When I was young I wept
Watching such beauty die,
And only now, grown old,
Know there's a reason why.

In a Summer Garden

A butterfly volplaning
From sunlight into shade,
Reminds me of those happy things
That die, but never fade.

Even the rose in fading
Is what no poet sings:
Death comes to take the butterfly
While still are bright its wings.

Departure of a Guest

Where will it go? It's only God who knows,
But why it goes is quite a simple matter:
It does not like the smell of crumbling houses
That groan and sigh with every wind that blows;
It hates and fears the loud heart-chilling clatter
That every footstep on loose boards arouses.

This place was once your inn and long ago,
A guest, you came with others through these doors
Into the warmth to join in song and wine;
But now there's only silence and the slow
Movement of shadows on the sinking floors
As only Desolation comes to dine.

Spirit of Beauty, I no longer may
Among these ruins be your smiling host,
To serve you with devotion masked as care;
Go, as you must, upon your destined way,
But do not haunt these ruins with your ghost
To mock me looking for you everywhere.

The Great Triad

Of Nature, God and Man
I know but little more
Than he knows of the sea
Who never left its shore,

But of that little this
I'm ready to declare
For Customs at the port
To which at last I fare:

Of Nature, how my sense
Loved well its lovely part,
While the death-nourished rest
With pity wrung my heart;

Of God, what I've been told
Is all that I can know,
And that He'll understand
My grounds for saying so;

And Man? How dear Man is
Even from his beginning,
With eyes fixed on a star
And some selective sinning!

Divestiture

Stop the long winnowing
For grain it doesn't bring,
And give the wind in pay
The chaff to blow away.

And then, to banish pain,
Be the glad child again
Who pauses not nor grieves
In Autumn, burning the leaves.

A Garden in April

How bright was that day, and how fresh!
But myself, as my arteries harden,
A worn cog and no longer in mesh
With the finely tuned needs of my garden.

So he came, a stout rollicking lad,
And away in a dance with my barrow
As he whistled a wild tune that had
The madcap that's Spring in its marrow.

And my hoe, of sedate an upbringing,
Sprang to life at the touch of a master,
And I'm sure there was joy in its swinging
To a tune of tumultuous disaster.

As he pulled up the flower and the weed
With a quite indiscriminate gusto,
How he laughed in the face of the creed
Of believers like me in the 'just-so'.

But there was no revolt in his manner,
Nor challenge to custom or reason,
So that I, with the brain of a planner
Saw how he belonged to a season.

When the cloud brings the hail-storm or shower,
And lightning companions the thunder,

And the heart leaps exulting in power
And the soul rides the Spring-tide of wonder.

So he came, and work done, went his way.
And I saw how my garden, though shaken,
Smiled out from a charmed disarray
As I've read lovers do when they waken.

And my garden went on through its year,
And I, too, but as now to remember,
With a passion how lost and how dear!
That April, this late in December.

To Nature

I

To see you in a blossom,
What rich variety!
For there's a bloom on every plant
For lovers' eyes to see.

To hear in April's bird-song
Your joy in every note,
Would be a tune more lovely
Than mortal ever wrote.

To find you in the fragrance
A garden wafts at night,
Would be as love a lover
Finds far from touch or sight.

To watch you every evening
For sleep compose the day,
Would make of even its sorrows
Children come in from play.

Yes, could the heart speak only
Of that which lovely is,
You would be Heaven's prelude,
Its overture to bliss.

II

But there's the voice of truth adjuring me
Not to be false to what too well I know,

How death may lurk within the fairest show
As in the fly-trap's scented witchery.

And of the bird song, still to keep in mind
The singer sings alone because he must
By Nature's law and procreation's lust,
And you but give the beauty which you find.

And of the fragrance which, entranced, you feel
Is love's own effluence borne upon the air
From a fair garden you but guess is there —
Don't trust the dark for what dawn may reveal.

And of the evening, that it serves to be
Usher of darkness and the noiseless flight
Of the sharp-taloned hunters of the night,
Whose touch is death, dealt, Oh, so stealthily!

III

From this ambivalence,
This war of heart and head,
Where darlings of the sense
By knowledge pierced, lie dead,
I longed to find release,
And in that freedom, peace.

And I have found a way
Nature, to live with you
On soulless terms which may
Render to each his due
And substitute for strife
An armistice for life.

You, "red in tooth and claw",
Ruled not by right and wrong
But by the primal law
Of victory to the strong;
Knowing not love nor hate,
Inscrutable as fate.

And I, beside you frail
As blossom to your frost,
How shall my strength prevail
Where all life-forms have lost
In bargaining with you
And passed in dust from view?

Whatever be your plan,
I can but play my part
And, standing as a man,
Blessed with this human heart
And strength that does not bow,
To you I make this vow:

That I will love and hold
Beauty wherever found,
(In you so manifold),
As Earth's most holy ground
Where all who sorrow, know,
Waters of healing flow.

Where thought is hushed to let
Its care-worn children sleep,
Truth willing to forget
To waken who must weep,
And consciousness possess
A heaven of quietness;

And in it beauty's power
To free the soul's delight
As from a seed the flower
And dawn from darkest night,
Although there only be
A birdsong from a tree.

And when I watch with fear
Your tiger launched in chase
Drawing so terribly near
In that smooth wave-like pace,
How glorious! Until
The slashing leap and the kill.

Then, then I turn my eyes
From that blood-tainted spot
Where killer and his prize
Work out the timeless plot
Which lays one torn and dead
That another may be fed.

And so my part in this,
(As Man, my right of choice),
One-sided armistice
In which you have no voice.

But, as you do your will,
Know that I love you still!

One for the Road

"Or leave a kiss but in the cup."
        — Ben Jonson (1573-1637)

When sadly I contrast
The present with the past,
My weakness with the power
Of a remembered hour,
And feel my day's decline
Nearing the summing-up;
Though water's in the wine
And not a drop to waste,
What joy it is to taste
Life's kiss left in the cup!

In Praise of Mirages

To me, a boy on Wimmera's plains,
Mirages quivering in the sky
Were not the spawn of addled brains
Nor agents of a cruel lie.

They were, as spirits, given me
A beauty that my eyes could know
When wonder was my empery
And summertime its Prospero.

Above a suffering Earth's distress
They floated, yet not quite aloof:
Of something left the heart to bless
They were the fair, the living proof.

The shimmering lake, the stately grove,
The dwelling at the water's edge,
To them I daily gave my love
With something stronger than a pledge.

They are the melody unheard
That, not embodied, cannot die;
The beauty for which there's no word
Yet given man to know it by.

And now, grown old, I bathe my face
In that far lake, and in that grove
And dwelling go to find the grace
Which brings renewal of that love.

On My Seventy-sixth Birthday, 1976
For Neiva

Love is the "many-splendored" thing
Whose protean forms and colors
Make mockery of the questioning
Of Seers and priests and scholars.

A boy, in Riverina skies
I watched the sunset flame
And strove in childish-eager wise
To give each hue a name.

My elders smiled at my despair:
"You'll know, when you grow old,
It is the dust from earth up there
The setting sun turns gold."

The dust of earth, the light of heaven,
The alchemy of hurtless flame:
Today I know why love is given
Its many-splendored name.

Verses for a Fiftieth Wedding Day Anniversary

*"Nature's first green is gold,
The hardest hue to hold."*

.   .   .   .   .

"Nothing gold can stay."
      Robert Frost

The gold went as it must.
We learned to prize the leaf
That, often dull with dust
And scarred by many a thief,

Bright-winged, moth-lovely some,
And others fat, obscene,
A caterpillar-scum
Moving upon the green,

Still rode the tides of air
Till Autumn's torch-fire came;
Then April's gold sang there,
A Phoenix in the flame.

Bedside Moment

I saw, with an awakening memory,
A light I'd seen far out upon the sea
Rising from the still deep mysteriously.

Her brow, that sometimes clouded with the pain
Of body and spirit, was now clear again
As skies that flood with sunshine after rain.

I spoke my joy. Her smile was soft and slow
And, like that light I'd seen so long ago,
Risen from depths not given me to know.

Dirge in Early Spring

Oroville, 1979

The early primrose lifts
Its swelling buds to greet the morning sun,
And soon the Iceland poppies in bright drifts
Will flash like dancing rivulets as they run.

Soon, well I know,
The birds she loved will come to mate and sing,
And I will hear her call, her eyes aglow,
"Come to the window; listen, it is Spring!"

I dreamt spring-song would be
Not what it is this turning of the year:
"We bloom as always but she cannot see;
We sing as always but she cannot hear."

White Violets

This Spring the white violets
Came early and everywhere
Greet me with their white expectant faces.
For years I'd kept them sternly in their places:
A rock-bowl here, a thin, neat border there.
They've broken lines and every boundary

A gardener sets for such;
Even the lawn, still winter-brown, is a sea
Foamed over by them and the warming air,
Filled with their scent, proclaims their empery.

Why did they come so early? Did they know
That one was on the way to still the hand
That bestowed blessings on them with its touch?
And why such masses? Did they fear
She might not see them with her pain-dimmed eyes,
Or, hastening on the way she had to go,
Would miss them at this turning of the year?

Grief to those questions asks for no replies.

Reverie

Tenderly as a bird
Covers her young,
Love, that most tender word,
Hallows my tongue.

.   .   .   .

Words of a myriad sort,
Old words and new,
Give to our every thought
Its shape and hue:

Words for the bitter-sweet
Taste on our lips
When joy and sorrow greet
Like passing ships.

Words for all things that are
Or yet to be,
The thought, the deed, the star
Of prophesy.

But fairest jewels of all
That Treasure-Chest,
Which Truth and Wisdom call
The priceless best,

To me are those that prove
What hearts profess:

That beauty born of love
Is loveliness.

   .   .   .   .

Tenderly as a bird
Covers her young,
Love, that most tender word,
Hallows my tongue.

Youth and Age

I

Time was, when I pulled on my socks,
Bedside, bent down at break of day,
My feet pressed to the starting-blocks
From which to dart upon their way.

And time was when I loved that pace
Because I thought it carried me
Past deserts of the commonplace
To some far-off epiphany;

Some revelation of that force
The rarest gift to humans given,
Which sets the hero on his course,
The humbler Saint on hers to heaven.

I traveled far, I traveled fast,
Only with weary eyes to see
The star I sought is, at this last,
As far as at my birth, from me.

II

And now I wear my socks all night
And at day's break explore,
My feet thus clad, to left and right,
For slippers on the floor.

Sometimes upon the polished oak
They slide till I grow weak
At helping in their little joke
Of playing hide and seek.

Until one morn in testy mood
I crawled upon my knees,
And there, deep in the shining wood
I saw the living trees!

Cloud-Shadows

I chased them when a boy
On feet as light as they:
Cloud-shadows were my joy.
And when I had to keep
A leaden-footed way
I chased them in my sleep.

There was no prize to gain
More than the joy of speed,
And memories that remain;
And where my feet were set
They left a print indeed,
But nothing to regret.

I ran, but not by law
From an appointed start
To what the race was for;
But in a child's employ,
Out of a happy heart,
Of innocence and joy.

And so to me was given
An amulet to wear:
This memory of heaven;
When sorrows would enslave
In service to despair,
How strong! How quick to save!

Count-down

When, like a child remembering, I am glad
Of the few certainties I still possess
Out of the many I once thought I had
With an assurance firmer than a guess;

But, doubting joy, when I begin to think
'Now, was that long ago or yesterday?'
What was a lighthouse beacon starts to blink
In warning that it, too, is on its way.

Then, still that child, how dear the little light
My candle gives as fearfully I mark.
By stars, the vast dimension of the night,
Filled with the nameless perils of the dark!

Preparation for a Quilting Bee

"A wandering minstrel I
A thing of shreds and patches."
　　　　　Author unknown to me.[22]

I

The more my heart lags
Let my fingers wax nimble
At sorting these rags
For needle and thimble.

Though fast fades my sight
After triumphs of seeing,
May it grow again bright
At these remnants of being.

And spirit, don't mumble
Like a player who's losing,
But, though weary and humble,
Be you bold at this choosing.

II

Dear ladies, here I give to you
This pile of patches that was I,
To shape into an image true
Enough for friends to know me by.

If you were gardeners I might plead
That these are seeds and ripe for planting,
With an admixture of the weed
To add some spice to the enchanting;

22　This, the source of which Moll did not know, is from the lyrics to Gilbert & Sullivan's musical *The Mikado* (1885), presumably by librettist W.S. Gilbert. It was also used in a 1948 cartoon by Herbert Block.

And then, with Spring and sun-bright showers,
Birdsong and joy — I'm still assuming —
An April breeze would move the flowers
Into an ecstasy of blooming.

But you, being human, will be making
Judgments as you select and sew,
And I'm afraid they'll lead to waking
And not the sleep 'twere good to know.

Therefore, with contrite heart I pray you,
Before such duty you espouse,
Let your gentleness betray you
To kindness more than law allows,

That, in forgetfulness of duty,
You blend the colors, shade with shade,
Till at some opalescent beauty
Joy fill your hearts at what is made.

And when the time has come for sleeping,
I, too, shall see the gleam you caught,
And take it with me for safe-keeping
Beyond the last frontiers of thought.

Dawn Watch

"…when unto dying eyes
The casement slowly grows a glimmering square."
from Tennyson's *The Princess*

With this much left me of the morning sky,
These moments in a timeless happening,
This little share in an eternal thing,
Let me not fog the window with a sigh,

But turn the bed-light out, as is most fit
Now this far visitor has come to me,
And with a welcome beyond courtesy
In gratitude lift up my eyes to it.

Reunion[23]

When I sat quietly,
As age has ruled I must,
I felt one come to me,
One I had thought had died,
A child with a child's trust,
To nestle at my side.

It was myself before
Instinct turned into thought,
And thought to reasoned law;
And thus made fugitive,
Outcast, but never caught,
Lived on to help me live.

That self that leapt and ran
With others of its kind
On the long road to Man
Before the rule of sense
Gave way to rule of mind
And thought's omnipotence.

The self that took delight
In all around it spread;
That borrowed the bird's flight,
From soaring hawk to dove,
And for a bird found dead,
Made a small grave of love.

That self that everywhere
Went out from deep within
Itself to find and share
With plant, and beast and star,
Not as a friend, but kin,
The loveliness they are.

.   .   .   .

Yes, at my side; and know
That he has come to stay,
And never again will go;

---

23   The word "delight" in the fourth stanza was printed as "desight" in the original. The word
    "desight" exists as an archaic usage for something unsightly, which seems the opposite
    of what Moll intended in this self-published volume.

But with me cease to roam
Till there will come the day
Together, we'll go home.

A View
From a Ninetieth Birthday

Sinking into the long-assured takeover,
The last surrender and folding of the arms
As there is nothing left them to recover —
Even that sinking has its sober charms.

It is the time of a fifth season's coming
That, without reference to the other four,
Follows a different calendar for homing
To lands where the four seasons come no more;

Or if they do, there'll be a different knowing,
Like that of trees conversing with the rain,
Or birds about their busy-body going
Telling the world it's nesting time again.

And I, who've felt so many Autumns gladden
Me with their color-language void of grief,
In that fifth season find no thought to sadden
As I rehearse in language of the leaf.

In the Season of Migrations
For more than sixty of my last years, in Oregon and in California, I have lived where in
Autumn and in Spring, great flocks of ducks and geese bring excitement to the sky as they
pass in their ages-old migrations. By day the sight, and at night the sounds of their going fill
an earth-bound observer with wonder at the answer being made by thousands of creatures at
the same moment to a call heard and understood by all. Theirs is a venturing among dangers
known from their own experiences and carried on in utter commitment to intuition,
evidently without hesitations and with a beauty which is an augury of success. [EGM]

Editor's Note: The original book contains many pages of notes and explications intended to
assist the reader in tracking Moll's allusions and meanings. These "Notes & Definitions for
the Convenience of the Reader" are not reprinted here, except for a couple that are removed
to the Glossary at the end of the collection. I have retained Moll's note on migrations.

Poems from *Recognitions at Ninety-three* (1993)

Editor's Note: Some long explanatory notes have not been reprinted in this collection.

Preface

Aging is like the breaking of a chain
In ever smaller pieces, till at last
Link parts from link, with custom dulling pain,
As all builds to the scrap-heap of a past.

And then I've felt the process gently change
From fragments falling, to a gathering in,
And a child's impulse eager to arrange
Them into forms and bid their lives begin,

Not now as links but as incipiences:
A thought just launched, like bird upon the wing;
A light just lit in the warm dark of senses;
A song begun, for silence left to sing.

Retrospect

> *Move upward working out the beast*
> *And let the ape and tiger die.*
> > Tennyson
> > In Memorium CXVII

> *Time is on the wing to bud*
> *Rose in brain from rose in blood.* *
> > George Meredith
> > The Woods of Westermain

I'm in and out of Nature as a cloud
Is in its life with rivers, lakes and sea,
But with the difference, of which Man is proud:
Beyond what is, the faith in what's to be.

For I must live by vision and my past,
The one for hope, the other for the strength
To follow it and to the way hold fast
No matter what its dangers or its length.

As in a caterpillar I've seen wings
Of a new, lovelier life, with joy I know
How beauty, rising from rememberings,
Inspires the blood to singing in its flow.

Tiger, there is a beckoner in your eyes
That has enticed me where thought cannot reach,
And into many an untamed enterprise
Whose management thought has no skill to teach.

Some of them were perfections unachieved,
Javelins thrown that never came to earth;
Insights that quickly faded, unbelieved,
Because I had no measure of their worth.

But thus it is that mind must seek a soul
To bring life's incompleteness to an end
Of fragments fused in a resplendent whole –
Oh, tiger, tiger, ever stay my friend!

And ape, who name was once of little worth
Except as something with near-human face
Down from the treetops, and a source of mirth
In the stock way of being out of place,

Did your eyes never turn that laugh to shame
By what seems yearning and a sorrow there?
Not fear, nor hate, not bitterness and blame
But a proud patience mastering despair.

Knowledge has shown, within your blood and mine,
The rose which time has budded in my brain
As beauty's symbol in a life's design,
While below thought for you its charms remain.

Stay with me now, and as I tend my garden
I will take grateful care that neither lack,
For it is you, even as my arteries harden,
Who help me up and on, by looking back!

> *To bud [in this context] is to insert a bud from one plant into the bark of another sort of plant.

(1)

We live by recognitions and rejoice
Best when by grace or fortune we can share
The meanings in the magic of a voice,
Or on our lowlands breathe the mountain air.

(2)

Beauty I knew by my own heart's desire,
Whatever form it took, was there to stay;
As, when a child watching the sky on fire,
I grieved to see its colors die away.

(3)

I who loved laughter, now it's growing late
And small time left for what I have to do,
Will laugh once more, but just to celebrate
The heart's-ease of it since my years were few.

(4)

After long life and much to mourn, I still
Find silence tells the all that death has done,
In light that's gone forever from a hill
Where two once walked, but now there's only one.

(5)

Earth's is a mighty vision in the root
Of life to rise between it and the sun:
Leafage and bloom, the benison of fruit,
And myriad lives, each with a course to run.

(6)

As from their pedestals the people spill
Upon the floor of Moscow's famous Square,
The bronze memorials to a tyrant's will,
How fair the path to freedom opening there!

(7)

I celebrate the triumph of old hands
Guiding their needles in a maze of lace
With genius in a touch which understands
How to make visions live in time and place.

(8)

False dawn we call it? But what joy to see
Something creep past the watchtowers of the night

To open heaven with a secret key
And let us, still in darkness, glimpse the light!

(9)

My thought, by old age gentled, fastens on
Its object not with ardor of a quest,
But as a butterfly that, chanced upon
A warm and windless spot, stops there to rest.

(10)

As wilting petals signal to a close
A blossom's dealing with the honey bee,
Our failing powers, as naturally as those,
Leave us shut in with our eternity.

(11)

The names I love are falling by the way
Beyond the reach of my remembering;
But in their place I feel a dearness stay
Like after-sounds when bells have ceased to ring.

(12)

As darkness pools upon our valley's floor
And the breeze dies into the waning light,
I like to wait for the first star before
I give myself entirely to the night.

(13)

With awe I heard a mountain tell the sun
The story of its life in the Design,
But through the violent courses it had run
Love waited till it told of its decline.

(14)

I lived with flowers to my heart's content,
And showed my love and joy in thought and deed,
But, mixed with sorrow, even deeper went
That which I felt for beauty in the weed.

(15)

How wise to keep a suburb of the brain
Where banned is all the tumult of the street
And one can still hear music in the rain
And hope for some wild songster to repeat.

(16)

We own the earth, but with a mortgage where
Are many items only Nature chose;
And if to play at trickery we dare,
She's ready and quite able to foreclose.

(17)

When Nature saw emerging something strange
In a life-form from others different,
Did she know that this creature would arrange,
Itself, the means to cancel the event?

(18)

For us, locked in survival's marathon,
Defeat's assured by liking become need,
Until, acquiring all we look upon,
We'll die beneath the burden of our greed.

(19)

Species in their existence upon earth
Ceaselessly struggle to prolong their stay;
Man, the inventor from his very birth,
Has to extinction built the shortest way.

(20)

*"The earth cannot provide infinite natural
resources or endlessly assimilate our wastes."*
    Maurice Strong, organizer
    of the International Earth
    Summit. (Quoted in the *San
    Francisco Chronicle,* June 11, 1992)

It was one thing to contemplate Man's end
Sharing the world's own ending, with a whimper;
But Oh to die, as all the signs portend,
Upon a garbage heap and with a simper!

(21)

Knowledge as power, by mankind wooed and won,
How fair the course, though perilous and far,
Could wisdom seal the contact thus begun
And make compassion evolution's star. ?

(22)

The tree of life asks of men's high ambition
To nurture growth, that knowledge never be
A parasite which, by the soul's attrition,
Brings a slow death that first deforms the tree.

(23)

Needless technology, success elated,
And by the wonders of invention fed,
Can be a fever-hunger never sated,
A spider with a plethora of thread.

(24)

There's an example that might profit us
As we build armaments against attack,
Of how a tortoise of Galapagos
Fares when he's rolled upon his mighty back.

(25)

When only trains went faster than a horse
I saw but little, but I saw it well;
Now that my speed outdoes earth's in its course,
How small the space is between heaven and hell!

(26)

Did I rise free from Nature only to
Fall back in worse than Nature's savagery,
With plans to kill and maim my fellows who,
Fear lets me know, have the same plans for me!

(27)

The ocean's tides are pulse-beats of a heart
Ageless and stronger than all measured powers,
And yet, in harbors, stage the small wave's art
Sundancing with the grace of wind-blown flowers.

(28)

Not just because there's absence of a breeze,
But for a reason which would make men wise
A lake in images tells what it sees
Only when clear and still the water lies.

(29)

Compassion without passion is a word
That keeps on beating like a metronome
Where there is not a note of music heard
And the musician long since has gone home.

(30)

I was content with Eden's apple tree,
Prizing it only for its bloom in Spring,
But when its red fruit dangled over me,
I,…well, that was a very different thing.

(31)

Re-reading, as I am obliged to do,
Words which I hoped had faded from the page,
Why must this be? Stand nakedly in view
Darker against its yellowing with age.

(32)

Young man, before you venture on confessing,
Be sure beyond a doubt that you possess
A sin that's truly somewhat of a blessing
And makes you rather proud as you confess.

(33)

I'm happy in this almost second childhood,
That valley where the rainbow used to sleep,
Where distant trees were a mysterious wildwood,
And all the stars in heaven were mine to keep.

(34)

An infant's smile to which our lips reply
Can cause on earth this heavenly consequence:
A turning of the road to travel by
To the lost Eden of our innocence.

(35)[24]

There is completeness in unhurting laughter,
Like a deep breath's of fresh but balmy air,
And starts no thought of a before or after,
But revels in the moment that is there.

(36)

The politician woos with voice and hands,
The voter answers him with hands and voice,
And, much or little that each understands,
Both find good reason loudly to rejoice.

(37)

Old age reliving infancy, in sport
What joy it is to see the ball we rolled,
By heroes hit, and kicked, and thrown, and caught,
And triumph in the triumphs we behold!

(38)

A baseball hero, getting set to hit,
First paws the earth as does a threatening bull,
Then, having briefly turned away to spit,
Stands like a statue poised and purposeful.

---

[24]   The second line "Like a deep breath's of fresh but balmy air," at first seems "off" in terms of grammar and scansion, but it matches Moll's tendency to use complex internal structures, in this case by hauling the word "completeness" into the meaning of the second line by way of the structure of the sentence, so it has been retained.

(39)

In youth I held that distance made for worth,
And soared in spirit as on eagles' wings;
Today, scarce able to lift foot from earth,
"Heaven it is to live at peace with things".*
           George Santayana

(40)

My chair, its fabric worn by time and me,
Now has its inner working showing through;
And I, in empathy with what I see,
Dread what may next be coming into view.

(41)

Nature has places which make Hell seem mild
But none to match the warrens of mankind
Where, even from birth with vileness reconciled,
Things human live to hopelessness resigned.

(42)

The laws of nature are described by men,
But none can be more feelingly expressed
Than is that hush from grass to treetop when
The mother bird sits watchful in her nest.

(43)

When sleep's been fitful in a winter's night,
How like a soothing hand to feel begun,
In thinning darkness and increasing light,
Earth's ever faithful turning to the sun.

(44)

There are life-meanings which we understand
When understanding's said a last goodnight
And our responses are unthinking and
As urgent as a plant's response to light.

(45)

I like to see great mountains at a distance,
And the same's true of heaven and things divine,
But I have found the loves of my existence
And all its warmth below the timberline.

(46)

A little ball of fluff, the killdeer's chick,
Came to me past its mother's warning cries,
And joy still moves my being to the quick
That I had won that best of all replies.

(47)

There is a knowing that cannot be willed
But, reached through wonder and the heart's desire,
Is passion of love and beauty, felt, and stilled,
On the last height to which man can aspire.

(48)

My past for virtue had a faith and heaven,
And unforgiven sins another place;
And for those absolutes there was no leaven
Of pity for the sorrows in a face.

(49)

Now in my landscape no more, grim and stark,
Looms Sin with, far off, the red glow of Hell,
I almost miss that never-changing mark
My forebears on their travels knew so well.

(50)

Change that has shaped the self I try to know
Has made self-knowledge a bewildering maze
Where self-love, fearful, begs me not to go,
But know myself by other's blame and praise.

(51)

As thought transcends the limits of the brute
An aspiration toward a soul is born,
Like the first flush foretelling the ripe fruit
Or day the bloom whose opening bud was dawn.

(52)

Substance as way and end, survival's plan,
May for subsistence be a proper goal,
But, in the wisdom which we claim as Man,
A nobler aim is graciousness of soul.

(53)

Soul is no hired accountant keeping score
Of what the sum at Heaven's gate will show
Of sin and virtue the dread less or more –
But is the energy which makes that so.

(54)

Belief, soul's climate in our mortal lot,
Can be a dreary, heavy-footed state,
Where winter's merely cold and summer hot,
Or one where both hold dreams to celebrate.

(55)

Soul is to substance a bloom's effluence,
A fragrance named, but not for any part;
And so to knowledge an unseen fountain whence
Flow waters of sweet meaning for the heart.

(56)

In light before full dawn what joy to see
Something creep past the watchtowers of the night
To open heaven with a secret key
And let us, still in darkness, glimpse the light!

(57)

In my first footstep was a flag unfurled
To fly above the waters of strange seas
Past islands of enchantments to a world
Far, far beyond the Straits of Hercules.

(58)

Old now I hear, close and yet far away,
And like a secret for just me to keep
Of instruments unknown as those who play
This hover-song above a sea of sleep.

Renewal

When the day's news disheartens, in my mind,
Like background music blurring out the page,
Opens and grows a vision of mankind
Dear as a story from another age

Told by some patriarch how in Nature's plan
Of change and growth a living form arose
To climb for eons toward the estate of Man
With a desire only the wild heart knows.

And how on the still sharply rising ground,
Delayed but never halted by defeat,
We struggle on through good and evil, bound
For where we know earth and a heaven meet.

And not far off in some eternity,
But where the sky fills with the stars we know;
Where our own joy in other's joy will be,
And hope itself grow nobler as we grow.

A place in which the strong will lift the weak;
Where those who suffer will be comforted;
Where beauty's vistas wait for all who seek;
The blind in flesh and spirit will be led.

Where, as when first we sped the mail by flight,
As we direct our vision and our force,
Our works will be our beacons in the night,
And listening, we'll know the plane's on course.

Note: In the original chapbook, "Renewal" was printed on the verso page facing Nos. 57 and 58 in the previous sequence. This appears to be a layout error so we have moved "Renewal" to the end position in this book.

Poems from *The Children of Somalia, 1992-1994 and Other Poems* (1994)

Fore-words

1

Old age had given my childhood back to me,
A happy gift, and so a glad receiving,
That from the dust I'd gathered set me free
Into the shining of that first achieving.

A farmer's child, I grew with things that grew
And reveled with them for sheer living's sake:
The wheat's green waves with every wind that blew;
The cockling his first crowing dawn awake.

The cabbage plants my father let me set
On promise I would tend them all their days,
And as they formed – I feel the wonder yet,
Even as I taste the sweetness of his praise!

So plants grew dear to me by tending them,
And animals, whose attitudes of joy
Made them with me as leaves on the same stem,
In different ways, all in the same employ.

And as that interchange, small part by part,
Was given back to me, though weak and bent,
I felt a splendid lifting of the heart
In gratitude for what that feeling meant.

It was the song the sunlight sings to roots
In the dark earth, of growth to ripening,
And Man, in deeds to pass those fairest fruits,
And drowsing then, I loved to hear it sing.

2

In our one-world I'd watched the news of it
Stream by in pictures, a kaleidoscope,
And, with the millions shaping views of it,
Rattled like dice between despair and hope.

Just now and then for me the stream was still
Or was of spoken words which stood alone
And made a claim upon my idle will
To let some joy or sorrow be my own.

In one such time, Somalia, your name
Was with me day by day until I knew
Your story, with its horror and its shame,
Deepening my fear to heart-break as it grew.

For I'd relived, with gratitude, my youth
And in your name had heard a lullaby
Like one I love**. Then came the bitter truth
To hear it sung where starving children die.

**A lullaby, whose music was composed by Brahms and whose words I know only in my hit-and-miss German, has had a charm and tenderness for me for longer than I can recall. It bids the child good night and to sleep well and sweetly in dream-paradise; and it assures the child that in the morning, as God wills, it shall wake again.

I

Somalia, heard as a lullaby,
Your name haunts me with fearsome power possessed
By tones which have the softness of a sigh
As life bends over infancy at rest.

A sigh the gentle language of lament:
"How fair you are! Sleep on – forever sleep,
For when you wake your part from heaven sent
Will for so short a time be yours to keep."

A sigh the testament of withering
Heard in the wind when turned to speech as though
A blossom full-blown to a bud should sing:
"Sleep, for the winds that rocks you still will blow,

That rocks you like a mother, terribly will
Be as you rouse a thirst death brings to slake
On fragrance only yours. Oh thwart it still
By sleep – and May God let you never wake!"

II

So from her ravished heart a mother made
Over her child the one prayer left to say

That death would come to take it, unafraid,
Safe from the waking to another day.

No power was there to stop the horror's course,
No government with armies to attack
And, with Man's holiest of hopes the force
To strike it down, or beaten, drive it back.

Drought, with its vampire sun sucked the earth dry
And all that lived became a withering,
Watched by a vast indifference of sky
Too old, too strong to pity anything.

And war, another vampire, sucked the blood
Of men who felt its lips as an embrace,
And thus dehumanized, from all the good
Mankind has won, turned with averted face.

Fathers, and other fathers and their sons
Grappled in hatred even as they bled,
While starving mothers to the sound of guns
Gathered doomed children to the already dead.

III

Then suddenly the world was at your gate,
Somalia, as nations came to you
With guns to silence those which made your state
A horror only Hell could boast as true.

What they uncovered there I, too, was shown,
And though with fear it moved me and dismay,
Being of human lives, it touched my own,
Any my heart would not let me turn away.

A place with shattered buildings filled the screen
Where, a voice said, an army had passed through,
And it seemed right that not a touch of green
Gave hope life there would start its course anew.

Alone, a woman in harsh sun glare stood,
A naked child in arms, on whose gaunt stare
Her look was that of stricken motherhood
Answering a plea for food with nothing there.

A ghost of beauty lingered in her face,
As in a dark rose blossom spent and dying,
And, as in that, of living the last trace
Was unstrung anguish of a mute complying.

And then behind her, moving like a wave —
How could I ever think my eyes would see
Children like skeletons come from a grave
Fixing their gaze, their all that lived, on me!

Cheeks fallen in, glances without surmise
From black eyes no more blinking at the sun,
Silent as beasts brought there for sacrifice
To die on some cursed altar, one by one.

Wherever shade was I saw bodies lie
Gruesome from thirst and hunger and their pain,
Their lips the moisture for the carrion fly
Brushed feebly off, only to come again.

Young men with rifles loitered here and there,
But none came near that place of pestilence;
With human lives their target, not their care,
Pity for them had lost its eloquence.

There anger stopped my viewing as I saw
That loveless, brainless travesty of might,
And, with a rifle as his God and law,
The crawl of Man from dawn back into night.

IV

But they still came, till I could watch no more;
Children who walked like creatures stupefied,
Or lay as vileness all who live abhor
Was closing on them slowly as they died.

The screen stayed blank, but they'd become a part
Of my own childhood, as though we were one
By interchange of smiles from heart to heart
In fellowship of living just begun.

Near my life's end, this seemed a glad returning
To memories that had ripened through the years
Like fruits of meaning in the warmth of yearning,
And in a climate not devoid of tears.

But truth in anger blamed me for that seeming
Of Solace in this place where I should see
The leer of treachery in such a dreaming
And blast it, not turn eyes away and flee.

For they who died were of the seed of Man
And as a living human I must bear,
Even though helpless, anguish for the plan
Which made of earth a hell, and put them there.

Contrite, I gave myself to thought's control,
That strength, when the heart listens to the brain,
To look on power that is without a soul —
The human face earth must not see again!

V

Forgive me that brief respite from your pain,
Children, for whom that waits till feelings end,
And I will walk with you the path again
Where only death can be your truest friend.

Like plants from seed which should not have been sown
By that blind sower, procreation's lust,
On stony ground where nothing can be grown
With wind for rain, and hope the blowing dust;

You shrink in vain from the sun's vampire touch
Upon the tender life to which you cling
In children's bodies till, how changed from such!
All that is left you is your withering.

And though there are green valleys where the breeze
Tells of crops ripening to be harvested,
War is the only harvester of these
And is the only hungerer that's fed.

A hungerer with countless gaping mouths,
All human, but of warring clans whose strife
Is for the power, the rights the gun allows;
A Nation's government, its law, its life.

Where in this place of crazed, triumphant hates
Can be a pillow for an infant's head?
To what but to the fate assigned that waits
Can its small blameless, trusting feet be led?

Oh, far away, but terribly in my sight,
There where hands that would help you could not save
But only place you in clean sacks of white
Cloth, your coffins for a common grave.

It is a mother's hands that place you there,
Each child so harmed death for it had no sting;
I see her bending to it for that care,
Dry-eyed in this, her love's last lingering.

After-Words

1

Our humanness, angel of good on Earth,
Is stricken at the heart-strings by the sight
Of children with their trust betrayed at birth
Into a darkness that is not of night.

That trust, a faith, and more, a contract known
As surely as one breathing knows the air;
A swelling seed the earth where it is sown;
The answered cry that help is coming there.

It is what mothers read in children's eyes
Before the children turn their glance away,
And, lingering still in sleep's dream-paradise,
Stretch hands to bring it closer yet by day.

It does not have a form in thought or word
Or signs we use in our rememberings,
But, like the poet's melodies unheard,*
It is of spirit when the spirit sings.

It is the call to selfhood children hear,
And where eyes lead, to find it they must go
Into the land of wonders growing clear,
As we who've made that journey still may know;

> *Heard melodies are sweet, but those unheard
>   Are sweeter; therefore, ye soft pipes, play on;
> Not to the sensual ear, but more endear'd,
>   Pipe to the spirit ditties of no tone.
>   *John Keats, Ode On A Grecian Urn.*

And then, as wonders were our world and we
Felt hands enfolding ours to warm and guide,
They learn – how slowly! – what it means "to be",
And all the fear, the pain, the joy, the pride!

2

Indwelling in that child-faith there was felt
An energy of life seeking control,
Holy as prayer when ancient pilgrims knelt
In suppliance to Love to make them whole.

It was like water to a thirsting one,
Somalia, and held by you in trust;
Thought cannot grasp the monstrous thing you've done,
Pouring it past those lips into the dust.

When nations came to you with arms held wide,
As Good Samaritans – Man's hope on Earth –
Their help unthanked, you struck their hands aside,
To keep as one the gates of Hell and Birth.

Now, in the empire where the gun holds sway,
You are, with Ethiopia, Sudan,
Another traveler on the downward way
Self-outcast from the fellowship of Man.

Down to the first, instinctive savagery,
For which survival was the whole of law,
And from which humankind is breaking free
To face the heights which we feel destined for;

Down to a deep where's still more depth below,
Down past the place where your dead children lie;
And do not ask for pity as you go –
It is our angel speaks, "I watched them die!"

Editor's Note: Two extracts from 1994 newspaper articles, provided as background, have been deleted.

Other Poems

April Revisited

How can one in the winter of his days
Lift head and heart in greeting to the spring?
Or from a throat that's withering sing praise,
To April's birdsong a fit answering?

As I become an April sky of moods –
Sunshine – clouds – storm, I am reproved by reason
For what I fondly call my interludes
Between the sessions of a sterner season.

Reason lays stepping stones to reach desire,
April's the time for leaping over brooks;
But I come from my winter to its fire
And musings in its quietest of nooks.

In one clear flame are melded all the changes
April has known, and in this harmony
Renewed, the deathless all-life spirit ranges
Out of the past devising what shall be.

From bits of all seasons put together
You are the varied splendor of them all,
With tides of blossoms changing with the weather
A joyous preview of the sadder fall.

Shakespeare, twice April's child, is with me here,
From where he went through human lives to roam,
And when in art he'd made their meanings clear,
Gave them to us. And here you brought him home.

When Chaucer, with his pilgrims and a plot
Fashioned for sober and for laughing eyes,
Began their journey – a chance-gathered lot –
It was in Springtime, under April skies.

Some of your ways, in human terms are cruel,
But as that's meaningless for Nature's ways,
For your glad songs of beauty and renewal,
My thanks and in my gratitude, your praise.

Editor's Note: Moll's notes explaining who Shakespeare and Chaucer were have been deleted.

Quatrains

Forms are just denser darkness in the night,
But with the dawn I watch them, one by one,
Win back themselves, as through all change a right
Of subjects with allegiance to the sun.

The dawn is a white seagull coming in
With wings locked wide above a treetop sea,
And as I watch the slanting-down begin,
I hope – not knowing why – that it sees me.

When sullen thoughts conspire with winter's cold,
They shut the door and lock it from inside;
But as they nod – for they are getting old –
My spy among them gently sets it wide.

I hate to watch my senses one by one
Packing like workmen to be on their way
Although the job is only half-way done –
But, as it happens, theirs is now the say.

I once played handball with the ball a thought
Struck against walls from which it veered in flight,
But having now no longer such a court,
All that I launch goes simply out of sight.

When age has stilled the care for consequence,
What joy it is with spirit ranging free
To think, feel, dream in untamed innocence
As children build sand-castles by the sea!

When I was young and in my choosing free,
I pushed the horizon back as on I stepped;
Now that I'm old, it turns the trick on me
And proves itself, Oh!, how much more adept!

My endings now outnumber my beginnings,
In the accounting at last quarter's end,
As do my losses far surpass my winnings;
But friends say not to worry, — it's a trend.

In Old Age Land, where danger waits in hiding,
Each step's an Everest from which to fall;
But Oh the joy, when luck some help providing,
I make it, upright, safely wall to wall!

Hunched in his chair before a sinking fire
An old man waves the proffered glass away,
And now that gesture of a lost desire
Deepens in meaning for me, day by day.

Whose life has changed to still-life, happy man
Who can remember something of the bloom
On deeds which, in this new housekeeping plan,
Are painted fruits, scentless in a dull room.

Where music leads we stumble as we go
Reaching for words to help our thought possess
Meanings to match the flight, the pause, the flow
Of sound, whose soul stays free in wordlessness.

We old ones touch our world with little force,
But well that little may be worth the knowing;
For it was we who helped design its course
And have our thoughts, long thoughts, about its going.

A politician plans a "gentler land"
Than men have dreamed of or have striven for,
Where every citizen, with gun in hand,
Will see to it that all obey the law.

I'd like to see the thousand points of light
Which that same Orator puts hope in, but
I must confess that I have had that sight
Once, on forgetting that a door was shut!

Three Poems [25]

"Man's happiness, his flaunting honey'd flower of soul,
is his loving response to the wealth of Nature.
Beauty is the prime motive of all his excellence,
his aim and peaceful purpose; whereby he himself
becoming a creator hath often thought to ask
why Nature, being so inexhaustible of beauty,
should not be all-beauteous, why, from infinite resource,
produce more ugliness than human artistry
with any spiritual intention can allow?"
Robert Bridges. The Testament of Beauty.

1

I dislike even necessary killing,
Though in my youth I played an eager part,
At hunting and at fishing ever willing,
But, toward the end, with sorrow at the heart.

And so in Nature, where the death of one
Most often is another's means of life,
Why is it that I turn from killing done
By tooth and claw as from a bloody knife?

I cannot watch the wildebeest brought low
And torn apart before allowed to die,
Though lioness and jackal like it so,
As do the vultures watching from the sky.

Killing, systemic in the struggle for
Survival in a never-ended fight,
With neither hate nor malice to deplore,
And only by succeeding counted right,

Would seem to make of earth a killing-field,
The ocean its companion in that state,
And death the reaper of what both may yield
As husbandman by sovereignty of Fate.

---

25 In the final quatrain of Poem No. 3 the line "As is one's own a silent, wordless prayer"
was printed "As in one's own…" in the print-shop edition of these poems. Moll hand-
corrected the copy he sent to long-time friend Thelma Greenfield; the corrected version
is used here.

But how the joy of living rises up
Against that seeming of a soulless power
To pledge in liquor from a victor's cup
"The force that through the green fuse drives the flower!"*

    *The first line of a poem by Dylan Thomas.

2

That is the force in Nature and in Man
Which makes us one with beauty's blossoming,
And for whose joyousness in being's plan,
As with the bird's, the hearts within us sing.

And to that happiness thought will return,
How eagerly!; like homing from a view
Of ugliness we cannot love nor spurn,
But in truth's wholeness know that it is true.

I watch a snake, that has for blood no thirst
And kills and dines, all in a single act
By swallowing its living meals headfirst –
And truth becomes life's mocker in a fact.

But less sight-shocking memories take me where
A stone-brown lizard on a sun-warmed stone
Sends out its tongue to reap in fields of air
A harvest its by right of skill alone;

And where a spider, plump and most polite,
"Please come into my parlour," begs the fly,
And then, as reason to assure delight,
"The prettiest that ever you did spy;"

And where a mantis, twig among the rest,
Sits posed and Oh, so stately, so serene,
So dignified while on a meal-time quest,
And gentle, as attests his coat of green!

Where there's no bond with killer or its prey,
Killing, though ugly, may seem like a sport
Where one in praise of competence may say
"Well hit," and follow quickly with "well caught!"

But when sweet-nectar is the killer's snare
For insects who bring pollen to make seed,
I feel a sickness of a spirit there,
And on death's face the ugliness of greed.

3

My onward going stopped, I stand quite still
Upon a ridge between the day and night,
While of my memories of good and ill
One grows in brightness in the fading light

Below me in the valley whence I came;
And my thoughts linger there because I know
The dark can only serve to feed its flame,
And if not seeing, I still will feel its glow.

One spring day in an open field a bird
Fell as from flight, before me in the grass,
And lay quite still, then of a sudden stirred
As though to leave the place where I would pass.

It was a killdeer, and I knew the text:
A nest somewhere I must not ever find
But be led wrong by a strategy perplexed
That was in Springs of long ago designed.

I was to her a danger, one of those
With fox and hawk and the snake slithering
Silently through the grass, by habit foes,
And her defence her cunning and her wing.

She lay there crumpled a few feet away,
One foot exposed, but limp; tail-feathers spread,
And all in what seemed painful disarray,
Except the small unruffled, watchful head.

Then, when I moved she wrenched herself upright
With a wing hanging as though broken, and,
Were I a fox, what an alluring sight!
She staggered wildly as she tried to stand.

But in that staggering she'd passed me by
Going the way I'd come from, and I turned
To see her fall again and crumpled lie,
But with, I knew a first small victory earned.

I made the expected rush, but quickly she,
The wing healed, struck with both, but the height gained
By wings which beat so weakly falteringly,
Though greatly needed, could not be maintained.

Falling once more, with little, broken cries,
She was a fledgling wandered from the nest,
Doubly desirable to hungry eyes,
And to pursuit a new and added zest.

And so we two contenders played our play,
But I as with an eager, gifted child,
Knowing, when laughter'd blown pretense away,
How dear would be the hug that reconciled.

From what is threatening the weaker flee;
But out from safety she of little force
Had come to meet what seemed her enemy –
A child, to turn a river from its course!

She played seductress well to hunger's eyes,
So small, so brave, so frighteningly alone,
That when at last I stood to watch her rise
She had become so utterly my own

As is one's own a silent, wordless prayer,
And she its emblem, to know beauty by
In the life-spirit, how triumphant there
That form in the immensity of sky!

Quatrains

I have loved knowledge as a liberator
From groping to a worthier human way,
But now it's killing's choicest tools creator
I live with fears reason cannot allay.

"I am," our flag, and there our yearnings rally
That, in some tongue, if spoken, still not heard,
On some far mountain top, or in its valley,
Will shine the meaning of what's there averred.

For My Daughter Carolyn

As when beneath the ashes there remain
Coals which a breath has started into glowing,
How often have your words waked hope again
When it seemed ash, or snow in winter's snowing!

Apologia

I lived with flowers to my heart's content
And showed my love and joy in thought and deed,
But, mixed with sorrow, even deeper went
That which I felt for beauty in the weed.

Old age my plea for all I've left unweeded,
I like to see what the chance winds have sown
For plants I now pass by as though unheeded
No matter how flamboyant they have grown.

And when I stroll where should be only roses
And see my wildlings matching their effulgence,
There's joy within me as my heart proposes
They pay in beauty for my sin's indulgence.

In a Ninety-Fourth Year

Watching the gulf upon whose brink I kneel
Widening between me and my yesterdays,
I shiver at the chilling breath I feel
As the far rim starts dimming out in haze.

Outlines remain, though faint, of what is there
And, like the horizon from mid-ocean seen,
Give to my eager eyes not anywhere
Joyous reunions with what has been,

But only unresponsive, featureless
Indifference as in that endless line
Where sky and ocean meet and I possess
Nothing that gives back what once was mine.

Not able to recall where I have been,
I can't set compass for the further going;
And even if I could, the new would mean
Only by what's already in my knowing;

And that's beyond the farther rim where I
See less and less in spite of all my trying,
While overhead the clouds go sailing by,
So bright, so fleet, so lovely in their flying!

Quatrains

Earth has a timeless contract with the root
For life to rise between it and the sun:
Leafage and bloom, the benison of fruit,
And myriad lives, each with a course to run.

A peasant's face, moulded by deed and thought,
Strong, elemental as the life she knew,
Bends over lace as frail as patterns caught
By dawn on cobwebs lightly gemmed with dew.

A wild duck from some willows at the shore
Moves out on sunlit waters of a lake
Bound for a reedbed where she will explore,
Her seven futures bobbing in her wake.

From *A Gleaner's Sheaf of Poems* (1995)

443

The Hidden Strength

In treasures which we hold
We think of no alloy,
Though, even in love's employ
It is the strength in gold.

It lets the gold endure
As love has shaped its form
In passion's darkest storm
An Image strong and pure.

Itself a commonplace,
Under the festive light,
Though hidden from the sight,
It is the life in grace.

Itself plain common sense
That asks for nothing more,
Yet ground from which wings soar
To beauty's eloquence.

And Oh, for love to win,
It is the glass kept bright
In windows on the night,
To let the stars shine in.

To Dance

Note: In Greek legend, Pygmalion, King of Cyprus, is also a sculptor. He fell in love with his beautiful statue of a maiden, Galatea, and Aphrodite endowed the statue with life. A happy story, and in addition, in it I find the concept of how art approved by love's goddess can make the beautiful a living part of human life. That thought leads on to Byron's lines about poets and their art:

> "Tis to create, and in creating live
> A being more intense that we endow
> With form our fancy, taking as we give
> The life we image."

"We receive but what we give," is from Coleridge's Dejection: An Ode.

This morning in our yard of shrubs and trees,
All blooming over, emptied every nest,
Life had gone elsewhere with its birds and bees,
And I was dull and listless with the rest,
When like a shout on that stagnating air
To strong-winged yellow butterflies were there.

In my upbringing dancing was a sin,
But in due time I saw it as the art
Of weaving human tapestries wherein
The dancers play a story-teller's part
By patterned moves and gesturings to show
The winds of passion working as they blow.

I'd watched the dance of humans and of birds,
Sun-dancing waves in harbors of the sea,
And, in those times when heaven smiled, of words;
And now was mine, quite unexpectedly,
To see once more, with old and failing eyes,
The summer dance of yellow butterflies.

And then I felt my heart rise to go out,
Eagerly as a child when called to play,
The one best summons children know about,
That has a charm on even the foulest day;
And hurried to a window for the view,
But not in quite the way that children do.

And as I made that passage cautiously,
By expectations light I lived ahead
To where, from all earth's bondages set free,
And by the spirit's-to-spirit music led,
Beyond the reach of weariness and pain
I'd dance with Nature's dancers once again.

Oh how those fragile wings have borne me clear,
In flight as bold as thought and just as fleet,
Above and past the open jaws of fear
To where for me the earth and heaven meet,
And in our human world of pain and strife
Pygmalion's Galatea comes to life.

The dance was on. I watched with hungry eyes
The nonsubstantial patterns being made
By swing and turn and swoop and dizzying rise
Weaving together sunshine and the shade
Tapestries by the art of matchless flight,
And smiled with pleasure at the charming sight.

And then…and then, Oh God! so speaks my heart,
That once could find no words for its delight
In being in that dance the human part
Where Man's own spirit and Nature's joy unite
In meanings glimpsed in being's finest hour
Of things eternal in their grace and power?

Truth answered, " 'We receive but what we give',
And you gave only weariness of soul,
A pillow for the sleep of all who live
When age becomes the giver in control;
And Man must steal, when beauty's his desire,
Like one, most famous, some of Heaven's fire".

Now afternoon. Some butterflies still there,
The oaks, the pines and the camellias stand
As a sea breeze is freshening the air,
Where, planted long ago by my own hand
To be, in age something to call my own;
But Galatea has gone back to stone.

Slumber Song

Desires remembered, but their clamor stilled
By age, are moths released from the cocoon
Where they grew wings, and with new ardor filled,
And beautiful, set out to reach the moon.

Not questioning their courage or their course,
And in their wings the ecstasy of flight,
Though they will never, never reach its source,
Their every move is hallowed by its light.

I do not know where dawn will bid them rest,
But every night a moon is in the sky,
In trust like theirs my slumber will be blessed
By the felt presence of their passing by.

Upwind to the Past

There's a cloud in the sky, but it's May
And the sun will be shining again,
So we sang in our Youth's pleasant day
As we danced in the sunshine and rain.

But the cloud in our hearts has its home
Now we're old, and so tutored by pain,
Our faith is, if joy still would come,
That sorrow must be its refrain.

So we gaze from our prison of thought
As a sailor might gaze from the shore,
With the wind in his face from a port
Where his boat will drop anchor no more.

But the sailor's more blessed in his star
Than are we, for that wind in his hair
Is his wings, and no matter how far
Be the port, in a breath he is there.

And I say to old-age's belief,
Let such wind be our wings once again
To the joys of our childhood, though brief,
But with dearness of life their refrain.

Quatrains

A small girl lost in heaven with her hands
Holding a tame dove in an ecstasy;
Oh life, be gentle as she understands
Of doves their holding and their setting free!

Imagination still is in their eyes,
And thought in them has yet not shed its wings;
The wonderful occasions no surprise,
The heart in them still dances as it sings.

To the hereafter we take separate ways,
But each can help his fellows in their going,
Sharing in humanness with joy and praise
The harvests all had helped with in their sowing.

Old age is like a river's whirlpool where,
Though it is no one's chosen place to be,
Just going round and round is all we dare,
For onward there's no way to pass the sea.

Geese Overhead at Night

I lived where geese in migratory flight
With bursts of talk electrified the night
Over high mountains and wide valleys, where
I'd rise to be a moment with them there
As they went North, far North to the one place
The fountain for renewal of their race,
Guided by stars to gain by strength of wing,
In Nature's creed, their sacrament of Spring.

Moving with them as though borne by a wave,
In flesh and soul I felt the power that gave
Stream up from sense to sensibility
And beyond that, from self I felt swept free
As my heart beat with those wild hearts as one
In what earth knows as heavenly unison.

But old, I cannot feel their bodies press
Against me, but I feel the tenderness
Of that instinct, their bond of each to each
In the great aim the stars still help them reach,
The loveliest instinct in all Nature's plan,
And firmest link with humanness in Man.

And now, as then, the night is still and deep.
As I begin to sink towards dawn in sleep.

De Senectute

> "Tears, idle tears, I know not what they mean,
> Tears, from the depth of some divine despair
> Rise in the heart and gather to the eyes,
> In looking on the happy Autumn fields,
> And thinking of the days that are no more."
> Tennyson, from The Princess

The fitful time has come:
The candle guttering,
And the soul sitting numb
In listlessness of wing.

The one, brief as a spark
Seen at the dead of night,
But still, against the dark,
A memory of light.

And the soul lifts its head
A last time to the sky
To glimpse, as once it read,
The road it traveled by.

And so we old ones share,
Beyond all storm and strife,
In a divine despair
What was divine in life.

Of Infirm Age and Doors

We old ones, it is clear,
Like the truth less as facts
Than as an atmosphere
With the sun at our backs
As we go slowly West
Towards shadowy hills of rest.

Or is it what we see
Comes veiled into our sight
Because reality
Softens its harsher light
In a kind enterprise
To comfort failing eyes?

Or is it, at play's end
Where each has had a part,
And all the world's a friend
With heart gone out to heart,
Life gives each in his place
This curtain call of grace?

But there's no veil, no doubt,
And well we understand
Where doors lead in, and out,
The dearness of a hand
That holds the door, and wide,
To let us pass with pride.

In the Close of a Ninety-Fifth Year

When dawn and I were friends
I'd say to night, "Don't stay;
I'll wait till dawn attends
To what I have to say".

That was because I knew
How dawn likes life with zest,
And so would hear me through,
As at a friend's request:

How plants need light to grow,
The bird its hour to sing,
And humankind to show
Out heart belongs to Spring.

The dawn and I stay friends,
But I am old and weak,
And since all zest now ends,
We try no more to speak.

The time has come to say
The fount of hope is dry,
And so tonight, please stay,
And dawn, go by…go by.

Variation on a Theme

At age ninety I declared:

> "Stop the long winnowing
> For grain it doesn't bring,
> And give the wind in pay
> The chaff to blow away.
>
> And then, to banish pain,
> Be the glad child again
> Who pauses not nor grieves
> In Autumn, burning the leaves."

And now at ninety-five:

As I sit by the ashes of desire,
Those of my spirits' and my senses' burning,
In the great stillness of the unreturning
There is not even a memory of fire.

Shut from the wind that winnows right from wrong
The ashes lie with touches of a grace
All being has when everything's in place
Like sound and sense in music of a song.

The grace which is when every part confesses
How that another helped it as it grew
Into the wholeness which the harvest knew
And man the reaper in his turn possesses.

So, when you come, wind, be the breeze again
That from the too-great ardor of the sun
Sheltered what in a blossom had begun,
And helped the chaff in nurturing the grain.

And I will watch them lying here together,
The chaff, the grain, and thinking of the flower
Which made them both, I'll bless that happy hour,
That pause of sunlight in my winter weather.

The Longer Reach

"If winter comes, can Spring be far behind?"
        Shelley, Ode to the West Wind

      No inner tension left
      To hold the parts together,
      I feel myself bereft
      Of seasons in my weather,
      Except for this one thing:
      There'll be no more a Spring.

In the silence of moth-wings in flight
As they move through the dark toward a light
Words settled themselves on a page,
And, though having the lilt of a song,
Their meaning was that of a sage:
"Seeing life as a self, you are wrong."

"For a bee of a sudden in May
Will turn to its fellows and say
'It is decking the orange tree now
With blossoms It made for each bough:
Come! I will show you the way'".

"And a bird, as a breeze at her breast
Moves the feathers to gentle unrest,
Will say to her mate, 'It is here,
The weaver of dreams that are dear;
We must help, It is building a nest!'"

Landscape with Sheep

If sleep comes hard, my elders used to say
Just counting sheep will often end the trouble.

I see them now in a familiar place;
A gently sloping hillside with gum trees,
And I breathe deep that fragrance on a breeze
Which cools the sun-warmth on my upturned face.

The sheep are settling down for the night's rest,
In scores but sinking slowly one by one
In a great confidence, as seems the sun
While pausing on a hilltop to the west,

With Earth its perch outlined against the sky,
To watch the flush of sunset rise and spread
Its colors in the heaven overhead
In both a benediction and goodbye.

So the day ends in beauty; and as one
Slips from the room where there has fallen asleep
A child for whom love has a watch to keep,
Silently from its hilltop slips the sun.

Hearing Spring Song When Deaf

I cannot hear you, Robin, but where bound,
As now I watch your lover's pilfering:
A twig, a straw, a dangling bit of string,
I know full well, and so without a sound,
They are for me the song you used to sing.

And Bewick's, as of old you've come as two
And I can read your quick, house-haunting eyes
Probing each nook to find if in it lies
April's own heaven, hidden out of view
But right for song and your own enterprise.

And if, come summer, sitting in this chair,
And Fortune still has left a smile for me,
I'll watch young purple finches from their tree
Launching short flights to test the summer air,
And that is now the song yours used to be.

Quatrains[26]

When trust stands baffled by complexity,
And clouds unmoving, keep the heavens dark,
A lovely legend gives my eyes to see
Noah's white dove returning to the ark.

There's nothing wrong in simple vegetating,
If like a plant, and only once a year,
We bear a blossom that is worth the waiting
To one we know will hold it more than dear.

---

[26] The penultimate line (next page) uses "caste off" in the original print-shop edition. This
    seems likely to be a mistake and is corrected here.

There is completeness in unhurting laughter,
Like a deep breath's of fresh but balmy air
That starts no thought of a before or after
But revels in the moment that is there.

The gallop was a wildly joyous flight
Away from every meaning but its own
Of heaviness cast off in the delight
Of racing blood and leaping flesh and bone!

Soul's Way

> *"An aged man is but a paltry thing,*
> *A tattered coat upon a stick, unless*
> *Soul clap its hands and sing, and louder sing*
> *For every tatter in its mortal dress."*
> William Butler Yeats

Ancient, like other Ancients, I have found
That scarecrow image most appropriate
And for the ways in which we are unsound
A proper likeness for our hapless state;
But my own soul, I must in sadness note,
Stays silent as though hiding in that coat.

It is a state no one would ever seek,
To be a sham to keep some birds away
By hanging on a stick, senseless and weak,
Where fruit is ripening on a summer day;
Then, in that image of what must depress,
Destiny rides upon a bold "unless"!

There shines the power and splendor of the soul
In office as we humans like to see,
The spiritual master of life whole,
One foot in time, one in eternity;
And by edict divine to mortals given,
The judge on Earth. And to be judged in heaven.

Of my first eighteen years five had been spent
Where was no science, library, or thought
To break the spell – not evil by intent –
Of rightness in the truth as it was taught,
And knowledge, with all said, had as its goal
At heaven's gate sure passage of the soul.

I liked the soul the poet saw and heard,
Though my own was, and is, harder to find;
More drawn to the small twittering of a bird
Than to the flags and trumpets of mankind;
And found, if in a tavern or a church,
Not quite what was expected in the search.

It was a life-force waiting as I grew,
Till in my twentieth year, with my world changed,
I felt it as a presence that I knew
But from which I had been for long estranged;
And joyously we locked our arms together
To face the hopes and fears of growing weather.

The climate of the book, the microscope,
With learning's sun warming the life in each
To thought with visions of tremendous hope,
An Everest, but with its top in reach,
And from its summit, as is all men's desire,
The dream of views from summits ever higher.

I learned from farm life that what I perceive
Is partly what I have bestowed in viewing,
And so what I have found there and believe
Is, in a measure, soul's creative doing;
A moving interchange, in peace and strife,
And, near my end, the story of my life.

Then came a need, reanimating age,
That, like a helper, as one reads a book
Has, quite unseen turned back the blurring page
To give the tired eyes the 'one more' look
Before the book is closed and laid away
By time, impatient from too long a stay.

Like buds on plants that bloom again in Fall,
My memories, one brighter Autumn day,
Seemed poised and set for answering recall
By opening where the sun paused on its way,
And my step quickened as I took my chair
For spirit to greet spirit warmly there.

With a soft blanket spread across my knees,
I closed my weakened eyes against the light
To give my inner self its way to please
With memories coming to the finer sight
As spirit with no longer need to pass
Through passion's smudges on the window glass.

They came and were, not presences but facts
In a procession to which I was host;
Persons I'd loved, their natures, smiles and acts,
Each in unlivingness not even a ghost
To break the spell of this grim travesty
Of what in life had been so dear to me.

So did the longing in my heart propose
In buds once more a festive blossoming,
And words re-read before the book must close,
When I of life had not enough to bring
Life back in them as relived memories
Real as the blanket warm upon my knees;

And it was that, reliving with no force
The rise of spirit naturally from sense,
And sending visions to be on their course
Shaping the transient into permanence
As floating sounds are given shape in song,
The heart had done itself a grievous wrong.

For in the chorus of forever Spring,
That mighty chorus of what is to be,
I have not left even a voice to sing,
And while men feast in hope's festivity
For each day more of life set free from fate,
I study patterns on my empty plate.

Breath of my flesh, soul, you've grown old with it,
I should have known. And though no tattered thing,
No more, as once, the fire by feeling lit
That warmed life even in its wintering.
Have you or not a rendezvous to keep,
Come as of old to sink with me in sleep.

For a Ninety-Fifth Birthday

My days, now downhill going, move so fast
I cannot tell my present from my past,
And, as for looking to what lies before,
I feel I'm stuck in a revolving door.

The time has come when there's no last or first,
No draught of wine to slake a spirit's thirst;
No livingness within my gazing eye
That in a blossom saw what cannot die;

No listener within my fleshly ears
Who once would note the singing of the spheres,
Or nearer home, when summer days were long
Brought joy to me in a bird's sleepy song.

My words, no longer vibrant, do not twine
To be on fact imagination's vine,
Transforming it from wood to living tree
With its calm beauty and its mystery.

But here breaks in a strong and strengthening thing –
The gratitude in my remembering
To those who lived with me the heart's content
In Love's embrace and friendship's testament

To you, the many, gathered to the dead,
And you who with me break life's daily bread,
Whether or not my birthday comes to pass,
Think of this poem as my lifted glass.

The Light that Does Not Fail

There's a light I can turn off or on;
At my touch it is there, and again,
With not given a chance to remain,
At my touch it is gone.

Its nature is of the machine,
Having life for a second, then dead,
Like a word that's forgotten when said,
With no pause in between.

Or its light which a city lives by,
Giving over itself to delight
By making a night out of night
With no stars in the sky.

Or it is, like a bird on a bough,
Adding life to the one that is there
With a song making brighter the air,
As silence knows how.

But when heaven bends down to the earth,
Dawn-light is a mother's eyes
To which everything living will rise
In the joy of rebirth.

Tell a Star

While you're young tell a star where you go;
Though it has for you never a care,
If in truth you do want it to know,
It will follow you there.

And should you be sad and alone
In a crowd in a city at noon,
Just recall what's up there, and your own,
And that night will be soon.

But never then pause in your walk
To look up with a smile at the sky
Lest a watcher should stop you to talk
Just to ask of you why.

And of you in your bond with a star
It is only who love you can know,
For they too seek gardens that are
Where the amaranths grow.

Insight

Before youth left me, from the road to Man
On looking back, so clearly in my sight
Were hills and valleys where the pipes of Pan
Played in such haunting witchery of light

All seemed like something found I should not keep
But hide, how marvelous but yet not strange;
Safe from the eroding touch of dreams in sleep,
Deep in my heart where it could never change.

Here, at great age, I pause to testify
In gratitude, to that experience
And others like it, how I learned thereby
At least awareness of "a soul in sense",

And humanness, torn by conflicting wills,
Finds singleness and peace and healing care
When memory, like a kindly host refills
The cup of hope to drink against despair;

For they are insights that cannot be willed,
And touching us, we cannot say from where,
Leave us with longings still to be fulfilled,
And in whose cause we hope, and strive, and dare.

Unpublished and Uncollected Poems

The following poem appeared in the *Bulletin* (Sydney), December 12, 1956. It was not included in any subsequent collections.

A Stone Bridge Built by Convicts

Bridges are flight caught up in steel and stone,
Twin-natured beings of a single birth
That range the sky yet never leave the earth
And speed forever yet are never flown.
And those who step on bridges feel the strength
Of Mercury rise in them and the glow
Of voyagers who at its launching know
Their journey will have splendor all its length.
Surely none ever built more sadly well
Than these who felt the whip, the ball and chain
Upon them, and who stood at last to stare,
With eyes too weary even to show pain,
At this stone arc firm-buttressed deep in hell
And leading from that nowhere to nowhere.

The following two poems were sent by Moll to his friends Stanley and Thelma Greenfield, fellow professors at the University of Oregon. I borrowed them from Thelma, a long-time friend, when I began work on this project. As far as I know they have never been previously published. It is not always possible to determine the chronological sequence of these poems, but they are generally dated at least by year.
–Ed.

Provincia Gallia Narbonensis (1994)

I. Les Baux

Its jagged bones rose high into the air,
Wind-swept and somehow brutal, hardly fair.
Lords lived here, proud and scorning servitude,
Feudal, medieval, with an attitude.
"Race d'aiglons, mais jamais un vassal!"
These words, recalled by Frédéric Mistral,
Proud poet of Provence, who loved Les Baux,
Captures its stark appeal.

II. Glanum

                    Then, down you go
To St.-Rémy where, level with the plain,
A Roman arch—inviting, almost sane—
Welcomes your steps into the ancient town
Of Glanum, whose as yet unearthed renown
Escaped the notice of Van Gogh's hot brush
Which rendered the Alpilles. Now, with a hush
Columns and stones rise gently to the feet
Of the Alpilles. Before Van Gogh, in the heat,
The Glanics first had settled here. They found
A source to worship. High up, on a mound
The Celtic vestiges remain. Then came
The Greeks north from Massilia, the name
Of old Marseilles. And then the Romans came,
Steady, pragmatic visionaries. Streams
Required, no longer, passive worship. Dreams
Were metamorphosed into aqueducts,
Conveying sea nymphs to these arid tracts.
A scene on the arch speaks Roman dominance,
Hinting compassion for the grave mischance
Suffered by those who struggle to withstand,
With noble fortitude, Roman command.
Thus Caesar strangled Vercengetorix,
The Hector of the Gauls, thereby to fix
The world's attention on the penalty
Of fighting to resist Rome's sovereignty:[27]
A fallen Gallic warrior, resigned
With awkward breeches, his hands tied behind
His back, shamed shoulders sloping in defeat;
A female captive makes the loss complete.

III. Aquae Sextiae

The cost was high, the massive deportation
Of native peoples; wars; civilization
Thus was achieved. Farewell, the severed head!
(The Gauls' obsession). Rome would choose, instead
Selected acts of measured cruelty.
A strangled Vercengetorix, a sea
of Christian blood left by the lion's maw
Joined Virgil's poetry and Roman law.

---

27   This line was hand-corrected by Moll from the original typed line "Of proudly fighting
        Rome's hegemony."

A weird mélange replaced the têtes coupée.
At Celtic Entremont, some skulls, they say,
Were found with nail holes drilled through ancient bone.
The vacant stare, eyes opened wide in stone,
The mouth slit thinly, silencing a groan:
These sculpted, severed heads are on display
In Cézanne's Aix, in the Musée Granet.
At Entremont, Cézanne's Mt. St.-Victoire
Sloping, leans and commands the valley, far
Yet dominant. There Marius crushed and spilled
The invading Teuton hordes and blood, which filled
The earth with gore, enriching all the fields,
As bumper crops poked through cracked, fallen shields.

The Life-Force (May, 1997)
(in a ninety-seventh year)

I

In the fall of a wave lies a power
That will help the next wave in its climb;
So I view my life force at this hour
In a glance from the small to sublime

From a space between waves to the form
Of an Everest vast in the sky
Where, the clouds, on the wings of a storm
Are driven in violence to die.

Or remember when still I could feel,
When the form lifted thought to its crest,
How I loved but could never reveal
The awe in that meeting expressed.

For the life-force there playing a part
Is of nature and has no concern
For the little, shy lives in my heart
For whose touch, ever closer, I yearn.

II

So I turn where they always rejoice
To the garden and every plant there
Which we know by that change for a voice
Its fragrance set free on the air;

By that, and its shape and the tone
Of its color, as red of the rose,
So in beauty none stands there alone,
But with friends, as a wise gardener chose.

There's a blue that is violet blue
And a gold that is sunflower gold,
And my heart opens wide to the view
And this memory from heaven to hold,

When my first love came down from the hills
In the time of aenemone skies,
And her step had the grace of the hills
And its light was the light in her eyes.

Then, for bloom that has died on a plant,
For our sorrow there's never a need,
As we know how the life-force will grant
A new life in the promise of seed.

And when birdsong seems over with Spring,
It has gone to new throats from a nest,
And in time with the seed it will sing
All the sweeter for winter and rest.

III

The life-force in the waves of the sea,
As I think of unmeasurable time,
Lets me glimpse how no ending may be
Of the fall lending power to the climb;

How eternity may be the dower
Of the life locked in seed by the plant,
And the beauty which lived in the flower
Heaven's gift with its fairest to grant.

Pain fishes with nets of small mesh,
From the prick of a pin to the break
Of a heart memory keeps ever fresh
As for timeless unpitying's sake.

And when hopes disappear in the sand
And we weep where our barren souls lie,
The long dreams of mankind understand
And send beauty to know heaven by.

It is beauty the life-force must gain
For the eye of its spirit to see,
As a rose bud the healer of pain
When it opens by living set free.

IV

As when heaven touched earth in the deed
When a traveler who answered the cry
Who was robbed and left roadside to bleed
And in pity would not let him die.

Or today when great ships of the air,
U.S.A. to Korea, loading wheat
To end the starvation that is there
And lets life have a future to greet.

For its spirit to see and rejoice
That for it there await to be won
More Edens of Man's noblest choice,
Awaking as night for the sun.

And of each human a sentient being
Who in excellence of beauty with grow
By sharing with others their seeing
In a joy which time lingers to know.

As my life-force now suffers decay,
I gather what memories grow bright,
Like some gems in a darkening sky,
And dream in the power of their light.

Oh how dear in its valleys and hills
And how sweet has been life's enterprise,
Which dying not ends but fulfills—
And I'm glad there are tears in my eyes.

THIS WAS THE LAST POEM ERNEST G. MOLL WROTE. [28]

---

28 Moll added a footnote regarding section IV: "The traveler: The Good Samaritan in the
story about him told by Jesus, as reported by Luke in the New Testament." This poem
was typed by Moll's daughter Carolyn from a holograph manuscript mere hours before
the poet died. Moll's handwriting in his last years was shaky and wandered a bit on the
page. This poem in typescript is signed at the bottom "Ernest G. Moll May 1997" in
Carolyn's handwriting, which suggests that the poet was too infirm to affix his own
signature, as he had for poems he distributed in 1995.

Glossary

Bewick's. Bewick's Wren, a North American bird known for probing into unlikely locations such as cars, planters, old clothing. It is common where Moll lived in Oregon and California.

Billabong. Aboriginal term in general use in Australia for a watercourse, often an old riverbend, usually still containing water but largely or entirely bypassed by its former feeder stream. In American usage this would be called an oxbow lake, often just an oxbow.

Boundary. In cricket, a long hit outside the delineated playing area that automatically generates multiple "runs" (either six or four depending on where the ball goes) without the batter actually running. Roughly similar in concept to a home run in baseball.

Bradman, Don. World-famous Australian cricket player.

Caravanserai. A camping area for travelers.

Cloudcap. A feature on the rim of Crater Lake.

Cootamundra. Town in the Riverina region of New South Wales, Australia.

Coulter. Part of a plow.

Crook. To "go crook" in Australian usage means to become angry and act badly or destructively.

Dam. In Australian and some British usage, the dam is the water behind the barrier, not the barrier itself as in American usage. An Australian dam is what an American would call a reservoir, sometimes a stock-pond or, less accurately, a lake.

Dream-time. An older usage for what today would be called the Dreaming, an important part of the creation story of many aboriginal people. Also known as the Alcheringa (spellings vary).

Duessa. Character in Spenser's Faerie Queene known for being a chimerical or false person.

Dutton cliff. A feature on the rim of Crater Lake.

Euro. In this context, an aboriginal name for the small kangaroo commonly called a wallaby.

Fossicking. Rummaging or digging about for objects, especially gemstones. Chiefly Australian.

Galah. Australian cockatoo, a parrot-like pink and gray bird known for odd distinctive behavior, such as briefly hanging upside-down. A mild insult if applied to a human.

Goanna. A type of large Australian monitor lizard.

Hillman. A feature on the rim of Crater Lake.

Honeyeater. Asian bird family physically similar to Western Hemisphere orioles, but generally less colorful.

Humpy. An Aboriginal living hut intended for temporary usage.

Kookaburra. A loud-voiced Australian bird related to kingfishers but more terrestrial in habits.

Llao. Llao (pronounced "lauw" as if it had only one "l") is a god of the Klamath
  tribe of Native Americans in Oregon. In Klamath mythology, Llao, god of the
  underworld, battled with Skell, the sky god, which resulted in the eruption of
  Mount Mazama in about 5600 B.C., creating Crater Lake.

Leather-head. Colloquial term for the Australian bird formally named Friarbird.

Lubra. Colloquial term for an aboriginal woman, today generally considered
  offensive.

Mopoke. This is a common colloquial pronunciation and spelling of the small
  Australian owl also called a Morepork or sometimes boobook after the sound of
  its call.

Mulga. A type of Australian acacia tree commonly found in farming and outback
  regions. Also used generally to describe rural scrubland.

Possum. In Australia, this name is used for a marsupial resembling a slender
  American mink. This is a different species than the Opossum of the Western
  Hemisphere.

Riverina. An agricultural region in southwestern New South Wales, Australia.

S.T.C. Presumably refers to Samuel Taylor Coleridge in this context.

Soldier-bird. Colloquial name for the Noisy Miner, an Australian honeycreeper
  with a partial black hood.

Stooks. Alternative for shocks, stalks or stands of grain.

Swagman, swaggy etc. A person, almost always male, who lives a wandering life
  but may choose to work at rural station sites or towns, usually for a short time.
  Less used in modern times.

Two-up. An Australian gambling game involving tossing coins.

Volplaning. Gliding, as by an aircraft with the engine off.

Waddy. Aboriginal term, now in more general use, for a small wooden club,
  roughly equivalent to the Irish term shillelagh.

Wagga. The city of Wagga Wagga in western New South Wales, Australia.

Warrigal. Most commonly used for the wild dog also known as a dingo, which is
  similar in size and some behaviors to the North American coyote. Also a
  modifier or general descriptor for other wild, particularly predatory, animals.

Watchman. A feature on the rim of Crater Lake.

Wattle. In this context, a type of acacia tree.

Wether. A castrated male sheep, equivalent to the term steer or ox for a bull. The
  term "bellwether" comes from this origin, as the lead male sheep in a flock.

Wimmera. A farming area in Victoria, Australia.

Wood-Reveler and **Knight's-Plume** mosses. "The two mosses named are
  beautiful and common in the fir forests of western Oregon." – *EGM*

Woomera. A spear-throwing stick.

Wried wood. The past tense of wry, rarely used, a term which appears in "A
  Gnarled Riverina Gum Tree" in the collection *Cut from Mulga.*

Yellow Bob. The Eastern Yellow Robin.

Yew. "I speak of it as "death's own tree" because it is often found growing in old
  cemeteries of England and Europe. Example: the poet Gray's reference to the
  tree in his "Elegy Written in a Country Church-Yard"." – *EGM*

Principal Contributors

Alan L. Contreras is a fourth-generation Oregonian and a graduate of the University of Oregon and its law school. He is retired from a career on the fringes of higher education. Contreras has published eight books as author, editor or co-editor with Oregon State University Press, plus several books with other publishers. Recent titles include *A History of Oregon Ornithology, Collected Poems of Ada Hastings Hedges, Edge of Awe: Experiences of the Malheur-Steens Country* and *Afield: Forty Years of Birding the American West.* He had the privilege of visiting Australia, all too briefly, in 2009.

Patrick Buckridge is a retired professor of literary studies at Griffith University, Brisbane, Australia. He has published widely on Australian literature and literary history, the history of Australian journalism, biography, and the history of reading. He was born and grew up in Brisbane, graduated from the University of Queensland (1968), and gained his doctorate in Renaissance literary studies from the University of Pennsylvania, Philadelphia (1975). For most of his career, he taught courses on 'Great Books', poetry, Shakespeare and Australian literature.

Hope Arnold was born and raised in the Pacific Northwest. She is a freelancer and the owner of Hope Helps, a small business in Eugene, OR. She is honored that she was asked to assist Alan Contreras with the transcribing and proofing process of this book. She looks back fondly on the summer she spent in Alan's living room reading Moll's poetry out loud during the final proofing process, and is proud to have contributed to increased knowledge of the incredible life and legacy of Ernest G. Moll.

The Ernest G. Moll Faculty Research Fellowship

The Ernest G. Moll Faculty Research Fellowship in Literary Studies at the University of Oregon is awarded to the most outstanding proposal(s) in the field of literary studies. In addition to the course release, the Moll Fellowship provides recipients with $1,000 in research support to be used during the fellowship year.

The Ernest G. Moll Research Fellowship was created in 2003 and endowed in 2006 through a generous gift to the OHC from UO English department alumna Maribeth Collins (BA 1940). Ms. Collins was a student of Ernest "Gerry" Moll, a UO English professor/poet who taught in the English Department from 1928 to 1966. Moll played a significant role in the development of Collins' life-long interest in poetry, and the two struck up a meaningful correspondence toward the end of his life. Ms. Collins established this fellowship to honor the memory of her favorite professor.

Awardees of the Ernest G. Moll Research Fellowship in Literary Studies, University of Oregon

2003-04	Evlyn Gould, Romance Languages: Turning Around Dreyfus: Educating Citizens During the Third Republic in France
2004-05	Dianne Dugaw, English: The Hidden Baroque in Britain and the Gendering of Literary History
2005-06	William Rossi, English: Clutching a Rainbow, Frying a Rat: Walden's Double Evolutionary Narrative
2006-07	Ellen Rees, German and Scandinavian: Genre and Space in Cora Sandel's Short Prose
2007-08	Cecilia Enjuto Rangel, Romance Languages: Cities in Ruins in Modern Poetry
2007-08	Katya Hokanson, Comparative Literature and REEES: Theatrical Asides: Gender and Nation in Russian Women's Travel Writing
2008-09	Deborah Shapple, English: Uneven Exchanges: Narratives of Realism in 19th-Century South Africa
2009-10	Soojung "Susanna" Lim, Robert D. Clark Honors College: Revolution and the Yellow Peril: East Asia and the End of Empire in Russian Modernism
2010-11	David Wacks, Romance Languages: Hebrew Literature and Hispanic Culture
2011-12	Leah Middlebrook, Comparative Literature and Romance Languages: On Muses and Mathesis
	Liz Bohls, English: African Exploration and British Slavery: Mungo Park's Coffle
2012-13	Michael Stern, German and Scandinavian: The Essential Gesture
	Courtney Thorsson, English: Revolutionary Recipes: Foodways and African American Literature
2013-14	Gina Herrmann, Romance Languages: Jorge Semprun: Duty of the Witness, Task of the Writer.
	Karen McPherson, Romance Languages: Growing Old and Realizing Life in Marie-Claire Blais's Soifs Cycle.
2014-15	Frederick Colby, Religious Studies: Spanish Muslim Visions of Heaven and Hell in the 13th Century CE.
	Evlyn Gould, Romance Languages: Salons and Cénacles in Fin de siècle Paris.
2015-16	Lara Bovilsky (English): Almost Human: The Bounds of Personhood in Early Modern England.

2016-17   Lanie Millar, Romance Languages: Disappointment in Cuban and Angolan Novels
           After Revolution.
           Mark Whalan, English: World War One, American Literature, and the Federal
           State.
2017-18   Tara Fickle, English: Serious Play: Assimilating Games in Asian America.
           Anne Kreps, Religious Studies: The Crucified Book: Sanctifying the Written Word
           from Valentinus to Constantine.
           David Wacks, Romance Languages: Spanish Crusader Fiction.
2018-19   Jeffrey Schroeder, Religious Studies. "Make-Believe Buddhism: Jodo Shin
           Thought and Politics, 1888–1965"
           Cory Browning, Romance Languages. "Terror, the Order of the Day: The French
           Revolutionary Terror and its Restagings"
           Mayra Bottaro, Romance Languages. "Scrambled Messages: Telegraphic Poetics
           and the New Atlantic Language"
2019-20   Michael Malek Najjar, Theatre Arts. "Middle Eastern American Theatre"
           Brent Dawson, English. "Worldly Muck: The Matter of Universality in English
           Renaissance Literature"
           Roy Chan, East Asian Languages and Literatures. "Sovereign Reorientations:
           Transnational Figurations and Global Forms in Modern Chinese and Russian
           Literatures"
2020-21   Jina Kim, East Asian Languages and Literatures. "Amplifying Voices: Auditory
           Texts in Colonial Korea, 1910-1945"
           Fabienne Moore, Romance Languages. "The Formation of a Multicultural
           Mediterranean in Chateaubriand's and Byron's Works"
           Timothy J. Williams, Clark Honors College. "Civil War Prisons and the Problem
           of Confederate Memory"
2021-22   Martha Bayless, English. "The Forgotten Queen: An Early Narrative of the
           Powerful Woman"
           Sharon Luk, Indigenous, Race, and Ethnic Studies. "Sea of Fire: A Buddhist
           Pedagogy of Dying and Black Encounters in Times of War"
           Analisa Taylor, Romance Languages. "Daughters of the Moon: Longing and
           Memory in Mexico's Lacandon Rainforest"
2022-23   Faith Barter, English: "Black Pro Se: Authorship and the Limits of Law in 19th-
           Century African American Literature"
           Stephanie Clark, English: "A King Must Buy a Wife: Purchase, Ownership, and
           Personhood in Early Medieval England"
           Sarah Wald, Environmental Studies and English: "Race, Recreation, and Public
           Lands: Storytelling in the Outdoor Equity Movement"
2023-24   Michael Allan, Comparative Literature: "A Pre-History of World Cinema"
           Katherine Kelp-Stebbins, English: "Draw for Your Lives: Comics Journalism and
           Human Rights"
           Thomas Glynne Walley, East Asian Languages and Literatures: "Eight Dogs Part
           Three"

Addendum (December, 2024 printing)

AUSTRALIA to ENGLAND
(For the Coronation of King George VI)

NOW with your trumpets lifted
And your proud flags unfurled,
Your praise by great winds drifted
In song around the world,
Hear it, though softly spoken,
Across far waters sped,
The word of faith unbroken
We would not leave unsaid!

For all that you have given
We give you thanks again:
Your sons whose hands have striven
With beauty not in vain;
Shakespeare, through you, our brother,
Wordsworth the calm and strong,
Milton and many another
Prince in the courts of song;

Bacon, the lord of reason,
And all who by his light,
Fearless in any season
Or depth of any night,
Seek Truth, the great queen, seated
Where the last star shines cold,
Who crowns the undefeated
With more than pearl and gold;

The just, the bold, the blameless,
Nelson and Nightingale,
And all the millions nameless
Whose labour shall prevail
To make your joy your glory
And peace your gem of worth,
And your best praise your story
The fairest told on earth.

And we? From Southern reaches
Of hill and curving plain
And warm white-sanded beaches
And uplands sweet with rain,
We send you what is dearest
Of us to make your own,
Youth, strength, and faith the clearest
Freemen have ever known.

Thus, now, we speak in gladness;
But should the dark hour come
When, stung with the old madness,
Men reach for sword and drum,
When anger rides the sky-way
And hatred rends the earth
And death in street and by-way
Makes mockery of birth;

Then, with your trumpets lifted
And your proud flags unfurled
Above the black smoke drifted
On thunder round the world,
Hear it, oh, clearly spoken,
Across far waters sped,
The word of faith unbroken
We will not leave unsaid!

From the *Sydney Mail* (NSW: 1912-1938), Wed 19 May 1937, Page 25.

INDEX of TITLES

The standard entry in this index gives the title of the poem, a code for the volume in which it appeared, and the page number in *TransPacific* on which the poem starts, e.g.

At the Grave of a Land-Shark (CFM) 109

Given that Moll republished some poems in different books and also used the same title for different poems, the index attempts to indicate the relationship between various poems in *TransPacific* which bear the same title. There are three categories:

1] Where two poems are the same except for accidentals or very minor substantive changes, they are given a single entry with both appearances listed. Thus, the two versions of the 9-line poem, "Bedside Moment" which differ only by the change of "rising" to "risen" are indexed thus:

Bedside Moment (TWS) (VNB) 383, 406

2] Where there are two instances of what is clearly the same poem, although revised for the later version, two entries are used and the second one includes the abbreviation "rev." Selectively, a note is added to explain the revision. The first stanza of "Dirge in Early Spring" was omitted when the poem was republished in *The View from a Ninetieth Birthday*. The versions are thus indexed:

Dirge in Early Spring (TWS) 381
Dirge in Early Spring rev.[3] (VNB) 406

with an endnote on the truncation.

3] Sometimes two poems share a title and nothing else. Such poems are listed separately, and the titles are followed by all or part of the poem's first line to distinguish or identify them. A good example is the two poems called "Farewell":

Farewell ("Slowly the waves") (LW) 17
Farewell ("Having been more than man") (BI) 84

List of Book Abbreviations

(BI)   *Blue Interval* (1935)
(BR)   *Briseis* (1965)
(BTC)   *Beware the Cuckoo and Other Poems* (1947)
(BW)   *Brief Waters* (1945)
(CFM)   *Cut from Mulga* (1940)
(COS)   *The Children of Somalia 1992-1994 and Other Poems* (1994)
(CS)   *Campus Sonnets* (1934)
(GSP)   *A Gleaner's Sheaf of Poems* (1995)
(LW)   *The Lawrentian* (1921-22)
(NM)   *Native Moments and Other Poems* (1931)
(RCL)   *The Road to Cactus-Land* (1971)
(RNT)   *Recognitions at Ninety-three* (1993)
(SF)   *Sedge Fire* (1927)
(TLS)   *The Lifted Spear* (1953)
(TRS)   *The Rainbow Serpent and Other Poems* (1962)
(TW)   *The Waterhole* (1948)
(TWS)   *The Well and the Star* (1983)
(UCP)   Uncollected Poems
(VNB)   *The View from a Ninetieth Birthday* (1992)

NB Endnotes in the following Index are separately numbered from those in the main text.

1 "A Pause" was titled "Pause" in BW. *TransPacific* follows the title used in *Poems 1940-1955*.
2 "Departure of a Guest" (VNB) 399 has two stanzas rewritten.
3 "Dirge in Early Spring" (VNB) 406 omits the first stanza of the earlier version.
4 "Snares for Beauty" (CFM) 104 retains and rewrites only one sonnet of the eleven in the original version.

www.ingramcontent.com/pod-product-compliance
Lightning Source LLC
Chambersburg PA
CBHW050750150726
48196CB00004B/412